INTRUSION DETECTION SYSTEMS

SECOND EDITION

INTRUSION DETECTION SYSTEMS

SECOND EDITION

ROBERT L. BARNARD

Butterworths

Boston   London   Durban   Singapore   Sydney   Toronto   Wellington

Library of Congress Cataloging-in-Publication Data

Barnard, Robert L.
  Intrusion detection systems.

  Bibliography: p.
  Includes index.
  1. Burglar-alarms. 2. Security systems.
I. Title.
TH9739.B37   1988   643'.16   87–13959
  ISBN 0–409–90030–3

Butterworth Publishers
80 Montvale Avenue
Stoneham, MA 02180

10 9 8 7 6 5 4 3 2 1

Printed in the United States of America

To my wife, Vivian, and children, Steven, Donna, Barbara, David, and Susan

Contents

Preface

Intrusion detection systems are an asset to effective security because they can alert security guards and responsible personnel to intrusions at protected facilities. I have found, however, that most security directors and managers and company owners, presidents, and vice presidents, the individuals who are responsible for protecting a company's assets, usually do not know enough about intrusion detection systems. Yet these are often the individuals who select the equipment or make critical decisions about their security system design. Consequently, many of these responsible individuals are buying intrusion detection equipment in a piecemeal fashion that usually precludes a totally integrated security system—that is, a security system that will adequately satisfy their security requirements in a way that is compatible with the facility's operational requirements and environmental conditions.

This book should help those individuals have a better understanding of how to design an intrusion detection system. It explains the basic operating principles and applications of intrusion detection equipment in an easy-to-understand text. But designing an intrusion detection system requires more than just understanding the equipment. It requires an adequate understanding of the security threat. This means the user must know, or at least be able to anticipate, the skills or modes of operation an intruder might use to gain access to valuable assets. Then he must be able to relate this threat to the facility or area he is protecting in order to establish the security requirements.

Part I of the book explains the importance of conducting a threat analysis and discusses factors that can influence the threat. The remainder of the section describes how to conduct a site survey and discusses factors that can adversely affect the site's security. Once the survey is completed, the security requirements have been established, and the decision to install an intrusion detection system has been made, sensors must be selected to detect intrusions at the barriers surrounding the assets or to detect motion inside the area requiring protection. Selecting sensors is the most critical function in designing an intrusion detection system, and selecting the wrong sensor with respect to the operating environment can result in an unmanageable number of nuisance or false alarms. Misapplying sensors is one of the major factors contributing to the false alarm problems in the security industry.

The threat is not always easy to define, especially for someone who is not experienced in conducting security surveys. It is even more difficult to relate the level of security necessary to neutralize or at least minimize the threat. Therefore, I have added a design guide in Part I that establishes four levels of security that should encompass most security application needs. It describes a generic threat for each level and suggests the minimal security measures necessary to protect against this threat. These measures are illustrated in Table 4–7, Threat/Physical Security Matrix, to assist managers in selecting the intrusion system and establishing the operating and control procedures for four types of sites: residential, commercial, industrial, and high-risk facilities.

The second, third, and fourth parts of the book describe the basic principle of operation and application of exterior sensors, interior sensors, and alarm transmission systems. The discussions on sensor operation describe how the sensors function and identify many of the stimuli that cause sensors to alarm. The discussions on applications give guidance on how the sensors should be deployed and describe typical applications for each type of sensor. After the sensors have been selected, the type of alarm transmission system for relaying the alarm information to the monitoring station must be selected. The discussion describes the types of alarm transmitters and monitors available and describes how the alarm information can be displayed so that the monitoring operator can effectively alert and direct the response force to the scene of the intrusion.

Part V discusses visual and television surveillance and alarm assessment, which is a major part of a fully integrated physical security system. Whether surveillance and assessment are accomplished by using guards alone or by using guards supported by television, proper lighting is required. Television and lighting systems require designers who specialize in these areas, but the security person also should have a basic understanding of these systems. Therefore, this section discusses the basic principles of operation and application of lighting and television equipment for the non-technical security person.

Part VI addresses access control to acquaint the reader with control techniques and vulnerabilities, along with the various types of access control systems and contraband search equipment used at critical facilities such as nuclear plants. Access control is a vital part of any security system, and if it is improperly designed, it might produce a false sense of security.

The first six parts of the book are filled with detailed information about the operation and application of intrusion detection, lighting, television, and access control equipment. Because the information is so specific and detailed, a seventh section on applications is included to give guidance on how to design an intrusion detection system. There are no step-by-step procedures for designing a security system because each application has its own unique requirements. There are, however, some general guidelines that should be followed. Instead of just listing guidelines for designing an intrusion detection system, the book relates some specific design ideas by describing the design considerations and equipment selection for three hypothetical facilities. The three sites are a school complex, nuclear power reactor, and high-rise office building. Each facility was selected to illustrate a different design concept and system application. All three examples illustrate how an intrusion detection system must be totally integrated with all other necessary security functions to satisfy the security requirements. Besides satisfying the security requirements, the system also must be manageable within the facility and functionally operate in its particular environment.

I want to emphasize that the material in this book is strictly limited to the author's opinions. It does not reflect the position of Belvoir Research, Development and Engineering Center, the Department of the Army, or the Department of Defense.

INTRUSION
DETECTION
SYSTEMS

SECOND EDITION

PART I

SECURITY SYSTEM INTEGRATION

There is no universal "best" security system for all applications. A security system should be designed adequately to safeguard valuable assets against the sophistication of those adversaries who pose a threat to these assets. Many different physical security devices and electronic surveillance systems are available that can be combined to form a security system. Physical protection is provided by locks, safes, vaults, and structural barriers such as fences, walls, and doors. Electronic surveillance is provided by interior and exterior intrusion detection sensors, access controls, television cameras and monitors, and alarm signal transmission and monitoring systems. The key to having the best security system is selecting the right security devices and systems and implementing adequate security controls and operating procedures to ensure the safety of your assets.

A physical security system consists of four equally important interacting functions—delay, detect, alert, and respond. The first function, *delay*, is provided by the presence of physical barriers protecting the assets, such as safes, vaults, walls, ceilings, doors, and fences. The second function, *detect*, is accomplished by intrusion detection sensors that detect the presence of an intruder. The third function, *alert*, is provided by an alarm transmission and monitoring system that annunciates and identifies the specific alarm location. And the fourth function, *respond*, is executed by the response force that responds to the intrusion alarm. If these four functions are not tightly integrated in the security system design, the assets might not be adequately protected. For instance, the assets can be surrounded with the best intrusion detection equipment available, but if no one hears and reports the intrusion alarm, and especially if no one responds to the alarm, the intrusion detection system is totally inadequate, except perhaps as a psychological deterrent.

Figure 1 is a simplified illustration of how these four security functions are combined in a security system. Mr. Ids (Intrusion Detection System), who will assist in illustrating the application and principles of operation of the intrusion sensors, is shown entering the front door of the jewelry store.

1

Figure 1   Intrusion detection system.

The door offers very little delay to Mr. Ids's crowbar, but the valuable jewelry is stored in a safe that will delay his mission. As Mr. Ids opens the front door, however, he is detected by an intrusion detection sensor. The sensor activates an alarm transmission device that transmits the alarm signal to the central station, where it is received, displayed, and annunciated to alert the central station operator. The operator then notifies the police of the intrusion, and they respond to protect the owner's assets and apprehend the intruder.

KNOW THE THREAT

Before an intrusion detection system can be designed to protect any assets, the designer should conduct a threat analysis to identify and determine the sophistication of the threat. The threat can be either internal or external to the organization, or both, and the skill level can be expected to range from unskilled to highly skilled. Knowing the threat is the primary prerequisite for designing an effective security system. Such knowledge should include consideration of the adversary's probable operational methods, as well as his technical equipment, resources, and overall ability to defeat or compromise security systems. These considerations will vary with the sophistication, skill level, motivation, and dedication of the adversary. Fortunately for our society, the skill level of most intruders ranges from unskilled to semiskilled.

Designing an intrusion detection system to protect valuable assets from an internal threat, especially a skilled insider, is a task requiring insight and careful deliberation. The skilled insider can be expected to have access to lock combinations and keys, to have a good working knowledge of the intrusion detection system capabilities and limitations, and to understand the overall operations and security measures of the organization. Therefore, adequate safeguards cannot rely solely on normal security measures such as good key control, equipment tamper protection, and alarm line supervision.

To protect against skilled insiders who have inherent advantages by virtue of their position within the organization, there should be continuous security checks and balances for the security procedures, and the installation should have an adequate security equipment maintenance plan and a standard operating routine. These procedures and controls should be integrated into the company's security plan, and the execution of these controls should be monitored by management to minimize the insider's advantage. For instance, the security equipment maintenance technician will probably have unlimited access to the company's intrusion detection equipment, and therefore could easily compromise the equipment when he is supposedly repairing it. To protect against this type of equipment compromise, there should be security measures requiring a guard or another responsible person in the organization to be present with the maintenance person during repair and to verify that the security system is operating satisfactorily after the equipment has been repaired. Although this security measure will not eliminate compromises, it will certainly complicate the execution of any compromise. This is just one example of the type of security measures that should be incorporated in a security plan to minimize the security system's vulnerability to an inside threat.

A major internal threat of a different type plaguing many organizations is employee theft, which ranges from theft of office supplies to embezzlement of corporate funds. For this type of threat, the employee usually does not have to be knowledgeable about the intrusion detection system because he probably accomplishes the thievery during working hours when the security system is in the access mode or turned off. Internal theft is a very real and very difficult threat to combat, but it can be minimized by implementing good security controls that check operations, materials flow, and accountability, and by means of credible accounting practices within the organization.

EXTERNAL THREAT

An intrusion detection system is used primarily during off-duty hours to detect penetrations by any external intruder. The skill level of the external intruder ranges from unskilled to highly skilled. An unskilled intruder is considered direct and obvious. He can be expected to gain entry into a building through the doors or windows after climbing over, cutting through, or lifting the fence fabric and crawling under it. A highly skilled intruder is considered very sophisticated and can have a devious approach. He can be expected to have the technical ability and equipment necessary to compromise the most sophisticated security system, either by directly defeating the intrusion detection equipment or by compromising the alarm transmission system. He can compromise even the most sophisticated lock and has the technical ability or assistance to breach any barrier given sufficient time.

As previously mentioned, the skill level of most threats ranges from unskilled to semiskilled. A semiskilled intruder can be expected to gain entrance into a building by circumventing any protected door or window, and he can be expected to generate alarms deliberately in an area where he wants to enter until the proprietor, the police, or whoever responds to the alarms and either ignores them or turns the system off. He can be expected to compromise unsophisticated line supervision devices by superimposing bogus signals on the supervised alarm transmission line to make the monitor appear normal. At this time, the intruder is undisturbed and free to carry out his mission. This method of compromising signal transmission systems is often referred to as *spoofing*.

The nature and skill level of the threat to most assets varies dramatically between geographic locations, especially worldwide locations. It also varies somewhat from city to city, from city to surrounding suburbs, and even between neighborhoods within the same city. Although the threat might vary geographically for most assets, some high-value items and strategically vital facilities attract skilled adversaries and dissident groups regardless of their geographic location. Banks are one example of a high-value target, and nuclear weapons plants are an example of a strategic facility. Other nuclear plants, such as those used for manufacturing nuclear fuel or nuclear reactors, also are attractive targets for both social and militant dissident groups. Therefore, these types of facilities require the highest level of security protection.

I have emphasized that a security system should be designed to protect the items or facilities from the known or anticipated threat. To achieve this goal, the security system designer should know what type of threat to expect. If he is not knowledgeable about the degree and nature of the threat, the best source of this information is local law enforcement agencies. But remember, like all other sociological problems, the threat is constantly changing and must be periodically reviewed. Potential adversaries are always obtaining technical information and learning new techniques for compromising security systems. What might have been an adequate security system 5 years ago might not provide adequate protection against today's threat. In fact, the system you are now designing might be inadequate in 5 years or less because today's adversaries are learning very quickly.

The first three chapters of this section discuss factors that should be considered when establishing security system requirements, selecting the security equipment and support elements, and coordinating the design within the organization. Chapter 4 is a design guide that establishes levels of security, identifies the internal and external threat for each level, and recommends the minimum security systems, procedures, and controls for each security level to minimize the effectiveness of the identified threats. The final chapter provides a list of questions pertaining to each topic to ensure total system integration.

Chapter 1

Design Requirements Survey

A threat analysis is a prerequisite to any security system design because this information is required for the site survey. A comprehensive survey should be conducted at the facility requiring protection to assess the vulnerability of the site with respect to the group size and sophistication of the anticipated threat. The threat is affected by psychological and physical factors related to the assets, such as their value, location, physical protection, and security systems. These factors should be evaluated during the facility survey and included in the security system design considerations. In the survey, the assets' value and geographic location are considered fixed parameters. The assets could possibly be redistributed or relocated to reduce the threat, but for this discussion they are considered fixed.

Physical factors that can affect the threat, such as fences, locks, walls, and doors, should be considered as areas where, perhaps, the protection for assets might be improved. Physical factors are easier to evaluate than psychological factors because their effectiveness can be measured in the time they delay an intruder, but the effectiveness of psychological factors is relative. Some psychological factors or deterrents that can affect the threat include the appearance of police, uniformed guards, television surveillance cameras, lights, mirrors, and warning signs. Psychological factors should be considered for their deterrent effect as possible methods of improving the overall asset protection.

The design considerations discussed in the following paragraphs are not all the factors that should be considered, but they are important considerations applicable to the design of any security system for most businesses and industrial facilities. These design considerations are not listed in any order of priority.

ASSET VALUE

The protection given a particular asset, whether it is a valuable object or a critically important facility, should be in keeping with its value. Value in this context is not just the monetary worth of the asset but includes its intrinsic value to the existence of the business to which it belongs or its importance to our national security. For instance, if a store handles merchandise that is hard to obtain or requires a long lead time to obtain and the value of the merchandise is being appraised, consideration should be given to how long it will take to replace the merchandise if it is stolen or destroyed. In considering the loss, consider what the customers will do when the store cannot fulfill their needs. They will probably go to a competitor, and the store owners may lose most, if not all, of their future business.

The intrinsic value of an asset or facility such as nuclear weapons, the facilities where they are manufactured, or other critical facilities such as nuclear processing and reactor plants is immeasurable. For this reason the facilities are the responsibility of the military and the Department of Energy, or they are controlled by the Nuclear Regulatory Commission (NRC) through regulations on those facilities doing business under a renewable license.

In determining realistic value, the cumulative cost of replacing stolen operating equipment, merchandise, and materials also should be considered. For instance, the principal of a school should consider the cost of replacing stolen operating equipment, such as typewriters or audiovisual equipment. The cumulative costs for a single year may or may not justify installing an intrusion detection system. But if the principal considers the cumulative cost of all the stolen equipment experienced or likely to be stolen over a 10-year period, the cost of replacing the stolen equipment will probably be exorbitant when compared with the cost of installing and maintaining an intrusion detection system during that period. (Ten years is the average life expectancy of well-maintained security equipment; however, it is not necessarily the number of years the system will adequately protect your assets.)

When you are considering how much security is needed in a security system, the major point is the long-term savings that may be obtained by installing an intrusion detection system. This consideration should include replaceable items and nonreplaceable business. Then establish a budget for the security system that is in keeping with the value of the assets. Limiting the expenditures could jeopardize the adequacy of the security system and the safety of the assets.

LOCATION OF ASSETS

Location of the assets is an important consideration in designing a security system for an existing installation. Location in this context refers not only to the assets' location in a high-threat area, but also to factors such as the nearness of human activity, the accessibility or vulnerability of the assets, the proximity of other buildings or businesses, the nearness of the alarm response force to the installation, and vehicle access roads leading to or passing the installation where the assets are located. If a move to a new location is being planned, these factors should be considered in selecting the new site.

Nearness of human activity is important because if there is always activity near the assets, the security system could probably be limited to local control devices and audible alarms. Local control devices are locks, television surveillance systems, and access control devices. Audible alarms are meant to alert those nearby to a problem. But if human activity is not always present, the security system will probably require additional security devices and protection, such as high-security locks, security containers, physical barriers, intrusion detection systems, and alarm transmission devices.

Accessibility and vulnerability of the assets are worthy of careful consideration. Assets such as jewelry or currency should be displayed or stored out of reach and protected from the public during operating hours. During nonoperating hours, they should be stored in a safe or vault to improve delay. Depending on the threat and the value of the assets, the safe or vault might justify installing an intrusion detection alarm system. For assets too large to be stored in vaults, the room or building in which they are located should be structurally sound to resist or discourage the anticipated threat. If the threat would not be discouraged by the structural integrity of the building, then an intrusion detection system should be installed to detect unauthorized entry. The penetration resistance of the room or building containing the assets should be adequate to deter or delay the intruder long enough for the alarm response force to respond to the intrusion alarm before severe asset losses occur.

Vehicle access roads leading to or near the building or area where the assets are located are important. For instance, if the assets are materials or equipment stored out-of-doors in a well-lighted fenced compound visible from the access road, the area can be observed for possible criminal acts by patrolling law enforcement officers. This type of visibility and exposure would be a deterrent to some unsophisticated threats. If the fenced compound is equipped with a perimeter alarm system, an access road reduces the response time for those responding to an intrusion alarm. Likewise, an access road leading to or past a protected building facilitates rapid response to an intrusion alarm or to any other type of emergency.

Nearness of other buildings or neighbor businesses could be an aid in terms of providing additional security. Or it could be a liability by increasing the threat to the assets because of the appeal of the neighbors' assets to an adversary. For instance, if the neighboring business is operated during the hours that the assets of interest are secured, the nearness of activity could be a deterrent and therefore a security asset. A liability to the assets in terms of neighboring businesses would be one with high appeal, such as a jewelry store. When establishing the design criteria for a security system or when selecting a new location, consider the impact of the neighbors' businesses on the threat to the assets being protected.

The nearness of the alarm response force is a primary consideration. Basically, the closer they are, the more rapidly they can respond to an intrusion alarm, and the better their chance to protect the assets and apprehend the intruder. The alarm response force and its timeliness of response are vital factors in establishing the design criteria for a security system. An intrusion detection system can only detect intrusions, and physical barriers can only delay intrusions. Intrusion detection systems and barriers provide protection if, and only if, they deter an attack on the assets or if they are properly supported by a reliable response force, which provides the primary asset protection.

PHYSICAL BARRIERS

Physical delay afforded the assets is another very important consideration in designing a security system. Physical delay can be provided by structural barriers such as fences, gates, walls, roofs, floors, doors, windows, or vaults and natural barriers such as rivers, lakes, cliffs, or any natural obstruction that is difficult to cross. Unsophisticated intruders, whose mode of operation is limited to forcible entry through doors and windows, will probably be discouraged by structurally sound barriers secured with high-security locks. But these barriers are only minor obstacles that impede the progress of the more sophisticated and dedicated intruder. A dedicated and skilled intruder will attack almost any barrier if he believes the rewards justify the effort and risk. Therefore, the degree of delay provided by the physical barrier is an important factor in either discouraging or impeding the progress of an intruder.

The length of time required for an adversary to penetrate the physical barriers is a function of its penetration resistance and the breaching method used. The time required to penetrate the physical barriers surrounding the assets should be considered along with the guard response time when designing an intrusion detection system. If the barrier can be penetrated before the guard can respond, either earlier detection, a closer guard force, or improved barrier penetration resistance is required.

Times required to breach chain-link fences and to penetrate various types of walls are discussed in the following paragraphs, based on actual penetration tests.

Fences

Fences are used to channel personnel and vehicles through designated entrances during normal operation and to discourage or deter entrance into the fenced area during nonworking hours. Fences may be considered a barrier to an unskilled intruder, but they are only minor obstacles to a more skilled or agile intruder. Fences are, however, usually considered the first level of protection in a security system. For this reason, fences are quite often protected with fence disturbance sensors. The most common type of fences are chain-link fences, like those installed around the perimeter of most industrial sites, utilities, and government installations. These fences are typically 7-foot-high woven metal fabric supported by steel posts and usually topped with either three or six strands of barbed wire supported by either a single or double V-shaped outrigger. A single-arm outrigger supports three strands of barbed wire, and a V-shaped outrigger supports six strands with three strands on each arm. The barbed wire topping increases the effective height of the fence to 8 feet.

A structurally sturdy, well-maintained fence provides a better barrier for fence disturbance sensors and will psychologically discourage intruders and resist penetration more effectively than a loose, poorly maintained fence. Here are some maintenance measures that should be taken: Keep the fence line free of brush and bushes; eliminate washouts under the fence that allow easy access by crawling; remove any objects from along the fence that could be used for gaining entrance by climbing; and secure all gate hinge hardware so that the gate cannot be easily removed even though it is locked.

Although the perimeter fence provides the first or outermost level of protection, fence penetration tests conducted by the U.S. Army and other government agencies have demonstrated that a standard chain-link fence can be climbed over or crawled under in about 2 to 5 seconds and cut through in less than 18 seconds. The results from these tests emphasize the ineffectiveness of chain-link fences against an agile intruder, especially one with prior training. The conclusion was that chain-link fences, even ones topped with barbed tape or concertina wire, serve as a psychological deterrent to the unskilled intruder but only slightly impede the progress of the trained intruder.

Sometimes the major advantage of a fence is that after the intruder crosses it to get in, he must retreat through or over the fence with the assets he is trying to steal. For some assets this might not be difficult, but if the intruder is trying to steal bulky materials or large objects, the fence might impede his retreat, limiting the thief as to how much he can take without opening the gate or cutting through the fence. Therefore, chain-link fences have some value in protecting bulky assets, assuming that the area is patrolled on some random schedule; otherwise, intruders would be undisturbed in executing their objective.

Overall, fences serve a useful purpose by defining legal boundaries, deterring the general public, and eliminating interference from wanderers and lowly motivated intruders. Defining the legal boundary around an installation is important. If, for instance, a guard or responding police officer finds someone inside the fenced compound, there is little doubt that the person realizes he is trespassing. The effectiveness of the boundary is enhanced if it is properly posted.

Walls

Exterior walls are usually considered the first level of protection for buildings not enclosed by a fence. Depending on the type of building, the exterior walls may vary from wood siding to thick granite walls seen in fortress-type banks and government buildings. The most common types of exterior walls are constructed from cinder block, brick, concrete, precast concrete, or any combination of these materials. Of course, concrete and precast concrete walls offer the greatest penetration resistance, but even they are vulnerable to penetration.

The National Bureau of Standards (NBS) and other contributing government agencies have conducted barrier penetration tests to measure the effectiveness of the barriers in resisting forced penetration using commonly available tools such as sledgehammers, rotohammers, diamond drills, burning bars, and saws. The resistance effectiveness was determined by measuring the time required to make a man-passable opening through various types of typical construction materials. A 96-square-inch opening with one dimension of at least 6 inches is considered large enough for a small person to wriggle through. Although the NBS has conducted many tests on specially constructed barriers, only the results from those tests conducted on typical exterior walls are discussed.

Using a 12-pound sledgehammer, a man-size hole was made in an 8-inch-thick hollow core cinder block wall in less than 2 minutes. Another hollow core concrete block wall, having blocks laid in line and No. 8 reinforcing bar and mortar in each core, was penetrated in less than 4 minutes. Even a brick-veneered hollow core concrete block wall with reinforcing wire and concrete filled cores was penetrated in less than 3 minutes with a 10-pound sledgehammer. Based on these tests, an intruder can make a man-passable opening in a standard concrete hollow core wall in less than 2 minutes using only a sledgehammer.

Two separate man-passable openings were cut through a wooden wall constructed from two layers of 1-inch-thick fire siding in less than 2 minutes. One opening was cut using an electric saber saw, and the other was cut with a radial saw. These tests demonstrated that even a well-constructed wooden wall can be penetrated in less than 2 minutes.

A man-passable opening was made through an 8-inch-thick reinforced concrete wall in less than 18 minutes using conventional tools. A similar penetration test was conducted on a 5½-inch-thick reinforced concrete slab roof. The man-passable opening was completed in less than 13 minutes. These penetration tests reveal the vulnerability of physical barriers that are often considered almost impenetrable, especially considering that the penetration times could have been reduced by using explosives.

The reason for describing these tests is to stress the vulnerability of common construction materials to penetration. For this reason, the structural integrity of the barriers protecting your assets should be carefully considered during your security requirements survey.

Operable Openings

Operable openings are doors, windows, transoms, or any device that can be opened to allow people, fresh air, or light to enter a room or building. They are the most common points of entry for intruders, especially ground-level doors and windows located in inconspicuous locations. Operable openings are also the hardest points to protect, simply because they are designed for allowing personnel access, in the case of doors, or for letting in daylight and fresh air, in the case of windows and transoms. In fact, any opening less than 18 feet from the ground and 14 feet from other structures should be physically covered with bars or grilles, equipped with intrusion detection devices, or both.

The first consideration in protecting an operable opening is to determine whether the opening is really needed. Many buildings, especially older ones, have windows and doors that are no longer used. The problem of protecting obsolete windows or doors can be eliminated by simply sealing them permanently in a manner that maintains the penetration resistance of the wall containing the opening. For instance, if the door to be eliminated is mounted in a brick wall, the door assembly should be removed and the opening bricked up, taking care to anchor the new construction properly.

Ground-level doors, especially accessible ones, are used for gaining entrance into a facility more than any other openings. Therefore, the door locks, mounting hardware, and door assemblies should be in keeping with the integrity of the walls in which they are mounted. Because of the high probability of an intrusion through a door, all exterior doors should have intrusion detection devices that will detect anyone opening the door. Since ground-level windows also allow easy access, they too should be physically secured and protected with intrusion detection devices.

Here are some physical security measures often suggested for securing doors and windows: Provide adequate locks on all operable openings; conceal or secure all mounting hardware, fasteners, hinge pins, etc.; install expanded metal grilles or bars over all accessible windows; replace glass windows with glass blocks or impact-resistant glass; and replace glass in or around doors where the glass can be broken to reach the door release. The door glass also can be replaced with an impact-resistant glass or a material that will maintain the penetration resistance of the door assembly and surrounding structure. Some of these recommendations may not be aesthetically pleasing, especially grilles over windows, but there are some very attractive window grilles that can actually enhance the appearance of the building.

DETERRENTS

A deterrent is defined as anything that will turn aside or discourage through fear, or prevent an action either by making the action difficult or inciting fear of the consequences. Deterrents can be classified as either physical or psychological. Physical security deterrents are highly visible devices or barriers designed to delay the entry of an intruder long enough for him to be apprehended. Such deterrents include locks, safes, window grilles, walls, and fences. The effectiveness of these deterrents for delaying an intruder must be discernible to the intruder and project as significant the time required to penetrate the protecting device or barrier. For instance, an 8-inch-thick reinforced concrete wall can delay a team of intruders using conventional tools about 20 minutes, while a hollow core concrete block might delay them only 2 minutes. In terms of the intruder's estimated penetration time, concrete walls are obviously much more effective as a physical barrier than cinder block walls and might obviate an attack on the concrete walls.

The physical effectiveness of security deterrents can be quantitatively measured in terms of penetration time and ranked as to the likely effect on delaying an intruder, but their psychological effectiveness against the intruder cannot be quantitatively measured. It can only be qualitatively stated or judged based on actual crime statistics. For instance, if stronger door locks and window grilles are installed on a facility with a high incidence of burglaries and the number of burglaries drops 30 percent in the first year after the improvements, then it can be judged with a high degree of probability that the physical barriers were psychologically effective in reducing the burglaries planned or attempted.

A very effective psychological deterrent for reducing crime is the presence of a law enforcement officer, even on a periodic but random basis. A police officer is a deterrent for almost any level of threat except the dedicated intruder or militant adversary who will risk the consequences of apprehension for monetary reward or for a "cause." Many department stores, industrial facilities, and institutions have recently hired uniformed guards, not only for maintaining order and traffic control, but also for their psychological effectiveness in deterring crime.

Some other psychological deterrents used by the security industry to deter crime are photographic and television cameras, shoplifting mirrors, intrusion detection devices, lights, warning signs, and watchdogs. Whether these deterrents are physical or psychological is not important. What is important is that any deterrent is effective only if it is perceived by the intruder as a deterrent. Therefore, to be effective, any deterrent must be made known to the intruder in an intentional way, preferably during his planning phase. In some cases, such as shoplifting, this could mean using the advertising media, such as television and signs, to project the message. Another example would be the permanent identification marking of valuable items to make fencing items more difficult because of traceability.

Again, the psychological effectiveness of these devices and strategies cannot be quantitatively measured. But because of their reported effectiveness in reducing crime, especially shoplifting, psychological deterrents should be considered in conjunction with the level of threat in your total security system design.

Chapter 2

Design
Philosophy

Once you have completed the design requirements survey, including evaluating all the features and circumstances affecting the threat, and have established the design criteria for your intrusion detection system, you are ready to begin assembling the components of the security system. This assembly involves selecting or identifying the delay elements and the alarm response force, if required, and establishing the system maintenance concept, as well as selecting the appropriate intrusion detection sensors and the alarm transmission and monitoring equipment.

Adequate selection of the security equipment to satisfy your system requirements is probably the most difficult task in designing an intrusion detection system. This is especially true for most users who attempt to design their own systems because it requires a basic understanding of the principles of operation, applications, and limitations of the security equipment.

Many security systems have been installed that do not adequately protect the assets they are intended to protect. This type of situation has resulted from the fact that the salesperson, equipment installer, or system designer did not fully understand the operation and application of the security equipment to the required level. This lack of knowledge also has contributed to many of the intrusion detection system false alarm, and especially nuisance alarm, problems that plague the security industry. This problem is worsened because most users do not understand the basic operation of their own system. Therefore, the basic operation and applications of the various types of intrusion detection equipment will be discussed in some detail in later chapters to help minimize these problems. Before presenting any security equipment discussions, however, several additional design prerequisites should be considered in addition to analyzing the threat. One such prerequisite is the intrusion detection system design philosophy. This means deciding on features such as what zone or zones of detection should be used to safeguard your assets adequately. Intrusion detection sensors are designed to provide one or more of five zones of detection. The first zone of detection, starting at the exterior boundary, is perimeter penetration detection; the second zone is exterior zone of detection; the third zone is building penetration detection; the fourth is motion detection; and the fifth is proximity detection.

After the zone or zones of detection have been established and the appropriate intrusion detection sensors selected, you should decide how the status of the intrusion detection sensors will be monitored. There are several possibilities: employ the services of a central alarm station; use a proprietary alarm monitoring system; use a telephone dialer; or use only a local audible alarm to annunciate the alarms. Any one or a combination of these monitoring techniques might satisfy your monitoring requirements. Whichever system you choose, its selection should be based on the value of the assets being protected and the sophistication of the anticipated threat.

Another prerequisite that must be considered is the alarm response force. The response force selection or identification will depend somewhat on the monitoring system, but especially on the allowable alarm response time. Local law enforcement officers or security guards, either central station guards or proprietary guards, are normally used to respond to intrusion alarms. A central station guard is usually accompanied or joined by a local law enforcement officer at the origin of the alarm. Regardless of who responds to the alarms, they must arrive at the alarm location before the intruder penetrates the physical barriers and absconds with the assets; otherwise the response force will be totally ineffective. For this reason, the designer should evaluate the penetration resistance of the physical barriers and the zones of detection selected for the intrusion detection sensors to determine the maximum allowable response time the response force has to respond to the alarm. They should be able to arrive at the asset location within this time. If not, either physical barriers must be added to delay penetration or another zone of detection must be added to provide earlier detection. Another possibility is for the response force to be relocated to improve their response time. This might not be possible, however, especially if the response is by local police.

Another often overlooked consideration of an intrusion detection system is how the equipment will be maintained and repaired and by whom. The maintenance concept should be established during the system planning phase. Once the intrusion detection system is installed, it will then be properly maintained. Maintenance can be contracted to an equipment installing company, or it can be performed by an in-house maintenance force. If the intrusion detection system is leased, maintenance should be part of the leasing agreement. Regardless of who maintains the equipment, care should be taken to ensure that their maintenance obligation is compatible with the user's operating schedule. Otherwise, the assets might be without protection or suffer degraded protection while the system is waiting for repairs.

ZONES OF DETECTION

Five zones of intrusion detection can be considered for an intrusion detection system design. The first and outermost zone, perimeter penetration detection, is usually at the perimeter fence. Fence disturbance sensors or fence-mounted electric-field sensors are intended to detect an intruder penetrating the perimeter fence either by climbing, cutting, or lifting the fence fabric. The second zone of detection, exterior zone of detection, is provided in the area between the fence or the property boundary and the assets or facility being protected. Exterior microwave or infrared invisible barrier detectors or buried sensors are intended to detect anyone running, walking, or crawling through this zone. The third zone of detection is the perimeter of the building or room protecting the assets. Structural vibration detectors, door contacts, window foil, and vibration detectors are intended to detect anyone penetrating the building or room. The fourth zone of detection is the interior of the building or room. Ultrasonic, microwave, sonic, or infrared motion detectors are intended to detect anyone who has entered the building and is moving within the zone of detection. The fifth and innermost zone of detection is at the item being protected. Capacitance proximity detectors and concealed pressure mats and switches are intended to detect anyone either approaching, removing, or attempting to remove protected objects or attempting to penetrate protected containers.

In terms of allowable response time for the response force, the first zone of detection at the perimeter fence allows the longest response time if the assets are located within a building that is enclosed by a fence. The third zone of detection allows the longest response time for a building that is not protected by an exterior intrusion detection system. The fifth zone of detection allows the least response time, and unless the assets are well protected in a safe or the response guards are in close proximity to the protected assets, the fifth zone of detection should be used only in conjunction with other zones of detection.

To safeguard your assets adequately, the selection of each zone of detection should be carefully considered in conjunction with the threat and the appropriate intrusion detection sensors.

INTRUSION DETECTION SENSOR SELECTION

To select the most effective sensor or sensors that will satisfy your protection requirements at the appropriate zones, you should be aware of the many available types of sensors and be knowledgeable about their basic principles of operation and application. Although the remaining chapters of this book are devoted to providing this information in some detail, the various types of sensors are described briefly in the following paragraphs to acquaint you with each type of sensor in relationship to the zone of detection where it may be used. Understanding the operation and applications of the various intrusion detection sensors is necessary to design an intrusion detection system that will satisfy the detect requirement of the four primary prerequisites—delay, detect, alert, and respond—that should be considered when designing an intrusion detection system. This discussion will acquaint you with the sensors and their zones of applicability with reference to the design of the total intrusion detection system.

Fence Disturbance Sensors

Fence disturbance sensors are used to provide the first zone of detection for perimeter fences. Several types of fence disturbance sensors are available. They include electromechanical switches, piezoelectric transducers, geophones, and electret cables. These sensors are used on chain-link fences similar to those installed around the perimeter of most military installations and utility companies. They detect the mechanical vibrations generated in the fence when an intruder climbs over, cuts through, or lifts up the fence fabric to crawl under. An advantage of fence disturbance sensors is that they are mounted directly on the fence following the fence contour. Because they are mounted directly on the fence, they do not occupy space inside the fence line.

In the application of fence disturbance sensors, remember that the intruder must come in contact with the fence to be detected. If he bridges over or jumps the fence without touching it, he will not be detected.

Electric-Field Sensors

The operating principle of the electric-field sensor depends on generation of an electric field along a combination of field and sense wires arranged in a horizontal fence configuration. As an intruder, crawling, walking, or running, approaches the electric field generated along the fence, his body distorts the electric field. The resulting distortions change the characteristics of the electric field, thereby altering the electrical signal on the sense wire. When the signal change satisfies the detector alarm criteria, an alarm circuit is activated.

The electric-field fence can be used to provide the first zone of detection when it is mounted on a perimeter fence or the second zone of detection when it is installed in a stand-alone configuration along a zone between the perimeter and the item or structure being protected. In the fence-mounted configuration, the sense and field wires are installed on insulated standoffs secured to the existing fence posts. In this type of installation, the electric-field wires follow the fence contour and occupy very little space inside the fence. In the stand-alone configuration, the electric-field wires are supported by fiberglass posts or by insulated standoffs on steel posts. These posts can be installed along the boundary, also following the ground contour, keeping inside the existing perimeter fence or boundary, or they can be installed in proximity to the item or facility requiring penetration detection.

Invisible Barrier Detectors

Invisible barrier detectors also provide the second zone of detection for exterior zones. Two types of invisible barrier detectors are available: infrared and microwave. Invisible barrier detectors generate an invisible beam of energy and are intended to detect intruders running, walking, or crawling through the beam. The barrier is formed by a transmitter emitting a beam of either microwave or infrared energy. A corresponding receiver, located in the line of sight of the transmitter at the opposite end of the beam, receives and monitors the transmitted signal for changes characteristic of someone penetrating the beam.

Both microwave and infrared detectors must be installed above level ground. Any obstructions such as lamp posts, trees, or hills between the transmitter and receiver will block the transmitted energy and make alignment difficult or impossible and detection unreliable. Likewise, if there are gullies passing through the zone under the microwave or infrared energy beam, they will not be covered, leaving an unprotected route for a crawling intruder.

Buried Line Sensors

Buried line sensors also provide the second zone of detection by creating a sensitive lane along the ground above the buried sensor. Three different types of buried sensors are available: pressure, electromagnetic, and a combined magnetic and strain. Pressure sensors include geophones and piezoelectric and balanced pressure transducers. The electromagnetic sensor uses ported coaxial cables to generate the electric field along the zone of detection. These sensors are intended to detect the seismic energy or strain induced in the ground by an intruder crossing the sensitive area along the ground and to detect disturbances in the electric field generated between the buried transmit and receive ported coaxial cables caused by anyone crossing the sensor zone.

An advantage to buried line sensors, other than the fact that they follow the ground contour, is that they are completely concealed from an intruder who might attempt to cross the protected boundary.

Building Penetration Detectors

Building penetration detectors provide the third zone of detection for building protection. Several types of penetration detectors are available, including vibration detectors, acoustical energy detectors, foil tape, and grid wire. One type of vibration detector used to detect penetrations through structural barriers detects the low-frequency, large-amplitude impacts generated during a forced penetration through walls or other building barriers. Another type of vibration detector detects the high-frequency vibrations generated by breaking glass and is referred to as a glass breakage detector. Acoustical energy detectors detect both sonic and ultrasonic acoustical energy generated by forced entry through physical barriers.

Foil tape has been used for many years to detect glass breakage, but it also can be installed along the insides of walls to detect penetrations. Grid wire also is used to detect penetrations. Grid wire is simply fine insulated wire that may be installed on walls and in screens or grilles that cover vents, windows, or other openings. Both foil tape and grid wire are electrically connected to a circuit that monitors their electrical continuity. When either the tape or wire is broken during a penetration, the monitoring circuit initiates an alarm.

Operable Opening Switches

Operable opening switches detect an intruder who opens a door or window to penetrate the building exterior, which is the third zone of detection. These devices include both balanced and general purpose magnetic switches, mechanical switches, and tilt switches. The balanced magnetic switch consists of an actuating magnet mounted on the door and a separate balancing magnet located inside the switch assembly, which is mounted on the door frame. When the door is closed, the balancing magnet(s) and actuating magnet hold the internal reed switch in balance. When anyone opens the door, the actuating magnet is moved, the switch becomes unbalanced, and an alarm is initiated.

The general purpose magnetic contact and tilt switches are very simple devices. The magnetic contact switch consists of an activating magnet and a reed switch assembly. The reed switch assembly is mounted to the door frame and the magnetic activating device is mounted to the door. When anyone opens the door, the activating magnet is moved away from the reed switch, initiating an alarm. Tilt switches consist of a free-moving switch mechanism with contacts that open or close when the switch is rotated. Tilt switches are installed on openings such as transoms. When the transom is opened, the switch initiates an alarm.

Operable opening switches should be installed on all doors and windows that can be opened to gain entry into a protected area. Crime statistics reveal that a very high percentage of intruders gain entry through doors and windows.

Volumetric Motion Detectors

Motion detectors provide the fourth zone of detection. Two types of motion detectors are available—active and passive. Active motion detectors fill the volume in range of the detector with either ultrasonic, microwave, or sonic energy. The transmitted energy forms a standing wave pattern as it reflects from the objects and walls in the room. Some of this energy is reflected back to the detector receiver, where it is received and processed. When there is a disturbance in the received signal due to someone moving within the protected area, the processor initiates an alarm.

Passive motion detectors do not transmit energy. They detect the energy generated by the intruder. Two types of passive detectors are available—infrared and audio. Infrared detectors detect the thermal energy emanating from an intruder's body, or they detect a change in the ambient thermal energy caused by the intruder moving through the protected area. Audio detectors detect the penetration noises generated by anyone entering the protected building or noises generated by activity inside the building

Combination active microwave or ultrasonic and passive infrared detectors also are available. These detectors take advantage of the differences in false alarm stimuli of the active and passive sensors to minimize false alarms in the combination sensors.

Interior Barrier Detectors

Although barrier detectors such as active infrared detectors or trip wires do not detect actual motion in the same sense as volumetric motion detectors, they can be used to detect people moving through interior zones of detection. Therefore, depending on where and how they are used, barrier detectors can be classified either as providing a fourth or fifth zone of detection. If they are installed at the perimeter across avenues of approach to a protected area, they could be considered volumetric. But when they are used to form an active barrier around a valuable object, they would be considered proximity detectors. Because of their application, barrier detectors are often referred to as traps.

Proximity Detectors

Proximity detectors provide the fifth zone of detection. Two types of proximity detectors are available—capacitance and pressure mats. Capacitance proximity detectors are used to protect metal containers that can be isolated from ground such as safes or file cabinets. These devices continuously monitor the net capacitance between the protected metal object and an electrical ground plane. An intruder approaching or touching the protected object causes a change in the net capacitance. When the capacitance change satisfies the detector alarm criteria, an alarm is initiated.

Pressure mats and switches also can be used to detect the presence of intruders when they approach or attempt to move protected items. For instance, pressure mats can be installed under the carpet around the protected item. Then anyone who approaches the item steps on the mat and initiates an alarm. Pressure switches are usually installed under the item requiring protection, and when the item is moved, the switch initiates an alarm. Vibration detectors and tilt switches also are used to detect anyone attempting to remove a valuable item.

ALARM MONITORING SYSTEMS

After the intrusion detection sensors have been selected, the system to monitor the status of the protected area must be selected. Selecting the proper alarm monitoring system to alert the response force is the second primary prerequisite when designing an intrusion detection system. The first prerequisite was to select the sensors to detect the intruder. Selecting the proper monitoring system is important because if no one hears or receives the alarm message, no response action is possible, and the system is totally ineffective, except perhaps as a psychological deterrent.

Sensor alarms can be simply annunciated by a local audible alarm such as a horn or siren, or a telephone dialer can be used to notify the proprietor or other responsible party of an alarm. Both these alarm annunciation methods rely on someone either hearing the audible alarm or being present at the designated telephone to receive the alarm-alerting messages. A more reliable alarm annunciation method is to have the alarm report to a central alarm station, either commercial or proprietary, where the security status is constantly monitored. With such a system, the operator alerts the response force to investigate the cause of the alarm. Alarm station operators are also available to monitor routine events such as openings and closings or access/ secure status, equipment tamper alarms, signal line supervision circuits, fire alarms, equipment operation status, and environmental controls.

Local Audible Alarms

Before you select a local audible alarm to annunciate your sensor alarms, you should consider its potential utility. As mentioned earlier, if a responsible individual who will alert the police to the alarm does not hear the alarm and report it, then the audible alarm is useless except as a psychological deterrent. For instance, how often have you been walking by a place of business where an alarm is sounding and heard someone say, "I wish someone would cut that noisy thing off"? In fact, how often have you ignored an audible alarm?

A local audible alarm can be used as a psychological deterrent for some levels of threat in conjunction with another more reliable alarm monitoring method. Of course, if apprehension of the intruder is one of the objectives of your security system, an audible alarm should not be used.

Telephone Dialers

Telephone dialers transmit a prerecorded voice message to a series of preselected telephone locations to alert the person receiving the message of the emergency. The dialer is a convenient method of transmitting alarms because it operates over ordinary telephone lines and does not interfere with normal telephone operation. But like local audible alarms, telephone dialers have their limitations. The first limitation is that someone must be present at the designated call location to receive the prerecorded alarm message. In order to alleviate this limitation, some telephone dialers can be programmed to dial several different telephone numbers and repeat the calls until someone answers.

Quite often, one of the preprogrammed telephone numbers is the police department. This is one way to alleviate the problem of getting a response. But before you arbitrarily program the police telephone number, contact their office and inquire of any local ordinance concerning the use of telephone dialers. Some cities have ordinances prohibiting telephone dialer calls, while others accept prerecorded calls but on separate telephone numbers so they will not tie up primary police emergency numbers. To be safe, check the use of dialers with your police department.

Alarm Stations

There are two basic types of alarm stations—commercial and proprietary. With regard to monitoring intrusion detection systems, the primary difference between the two is that commercial stations are usually farther from the protected area, while proprietary stations are normally located within or near the protected facility. However, some institutions use a single proprietary alarm station to monitor the status of a number of different remotely located facilities. For instance, many school districts use a single proprietary alarm station to monitor the alarms of all their protected schools.

If you plan to employ a commercial alarm station or have a remotely located proprietary station monitor your alarms, you should review their method of transmitting the alarm signals. This review is especially important if there is more than one area within a single facility requiring protection and each area requires separate identification. Some monitoring systems use a dedicated pair of metallic conductors or a dedicated voice-grade telephone line for each protected area. Other systems use a single dedicated metallic pair transmission line to carry the information for many individually protected areas, while still maintaining individual area identification. Still other systems, like the digital dialers, require only standard operational telephone lines for transmitting alarm messages. Radio alarm transmission systems are becoming popular, especially in those areas where telephone lines are difficult to obtain and where the protected area is remotely located from telephone service.

The primary reason for reviewing the alarm station monitoring and alarm transmission method is to find out whether a dedicated telephone line is required for each protected area or whether all areas can be monitored using a single dedicated line. This information is needed to establish the number of telephone lines that must be allocated for your intrusion detection system. If telephone line allocation is a problem because of insufficient capacity, you might want to consider the services of a central alarm station that uses multiplexed, digital dialer, or radio alarm transmission systems.

Several alarm signal transmission techniques are used by central alarm stations. They are briefly described here to acquaint you with their operating technique.

McCulloh Circuit

One of the oldest but still used methods of transmitting alarm signals is the McCulloh circuit. This transmission technique uses a dedicated metallic conductor connected in series to a number of protected facilities or customers. The limiting factor in determining the number of customers that can be connected to a single McCulloh loop is the total loop resistance that reduces the current available for transmitting the message. The number of protected areas on a single loop usually ranges from about fifteen to forty-five.

To identify the individual customers, each one is assigned an identification number. When there is an alarm, this number is dispatched as a series of "ground" and "break" pulses from the transmitter located at the customer's facility. These coded pulses are received by the monitor at the central alarm station, where they are decoded and printed.

An application consideration of most McCulloh circuit transmission systems is that they provide little or no line supervision. They can detect line faults, but in most McCulloh systems, the alarm station operator has no way of knowing whether a customer's unit is operating except when it is activated during routine business opening and closing.

Direct Current System

Direct current (DC) alarm transmission systems require dedicated metallic conductors between the sensor or protected facility and the monitor panel in the alarm station. An advantage of the DC systems is that they provide a level of line security against tampering by applying a low-level DC voltage to the transmission line. They then monitor the current flow in the transmission line through a balanced resistive bridge network in the control panel. If the current varies beyond a preset limit, due to either a sensor alarm or someone tampering with the transmission line, the resistive bridge becomes unbalanced and an alarm is activated.

An application consideration of DC systems is that dedicated metallic transmission pairs are becoming very difficult to obtain. In fact, telephone line leasing in general is becoming a major problem in most areas.

Another consideration of DC systems is that inclement weather can cause electrical changes in the transmission lines that may unbalance the resistive bridge and activate an alarm. For instancse, moisture in the transmission line or junction boxes can alter the line leakage to ground, which in turn changes the line current. Electrical fields generated by lightning also can induce current changes on the transmission line. In these environments, when the current change exceeds the preset limit, an alarm is activated just as if an actual intrusion occurred or someone tampered with the transmission line.

Alternating Current System

Alternating current (AC) alarm transmission systems are similar to DC systems except that they offer a slightly higher level of line supervision and the alarm signal can be transmitted over voice-grade telephone lines. This system essentially replaces the DC balanced bridge with an AC balanced bridge and the DC current with an AC signal; the DC transmission line termination is replaced with an equivalent AC termination. As with the DC system, a sensor alarm or anyone tampering with the transmission lines unbalances the AC bridge and initiates an alarm.

Like DC systems, AC systems require dedicated transmission lines, but an advantage of AC systems is that they do not require continuous metallic conductors. That is, the alarm signals can be transmitted over voice-grade telephone lines because an AC signal can be transmitted as an audible tone on the lines.

Multiplex System

Multiplexing is basically a method of transmitting multiple information signals over a single communication channel. The communication channel can be a twisted wire pair, telephone line, microwave link, or any combination of these signal transmission paths.

Two types of multiplexing techniques are available. One technique is called frequency division multiplexing (FDM) and the other, time division multiplexing (TDM). Frequency division multiplexing means that a single communication transmission line is subdivided into a number of separate frequency channels. Each customer is then assigned a separate frequency channel for transmitting alarms and systems status information. The number of frequency channels is a function of the type of communication path—metallic conductor, voice-grade telephone line, or radio. In TDM each user is assigned a short interval of time at a particular time interval or time slot in the transmitting cycle to transmit the status information.

Multiplexed systems can provide a high degree of transmission line security if the message is enciphered using either random or pseudorandom encoding techniques.

Digital Dialers

Digital dialers are similar to telephone dialers except that they transmit their information in a digital message rather than a prerecorded voice message. These digital words are transmitted as AC tones over standard voice-grade telephone lines in a manner similar to that used for multiplex systems. Because the transmitted message is in the form of digital words, digital dialers must communicate with a compatible receiver at the alarm station that can decipher the digital message and display the information. The minimal information transmitted by most digital dialers identifies the location and the access, secure, or alarm status of the protected area. Digital dialers also can be used for transmitting other signals such as duress alarms, fire alarms, and equipment malfunction alarms.

An advantage of the digital dialers, as with the telephone dialers, is that they can operate through the public telephone network. Another advantage of some digital dialers is that the alarm station operator can listen in over the telephone line for unusual noises, which would be associated with an intrusion occurring at the area where the alarm originated. The listen-in feature can assist a trained operator in verifying actual intrusions.

Alarm transmission devices transmit the security alarm status of the protected area to an alarm station, where it is displayed on a monitor. Dedicated monitors are available, as are monitors that display the status of all the protected areas separately but on a common numeric-type display.

Dedicated monitors monitor the status or each protected area's transmission device, with the status information on a single display panel dedicated to that particular area. Dedicated monitors are used to monitor DC alarm transmission devices. The more common DC monitors use a milliammeter to monitor the current on the transmission line and indicate an alarm when current changes exceed a preset level. An audible tone is simultaneously annunciated when the alarm is indicated, to alert the monitor operator.

Newer dedicated monitors use lighted displays to indicate the status of the protected areas. While the older dedicated monitors indicated only alarms and transmission line problems, the newer monitors indicate the access, secure, and alarm status of the protected areas. Access is indicated by amber lights, secure by green lights, and alarm by red lights. Some monitors also indicate the status of the primary power at the protected area. The alarm station operator then knows whether the protected area intrusion detection system is operating from primary AC power or standby DC power. These monitors also have an audible annunciator to alert the operator when any change occurs in the security or power status of the protected area.

Many alarm transmission devices collectively monitor the status of many different sensor alarm points at the protected area and transmit this information to the alarm station, where it is individually displayed on a single monitor display panel. This type of monitor displays the protected area identification number on a numeric display and prints the identification number, along with the status change information, time, and calendar date, on paper tape. The information on the paper tape serves as a record that can be used to verify any status changes at a protected area and the time the changes occurred.

Computers are used to manage alarm station monitoring systems, especially at those stations with large customer accounts. The question "What is a large account, and when should an alarm station invest in a computer system?" is difficult to answer. The decision requires a rather extensive cost analysis that includes reviewing the station's income and operating costs and evaluating these costs in conjunction with the computer equipment, installation, and maintenance costs and the cost to train the operators. The analysis also should include the station's anticipated growth over the expected life of the computer.

Computers are very able machines with the capability of performing many monitoring and command functions. In the security industry, computers are used to monitor the status of intrusion detection systems, environmental controls, fire alarms, duress alarms, or any equipment sensors. Along with the monitoring function, computers can initiate commands, such as giving the alarm station operator response instructions when an alarm or change in status occurs. They also can control the functions of environmental equipment and deterrent devices. The operator instructions can be displayed on a cathode ray tube (CRT) or printed on a line printer, in which case the printed message serves as the event record. This information also can be stored in the computer's memory for future reference.

Because computers are programmed and accept their instructions in a digital format, they can operate with any multiplexed transmission system or digital dialer. In fact, they can be used with any transmission devices with proper interfacing equipment.

Alarm Response Force

Operating in close conjunction with the intrusion detection and alarm monitoring systems is the alarm response force. Selecting and identifying the alarm response force is the third primary prerequisite in designing an intrusion detection system. The first two prerequisites were detect and alert, and now response is needed. Local law enforcement officers provide the primary response for many protected facilities and serve as the secondary response for most other sites.

Some commercially operated alarm stations use their own guards, who respond to their customers' premises to assist the local law enforcement officers when there is an alarm. Security guards usually check the facility for possible clues as to the cause of the alarm, admit the law enforcement personnel to the facility, and assist them in searching the area. The actual authority of the security guards with respect to apprehension is limited and could vary from city to city. Therefore, the user should carefully assess the services provided and the functional limitations of the security guards.

Some facilities with proprietary alarm stations rely on local law enforcement officers to respond to system alarms. Many others use their own guards for the primary response and request local law enforcement assistance only if it is needed. Guard service organizations supply guards for many installations; other installations hire and train their own. The determining factor in deciding whether a facility should use a guard service or hire its own guards is the availability and cost of the trained service guards versus the cost to hire, train, and maintain its own. Other factors that influence the decision are the number of guards required, their duty functions, initial and continued training costs, and how long guards will be needed. Liability is still another very important consideration when deciding whether to use proprietary guards or a guard service. The company supplying the guards is liable for their actions. Installations where the guards must interact with the public should certainly consider their liabilities.

Regardless of who responds to intrusion alarms, they must arrive at the property before the intruder penetrates the physical barriers surrounding the assets, completes his mission, and escapes. If the guards do not respond in this time, the security system is basically worthless, except that it might serve as a psychological deterrent to some threats. Therefore, the physical barriers surrounding the assets should be evaluated to determine whether their penetration resistance is adequate based on the anticipated threat. Estimate the time required to penetrate the barrier, then select the sensors that will provide the earliest warning of a penetration attack. Finally, measure the time required for the response force to arrive at the protected site. If they are likely to arrive before the barrier can be penetrated, the system should function effectively. But if the response force cannot arrive in the allotted time, then one or all of the following improvements should be considered: Improve the physical barriers around the assets; provide earlier warning of a penetration; change to a response force located closer to your site; consider using on-site guards.

If a commercial alarm station is used to monitor the intrusion detection system, the system designer will have to consider who will unlock the protected facilities for the law enforcement officers when there is an alarm.

Ordinarily, when an alarm occurs, the station operator notifies the law enforcement function and then the proprietor of the facility. If the alarm station does not have a key to the facility, the proprietor will have to go to the site and open the door for the police, and probably escort the officers through the facility. But if the proprietor arrives at the site and the police are not there, he should not enter the facility or try to apprehend anyone but should wait for the police and then assist them in any way possible. (The proprietor should *not* try to be a hero!)

If a commercially operated alarm station is used to monitor the intrusion detection system and the station uses security guards, the property owner should consider having the alarm station operator keep the keys to the premises. Most alarm stations maintain strict control of keys, but their procedures should be reviewed to ensure that they satisfy the property owner's security requirements. Whether or not the owner gives the alarm station operators the keys to the facility is certainly the owner's decision, but he should realize the inconvenience and the limited effectiveness of the law enforcement officers if they must wait outside the facility until the owner arrives to let them in.

On-site guards, whether they are proprietary or commercial, generally provide the most effective response force, especially in terms of response time. They should know the facility layout and be trained to respond swiftly if there is an intrusion alarm.

The remaining considerations and suggestions pertain primarily to on-site security guards. Such guards are used for every security function, from performing menial duties as a night guard to maintaining security at nuclear plants. Guards used for security at high-security plants must comply with special training requirements. The key to an effective security force is training. The discussion on training provided here pertains primarily to the training required for interfacing security guards with the intrusion detection system. It is intended to identify some of the subjects that should be addressed in a security force training program with regard to the intrusion detection system.

Before discussing the training for intrusion detection system interfacing, it is important to realize that security guards should know and understand their company's overall security plan. They should especially know and understand the security plan of the installation to ensure the safety of the personnel and the safeguards of the assets under all circumstances. Therefore, it is important for management to have the security procedures conveniently available to the guards at all times and to have an ongoing training program to ensure that there is a continuity of understanding to maintain the integrity of the guard force.

Each security guard should know the location of all the protected areas and the most direct routes to each area from any position in the installation, especially from the alarm station. This knowledge is required to speed the guard's response to emergencies. The security plan should include maximum allowable times for guards to respond to alarms from each protected area. This is especially important if the installation is large. Varied response times could be allowed for different locations within larger facilities. Guard training could be improved by simply having unscheduled drills to determine the time required for the guards to arrive at selected alarm locations. This type of performance verification must be carefully considered with respect to the guards' response action.

Security guards should know the types of intrusion detection sensors used in each protected area, where they are physically located, and their basic limitations and operating principles. With this knowledge, a guard touring the protected areas might recognize potential problems that could cause a sensor to false alarm or prevent associated equipment from operating properly. For example, if during the day someone piles boxes in front of an ultrasonic transceiver in an area protected by an ultrasonic motion detector, the boxes will block the ultrasonic energy, leaving the area behind them unprotected during the night. A well-trained security guard would probably recognize and correct the problem.

Another more subtle problem could occur if a clerk left a large, flimsy piece of cardboard near the transceiver in a position where it could move or perhaps even fall over when a heater blower turned on. Any motion of the cardboard, especially if it fell over, could cause the ultrasonic motion detectors to give a false alarm. The guard who understands the basic operating principles of ultrasonic detectors might recognize the cardboard as a potential problem and remove it. There are many similar problems that can exist, especially with motion detectors. With proper training, the guards could alleviate many of them.

During nonworking hours, when the protected areas are secured, it is recommended that the status of each area be kept in the secure mode at the alarm station while the guard conducts an inspection of the area. In this way the guard can quickly check the operation of the sensors while making a tour. The guard should carry a radio to alert the central alarm station operator that he is entering the protected area. He also can verify the fact that the sensors initiated an alarm. For instance, the guard can check the door switch when opening the door to enter the area and then walk-test any motion detectors in the area to check their performance. During these checks the guard might detect an equipment failure or abnormality that would otherwise go unnoticed until the normal maintenance check.

Officials who are responsible for maintaining a high level of security, such as those employed by nuclear plants, may be required to enforce the two-man rule to protect against the insider threat. The two-man rule contained in the licensee agreement between nuclear facilities and the NRC is representative. The rule simply means that no less than two authorized employees can be permitted to enter a restricted area together to work, remove materials, maintain equipment, and perform other functions. The two-man rule was implemented to negate the advantage one insider would have if he were left alone with unwitnessed freedom to divert vital materials or sabotage equipment.

The security guard often serves as the second person when a maintenance person enters a restricted area to repair or maintain security equipment. If the maintenance person is the inside threat, he could probably disable any sensor unbeknown to the guard, despite his knowledge of the equipment operating principles. Therefore, after the equipment enclosure is closed, the security guard should verify that the equipment is operationally tested and working correctly. This type of system checking does not preclude a possible equipment compromise, but it does provide an excellent security measure to minimize the vulnerability of physical security systems to inside threats by maintenance technicians.

A correct operational test is performed by first changing the status of the protected area from access to secure on the alarm station monitoring panel. The repaired sensor is then operationally checked to verify that it initiates an alarm at the monitoring panel. For instance, if an ultrasonic motion sensor is repaired, the security guard should ask the monitoring operator to change the area status to the secure mode. If other employees are in the area, they should be asked to stand still while either the maintenance person or the guard conducts a walk test. With proper training, the guard will know the detection range of the sensor and how the walk test should be performed. Such training will enhance the security guard's proficiency in maintaining an effective intrusion detection system.

In case of the proprietary alarm stations, each security guard should know the basics of how to operate the alarm station monitoring and surveillance system; whom to alert in case of intrusion alarms, fire, or ambulance emergency; and what action to take in the case of a security equipment failure. Standard training should require that each guard understand the fundamentals of how the equipment operates. He should then, if possible, have an opportunity to work in the alarm station, assisting the regular station operator with his duties. This training will ensure a smooth transition from regular guard duties to those of the alarm station operator in case there is a need for another operator. It also should improve the operational relationship between the station operator and the other security guards by making all of them aware of the total security operation.

In installations where the guards are required to use special security equipment such as metal and explosives detectors, they should understand the operations, capabilities, and limitations of the equipment. All sensors are limited to some degree in their performance; it is important that these limitations be stressed and even demonstrated during training sessions. This will help ensure that guards will not be lulled into a false sense of security and, as a result, be less than thorough in performing their duties. For instance, if incoming personnel are inspected with portable metal detectors, the guard should be aware that the metal detector must pass very near (within a few inches) the item to be detected. This means that the guard should pass the metal detector over both the front and back, including the arms and legs, of the incoming person to maximize the probability of detection.

The security guards also should have a basic knowledge of the facility's or plant's overall operation, the production equipment, the utilities, and any other equipment vital to the plant's operation. With this knowledge the security guard will be more effective during plant tours by being able to identify unusual conditions. This is especially true on weekends and holidays, when most employees are off and the plant is unoccupied. In these circumstances a guard might detect a potential equipment malfunction and alert the maintenance supervisor to repair the equipment before a major breakdown occurs.

Security guard training should be encouraged and supported in every organization using proprietary guards. Many guard functions can be identified and explained during training sessions. However, since would-be intruders choose their own modes of attack, guards are expected to make judgments on their own to confront a multitude of possible situations. Well-trained security guards are better equipped to exercise good judgment and thereby enhance the overall effectiveness of the proprietor's security plan.

EQUIPMENT MAINTENANCE PROGRAM

The security equipment maintenance program should be planned along with the design of the intrusion detection system. The first consideration in planning a maintenance program is to decide who will perform the maintenance routines and procedures. Maintenance in this context includes not only equipment repair but also operational testing and preventive maintenance inspections. Several maintenance possibilities can be considered. One possibility is to have all the maintenance performed in-house. This concept is feasible if there is an electronics technician or an employee having equivalent training and experience in the maintenance department. Another possibility is to hire someone with the necessary knowledge and skills to perform the maintenance. The decision to hire a technician will depend primarily on the size of the intrusion detection system and the availability of other maintenance options. A third possibility is to have the maintenance contracted to a service company.

A choice often used by facilities that have special security equipment, such as closed circuit television (CCTV) surveillance devices and computer-managed monitoring systems, is to divide the maintenance duties. The intrusion detection equipment maintenance is performed in-house, and the CCTV surveillance devices and computer system are maintained by an outside company under a service contract.

When contracting maintenance to a service company, there are at least three key issues besides cost that should be clarified in the contract. One issue is to establish the maximum allowable time for the service personnel to arrive at the facility once the service company has been notified of the equipment problem. The second issue is to establish a reasonable length of time for completion of equipment repairs. These two issues can be combined by establishing a total length of time for the equipment to be out of service once the service company has been notified. These are especially important issues for facilities that must maintain a high level of security because when any of the security equipment is out of service, especially the computer or CCTV system, additional guards will probably be required to maintain the company's required security safeguards. The contract also should clarify who bears financial responsibility for the additional guards or inconvenience if a conflict should arise.

The third issue is to establish the availability of the maintenance service when repairs are required. In other words, will the service be available 24 hours a day, 7 days a week, or will it be available only during the service company's normal working hours? These are key issues that often cause much conflict between service companies and their customers. Be sure that your service contracts satisfy both your security and routine plant operational requirements.

Equipment Repair

There are two basic equipment repair concepts that can be used to maintain the security equipment. One concept is to repair the malfunctioning equipment on location. This means diagnosing the circuit problem and immediately replacing all discrete faulty components to repair the circuit. The second concept is to locate the malfunctioning circuit module and replace it with a spare module. This concept is becoming very popular because many manufacturers now use plug-in circuit modules in their equipment, primarily to facilitate modular replacement. For this type of equipment, the serviceman simply locates the faulty module, possibly using special diagnostic equipment or techniques, unplugs it, and installs a new unit. Other equipment manufacturers facilitate modular replacement in their equipment by connecting the circuit board input connections to a terminal strip. The circuit boards are functionally designed so that only a few wire leads have to be disconnected from the terminal strip and several mounting screws have to be removed to replace individual boards.

An advantage of the modular replacement repair concept is that it keeps the security equipment in service while the faulty circuits are repaired at some later time. The repair can be performed in-house, or the faulty modules can be returned to the manufacturer. The most popular method is to return faulty modules to the manufacturer, where they are repaired or, if necessary, replaced with other units. The modular replacement repair concept minimizes the equipment downtime; this is especially important for those facilities operating with the two-man rule. In these facilities it reduces the actual time two persons are required in the restricted areas, thereby reducing labor operating costs. To support this repair concept satisfactorily, a reasonable number of spare modules must be maintained in inventory to facilitate immediate replacement of nonworking units.

Operational Tests

The maintenance program also should include periodic operational checks, performance tests, and inspections of all security equipment. Operational checks are performed to verify that the security equipment is operating satisfactorily. Most of the operational checks can be conducted by the security guards during their patrols, but there are usually some equipment checks that will require the skills of a maintenance technician. Operational checks include checks of all protected doors, motion detectors, metal detectors, perimeter detection devices, and emergency generators. An operational check for a protected door can be conducted by having the guard simply open the door and verify with the central alarm station operator that the protecting device initiated an alarm at the monitor. A volumetric motion detector operational check can be performed by having the guard walk through the protected area when it is in the secure mode and again verify with the monitor operator that the motion detector initiated an alarm.

Exterior perimeter intrusion detection systems can be checked when the guard patrols the perimeter. If fence disturbance sensors are installed on the perimeter fence, the guard can shake the fence fabric at several locations in each zone and verify that the sensor initiated an alarm. If the perimeter is protected with invisible barrier detectors, the guard can penetrate the barriers by crossing the protected zones and verifying detection with the monitor operator. Operational checks on equipment such as emergency generators will probably have to be performed by maintenance personnel.

Performance Tests

Performance tests are more detailed than operational checks and therefore would probably be carried out by a maintenance person. For instance, the performance test for a protected door would require measuring the distance the door must open to initiate an alarm. In this test the door should be slowly opened until it initiates an alarm; then the space between the door jam and the door should be measured. This distance should be in compliance with the distance specified in the company's security plan; it is usually between 1 and 2 inches. If the test results do not comply with these requirements, the door switch should be adjusted and retested.

Performance tests for motion detectors can be conducted by having the maintenance person walk through several strategic locations in the protected area while noting the number of steps taken before being detected. Usually motion detectors are specified to detect a person within three to five steps while walking at a rate of one 30-inch step per second. The maximum number of steps allowed before an alarm is initiated could vary with the required level of protection.

A preferred way to walk-test an active motion detector, such as an ultrasonic or microwave detector, is to walk with the arms folded across the chest. This method eliminates the Doppler frequency shifts produced by the swinging of arms and results in a more repeatable test. In other words, the second time the walk-test is performed in the same area, the detector performance should be very similar to the first test. If it is not, in all probability the sensitivity of the detector has changed. The motion detector's sensitivity or orientation should be adjusted and the test repeated. The walk-test should be conducted in several different locations within the protected area to evaluate the overall volumetric protection.

In general, performance tests should be conducted at least semiannually on all intrusion detection equipment to ensure that the level of protection remains adequate.

Inspections

Preventive maintenance inspections also should be conducted on the security equipment. The inspections should include, as a minimum, checking the standby batteries, verifying the enclosure tamper protection, cleaning the detector circuits and enclosures, checking for damaged or loose wiring or damaged components, and checking to ensure that the detectors are securely mounted and aligned. Each equipment manufacturer's operational manual should be reviewed to determine whether any special maintenance is required for the equipment. This review is especially important for any special security equipment such as CCTV surveillance cameras, computerized monitoring systems, metal detectors, or generator sets.

Tamper protection circuits located within sensor and processor enclosures can be checked by slowly opening the enclosure cover until the tamper switch initiates a tamper alarm. The alarm should occur before the cover is opened far enough to allow compromise of the tamper circuit or other circuitry. This distance is usually about ¼ inch. The tamper test should be conducted with the alarm monitor in the access mode. This is the operating mode in which the detector would be most vulnerable to a tampering attempt, since the individual could move freely in the vicinity of the units without fear of detection.

When an enclosure is open, it should be cleaned and inspected. Cleaning is especially important for out-of-doors equipment. Insects usually find their way into most enclosures. Dust also gets into enclosures, where it coats the circuits and critical components. Both insects and dust can create operational problems if they are allowed to collect, especially around the sensors of motion and barrier-type detectors.

The detector enclosures, especially the sensor enclosures, should be inspected to ensure that they are securely mounted. If a sensor becomes loose, external forces could cause the sensor to vibrate or lose alignment, and excessive vibrations may in turn cause false alarms.

After a detector has been cleaned, the circuit should be inspected for damaged components and loose or damaged wires. As simple as this inspection is, it may prevent future equipment malfunctions that could occur at some inconvenient or critical time.

Every detector standby battery also should be inspected and tested while its enclosure is open. Gelled electrolyte batteries are used as standby batteries by many intrusion detection equipment manufacturers. These batteries are sealed and consequently are relatively maintenance free. However, the battery terminals should be inspected to ensure that they are clean and free of corrosion, and the battery cells should be checked for ruptures. Of course, any battery that is damaged or ruptured should be replaced.

When a battery is first installed and at each subsequent inspection, the AC power should be removed from the detector as a test to ensure that the detector will operate satisfactorily on standby power. When the AC power is turned off, the detector should demonstrate that it can automatically shift to the standby battery without initiating an alarm. Likewise, it should not initiate an alarm when the AC power is restored. To complete the test, the detector should be operationally tested while it is powered by the standby battery.

Gelled electrolyte batteries have an average service life of 2 to 4 years when operated within the manufacturer-specified temperature limits. After the maximum service time designated by the battery manufacturer, the battery should be replaced because its capacity could be marginal in terms of operation time. To eliminate keeping records of how long a battery has been in service, the date of installation should be marked on each battery. Then the date can be conveniently checked at each inspection.

Training

Maintenance personnel who are responsible for maintaining the intrusion detection equipment should have a basic working knowledge of electronics. They also should possess the knowledge and skill needed to operate a volt/ohmmeter and perhaps an oscilloscope; this depends on the sophistication of the security equipment and the particular maintenance concept. Having such knowledge, the maintenance personnel should be able to maintain most types of intrusion detection equipment by using the manufacturer's operation and maintenance manuals. However, the more sophisticated equipment, such as CCTV cameras and computer-managed monitoring systems, will probably require additional training and possibly special diagnostic hardware or software.

Many manufacturers conduct short training courses related to the operation and maintenance of their equipment. It is recommended that maintenance personnel take advantage of these courses. This recommendation is especially applicable to those facilities that must maintain an excellent security posture while relying on service contracts for maintenance. For instance, if a computer-managed monitoring system is opened for checks and repair by an outside technician, the computer could be vulnerable to compromise by the outsider, who could modify the memory so that the computer would ignore certain protected areas at some later time, thereby leaving those areas vulnerable to penetration by an adversary. This type of compromise would not necessarily be detected by the normal performance verification tests of the types discussed earlier. Because of the complexity of the computer and the fact that the system could be compromised by a knowledgeable individual, the maintenance person monitoring the contractor technician must be reasonably knowledgeable of computer principles of operation and understand the basic functions of each computer module.

Therefore, it is recommended that the individual responsible for monitoring computer maintenance should attend the relevant computer training courses offered by the system manufacturer unless he already possesses extensive computer knowledge. Having this training might not prevent a compromise, but it certainly lessens the chances of its happening.

Chapter 3

Design Coordination

The designer should continually coordinate his intrusion detection system design and maintenance concepts with those individuals who will be affected by its implementation. These are the individuals who must operate and maintain the facility's performance within any restrictions that might be imposed by the security system. The designer also should be concerned about those individuals who are responsible for the safety of the employees and other occupants of the premises. These are the same individuals who are usually forgotten by the security system designer until the system is already installed or in the process of being installed. Then, much to the designer's dismay, the operations manager says, "You can't install that equipment there because—." Or the safety officers say, "That door can't be locked during the day because—." And then the designer's problems really begin.

This type of problem can be eliminated if the security system design is properly coordinated before the fact. Another benefit is that the individuals who participate in the system design will have a personal interest in its implementation and acceptance by both the employees and management. Management support is needed for the security system to be successful. Management must set an example by following the security procedures themselves, as well as insisting that all security procedures be followed by others and that all systems be maintained in operations.

Operations is defined as the group composed of people who manufacture the products, refine the minerals, generate the electricity, operate the department store, manage the office building, etc. In other words, these are the people who are responsible for the existence of the assets the intrusion detection system is being designed to safeguard. Therefore, time should be taken to understand their requirements and to review the proposed system design with them. As obvious as this recommendation appears, many systems are designed without giving any consideration to the operator or user. The design review should start with the initial system concept and continue through the final system design and installation. Follow-up reviews after installation will alert the designer to system problems that could be detrimental to the maximum effectiveness of the system if they are not corrected. These include not only hardware and operating problems, but also problems associated with management and employee acceptance of the intrusion detection system.

A general training session should be conducted before the system is operational to apprise employees of the need for the security system, acquaint them with the equipment, and instruct them regarding proper system operations. The training session could be highlighted by a tour of the facility to demonstrate, if possible, the operation of each piece of equipment. A well-conducted training session will eliminate many day-to-day problems and improve employee acceptance of the system. The acceptance might be enhanced even more if a responsible individual from management attends the training session and addresses the importance of the security system.

Additional training might be required for those employees who must comply with special operating procedures as a result of the new security equipment. For instance, if a system is installed to limit access to controlled areas, the employees affected by this system would require special training in its operation.

FIRE AND SAFETY OFFICERS

Since the fire and safety officers are responsible for the safety of all occupants of the facility requiring the intrusion detection system, they should be included in the system design coordination. Both the fire and safety officers will be concerned about the types of locking and access control systems and bars and grilles installed on windows and doors.

MAINTENANCE DEPARTMENT

Probably the most overlooked department with respect to being consulted on any system design project is the maintenance department. Yet these are the individuals who will probably be given the responsibility of maintaining the equipment after it is installed. Therefore, rather than just handing them the responsibility of maintaining your security equipment, give them the opportunity to participate in the system design. They should participate in selecting the equipment location within the facility, routing the equipment's interconnecting cables, and selecting the system maintenance concept, including the confirmation of estimated maintenance costs.

Quite often the plant drawings are not kept up-to-date to depict the latest equipment locations, additions, or deletions, or they do not show the new wall or the fact that new plumbing has been added. Sometimes these changes, especially the obvious ones, can be noted during a walk-through survey; but many of the subtle changes, such as the additional plumbing or cable trays, will probably be overlooked. The maintenance people will probably be familiar with most of these changes and additions and therefore will be helpful in locating the security equipment and especially helpful in selecting the best cable routes.

The maintenance supervisor should be consulted with regard to selecting the most appropriate maintenance concept for the intrusion detection system. The supervisor understands his employees and knows their technical qualifications and skills. The supervisor will sometimes misjudge their ability to maintain the security equipment, however. The usual first impression is that anything containing electronic circuitry is too complicated for his people to maintain. He might be right, but more often than not, the department can perform the maintenance if given sufficient training.

If the maintenance department has qualified electricians or electronics technicians who can operate a volt/ohmmeter and have the manual dexterity to work with small electronic modules, then they should be able to perform most maintenance on equipment using the modular replacement concept. Sometimes it is helpful to demonstrate the equipment operation and perhaps give the supervisor a hands-on demonstration of how to troubleshoot and repair the equipment. With this demonstration, and since most manufacturers have maintenance manuals and on-site instructions on operation, the supervisor should be less apprehensive about the maintenance and repair of the equipment. Another suggestion is to offer additional training for the maintenance personnel or hire an electronics technician who could perform the maintenance.

Sometimes the maintenance supervisor is still apprehensive and recommends that the maintenance be contracted. Quite often after the maintenance has been contracted and the maintenance supervisor has an opportunity to witness maintenance operations during the duration of the contract, however, he will reconsider and accept the maintenance responsibility instead of renewing the contract.

Chapter 4

Design Guide

An intrusion detection system should be designed to provide the response guards with the earliest possible warning of an unauthorized intrusion. It follows that before an intrusion detection system can be optimally designed, the designer must understand the operational capabilities and limitations of the security equipment and be knowledgeable about the threat to the assets or facilities requiring protection. The equipment's capabilities and limitations will be discussed in detail in the remaining chapters of the book. The intent of this chapter is to provide guidelines for determining intrusion detection system requirements for levels of security that can be assigned to the assets requiring protection; identify security procedures and controls that should be considered to minimize the effectiveness of the inside threat; and define the internal and external threat skills as they pertain to the different levels of security.

LEVELS OF SECURITY

Assets in most facilities or areas requiring protection can be classified as belonging in one of the following four security levels: Level A, Level B, Level C, or Level D. Level A suggests the minimum level of protection against a highly skilled adversary, while Level D suggests the minimum level of protection for an unskilled adversary.

This guide recommends the types of security equipment that should be considered for detecting intrusions by the threat identified for each level of security. If additional intrusion detection equipment or security measures are required to minimize the effectiveness of a perceived threat for a specific facility, they should be incorporated into the system design.

Individual facilities will require a security system incorporating some or all of the recommended intrusion detection equipment and security measures to protect their particular assets. The level of security for each protected area should be based on the criticality of the assets requiring protection, the vulnerability of the assets, and the skill level of the perceived threat. The threat could be any combination of internal and external, with a skill level ranging from highly skilled to unskilled, depending on the hostile intent and the value, monetary or intrinsic, of the assets being protected.

The design philosophy for each of the following levels of security is based on the adversary threat and skill levels shown in Table 4–1. The following security level descriptions are provided to assist in specifying the required security levels.

Level A (Maximum Level Security)

This level of security is suggested for areas containing high-value monetary and intrinsic resources, the compromise or loss of which would have a permanent or long-term effect on the operation or existence of the business or operation. Unauthorized access to the area could result in destruction, disclosure of information, or loss of control of the resources. A security system should ensure to the highest degree possible that only those persons who actually require entry and who have appropriate need should be allowed entry. The total security effort for the area should provide the highest probability of detection, assessment, and prevention of unauthorized access to the protected items. The intrusion detection system should detect any unauthorized penetration of the boundaries of the protected area—fences, walls, ceilings, doors, or windows—because the mere presence of an intruder in the protected area would be unacceptable. Visual surveillance and alarm assessment of the protected areas should include CCTV for the monitoring guards. The response guards should be adequate in numbers, well trained, and capable of protecting the assets from the highly skilled intruder.

Suggested intrusion detection systems for Level A areas include two complete levels of penetration detection of the exterior perimeter and building or protected area barriers. Motion sensors might be omitted from internal Level A areas if access control precludes "stay-behind" intruders. In areas where stay-behinds could be a threat, however, motion detectors should be used. The alarm monitoring system's signal transmission line supervisory or signal authentication technique should neutralize to the highest degree possible, possibly with a key-changeable code, the effectiveness of the highly skilled threat. Determination of the exact type and level of detection capability is at the discretion of the owner or proprietor of the assets requiring protection (or his designated representative).

Table 4–1   Level of Security Based on Threat

	Internal Threat	External Threat
Level A	Highly skilled	Highly skilled
Level B	Highly skilled	Skilled
Level C	Skilled	Unskilled
Level D	Unskilled	Unskilled

Other security measures that should be considered for physical and psychological effects for Level A areas are:

1. Multiple perimeter barriers
2. High-security locks
3. Structurally sound door assemblies, walls, floors, and ceilings
4. Window grilles
5. Safes and vaults
6. Security lighting
7. Television and visual surveillance for alarm assessment
8. Access control
9. Active random patrols
10. Trained dogs
11. Well-trained and armed response forces

Level B (Advanced Level Security)

This level of security is suggested for areas containing high-value monetary and intrinsic resources, the compromise or loss of which would have a short-term effect on the operation or business. The total security effort for this area should provide a high probability of detection/assessment or prevention of unauthorized penetration or approach to the protected items. The security system should detect any unauthorized penetration of the boundaries of the protected area that could result in removal of or damage to sensitive items within the protected area.

Suggested coverage for Level B areas includes one level of penetration detection at the exterior perimeter and building or protected area barriers, full volumetric motion detection around protected items and along anticipated intrusion paths, and point detection for appropriate items.

The alarm system's signal line transmission supervisory or signal authentication technique should be capable of neutralizing the effectiveness of a skilled external adversary attempting to compromise the monitoring system. Again, the level of coverage is at the discretion of the owner, proprietor, or a designated representative.

Other physical and psychological security measures that should be considered for Level B areas are the same as those for Level A areas.

Level C (Intermediate Level Security)

This level of security is suggested for areas containing pilferable material or sensitive items that attract the intruder because of monetary value. The total security effort for the area should provide a good probability of intruder detection to prevent unauthorized penetration and removal of the protected items. Coverage for Level C areas should include penetration detection at the perimeter fence when valuable assets are stored outside buildings. When the assets are stored inside, penetration detection should be provided on all doors and windows, motion detection should be used along avenues of approach and around protected items, and point detection should be employed on appropriate items.

The alarm monitor's signal transmission technique should be adequate to detect an unskilled external adversary attempting to compromise the monitoring system. The level of coverage is at the discretion of the owner, proprietor, or a designated representative.

Other physical and psychological security measures that should be considered for Level C areas are:

1. Physical barriers
2. Good locks and door assemblies
3. Window grilles
4. Local audible alarms
5. Warning signs
6. Random patrols by police

Level D (Basic Level Security)

This level of security is suggested for administrative control and in buffer areas providing security restriction for areas of a higher security category. Pilferable items within the area should have the same physical protection as those in Level C. The security system should detect any unauthorized penetration of a protected area that could result in removal of a protected item. The alarm monitoring system's signal line supervisory technique should detect an unskilled adversary attempting to compromise the signal transmission.

Suggested coverage for Level D areas includes penetration detection on doors and windows, motion detection around protected items or along avenues of approach to higher-level areas, and point detection on appropriate items. The level of coverage is at the discretion of the owner, proprietor, or a designated representative.

Tables 4–2 through 4–5 are a summary of the recommended detection considerations for the associated security levels. Table 4–6 suggests related security procedures that could be beneficial.

THREAT

The nature and degree of the security threat ranges from a casual incident to a sophisticated attack and varies with respect to geographic location, demographics, level of hostile intent, and criticality and vulnerability of the target.

Table 4-2 Intrusion Detection System Recommendations: Level A

Maximum Security	IDS Requirements		
	Penetration	Motion	Point
The security system should provide the highest probability of detection/assessment and prevention of unauthorized access to the protected items. It should be capable of detecting the actions of a highly skilled external threat penetrating or moving within the protected area for the purpose of sabotage or theft of the assets and a highly skilled internal threat tampering with or attempting to compromise the intrusion detection system for future asset sabotage or theft.	Penetration sensors should detect the physical act of climbing over or under perimeter barriers, making man-size openings through structural barriers, and opening of doors into protected areas. Multiple levels of penetration detection should be considered. This requires total penetration detection for each level by sensors that detect someone crossing the perimeter barriers, crossing the area between the perimeter barriers and facility, and penetrating the facility's structural barriers and opening any door.	Motion sensors should detect anyone moving inside the protected area.	Proximity sensors should detect anyone touching or removing protected items.

Table 4–3 Intrusion Detection System Recommendations: Level B

Advanced Security	IDS Requirements		
	Penetration	Motion	Point
The security system should provide a high probability of detection/assessment and prevention of unauthorized access to the protected items. It should be capable of detecting the actions of a skilled external threat penetrating or moving within the protected area and a highly skilled internal threat tampering with the intrusion detection system for future asset theft.	Penetration sensors should detect the physical act of climbing over or cutting through the perimeter fence or crossing the perimeter boundaries, making a man-size opening through a structural barrier protecting the assets, opening any door or window into the protected area, and penetrating the walls or structural barriers protecting the assets.	Motion sensors should detect the presence of anyone moving inside the protected area.	Point sensors should detect anyone touching or removing a protected item.

Table 4–4 Intrusion Detection System Recommendations: Level C

	IDS Requirements		
Intermediate Security	*Penetration*	*Motion*	*Point*
The security for this area should provide a reasonable probability of detection and prevention of unauthorized penetration, approach, or removal of protected items. It should be capable of detecting the actions of a skilled external threat entering through any door or window and moving toward or removing the protected item, and a skilled internal threat tampering with the intrusion detection equipment.	Penetration sensors should detect the physical act of climbing over the perimeter fence or opening a door or window leading to the protected area.	Motion sensors should detect the presence of anyone moving toward or in the area of the protected item. Only the avenues of most likely approach or areas around the most valuable items require protection.	Point sensors should detect anyone touching or attempting to remove a protected item.

Table 4–5 Intrusion Detection System Recommendations: Level D

Basic Security	IDS Requirements		
	Penetration	Motion	Point
Security for this area should provide a reasonable probability of detection or prevention of unauthorized penetration, approach, or removal of the items protected. It should be capable of detecting the actions of an unskilled external threat entering through a door or window or moving within the protected area for the purpose of theft and an unskilled internal threat tampering with the intrusion detection equipment.	Penetration sensors should detect the physical act of opening any door or window leading to the protected area.	Motion sensors should detect the presence of anyone moving toward or in the area of the protected item. Only the avenues of most likely approach or areas around the most valuable items require protection.	Point sensors should detect anyone touching or attempting to remove a protected item.

Table 4–6 Suggested Security Operational Procedures

Key Control. Keys should be controlled by an authorized individual and stored in a secure cabinet or safe.

Lock Rotation. Key and combination locks should be changed or rotated periodically and when anyone with possession of a key or knowledgeable about the lock combination leaves the organization.

Two-Man Rule. Two authorized individuals should be required to simultaneously occupy protected areas for operations and maintenance.

Patrols. Protected areas should be patrolled on a random but regular basis by trained guards.

Response Force. The size and training of the response force should be commensurate with the level of security.

Response Time. The response force should respond to a protected area in alarm in time to prevent the adversary from accomplishing his mission.

Personnel Reliability Program. Operators and maintainers should have a satisfactory background as determined by a systematic investigation.

Drawing Control. "As-built" intrusion detection system drawings should be controlled and stored in secured containers.

Sensor Testing. All sensors should be operationally tested often enough to ensure that the detection remains commensurate with the security level. Tests should be conducted at least semiannually.

Variations in the threat also are dependent on political or social unrest, world tensions, and economic factors. The threat can be internal or external, vary in intensity, and range from highly skilled to unskilled depending on the motivation. The motivation might be pilferage, theft, sabotage, espionage, extortion, or vandalism for monetary gain, self-esteem, social change, or political and ideological purposes.

A casual incident could occur when premises or articles are left unlocked and unprotected and the intruder becomes aware of their vulnerability by accident or coincidence. A sophisticated attack could occur when an organized and very capable group plans and implements an attack on patrolled and monitored facilities. Capability, motive, and the likelihood of success are factors that help determine whether an attack will be attempted. The intruders are more likely to be deterred when the value of the prize is small and the risk of detection and capture is great. There are instances, however, where terrorists might regard publicity resulting from an attempt as adequate reward regardless of the success or failure of the attack. In these cases no amount of known surveillance and detection equipment would deter the attacker, and only strong defensive means would be effective.

In general, the amount of protection required for a facility is determined by the value of the material and facility to be protected and by the expected competence of a perceived attacker. In many cases the level of protection used is determined by its cost when compared to the value of the potential loss and the probability that the cost incurred would be adequate to deter an intruder.

Probably the most difficult aspect of determining the level of protection required is to predict the capability and persistence of an intruder. If the perceived reward is great enough, no amount of protection short of a heavily armed defense team would discourage an attack.

Other factors affecting the level of protection are government regulations and codes or requirements imposed by insurers. These factors must be considered in the threat and protection assessment of any site. A description of each external and internal threat level follows.

External Threat

The external threat can generally be divided into three categories: highly skilled, skilled, and unskilled.

Highly Skilled

These intruders attempt penetrations for the purpose of conducting paramilitary operations, espionage, sabotage, or theft or compromise of sensitive or high-value items. They can be expected to plan their entry thoroughly, select the time and method of entry with care, and be very sophisticated and devious in gaining access into fenced compounds having perimeter intrusion detection systems and into buildings protected by intrusion detection systems. Highly skilled intruders would be likely to have support from staff research mathematicians, computer scientists, or electronics engineers with M.S. and Ph.D. degrees or with equivalent knowledge and understanding of advanced cryptanalytic techniques. They would probably attempt to defeat the alarm transmission system and other physical protective measures to gain surreptitious access to the protected facility. A vulnerable part of any intrusion detection system is the alarm and signal transmission links, especially when the communication lines leave the protected site and travel through open areas to reach the alarm monitoring station.

The highly skilled threat can be expected to have knowledge of the site's guard patrol and response routine, the physical configuration and topography, and the location of the target and its physical protection, including the intrusion detection sensors' locations, capabilities, and limitations. They can be expected to attempt to compromise any perimeter sensors by penetrating the exterior barriers at the most vulnerable locations—for instance, where sensors are improperly applied, illumination and surveillance are marginal, physical resistance is least, or guard response is difficult. Intruders can be expected to attempt to compromise the perimeter fence disturbance sensors by avoiding the fence while going over or under it or by cutting the fence fabric in such a manner as to defeat the detection logic. They might skillfully traverse the area between the perimeter barrier and the targeted facility using stealthy maneuvers to avoid visual detection, or they might circumvent or penetrate physical barriers using sophisticated, fast-cutting, low-energy-producing cutting devices to gain access. Once inside, they might cleverly maneuver to reach the targeted item without being detected and then defeat the most sophisticated locks or penetrate the barriers to minimize detection.

The highly skilled intruder can be expected to move very quickly or slowly because interior motion sensors can theoretically be defeated by very fast or slow movement. Sustained activity at very fast or slow speeds is difficult to maintain inside the protected area without detection, however. The sophisticated intruder should be expected to compromise the intrusion detection system by attacking alarm signal transmission lines with data substitution techniques aimed at preventing transmission of the alarm signal. They might attempt to cause massive disruption of communications, cut off AC power to the intrusion detection system to destroy its effectiveness, or bridge protected ground lanes to defeat sensors. They might move very slowly or quickly to escape detection by velocity-sensitive motion detectors or tunnel under barriers to gain access to interior zones within critical storage facilities.

Skilled

These intruders might attempt penetration solely for the purpose of theft for personal gain. They can be expected to attempt entry with some planning but with less technical and financial support than the highly skilled threat. They can, however, be expected to have technical support (mathematicians, computer scientists, or electronics engineers with a B.S. degree or equivalent knowledge) and have financial resources to obtain the necessary equipment to compromise an intrusion detection system monitoring system using less than the NBS algorithm signal authentication technique. They can be expected to evaluate the security posture by considering appropriate time factors, location vulnerability, and personnel/guard presence. They also can be expected to circumvent an unsophisticated or improperly installed perimeter intrusion detection system, gain access to any building by compromising most locking systems, and avoid detection by unsophisticated intrusion detection devices.

The primary differences between the highly skilled intruder and the skilled intruder are their technical understanding of the intrusion detection system capabilities and, in particular, the available resources and knowledge necessary to compromise line supervision using less than pseudorandom signal transmission from the protected area.

Unskilled

These intruders would attempt penetration for the purpose of theft and monetary reward without detailed planning or highly sophisticated equipment. They can be expected to gain access into fenced compounds or buildings by brute force, probably through the doors or windows after climbing over, cutting through, or lifting the fence fabric and crawling under it. Unlike highly skilled and skilled intruders, they can be expected to have only limited knowledge of intrusion detection system capabilities. They can, however, be expected to avoid being detected by circumventing fences and doors or windows that are obviously protected with intrusion detection sensors.

Internal Threat

The internal threat is inherently much more insidious than the external threat because the insider has authorized access to protected areas. For example, the equipment maintenance person often has free access to the intrusion detection system, where he could compromise critical equipment. The most cost-effective way of neutralizing or minimizing the internal threat is to incorporate control procedures, as indicated in Table 4–7, that will limit access to the protected areas, items, and intrusion detection equipment.

Like the external threat, the internal threat includes highly skilled, skilled, and unskilled individuals. A discussion of the capabilities of each skill level follows.

Highly Skilled

The primary difference between the external and internal threat is that the internal threat is likely to have complete access to the intrusion detection equipment and, in particular, to the sensor signal and alarm transmission lines. This will be supported with knowledge of local security procedures. Insiders possess the same technical and financial support as skilled external threats. Skilled insiders can be expected to employ several deliberate techniques to compromise the security of a protected area. They might modify sensor communication lines to inhibit alarms if security procedures do not require tests after maintenance work. They might adjust or alter the sensor processor to reduce sensor sensitivity. They can learn the sensor detection pattern and identify associated weaknesses in system performance. If they can find no unprotected areas, they might shield or isolate motion sensors to create "dead zones." They also might attempt to avoid motion detection by moving through the protected area too slowly to be detected by the sensor and by moving in such a way as to minimize the effective target area projected toward the sensor.

Table 4–7 Threat/Physical Security Matrix

Protected Site	Threat		
	Unskilled	Skilled	Highly Skilled
Residential			
Physical	Good door and window locks Solid doors Lighting	High-grade door and window locks Structurally sound barrier and door assemblies Window grilles Interior and exterior lighting	Rewards probably not worthy of their effort
Detection	Mechanical or magnetic door contacts Pressure mats	Interior and exterior perimeter IDS Balanced magnetic door contacts	
Alarm transmission	Local audible alarms		
Annunciation			
Miscellaneous	Pet dog or recorded sounds Timed lighting Warning signs Neighborhood watch Police patrols Safes	Interrogate/response DC or AC transmission Watchdogs Police patrols Safes/vaults	
Commercial			
Physical	Good door and window locks Solid doors Lighting Perimeter fence	High-grade door and window locks Structurally sound door assemblies, walls, and ceilings Window grilles Safes/vaults	High-grade door and window locks Structurally sound door assemblies, walls, and ceilings Window grilles Safes/vaults

Table 4-7 (continued)

Protected Site	Threat		
	Unskilled	Skilled	Highly Skilled
Commercial (cont.)			
Exterior detection	Fence strain wire sensors Fence disturbance sensors	Interior and exterior lighting Perimeter fence or barriers Fence disturbance sensors Invisible microwave or infrared barriers Buried line sensors	Interior and exterior lighting Perimeter fence or barriers Fence disturbance sensors Invisible microwave or infrared barriers Buried line sensors
Interior detection	Magnetic door contacts Window foil Glass breakage detectors	Balanced magnetic switches Barrier penetration sensors Glass breakage detectors Volumetric motion detectors Capacitance proximity sensors	Balanced magnetic switches Barrier penetration sensors Glass breakage detectors Volumetric motion detectors Capacitance proximity sensors
Alarm transmission	Local audible alarms McCulloh alarms Digital dialers	Interrogate/response with coding AC transmission	Interrogate/response with pseudorandom coding AC transmission
Miscellaneous	Warning signs Television surveillance Watchdog	Attack dogs or watchdogs Full-time guards Television surveillance and alarm assessment	Attack dogs or watchdogs Full-time guards Television surveillance and alarm assessment
Industrial			
Physical	Perimeter fence High-security locks Structurally sound door assemblies Window grilles	Perimeter fence High-security locks Structurally sound door assemblies Window grilles	Rewards probably not worthy of their effort

Category			
Exterior detection	Safes/vaults Lighting Fence disturbance sensors Fence strain sensors	Safes/vaults Security lighting Fence disturbance sensors Invisible perimeter barriers (microwave or infrared) Electric-field sensors Buried line sensors	
Interior detection	Magnetic switches Glass breakage detectors Photoelectric barriers Breakwire detectors	Balanced magnetic door switches Capacitance proximity detectors Volumetric motion detectors Vibration detectors	
Alarm transmission	Digital dialers McCulloh alarms DC or AC transmission	Interrogate response	
Miscellaneous	Guards Police patrols Warning signs Local audible alarms	Attack dogs or watchdogs Armed guards Television surveillance and alarm assessment	
High-Risk Facilities	Would not consider the risk of being caught		
Physical		Multiple fences High-security locks Structurally sound door assemblies Window grilles Safes/vaults Structurally sound walls and ceilings Security lighting	Multiple perimeter barriers High-security locks Structurally sound door assemblies Window grilles Safes/vaults Structurally sound walls and ceilings Security lighting

Table 4-7 (continued)

Protected Site	Threat		
	Unskilled	Skilled	Highly Skilled
High-Risk Facilities (continued)			
Exterior detection		Fence disturbance sensors Invisible barriers (microwave or infrared) Electric-field sensors Buried line sensors	Fence disturbance sensors Invisible barriers (microwave or infrared) Electric-field sensors Buried line sensors
Interior detection		Balanced magnetic door switches Volumetric motion detectors Vibration detectors Television with automatic motion detection Capacitance proximity detectors	Balanced magnetic door switches Volumetric motion detectors Vibration detectors Television with automatic motion detection Capacitance proximity detectors
Alarm transmission		Interrogate/response with pseudorandom coding	Interrogate/response with pseudorandom coding
Miscellaneous		Armed guards Watchdogs Television surveillance and alarm assessment	Armed guards Watchdogs Television surveillance and alarm assessment Response force

Skilled

This threat will have the same technical and financial support as the external skilled threat, while having an insider's advantage. Skilled internal intruders might be expected to use most of the same techniques mentioned for highly skilled internal intruders. Their probability of success will be lower because their technical skills and knowledge are not as great.

Unskilled

This threat will have the same knowledge as the unskilled external threat but will have an insider's advantage. Unskilled internal intruders, like unskilled external intruders, will have only limited knowledge of the intrusion detection system's capabilities. They will, however, have the opportunity to observe internal security measures, such as guard schedules and maintenance activities. They can be expected to use this knowledge to attempt intrusion at a time when areas might be unprotected or the detection system is not operating.

Table 4–7 lists the types of protective measures that should be considered when designing a security system. The matrix is developed for four types of facilities (residential, commercial, industrial, and high risk).

Chapter 5

Design Considerations

Designing an effective security system requires the total integration and coordination of all the user's security and operational requirements with the appropriate security systems and procedures that will effectively satisfy these requirements. The primary requirement for the security system is that it must be designed adequately to safeguard the user's assets against an anticipated threat. The threat can be internal or external to the organization, but the security systems and measures discussed in these guidelines pertain only to an external threat.

The following questions are included as considerations to assist managers in analyzing the threat, establishing the security requirements, conducting a site security survey, and selecting security systems and the necessary support services. The questions apply to designing a security system for facilities with buildings that require exterior perimeter and internal protection. Many of them might not be applicable to your specific security requirements. They also are not necessarily designed to elicit a yes or no answer but to stimulate your imagination, especially during the initial phase of your security system design.

THREAT ANALYSIS

The first phase of the threat analysis should be to interview the user to determine his security concerns and concept of the threat. Following are some questions that should be addressed during the interview:

1. What are the assets or facilities that require protection?
2. What is the monetary and intrinsic value of the assets?
3. What do you—the user—perceive the threat to be?
4. Are your assets an attractive target for terrorist activities or those of a dissident group?
5. Where are the assets located with respect to likely entrance points?
6. What are the crime statistics in the neighborhood?
7. How effective is the local law enforcement agency?

8. How fast and dependable are the police in responding to your facility in an emergency?
9. What is your present security system?
10. If intrusion alarms will be part of the security system, who will respond to assess the alarms?
11. How long will it take the response force to arrive at the site when there is an alarm?
12. Who are your neighbors, and how dependable are they?
13. What effect will the presence of your neighbors or their type of business have on the threat?
14. Do the local police patrol the site?

LEVEL OF SECURITY

Once the user has identified the characteristics of the threat, they can be compared to the threat levels defined in Chapter 4. Based on the threat and the value of the assets requiring protection, a security level can be established.

Following are some questions that will serve as a reminder and assist in establishing the required threat and security level. The highest security level in which the answers to all the questions are yes should be the minimum security level for the area or assets requiring protection.

Level A (Maximum Level Security)

1. Does the area contain high-value monetary or intrinsic resources where compromise or loss would have a long-term effect on the business or operation?
2. Can unauthorized access result in destruction, disclosure of information, or loss of resources?
3. Should the security system allow entry, to the highest degree possible, only to authorized persons?
4. Should the intrusion detection system detect any penetration of the boundaries with the highest probability of detection?
5. Is CCTV or a permanent guard required to safeguard the assets?

Level B (Advanced Level Security)

1. Does the area contain high-value monetary or intrinsic resources where compromise or loss would have a short-term effect on operation?
2. Should the security systems ensure a high probability of detection of unauthorized penetration of any boundary and movement within the protected area?

Level C (Intermediate Level Security)

1. Does the area contain pilferable material or sensitive items?
2. Should the security system provide a good probability of detecting any-one removing the protected item or items?

Level D (Basic Level Security)

1. Does the area need only administrative control?
2. Does the area provide a buffer zone for higher security areas?
3. Should the security system detect the presence of anyone moving in the area?

SITE SURVEY

The security site survey is a primary and essential prerequisite in designing a physical security system. This is the time to assess the entire facility requiring protection to evaluate its vulnerability to the perceived threat. Site surveys should be conducted with either the owner, the manager, or one of their representatives who is knowledgeable about the security needs. The survey team should be accompanied by someone who is knowledgeable about facility operations, especially if it is a manufacturing or utility facility.

The survey should start at the perimeter fence by examining the entire length of the fence, the area outside and inside the fence, and the exterior grounds between the fence and buildings. It should conclude with a detailed examination of the outside and inside of the building or buildings requiring protection.

The site survey should be conducted after the designer has interviewed the owner and other individuals who can contribute to improving the designer's understanding of the security requirements. The designer should have site drawings that show the perimeter fence, grounds, building positions, and basic floor plan of the buildings. Specific site information can then be referenced on the drawing during the site survey.

Following are some questions that should be answered by close examination of the items or areas involved in the security system design. Also included are other general questions that might be applicable to your security system design. The survey questions are divided into separate areas of concern.

Perimeter Fence

1. Is the fence high and secure enough to be effective against the anticipated threat?

2. Is the fence fabric tight, and are the posts well anchored?
3. What is the length of the fence along each side?
4. Are there gaps or washouts under the fence where an intruder could crawl under?
5. Are there trees or structures near the outside of the fence that could aid an intruder in climbing over the fence or avoiding contact with the fence if it is protected by intrusion alarms?
6. Are there materials or other items piled near the inside of the fence that could assist an intruder retreating from the site?
7. Are there weeds or bushes growing along the fence line that could interfere with guard surveillance or cause nuisance alarms if the fence is protected with fence disturbance sensors?
8. Are there signs loosely mounted to the fence that could rattle the fence and cause nuisance alarms if the fence is protected by sensors?
9. Are all the gates properly locked and secured so they will not rattle if the fence is protected by sensors?
10. Have unnecessary gates been eliminated?
11. Is the gate-mounting hardware secured so it cannot be easily unfastened to remove the gate?
12. Are the gate keys in the possession of authorized people?
13. What is the distance between the fence and the buildings requiring protection?
14. Where are likely places an intruder might attempt to penetrate the fence?
15. What are the weather conditions at the site—snow, rain, humidity, and temperature, both high and low?
16. Does snow accumulate along the fence to heights that will compromise the fence's effectiveness?

Exterior Grounds

1. Is the terrain level, especially around the perimeter where barrier-type intrusion detectors might be installed?
2. What is the ground cover (grass, brush, or trees), especially around the perimeter?
3. Are there obstacles around the perimeter that would interfere with invisible barrier-type sensors?
4. Are there trees or telephone poles near the perimeter that could interfere with buried seismic sensors?
5. Are there lights on the grounds, and if so, what is the type of lamp, lamp wattage, illumination level, and illumination uniformity?
6. Are there roads around the grounds or along the perimeter that could be used for patrolling?
7. Do domestic animals graze inside the site, or do wild animals penetrate the perimeter barriers?

Building Exterior

1. Is the structural integrity of the building, including the sides, roof, doors, and windows, capable of resisting or delaying the anticipated threat?
2. Are door hinges installed so that the hinge cannot be easily removed to open the door?
3. Are there glass panels in or near the door that could be broken to reach any lock releases?
4. Are all unnecessary doors permanently secured or removed and filled in?
5. Are the door keys issued only to authorized personnel?
6. Are the exterior doors protected with intrusion alarms?
7. If door switches are used, are the signal wires accessible?
8. Are all windows within 14 feet of the ground capable of resisting the anticipated threat?
9. Are all nonessential windows permanently secured or removed and filled in?
10. Are the windows protected by intrusion alarms?
11. Are the signal wires accessible?
12. Can grilles or bars be added over the windows to improve their penetration resistance?
13. Can security glass be used to improve the window penetration resistance?
14. Does the exterior of the building have any low roofs or protruding surfaces that could be used to reach unprotected windows?
15. Can entrance to your building be gained from an adjoining building?
16. How accessible is the main roof?
17. Are there exterior ladders on the building for access to the roof?
18. Are there skylights, hatches, air-conditioning ducts or vents, or any openings greater than 96 square inches with a minimum dimension of 6 inches through which a small person could squeeze?
19. Are these openings protected by bars or grilles?
20. Is the roof construction capable of resisting or deterring the anticipated threat?
21. Are there cable entrances, sewers, or tunnels leading into the building from outside?
22. Besides protecting all the building's exterior doors and vulnerable windows and vents with intrusion alarms, should the exterior walls be protected with barrier penetration detectors?

Building Interior

1. Where are the assets located inside the building or the areas that require protection?

2. Are the assets located in a safe or vault?
3. What is the construction or penetration resistance of the room or vault containing the assets?
4. How long will the structure delay a determined intruder, or is it adequately constructed to deter the anticipated threat?
5. Can the structure's penetration resistance be improved?
6. Where are the avenues of approach through the building leading to the assets?
7. Are there other rooms or doors through which an intruder must pass to reach the assets?
8. Will intrusion alarms, placed in strategic locations inside the building, improve the security?
9. Could barrier penetration detectors be used on the walls to improve detection?
10. Can interior motion detectors inside the room containing the assets or along avenues of approach be used to improve the security?
11. Is the environment in the building sufficiently stable for motion detectors?
12. Are the building configuration and furniture, equipment, or materials arrangement conducive to effective operation of motion detectors?
13. Will invisible barrier detectors, strategically located along avenues of approach to the assets, significantly improve early detection?

Security System

Security system design with respect to intrusion detection systems will be discussed in detail in the following chapters. Therefore, the following questions are general in nature and address security sensors in terms of levels or zones of detection and ancillary equipment that could contribute to the security system effectiveness.

1. Would perimeter intrusion detectors be effective in providing early warning of someone penetrating the perimeter?
2. Is there a chain-link fence that is in good repair around the facility?
3. Could the fence be protected by fence disturbance sensors?
4. Is the fence configuration such that the fence can be divided into reasonable sensor zones?
5. Is the terrain around the perimeter level enough to use invisible barrier detectors?
6. Are there trees or telephone poles near the perimeter that could interfere with the performance of buried seismic sensors?
7. Is the perimeter illuminated so that guards can properly assess the cause of any alarms?

8. Can the sensor zones of detection be divided so that a guard can have full view of a zone from any point along that zone?

9. Would CCTV be an effective way to monitor the perimeter and make alarm assessments?

10. If CCTV cameras are used, is the illumination level adequate?

11. If CCTV cameras are used, where are they monitored, and who does the monitoring?

12. Would an access control system at the perimeter fence entrance gate be helpful in improving security?

13. Can all exterior doors be protected with operable opening switches?

14. Can all vulnerable windows be protected with foil tape or vibration sensors?

15. Would volumetric motion detectors be desirable to protect the interior of the building?

16. Could an access control system be used to limit access to the building or control access inside the building?

17. Would additional lighting on the exterior or interior of the building be a deterrent to the anticipated threat?

18. Would interior barrier detectors strategically located in walkways or along avenues of approach improve detection?

19. Would proximity detectors on safes or valuable items improve protection?

20. How will the sensors be monitored—central station or proprietary?

21. If a central station is used, are the alarm and control signals transmitted over telephone lines?

22. Do the telephone lines have to be metallic, or can they be voice-grade lines?

23. Is a single pair of telephone conductors required for each transmitter or control unit?

24. Are an adequate number of telephone pairs available in the building requiring protection?

25. If a proprietary central station is used, could the alarm monitoring system be used to monitor fire alarms and environmental or equipment controls?

26. Will the security equipment maintenance be performed in-house or contracted?

27. How long should the repair take?

28. After the equipment is repaired, will an equipment test be witnessed by a security guard?

29. How often will the intrusion detection sensors be operationally tested?

30. Is the security equipment battery operated in case of an electrical power failure, or is it operated from an emergency generator?

31. Are the exterior lights and CCTV cameras and monitors operated by an emergency generator in case of a power failure?

Security Guards

Security guards, whether they are proprietary or contracted, perform essential functions in most large installations, especially those with intrusion detection systems. Local police are often used to respond to smaller facilities that do not need a full-time guard force. Local police are also used to support the proprietary and contract guards in case of an emergency or when law enforcement is required.

Following are some questions to stimulate thought in deciding whether to use proprietary or contract guards, or whether local police might fulfill your security needs. They also should help in organizing a security guard force and evaluating an existing force.

1. What are the functions of the security guards—to patrol the protected facility either randomly or continuously, provide access and egress control, control traffic, enforce company security, monitor intrusion alarms, respond to security alarms?
2. If intrusion detectors are used, will they be monitored by a central station or a proprietary alarm monitoring system.
3. If a central station is used, how long will it take for the guards to respond to the protected site?
4. What is their function when they arrive at the site?
5. Can they enter the facility, or must they call the owner to be let into the site?
6. What are their jurisdictional limitations?
7. If local police will provide law enforcement jurisdiction for the contract guards, how long will it take for the police to arrive at the site?
8. If local police will respond to the alarms alone, how long will it take them to respond?
9. Who will admit the police to the facility once they arrive?
10. Will the local police or contract guards randomly patrol the facility?
11. How familiar are the response guards with the facility layout?
12. Are the response guards provided with radio communication with the central station?
13. Are the guards knowledgeable about the security equipment?
14. When there is a security equipment failure, what action will the security guard take?
15. Will the failed equipment be replaced by a guard until it is repaired?
16. What is the security guard's function in case of fire and other emergencies?

PART II

EXTERIOR INTRUSION DETECTORS

Exterior intrusion detectors are designed for outdoor applications, just as interior intrusion detectors are designed for indoor applications. But unlike interior detectors, which are limited only to interior applications, exterior detectors can certainly be used indoors. Exterior detectors must be designed not only to survive the rigorous out-of-doors environment, but also to detect intruders under these rigorous conditions. They must perform this detection function with minimal false alarms caused by inclement weather, animals, or other stimuli. If exterior detectors can satisfy these rigorous out-of-doors requirements, they can certainly be used to protect interior boundaries with very little risk of false alarms.

Before continuing the discussion on exterior intrusion detectors, let's define the term *false alarm* as it is used in this book. A false alarm is any alarm that is not attributable to adversary activities or deliberately activated for test purposes. It can be caused by an equipment malfunction or failure, environmental conditions, animals, man-made disturbances, and operator or user error. Environmental conditions such as rain, snow, wind, and lightning can interfere with a detector's operation and initiate a false alarm. An owner entering the protected facility without exercising the proper procedures might activate an alarm. In both cases the alarms are classified as false alarms, even though in the first case it was environmentally induced and in the second it was a user error.

Sometimes it is desirable to categorize an alarm as a nuisance alarm if the cause can be identified. For instance, if an external perimeter detection zone is penetrated by a large animal, the animal will initiate an alarm just as if the zone of detection was penetrated by an intruder. The detector cannot differentiate between a large animal and an intruder. In this case, when the response force arrives at the protected perimeter and finds the large animal, the alarm can be justifiably recorded as a nuisance alarm. Another example is when a user fails to follow the proper opening or closing procedures and initiates an alarm. This can be classified as a user error or a nuisance alarm.

The purpose of this book is not to identify or differentiate between the categories of alarms but to identify the various causes so they can be alleviated or compensated for in the intrusion detection system design.

EXTERIOR DETECTORS

The exterior intrusion detectors discussed in this section are the devices used to detect an intruder or intruders crossing a boundary around the perimeter of the area being protected. In this application, they are referred to as perimeter intrusion detectors and provide the first or second level of detection. Detecting intrusions at the perimeter of a protected facility gives the response guards the maximum time to respond to an intrusion before the intruder can reach the protected building. A perimeter intrusion detection system can be used to protect valuable or vital materials and equipment stored outdoors inside a protected boundary; or it can be used to provide perimeter detection for buildings or other facilities.

The boundary around the perimeter of a protected area can be defined either by a physical barrier such as a wall or fence, or a natural barrier such as water, or it can be just an imaginary property line. The types of exterior intrusion detectors available to protect these boundaries are categorized as fence disturbance sensors, invisible barrier detectors, buried line sensors, and electric-field sensors.

Fence Disturbance Sensors

Chain-link fences typical of the type installed around the perimeter of most military installations, industrial sites, and utility complexes can be protected by using fence disturbance sensors. These devices can detect the mechanical forces induced in the fence by an intruder either climbing over or cutting through the fence, or they can detect forces generated when an intruder lifts the fence fabric to crawl under. Regardless of the intruder's method of penetrating a fence, the act of penetration impacts the fence with mechanical vibrations that are larger in amplitude and usually higher in frequency than the vibrations induced by naturally occurring phenomena such as wind. Fence disturbance detectors detect these induced fence vibrations or impacts and initiate an alarm when the magnitude and duration of the signals satisfy the detector's alarm criteria.

Invisible Barrier Detectors

Exterior perimeters with level ground can be protected by invisible barrier detectors, which generate a narrow beam of electromagnetic energy. An intruder who runs, walks, or crawls through the beam either interrupts or distorts the energy pattern. When the disturbance satisfies the alarm criteria, the detector initiates an alarm. The energy barrier is formed by a transmitter emitting a beam of either microwave or infrared energy, which is received by a corresponding receiver. The receiver is in the transmitter's line of sight and is located at the opposite end of the zone.

Separation between the individual transmitter and receiver is a function of the detector's application, the terrain, the operating environment, and certainly the type of detector (infrared or microwave). But under ideal operating conditions, infrared detectors can protect zones between 300 and 1,000 feet long, and microwave detectors can protect zones between 500 and 1,500 feet long, depending on the individual detector model.

Buried Line Sensors

Perimeter boundaries can be protected by buried line sensors. These sensors form a narrow sensitive area along the ground above the buried sensor line and detect intruders crossing this sensitive zone. Passive buried line sensors are available to detect seismic, pressure, and magnetic phenomena. Seismic energy induced in the ground by an intruder crossing the buried sensor (propagated energy) is usually a far-field phenomenon, while pressure (soil deformation) is a near-field phenomenon. Magnetic sensors detect the presence of ferrous materials either worn or carried by the intruder while crossing the protected zone. Active buried line sensors generate an electromagnetic field above the ground and detect perturbations caused by someone crossing the sensitive area. Both types of buried line sensors can protect a zone at least 300 feet long.

Electric-Field Sensors

Perimeter fences and boundaries also can be protected by electric-field sensors. These sensors generate an electrostatic field along a combination of parallel field and sense wires. The field and sense wires are secured to separate fence posts to form a stand-alone electric-field fence, or they are secured to standoffs mounted to existing fence posts to form a protected barrier that is part of the existing fence. As an intruder approaches the electric-field sensor, his body distorts the electrostatic field generated by the field wire. These field distortions alter the normal electrical signals on the sense wire. When the change in the signal characteristics satisfies the detector's alarm criteria, an alarm is initiated. Depending on the electric-field sensors' configuration, a single detector can protect a boundary section as long as 1,000 feet. A dual zone differential capacitance sensor can be installed on top of fences or other barriers or walls to detect anyone climbing over the barrier. The sensor generates an electric field between two equal-length wire arrays and the electrically grounded fence. Anyone touching the capacitance sensor changes the capacitance and initiates an alarm.

EXTERIOR SENSOR APPLICATION CONSIDERATIONS

Exterior intrusion detection systems using one or more of these detection techniques are usually required to satisfy all the different detection and operation requirements for the numerous exterior intrusion detection system applications. Even though the detection requirements for many applications might be similar, the perimeter of each installation requiring protection has its own unique physical characteristics. These dictate the type or types of detectors required to provide adequate and economic intrusion detection for the installation.

The application of exterior detectors is affected by the terrain contour, ground cover, animals, climate, weather, and perimeter configuration. For instance, if the terrain along the perimeter is level, a microwave or infrared invisible barrier-type detector could be used to detect intrusions along the boundary. But if the terrain is hilly, it would be economically impractical to use microwave or infrared barrier detectors. Electric-field sensors, buried line detectors, or fence disturbance sensors would be more applicable for uneven ground.

Ground Cover

Vegetation is a severe problem with all exterior detectors. If grass is allowed to grow much above 4 inches in the area between microwave or active electromagnetic field detectors, it can cause distortions in the energy pattern that could result in false alarms. Grass can interfere with the operation of infrared detectors, depending on the height of the grass with respect to the lowest infrared energy beam. Vegetation growing under the electric-field sensor can cause severe false alarms if it is allowed to grow long enough to touch the sense wire. Even the fence disturbance sensors can be affected by large weeds or bushes if they are allowed to rub against the fence. Thus, vegetation in the area of perimeter sensors can be a real problem that must be considered when designing any exterior intrusion detection system. In all these detector applications, the vegetation must either be eliminated or kept under control.

Animals

Wild or domestic animals, especially large animals such as cows, horses, deer, or large dogs moving through, going over, or rubbing against perimeter intrusion detectors can be detrimental to the system's performance. Intrusion detectors designed to detect physical phenomena generated by a person cannot differentiate between the stimulus generated by a person and that generated by a large animal, unless the signal processor uses some sophisticated type of signature analysis. Therefore, when an animal moves through a protected zone, it generates an alarm just as if a human intruder had crossed the zone.

Animals in and around the perimeter requiring protection are a primary consideration when selecting and designing exterior intrusion detection systems. The only type of system that is not affected by animals, unless the animal is wearing ferrous metal, is a buried magnetic detector.

Climatic Conditions

Intrusion detector applications are certainly restricted by climatic conditions. For example, if an installation is subject to heavy fog, rain, dust, or snow, these conditions can interfere with the operation of infrared detectors. The particles of moisture or dust diffuse or block the beam of infrared energy, sometimes reducing the signal level in the receiver until the detector becomes inoperable. Snow accumulation can affect the performance of both infrared and microwave detectors if it becomes deep enough to affect the energy pattern. Another climatic limitation applicable to seismic and pressure-type buried line detectors, which can jeopardize their ability to detect intruders, is that they become less sensitive in frozen ground. This deficiency can be somewhat compensated for by seasonally adjusting the detector's sensitivity. For the above reasons, climatic conditions should be considered when selecting exterior detectors.

Vehicle Traffic

In addition to climatic, terrain, and animal limitations, an installation's normal operational activities can impose restrictions on the use of certain detectors. For instance, vehicle traffic moving in close proximity to the perimeter could prohibit the use of both microwave detectors and buried line sensors. If the microwave energy pattern from the detector is projected close to the road, reflections from the moving vehicles might cause a false alarm. Seismic energy generated by the moving vehicles also might cause seismic sensors to alarm.

Detector Zone Length

Another consideration in designing a perimeter intrusion detection system is the length of the zone of detection. The zone length for a specific type of detector is not necessarily some fixed distance or the distance advertised by the manufacturer. The length can vary from site to site, and it can even vary along the perimeter of the same installation. Variation can be caused by operational activities along the perimeter, terrain contour, or the physical configuration of the perimeter. The length of any single zone of detection, however, should not exceed 300 feet. If the zone is much longer, it will be difficult for the response force to identify the intrusion location or the cause of any nuisance alarm. This is especially true at night if the area is not well illuminated.

Equipment Features

Some very important equipment features should be considered when selecting exterior detectors. They include weatherproof enclosures, conformal coating, and tamper protection. Since the detectors are installed out-of-doors, their electronic processor and power supply should be protected in a weatherproof enclosure. The enclosure should be locked and have tamper protection to detect unauthorized openings. It is also recommended that the electronic circuitry be coated with a conformal plastic coating to protect it from moisture deterioration, as moisture can shorten the life of the components. For this same reason, only hermetically sealed alarm relays should be used in exterior detectors.

Operating Temperature

Another very important consideration when selecting an exterior intrusion detection system is the detector's operating temperature. The operating temperature for most exterior detectors extends from $-30°F$ to $+150°F$, which is quite adequate for applications in much of the country. But there are areas where the temperature gets much colder than $-30°F$. In these areas, the signal processor must be installed indoors or in an enclosure with thermostatically controlled heaters to prevent the enclosure temperature from dropping below the detector's operating temperature.

There are also circumstances when the temperature inside the enclosure might exceed $+150°F$. For instance, if the detector is exposed to the summer sun for long periods of time, the temperature inside the enclosure can easily exceed $+150°F$. In these applications, a sunshield can be installed over the detector, leaving some space between the detector and shield for air circulation, to help reduce the radiant energy. If additional cooling is required, a thermostatically controlled blower can be installed inside the enclosure to circulate air over the electronic components. If blowers are required, the detector's processors will probably have to be installed in a larger weatherproof enclosure to accommodate the blowers.

GENERAL SENSOR APPLICATION CONSIDERATIONS

Exterior intrusion detectors will be discussed in detail in the following chapters, but before discussing the individuals sensors, let's look at some important design features applicable to both interior and exterior sensors. These features are enclosure tamper protection, signal line supervision, and electromagnetic shielding. Both tamper protection and signal line supervision are especially important for interior detectors because the detectors and the signal lines are often located in out-of-the-way places in the protected facility. With the detectors and signal lines out of sight, they could be vulnerable to compromise either by an inside threat or by anyone who would have access to the system during working hours. Electromagnetic shielding is important because electromagnetic energy emanating from electrical equipment or radio transmitters is a common cause of false alarms for intrusion detectors and alarm transmission systems.

Tamper Protection

Surreptitious attacks on the detection system should be detected. Tamper protection will minimize the threat of anyone escaping detection while attempting to open a detector enclosure. To be effective, the tamper protection should be monitored on a 24-hour schedule. Too often protection circuits of this type are connected to the primary alarm circuit. In this type of hookup, the circuits are monitored only when the overall detection system is in the secure mode during nonworking hours. There should be little need to monitor the protection circuits during secured hours if the facility is adequately protected because presumably no one could reach the detector or signal lines without being detected. Therefore, for maximum protection, tamper circuits should be monitored continuously, especially during working hours when the system is in the access mode.

Tamper protection for each processor and transducer enclosure can be a mechanically actuated plunger-type switch. The tamper switch should activate an alarm when the enclosure cover is removed between 1/8 and 1/4 inch or before the cover is removed far enough to defeat the tamper switch. The tamper switch should not be too sensitive because it might initiate an alarm with only minor movements of the mounting structure.

Not only should the equipment enclosure cover be protected, but any detector or transducer that can be compromised by removal from the mounting surface also should have tamper protection. The tamper switch should activate an alarm if the sensor is pried off or removed from its mounting surface. An example of such a device is the vibration transducer. If a vibration transducer is removed from the surface it is supposed to protect, there is no way it can detect a forcible entry.

Signal Line Security

The security of the interconnecting cables between the alarm transmitter, the detector's control unit, and the associated transducers is a very important consideration. If a signal line is compromised, the control unit will not receive an alarm signal, even if the detector is functioning properly. The minimum acceptable line supervision should detect an open or shorted signal line. Since most signal transmission system transmitters recognize an open circuit as an alarm signal, the line supervision circuit need only detect someone trying to compromise the detection device by electrically short-circuiting the alarm contacts. To minimize signal line compromise, signal line supervision should be monitored on a 24-hour schedule.

A line supervision circuit that will detect open and shorted circuits is probably adequate for many installations; however, for facilities requiring higher security, the signal line supervising circuit should recognize and initiate an alarm to any signal line impedance changes on the order of 5 to 25 percent. Although a system using a 5 percent current change to initiate an alarm appears to offer more line security than a circuit using a 25 percent change, in reality the 5 percent circuit is only slightly more difficult to defeat. Monitoring the signal line for changes in the impedance is just one line supervision method for improving signal line security. The line supervision just described is for the interconnecting cables inside the protected area and not for the signal lines between the protected facilities and the central station. Buried cables between exterior detectors and the central station should be routed through conduit, or the cables should be designed for direct burial.

Another consideration for improving signal line security inside the protected area, especially in areas of high security, is to install the signal cables in sealed metal conduit. Conduit will help protect the signal cables from compromise as well as from day-to-day abuse. There are two types of conduit: electrical metallic tubing (EMT) and heavy wall conduit. The EMT conduit is much thinner than the heavy wall conduit and therefore does not provide as much penetration resistance. EMT conduit is connected with slip couplings and secured in place with set screws. The heavy wall conduit is connected with threaded couplings.

Like any other design consideration, the type of conduit used to protect signal cables depends on the application. The heavy wall conduit provides greater penetration resistance than the EMT because it has a heavier wall and the conduit sections are threaded together. The slip joints of the thin wall conduit can be easily separated to expose the cable simply by loosening the retaining set screw and pulling the joints apart. To decrease this vulnerability, the slip joints can be tack-welded or bonded together.

Another vulnerability of both types of conduit is that some of the fittings have access openings for pulling cables, and the covers to these fittings are secured only with screws. Anyone removing a cover would have free access to the cable; therefore, the covers should be tack-welded or bonded to the fitting to maintain the penetration resistance of the conduit.

If the signal lines are not supervised or physically protected, the intrusion detection system could be very vulnerable to compromise. For instance, if an entrance door switch to a protected facility is connected to an unsupervised alarm transmission circuit, an intruder could be browsing around the facility during the day and, unbeknownst to the proprietor, place an electrical short across the switch contacts, compromising the door's protection. Then after the store is closed, the intruder could return and enter undetected. As vulnerable as this system is, there are many facilities protected with such systems. In conclusion, the signal line supervision and the physical protection for the signal cables should be adequate to protect the signal lines against the anticipated threat.

Electromagnetic Interference

Electromagnetic interference (EMI) is a major operational problem with almost all electronic equipment unless the enclosure is properly shielded and the power and signal lines entering the enclosure are adequately filtered. For instance, the noise you hear on your car radio, especially an AM radio, when you pass under high-power transmission lines is caused by EMI. The interference you see and hear on your television when someone is operating electrical appliances nearby is the result of EMI. The radio and television interference is annoying when it happens, but it soon goes away when the EMI source is turned off. If the electromagnetic energy interferes with an intrusion detector or signal transmission system, however, the result might be a false alarm. Therefore, an electromagnetic shield and signal and power line filter or shield should be considered in the selection and installation of an intrusion detection system.

Besides high-power transmission lines, electromagnetic energy is generated by radio and television transmitters, radar systems, electric heli-arc welders, electrical substations, and power plants. These are some of the large sources of electromagnetic energy; smaller energy sources such as electric motors and mobile radio transmitters also can cause interference problems. Most sources of electromagnetic energy can be identified within or near the facility being protected. But at least one energy source often overlooked is the mobile transmitter, such as those used in police cruisers.

These sources of EMI are sometimes difficult to identify unless you are aware of their existence and potential for causing alarms.

Intrusion detectors can be susceptible to interference from both radiated and conducted electromagnetic energy. Radiated interference is a result of radiated electromagnetic energy coming in direct contact with the electronic equipment, signal lines, and power and signal lines. If the enclosure and cables are not properly shielded, the radiated energy electrically couples to the electronic circuitry and cables and induces electrical signals in the signal processor. These induced signals could be interpreted as valid signals, resulting in false alarms.

Signal processors can be shielded from radiation by installing the circuitry in a metal enclosure with radio-frequency interference (RFI) gaskets between the cover and enclosure. Radiation susceptibility of the signal cables can be reduced by using electrically shielded cables or twisted wire pairs, depending on what the equipment manufacturer specifies. If shielded cable is specified, then shielded cable should be installed. Otherwise, the signal cable would be like a long antenna picking up radiated energy that could initiate false alarms. Installing the signal cable in conduit also will improve the EMI shielding.

Conducted interference is a result of electrical signals being induced on the power lines by electrical equipment, large sources of electromagnetic energy, and lightning. Lightning strikes produce large electromagnetic fields that can induce high-voltage spikes on the power lines. If these conducted signals are allowed to enter the signal processor on the power line, they might cause it to false alarm (if they did not destroy the detector). Depending on the magnitude, the conducted signals can be eliminated, or at least reduced, with proper filtering. EMI shielding and filtering should be included in any intrusion detection system design.

Detector Sensitivity

An important operational feature applicable to any intrusion detection system is the detector's sensitivity adjustment. The sensitivity should be adjusted in accordance with the manufacturer's installation procedures to a level that is adequate to satisfy the application requirements. Increasing the sensitivity, especially increasing it beyond the application requirement, substantially increases the probability of false alarms. The sensitivity of each detector or zone of detection also should be checked on a periodic schedule at least once a month at several locations along each detector zone. This recommendation is especially applicable for exterior systems because they are exposed to the weather and must operationally survive the changing seasons.

Primary Operating Power

Power supplies are usually taken for granted by most intrusion detection equipment users or, for that matter, by most users of any electronic equipment. But both the primary and secondary power supply's operating features should be reviewed to ensure that they will satisfy your intrusion detection system's operating requirements.

The primary power for active detectors operating in the United States is a nominal 115 volts/60 cycles per second supply. Although the frequency of the power is consistently stable at 60 cycles, the voltage in some areas can vary from a nominal 115 volts to as high as 130 volts and as low as 100 volts, and in some locations to even greater extremes. Such voltage variations can appreciably affect the detection capability and sensitivity of some detectors, especially active motion detectors. At low voltages a detector's range might be reduced to half its normal distance. Conversely, high voltages, if they do not cause catastrophic failures, might cause a detector to become supersensitive and therefore very susceptible to alarm. Voltage variation problems are usually compensated for by regulating the detector's operating voltage, but sometimes the regulation is not adequate to compensate for the wide variations. Therefore, the detector's maximum and minimum operating voltage characteristics should be reviewed to make certain the detector will function properly when exposed to local voltage variations.

Intrusion detectors are usually supplied with a separate step-down transformer to reduce the 115 volt line voltage to approximately 12 volts for the detector control and processor circuits. The step-down transformer is normally installed adjacent to the primary AC power supply to eliminate the necessity for using heavy power cables between the power source and the detector. By locating the transformer at the power source, the detector's operating power can be carried over smaller wire such as 18 or 20 gauge. All wiring should be installed in accordance with the Electrical Wiring Code.

Standby Batteries

Any area protected by an active motion detector or other intrusion detection equipment should have standby batteries for emergencies when primary power is not available. Detectors using standby batteries should have a trickle charging circuit to recharge the battery and maintain the charge for continual readiness. The detector should be able to switch automatically from AC power to battery power and vice versa without causing an alarm. It is highly desirable that the detector be equipped with a method of indicating when it is operating on standby power. Also, if the battery discharges during emergency operations, an alarm should be generated to notify the central station that the detector is not operating.

Another very important battery consideration is the battery operating time. Most detectors have a specified battery operating time of about 4 to 6 hours. Some detectors have operating times as long as 72 hours. Whatever the operating time, it is usually the operating time at room temperature. This specification is sometimes misleading because when the operating temperature decreases, the battery operating time decreases. In fact, at 32°F the output of some batteries decreases by as much as one-half their original rating. At lower temperatures the battery might last only a short time or might not operate the detector at all.

Larger-capacity batteries might be required to satisfy low-temperature operations. In this case the size of the standby battery might be too large to fit inside the detector's enclosure. For these applications, the battery can be installed in either a separate weatherproof enclosure adjacent to the detector or in a larger enclosure that can accommodate both the detector and battery. In applications where heaters are required, the heaters can be intalled in the larger enclosure to maintain the operating temperature for both the detector's processor and the battery.

If the temperature is so cold that the detectors require heaters to prevent the operating temperature from dropping below their operating temperature, emergency generators will be required to supply the equipment power and especially the heater power. It would be impractical to operate the heaters from batteries, especially for any reasonable time. If emergency generators are not available, other security measures should be taken when the power is off and it is too cold for the detectors to operate.

If the intrusion detection system is inside, the user might underestimate the temperature extremes, especially the low temperatures. But when primary power is off, the heating system is probably not operating and the area could become very cold. Therefore, when selecting a detector, even for inside applications, specify the standby battery operating time for the lowest required operating temperature.

If the battery operating temperature or storage temperature exceeds the maximum operating temperature of about 130°F for any extended period, the heat will reduce the battery's operating life. Therefore, batteries should not be stored in overheated locations. If the equipment is operated in a high-temperature environment, the battery should be located in the coolest area possible. The enclosure should be well ventilated, and perhaps blowers could be installed inside the enclosure to remove internally generated heat.

These are just some of the more general application considerations for both interior and exterior intrusion detectors. Other specific sensor application considerations will be discussed in the appropriate chapters, along with the basic principles of operation and limitations of the sensors that should be considered when designing an intrusion detection system.

Chapter 6

Fence Disturbance Sensors

Fence disturbance sensors detect the act of an intruder either climbing over or cutting through a fence or lifting the fence fabric to crawl under. These acts of penetrating the fence generate mechanical vibrations or stresses in the fence fabric that are usually higher in frequency and have larger acceleration amplitudes than the vibrations or stresses generated by naturally occurring phenomena such as wind and rain. Fence disturbance sensor manufacturers capitalize on these fence characteristics by designing their sensors to discriminate against low-frequency, naturally occurring vibrations and low-amplitude accelerations, and to detect higher-frequency fence penetration vibrations and larger impacts. These fence vibrations are detected by electromechanical switches, piezoelectric and geophone transducers, and electret transducer cables. Electrical signals from the transducers are sent to the signal processor, where they are analyzed.

The signal processing technique used by each detector depends on the type of sensor or transducer used to detect the accelerations in the mechanical forces generated in the fence. If the sensor is an electromechanical switch that opens on impact, the signal processor usually has a pulse accumulation circuit that recognizes a momentary contact opening as a single pulse. When the number of pulses satisfies the preset number of contact openings within a specific period, the detector initiates an alarm. If the sensor is a piezoelectric- or geophone-type transducer, the signal processor responds to the amplitude, frequency, and duration of the electrical signal generated by the act of penetrating the fence. When the characteristics of the signal satisfy the processor alarm criteria, the detector initiates an alarm.

The signal processors for most other exterior detectors are installed outside, along with the detector sensors, but the processors for most fence disturbance sensors are actually part of the alarm display panel located inside the central alarm station. Therefore, some detector alarm annunciation and display panels have special features, such as provisions to listen to the audible impact sounds from the fence sensors, to change the number of signal pulse counts and the count accumulation time interval required for the count accumulator to initiate an alarm, and to provide warning indications of possible alarms.

Mr. Ids is shown in Figure 6–1 cutting individual strands of chain-link fence to gain entrance. When he cuts through each strand, the wire snaps, relieving the inherent internal stresses generated in the fence fabric during the fabrication process. This snap generates a high-frequency pulse that travels up the wire strand toward the fence sensor. Because the fabric is reasonably tight, or should be, part of this energy is mechanically coupled to the adjoining wire strands. The energy continues to spread as it travels toward the transducer. The transducer detects and converts the mechanical energy into electrical signals that are sent to the signal processor, where they are analyzed and counted on an accumulation circuit. Mr. Ids must cut several strands of the fabric before the detector initiates an alarm. Based on the fence penetration tests discussed in Part I, Mr. Ids must cut at least thirteen strands of fabric to make a large enough opening to crawl through an unanchored fence.

Fence disturbance sensors can detect the act of cutting, climbing, and lifting the fence fabric best if the fabric is reasonably tight and the posts are well anchored. If the fabric is loose, the high-frequency vibrations and mechanical noises might be attenuated in the fence fabric before they reach the sensors. This attenuation reduces the probability of detection.

Another phenomenon that can cause false alarms is the wind-induced vibration from loose objects striking the fence. All loose signs, especially metal signs, should be removed from or secured to the fence so they cannot rattle. Rattling signs induce high-frequency vibrations in the fence similar to a cutting penetration. Since the sensors cannot differentiate between high-frequency vibrations caused by rattling signs, loose gates, vegetation, or any other objects banging or rubbing against the fence, the sensors can alarm to this type of stimuli. As previously mentioned, these sources of false alarms

Figure 6–1   Fence disturbance sensor.

can be corrected by either removing them from the fence or securely fastening them to the fence fabric or posts so they cannot rattle and interfere with the operation of the sensor.

Some fence disturbance sensor transducers can be installed on up to every third fence fabric section or fence post. But the probability of detecting an intruder penetrating the fence is a function of the sensor sensitivity and the sensor spacing along the fence. In other words, these sensors might be able to detect many types of penetrations at this spacing, but the farther apart they are, the lower the probability of their detecting all penetrations. This is especially true if an intruder cuts the fence fabric or lifts the fabric to crawl under midway between the sensors. Therefore, areas requiring a high degree of security should install individual transducers on every fence fabric section or fence post unless the manufacturer can ensure an adequate probability of detection with the sensors installed farther apart. Of course, installing the sensors closer together will increase the system cost, which should be considered along with the anticipated threat.

The major objection to using a fence disturbance sensor to detect penetrations through perimeter fences is that an intruder can either tunnel under or bridge over the fence without being detected. But the fence's effectiveness can be enhanced to reduce these threats. The threat of tunneling can be reduced by extending the bottom of the fence into the ground, by installing another barrier in the ground along the bottom of the fence, or by captivating the bottom 2 to 4 inches of the fence fabric in an asphalt or concrete sill. An asphalt sill that extends from the fence approximately ½ to 1 foot on each side reduces the tunneling threat, while facilitating mowing operations along the fence. Adequate drainage must be provided under or over the asphalt to eliminate erosion and standing water.

The threat of bridging over the fence can be reduced by extending the effective height of the fence with additional fencing or by adding barbed wire or rolls of barbed tape on top of the fence. Adding barbed tape to the fence improves its deterrent effect, but it could make the fence sensors more susceptible to false alarms in wind.

These are a few of the applications and installation factors that must be considered when selecting a perimeter fence disturbance sensor system. All these factors must be evaluated in terms of the anticipated threat, the type of fence surveillance system, and the cost to enhance the fence's penetration resistance.

If the anticipated threat is not likely to tunnel under or bridge over the fence, there are several advantages to protecting the perimeter fence with fence disturbance sensors. A major advantage is that the fence sensors are mounted directly on the fence; therefore, they do not require additional space inside the protected area, as do invisible barrier detectors, buried line sensors, and electric-field sensors. Another advantage of the fence disturbance sensor is ease of installation. The interconnecting cables can be mounted directly on the fence along with the sensor, following the fence contour up and down hills and around corners.

It is recommended that fence sensors be installed in sealed electrical junction boxes and that the interconnecting cables be installed in sealed conduit, provided the conduit or junction boxes will not interfere with the operation of the sensors. Although it is initially more expensive, the conduit provides additional tamper protection and electromagnetic shielding for the sensors and signal cable. Tamper protection exists because anyone trying to cut through the conduit for access to the cables will be detected by the sensors just like an intruder cutting through the fence. The conduit also protects the cable and sensors against weathering and day-to-day abuse, thereby reducing long-term maintenance problems.

Fence disturbance sensors can provide fence penetration protection for many industrial and commercial applications, depending on the anticipated threat. If the threat can be expected to climb over, cut through, or crawl under the fence, then fence disturbance sensors are good candidates to satisfy the detection requirements. They do offer several desirable application features that are summarized below:

1. Fence disturbance sensors detect intrusions at the perimeter fence before an intruder has the opportunity to penetrate the fence.
2. Since the sensors are mounted directly on the fence, they do not occupy space inside.
3. The perimeter detection zones do not have to be adjusted to compensate for ground contours or corners and offsets in the fence.

All these features are desirable, but remember, the intruder must come in contact with the fence to be detected. If the intruder can be expected to bridge or jump over the fence without touching it, then fence disturbance systems alone are not adequate to satisfy the detection requirements.

The basic principles of operation as well as application considerations for the individual fence disturbance sensors will be discussed in the following paragraphs.

ELECTROMECHANICAL TRANSDUCERS

Electromechanical fence disturbance transducers are usually normally closed switches, but normally open switches also are available. Normally closed switches initiate an open-circuit pulse when the switch is acted upon by accelerations generated in the fence fabric during penetration. Forces with adequate accelerations cause the electromechanical switch to momentarily open and close in a series of short pulses. The pulse rate corresponds to the frequency of the induced vibration. The number of pulses and the pulse rate depends on the attack method and the time required for the intruder to penetrate the fence. For instance, if the fence is cut, there will be a number of distinct pulses, one for each time the fabric is cut. If the fence is climbed over, there will be several seconds of continuous open-circuit pulses. These pulses can be recorded in a pulse count accumulator circuit, or they can activate an alarm circuit directly. Pulse accumulators are recommended because they will minimize the number of false alarms from single impacts on the fence, such as from debris blowing against it.

There are two basic types of electromechanical switches. One uses mechanical inertia switches, and the other uses mercury switches. A mechanical inertia switch consists of a single or double metal seismic mass that rests on two multiple contact rods or two or three electrical contacts in the normal or no-alarm position, creating a normally closed switch. The switch assembly is enclosed in a plastic case that captivates the movable mass, restricting its movement so that it always returns to rest on the contacts. The plastic case also seals the switch mass and contacts from moisture. To prevent corrosion and ensure a long contact life, the contacts and seismic mass are gold plated. These switches are typical of the interior mechanical vibration detectors discussed in Chapter 14, "Barrier Penetration Detectors." In fact, at least one manufacturer uses the same basic inertia switch for protecting fences, walls, and windows. The movable seismic mass in the switch reacts to the minute accelerations in the vibrations generated in the fence during a forced penetration. In some inertia sensors, the seismic mass is unrestricted so that it can react to forces slightly greater than its own weight. In other inertia sensors, the movable mass is restricted by some internal force, therefore requiring a larger force to move the mass off the contacts. Inertia switches with restricted mass are not as sensitive as unrestricted movable mass switches and are therefore used to protect fence gates or fence sections that have excessive movement where the undamped sensor might be susceptible to false alarms.

Mercury switches are normally open and make momentary contact on impact. The switch consists of a glass vial containing a small amount of mercury with two electrical contacts in close proximity to the mercury. Mercury is a liquid conductor that provides electrical continuity between the two conductors. Each switch assembly is enclosed in a small tamper-protected case that should be mounted in a nearly vertical direction on the fence to function satisfactorily. On impact to the fence, the mercury is displaced from its normal rest position and makes contact with the electrical contacts, generating a momentary closed circuit.

Mechanical fence disturbance switches can activate an alarm circuit directly, or they can be connected to a pulse count accumulator circuit. An accumulator circuit counts the open-circuit pulses and activates an alarm after it has accumulated the preset number of pulses in a specific time period. Depending on the intruder's method of penetration, he will generate a large impact on the fence, such as when hurriedly climbing over, or a series of small impacts, such as when cutting the fabric. Some accumulator circuits can respond to both the long-duration pulses generated by a hurried climb and the short-duration pulses generated by cutting. This circuit initiates an alarm momentarily after only several long-duration pulses, but a greater number of short-duration pulses is required to initiate an alarm. Regardless of the counting method, the circuit should automatically bleed off the pulse counts accumulated if an insufficient number of pulses are not accumulated within the preset alarm time period.

Applications

Mechanical sensors can be installed on every fence post or up to every third fence post, depending on the manufacturer's recommended method of installation. Each sensor is connected in series along the fence with a common cable, similar to a string of Christmas tree lights, to form a single zone of protection. The individual sensors are electrically wired either in series or in parallel depending on whether the switch is normally open or normally closed. The maximum number of sensors that can be connected together in a single zone is a function of the resistance in the interconnecting cable between the signal processor and switches, the resistance of the cable terminator, and the criticality of the signal transmission. These limiting parameters should be specified by the manufacturer. Regardless of the number of sensors that can be connected together in a single zone, it is recommended that a maximum single detection zone length of 300 feet be maintained. This zone length will not only improve the response force's ability to locate an intrusion or cause of an alarm, but it also will facilitate maintenance by reducing the time required to locate a bad switch in the zone.

The sensor cable can be routed along the fence, and the cable from each zone of sensors can be routed underground to the central alarm station. Again, it is recommended that the cable on the fence be routed in sealed conduit and the sensors be installed in electrical enclosures, provided the enclosure and conduit will not interfere with the sensors' performance. If the cable is installed underground, it should be either routed in conduit or be direct burial cable.

PIEZOELECTRIC TRANSDUCERS

Piezoelectric transducers convert the mechanical impact forces generated in a fence during a penetration attack into electrical signals. Unlike the mechanical switches that respond to the mechanical forces by generating a series of open-circuit pulses, piezoelectric transducers generate an analog signal. The signal varies proportionally in amplitude and frequency to the amplitude and frequency of the mechanically induced vibrations. The analog signals from all the transducers are collectively processed and analyzed in the signal processor.

The piezoelectric crystal, which converts the mechanical forces into proportionate electrical signals, is usually a thin slab of quartz. The quartz is physically ground to a thickness that will respond to the vibrational frequencies generated in the fence during an intrusion. This thin crystal is secured to the transducer enclosure so that it can respond to the mechanically induced forces. The induced mechanical stresses distort the crystal, generating an electrical signal that is proportional to the induced stresses. The resulting signals are amplified and sent along the interconnecting cable to the signal processor.

Typically signals from the transducers enter the signal processor through a bandpass filter. This filter passes only those signals that correspond to the energies with vibration frequencies characteristic of the vibrations generated during a fence penetration attack. The bandpass of the filter is selected by the manufacturer after conducting penetration tests and measuring the resulting frequencies. The filter is then designed to pass those corresponding signals with the best signal-to-noise ratio. Filtering reduces the susceptibility to false alarms resulting from low-frequency vibrations induced by low-velocity winds. But higher-velocity winds, above about 20 to 25 mph, generate high-frequency vibrations that are within the bandpass of the input filter. Since the processor cannot always differentiate between the valid intrusion signals and the wind-induced signals, the results are false alarms.

Applications

Depending on the detector model, the transducers can be mounted on the fence fabric or posts. The transducers can be mounted as far as about 30 feet apart on every third fence post or fabric section. Depending on the protection requirements for the anticipated threat, however, the transducers might be positioned closer together to improve the probability of detection, especially if the fabric is cut or lifted midway between the transducers. The improved detection results from the fact that the mechanical vibrations do not have to travel as far to reach a transducer. Reducing this distance improves the signal-to-noise ratio at the transducer.

In general, improving detection also increases the detector's susceptibility to false alarms, but this is not necessarily true. If the detection is improved by increasing the detector's sensitivity, then the detector will be more susceptible to false alarms. But when the detection is improved by improving the signal-to-noise ratio, then false alarm rates should decrease.

Positioning the transducers closer together does mean that additional sensors will be required to protect the same length of perimeter fence. However, additional transducers above the manufacturer's maximum recommended number should not be added to a single zone of detection to extend the coverage. Increasing the number of transducers could increase the ambient background noise and negate the advantage of placing the sensors closer together by reducing the signal-to-noise ratio in the signal processor. In this case the signal-to-noise ratio is reduced because the background signals from the additional transducers is added to the signals already present from the approved number of transducers. This additional noise would tend to mask the valid signals.

Piezoelectric transducers are electrically wired in parallel to the signal processor with shielded cable. Shielded cable minimizes the possibility of external electrical interference inducing signals onto the cable, which might be interpreted by the signal processor as valid signals. Additional shielding, line supervision, and physical protection from the weather will be provided by installing the interconnecting cable in sealed conduit.

GEOPHONE TRANSDUCERS

Geophone transducers detect the mechanical vibrations generated in the fence during a forced penetration and convert these energies into analog electrical signals that are proportional to the induced forces. A geophone transducer consists of a tubular seismic mass wound with a coil of fine wire and a cylindrical permanent magnet. The magnet is fixed to the geophone housing, and the seismic mass is suspended in spring balance around the magnet. When the geophone is acted upon by external mechanical forces, accelerations from these forces displace the housing and permanent magnet, while the seismic mass remains at rest. As the permanent magnet moves through the coil, the windings cut the magnetic lines of force. As the windings pass through the magnetic field, an electromotive force (EMF) is induced in the coil. The magnitude and frequency of the induced analog signal is proportional to the magnitude and frequency of the external accelerations.

These signals are then amplified and sent to the signal processor, where they pass through a bandpass filter, just as the signals from the piezoelectric transducers do. Sometimes multiple bandpass filters are used to pass energies in different frequency bands for improved signal recognition and to reduce false alarms from wind and other seismic energy sources. The signal processor analyzes these signals and initiates an alarm when the signal amplitude and duration satisfy the alarm criteria.

Applications

Geophone transducers are usually mounted to the fence fabric approximately 20 feet apart in the center of every other fence fabric section. They are mounted so that the axis of vibration is in the vertical direction. Mounted in this direction, the geophones are more sensitive to vertical accelerations produced in a forced penetration than the horizontal acceleration generated by wind blowing against the fence.

ELECTRET CABLE TRANSDUCER

The electret cable transducer is a specially sensitized coaxial cable. The cable's center conductor is covered with a low-loss dielectric material processed to carry a permanent electrostatic charge. A braided wire shield encloses the dielectric material. This cable assembly is covered with a weather-resistant plastic jacket. When the cable is subjected to mechanical distortions or stresses resulting from fence penetration, electrical analog signals are induced in the transducer cable proportional to the mechanical stresses.

These signals are sent along the transducer cable to the signal processor, which is usually mounted to the fence at the beginning of a detection zone. Incoming signals pass through a bandpass filter that passes only those signals characteristic of fence penetration signals. The frequency band of the bandpass filter was selected by the manufacturer based on frequency measurements made while conducting forced penetration tests. Processing only those signals within the bandpass of the input filter improves the signal-to-noise ratio. As previously mentioned in the discussion of piezoelectric and geophone transducers, improving the signal-to-noise ratio of the processed signal improves the detector's detection capability and reduces its susceptibility to false alarms.

An optional listening feature will enhance the central station operator's ability to verify actual intrusions. It allows the operator to listen to the fence noises causing the alarm to determine whether they are naturally occurring sounds from wind or rain or an actual penetration. Some sounds, such as an animal climbing or bumping the fence, will be difficult to differentiate from penetration sounds. But a trained operator can differentiate between most naturally occurring noises and the noises generated during an actual penetration. The listening feature is made possible because the transducer cable is microphonic—that is, it acts like a microphone.

Applications

Transducer cables are available in lengths up to 1,000 feet; however, a maximum detection zone length of approximately 300 feet should be maintained to facilitate the response force's reaction. The transducer cable is secured to the chain-link fence with plastic ties about halfway between the bottom and top of the fence fabric. The ties should be spaced about 18 inches apart, and care should be exercised when tying the cable to prevent damage. One end of the transducer has a connector to interface with the signal processor's enclosure, and the opposite end is terminated with a resistive load. The resistive load provides line supervision against cutting or electrically shorting the transducer cable or disconnecting the coaxial connector from the electronic processor.

Additional tamper protection can be achieved by installing the transducer cable in metal or hard plastic conduit mounted directly on the fence fabric. In this installation the mechanical energy induced in the fence fabric is transmitted to the conduit and on to the transducer cable resting inside the conduit. The conduit not only provides tamper protection, but it also protects the cable from the environment and from physical abuse. Expansion joints must be included in the conduit run to accommodate expansion and contraction of the conduit during seasonal temperature changes.

The signal processor is enclosed in a heavy-duty weatherproof enclosure with electromagnetic shielding. The enclosure is mounted on the fence at the beginning of a detection zone. The transducer cable is connected to the enclosure and then secured directly to the fence fabric or installed in the fence-mounted conduit. Power for the signal processor is routed through a multiconductor cable to the signal processor. This cable also carries the alarm relay signals from the signal processor to the display unit located in the central alarm station. Standby rechargeable batteries in the signal processor provide up to 8 hours of operation in case of a power failure.

The display unit annunciates and displays all alarms from the remotely located signal processors. Each sensor zone alarm is identified by a separate indicator lamp. If the alarm verification option is used, the desired sensor zone can be selected by a rotary switch on the display panel, and the audio sounds from that fence zone will be annunciated on a speaker.

TAUT-WIRE SWITCHES

Taut-wire switches do not detect mechanical disturbances in chain-link fences as mechanical, piezoelectric, and geophone transducers do. They are used in conjunction with barbed wire barriers to detect anyone penetrating the barrier. Taut-wire switches consist of a movable center rod that forms one contact of a normally open switch and a cylindrical conductor that forms the other contact. In the neutral or no-alarm switch position, the center rod conductor is in the center of the switch, not touching the cylindrical contact, thus forming the normally open switch. The switches are mounted inside a tamper-protective enclosure that is installed on a fence post near the middle of the sensor zone. The enclosure extends the full height of a standard chain-link fence and can project out over the fence to include the fence outriggers if desired. Switch assemblies are available for other fence configurations including just the outriggers. The switches are mounted in the enclosure in a vertical line separated by approximately 6 inches to

Figure 6–2   Strain-switch fence detector.

form the wire barrier. Anyone cutting, pulling, or stepping on the individual strands of barbed wire pulls the switch center conductor rod into contact with the cylindrical conductor, closing the switch and initiating an alarm.

A unique feature of the taut-wire switch is that the switch assembly is supported in its housing by a pliable plastic material. This material exhibits cold-flow properties that allow the switch assembly always to assume a neutral force-free position when the switch housing is acted upon by gradual external force. External stresses could be caused by the fence settling or moving during the freezing and thawing seasons. This feature prevents the switches from becoming prestressed, which alters their response to intrusion by changing the relative separation between the switch's movable center conductor and the fixed cone-shaped conductor.

In Figure 6–2, Mr. Ids demonstrates how a free-standing barbed wire fence protected with taut-wire switches detects a penetration. As Mr. Ids pulls up on one barbed wire strand and steps down on the other to step through the fence, he displaces the center conductor rod of the tout-wire switch attached to the strands. The center conductor makes contact with the cylindrical contact. The switch closure signal is transmitted to the annunciator panel. With this system, the first switch closure initiates an alarm. The switches should not be connected to a count accumulator because only one switch closure would be generated in a penetration if the intruder displaced only one strand or barbed wire to gain entry. For instance, he could lift just the bottom strand of wire to crawl under the fence and activate only one taut-wire switch. Although the taut-wire switches activate an alarm on the first closure, they are not subject to nuisance alarms from wind because a very firm pull is required to initiate an alarm.

Applications

In an installation, the strands of barbed wire in a single zone are supported at each fence post, except the switch assembly post, by a supporting bar and are held in tension by terminators. The supporting bars loosely support the strands of wire, allowing them to move freely to activate the taut-wire switches. The switch assembly and supporting bars space the barbed wire strands at about 6-inch increments starting about 4 inches from the ground. Barbed wire separation above about 3 feet can be increased to 8 to 10 inches, but the barbed wire separation for the lower strands should not exceed 6 inches because a small person might crawl between the wires without being detected.

Taut-wire switch fence assemblies can be used in many industrial and commercial applications if the threat is expected to climb over or cut through the fence to gain entry. Taut-wire switch assemblies also can be used in conjunction with the barbed wire outriggers installed on top of most chain-link fences around industrial installations to detect anyone climbing over the fence.

Taut-wire switch fence barriers have the same limitations, in terms of detection, as fence disturbance sensors. To be detected, the intruder must come in contact with the fence, either by cutting, climbing, or pulling on the barbed wire. If the threat can be expected to bridge over or tunnel under the fence, other types of perimeter protection will be required to detect intrusions.

Chapter 7

Invisible Barrier Detectors

Invisible barrier detectors generate a narrow invisible beam of electromagnetic energy and detect a disturbance or reduction of the energy caused by an intruder running, walking, or crawling through the protected zone. The energy barrier is formed by a transmitter emitting a beam of energy to a corresponding receiver, located in the line of sight and aligned with the transmitter, at the opposite end of the zone. The distance between the transmitter and receiver pair is a function of the type of detector, the application, and the operating environment. There is one primary application requirement for an invisible barrier detector to be effective: The terrain between the detector transmitter and receiver must be flat, free of obstacles, and free of vegetation, or the vegetation must be maintained at a length of about 4 inches or less so that it will not interfere with the detector's performance.

There are two general types of active invisible barrier detector. One type operates at microwave frequencies, and the other operates in the infrared frequency spectrum. Microwave detectors generate a beam of microwave energy and detect either a reduction or distortion in the received energy caused by an intruder blocking the transmitted energy by running, walking, or crawling through the beam. Basically, pattern distortion results from a change in any microwave energy multipath signals arriving at the receiver. The receiver signal processor detects either a reduction in the received signal or a multipath signal change, and it initiates an alarm when the change satisfies the alarm criteria.

Infrared detectors generate a multiple-beam pattern of modulated infrared energy and detect an interruption of the received energy or a change in the beam's modulation frequency. An interruption in the received energy is, of course, caused by anyone passing through the beam. A change in the modulation frequency could be caused by an intruder attempting to substitute another infrared source to compromise the detector.

Although both the microwave and infrared transducer are similar in principle, there are several basic differences in their modes of operation. For instance, microwave energy beams are much broader than infrared beams;

therefore, infrared detectors can usually be installed closer to fences or buildings requiring protection. An infrared detector should not be installed so close to a fence or barrier, however, that an intruder can jump over the energy beams from the fence without being detected.

Infrared detector receivers and transmitters can be stacked together to form a vertical column of detectors of any height. For most applications, the arrays are stacked from ground level to a height from about 4 to 6 feet, high enough so that an intruder cannot simply jump over the beams.

The bottom infrared beam should be low enough, about 6 inches above the ground, so that an intruder cannot crawl under the beam without being detected. Single-direction infrared columns should be overlapped at the corners of an installation and where zones of detection interface. Overlapping the zones of detection will prevent someone from climbing or vaulting over the detector without being detected. If two adjacent infrared columns of detectors are installed in the same enclosure, the top of the enclosure should be protected with a pressure switch or some method to detect anyone trying to climb over the detector column to avoid crossing the infrared beams.

Microwave detector antennas are considered point-source arrays, meaning that the energy emanates from a single point. Since they are usually mounted about 2 to 3 feet above the ground, depending on the terrain and ground cover, the area in front of and just below the antenna is unprotected. Therefore, to maintain full coverage between individual zones of detection and in the corners, the microwave transmitters and receivers must be overlapped. The overlap must be adequate to detect a low-crawling intruder midway between the overlapping zones and at the beam intersection in the corners. Microwave beams are usually broad and high enough that the transmitters and receivers do not have to be stacked in columns.

Because of the broad microwave energy pattern, the alignment between the transmitter and receiver is not as critical as the infrared transmitter and receiver alignment. Movement in the ground during spring thaw or winter freeze might cause the infrared transmitters or receivers to become misaligned to the point that the detector will not function and the units will have to be realigned. Because of their broad detection pattern, these types of movement usually do not affect the performance of the microwave detector.

The wavelength of infrared energy is just below visible light in the electromagnetic spectrum. Like visible light, infrared energy is very much affected by rain, fog, and snow. Precipitation reflects or diffuses infrared energy similar to the way fog reflects visible light. This is an effect that most drivers have experienced when driving at night in heavy fog. Because of this phenomenon, if the area requiring protection is subject to heavy fog, rain, or snow, the effective range of the infrared detectors might be reduced appreciably. Microwave energy is much lower in frequency than infrared energy and is less affected by precipitation. Therefore, the operating range of the microwave detectors is less affected by rain, snow, and fog.

There is a basic application requirement for both microwave and infrared detectors. The detectors are line-of-sight devices, and their energy will not penetrate the ground. If there are any hills or other obstructions such as lamp posts or trees between a transmitter and receiver, they will block the transmitted energy, leaving the area on the opposite side of the obstruction unprotected. Also, if there are gullies passing through the detection zone under the microwave or infrared energy beam, they will not be protected, leaving an unprotected route for an intruder.

Another application consideration for both infrared and microwave detectors is the problem with snow accumulation. A small accumulation of snow, 1 to 2 inches, should not affect the performance of either the microwave or infrared detector. But if the snow is allowed to accumulate above the bottom infrared beam, an intruder can crawl through the snow with a very low probability of being detected. Snow accumulation is a very real problem that must be considered in the application of both infrared and microwave perimeter barriers.

If microwave or infrared detectors are installed in areas where the snow accumulation, especially wet snow, will exceed 1 foot, consideration must be given to removing the snow from between and around the transmitters and receivers to maintain system performance. In this case the detectors should be installed far enough away from fences, buildings, or other objects that might interfere with snow removal. A similar maintenance problem exists if grass is allowed to grow in areas of microwave or infrared detectors. In this operating environment the detectors should be installed far enough away from any objects that might interfere with mowing. If the intrusion detection equipment interferes with any perimeter maintenance or site operational functions, it will probably receive severe abuse from the operating equipment until the detectors are either moved or destroyed. For this reason, perimeter maintenance and operations are very important considerations when designing a perimeter intrusion detection system.

The principles of operation, along with important application considerations of the microwave and infrared detectors, will be discussed in the following paragraphs.

MICROWAVE DETECTORS

Exterior microwave transmitters generate a narrow beam of microwave energy that is received by a corresponding receiver located in the transmitter's line of sight at the opposite end of the beam. When anyone passes through the beam, the receiver detects the perturbations in the energy pattern and initiates an alarm when the resulting signals satisfy the detection alarm criteria. The maximum separation between the detector transmitters and receivers to achieve reliable detection is primarily a function of the antenna configuration because both the operating frequency and the field strength are regulated by the Federal Communications Commission (FCC).

The FCC has allocated five frequency bands for operating exterior microwave detectors. These are the same frequency bands allocated for the interior detectors. Of the five available frequencies, the exterior detectors currently available operate at next to the highest allocated frequency, 10,525 ± 25 MHz. This frequency is used because the higher-frequency microwave energy is more directive than the lower-frequency energies, and the energy pattern is less affected by moving or blowing grass in the area between the transmitter and receiver. Detectors operating at 10,525 MHz are restricted to a maximum field strength level of 250,000 microvolts per meter at a range of 30 meters for unlicensed use.

The narrow shape of the microwave energy beam and the maximum separation between the transmitter and the receiver are functions of antenna size and configuration. The various antenna configurations used by microwave detector manufacturers include parabolic dish arrays, waveguide horns, strip-line arrays, and slotted arrays. The maximum range of detection for these microwave detectors varies from approximately 200 to 1,500 feet. A 1,500-foot range is difficult to cover, except perhaps to detect upright walkers.

The parabolic antenna array consists of a microwave feed assembly that is located at the focal point of a metal parabolic reflector. The microwave feed and reflector assembly are covered by a radome that protects the antenna assembly from the weather. A radome is a dielectric cover invisible to microwave energy. In this detector, the microwave energy is transmitted from the microwave feed toward the parabolic reflector, where it is reflected to form a beam-shaped pattern that is directed toward the receiver. The shape of the transmitted beam is a function of the shape and size of the parabolic reflector.

The transmitted energy then enters the receiver's acceptable field of view, striking the parabolic dish, where it is reflected toward the receiver's microwave feed. The received energy excites a crystal oscillator in the feed, which converts the microwave energy into an electrical signal proportional to the received signal. This signal is then processed and monitored by the signal processor. In general, the larger the reflector, the more needle-shaped the detection zone and the farther apart the transmitter and receiver can be. The zone of detection will be narrower, however.

The waveguide antenna array consists of a waveguide horn mounted to a waveguide cavity feed. This assembly is enclosed in a metal housing that has a radome covering the aperture of the horn to protect the antenna. As with the parabolic antenna, the shape of the transmitted energy pattern and the separation between the transmitter and receiver are functions of the shape and size of the waveguide horn. Again, the larger the horn, the greater the received signal strength and the farther the detector transmitter and receiver can be separated. In the waveguide horn array, the microwave energy emanates from the transmitter feed and is directed toward the receiver by the waveguide horn. Transmitted energy entering the receiver's field of acceptance enters the waveguide oscillator, where it is converted into an electrical signal that is monitored by the signal processor.

For this explanation, the energy pattern of both the parabolic antenna and waveguide horn array is symmetrical about the center line between the transmitter and receiver. The detection pattern is truly symmetrical only in free space, as in real applications, the pattern is distorted by the ground and any surrounding objects. Ignoring the distortions, the energy beam pattern is basically as wide as it is high and is widest in the middle between the transmitter and receiver. Of course, the farther the transmitter and receiver are apart, the wider the energy beam is. In these arrays, the detection pattern not only is symmetrical about the center line, it also is symmetrical between the transmitter and receiver. This symmetry results from the fact that both the transmitter and receiver use the same antenna configuration. To help visualize the energy pattern, imagine a nearly deflated football lying on the ground with a transmitter at one end and a receiver at the opposite end. In this representation, the football is flat on the bottom, but the remaining part of the ball is nearly symmetrical, especially about the center line, perpendicular to the ends of the football.

The strip-line antenna array consists of a narrow copper conductor radiator etched on a laminated sheet of low-loss dielectric material. The radiating element is mounted in front of a trough line reflector, and this assembly is covered with a cylindrical radome. The strip-line antenna generates a nonsymmetrical detection pattern that is narrower in the horizontal direction than it is in the vertical. An advantage of the narrow beam is that the detector can be installed closer to the perimeter fence or other objects, with less chance of electrical interference from the fence.

The slotted antenna array consists of a slotted waveguide feed mounted along the focal line of a one-dimensional parabolic reflector of the same length. Microwave energy is transmitted from the slotted waveguide feed along the total length of the reflector. The energy strikes the parabolic reflector, where it is reflected to form the detection pattern. The one-dimensional reflector looks like one half of a cylinder cut longitudinally, except that the curved surface is not circular but parabolic. Like parabolic dish-shaped antennas, the width of the microwave beam in the middle is a function of the shape of the parabolic reflector and the separation between the transmitter and the receiver. The shape of the beam pattern formed by the slotted array is similar to the pattern generated by the strip-line antenna except that it is wider than it is high.

During the discussions of the various types of microwave antennas, one might wonder why the energy pattern is always symmetrical between the transmitter and the receiver. The symmetry results from the fact that the receiver and transmitter antennas are identical, and although the receiver is passive, it has a field of acceptance identical to the transmitted detection pattern. Using the football again to represent the microwave detection pattern, one half of the football represents the detection pattern generated by the transmitter from the location of the transmitter to midrange between the transmitter and receiver. The other half of the football represents the shape of the corresponding receiver's field of acceptance.

Regardless of the type of antenna, the microwave detector's transmitted energy is modulated to improve signal processing and analysis for detecting characteristic changes in the detection pattern caused by someone penetrating the detection zone. The receiver demodulates the signal and automatically adjusts the signal level with respect to the alarm threshold. The signal level is adjusted by an automatic gain control (AGC) circuit. By using an AGC circuit, most microwave detectors do not require field sensitivity adjusting. Some detectors, however, have several selectable AGC ranges to satisfy the different application requirements. After the received signal is demodulated and adjusted, any changes in the signal are analyzed by the signal processor, and when the changes satisfy the detector's alarm criteria, the processor initiates an alarm. The most difficult task in designing any detector, especially exterior detectors, is to establish the alarm criteria so that characteristic changes in the received signals used to initiate an alarm are representative of the changes caused by an intruder and not by some small animal or other stimuli.

Probably the most popular signal processing technique is to detect a partial or total loss of the received signal and activate an alarm when the loss of signal exists for a preset period of time. Another signal processing technique uses a combination of loss of signal and phase distortion to detect an intruder. This processor detects a loss or reduction in the received signal and also detects a change in the microwave multipath signal. The multipath signals are the signals reflected from the ground or from other objects located in the microwave pattern. In other words, most of the transmitted energy arrives at the receiver directly, but some of the energy is reflected toward the receiver. The signals arriving at the receiver via these alternate paths are called multipath signals. Still another processing technique is to use a phase-lock loop detection circuit that can compensate for slow atmospheric changes caused by fog, rain, snow, etc.

The microwave detectors described thus far amplitude-modulate the carrier frequency; another type of detector pulse-modulates the carrier frequency with a 1,000 Hz pulse tone. This detector then monitors the level of the tone and initiates an alarm when there is either an increase or decrease in the received signal and when the signal level exists for a preset period of time.

A decrease in the signal level can be caused by an intruder blocking the transmitted energy, but an increase in the signal level is a little harder to visualize. An intruder who enters the energy patterns not only blocks the energy, but also distorts the signal path, causing a change in the signal's phase at the receiver. If the phase of the received signal coincides or is in phase with the uninterrupted signal, the signal levels add together, generating a stronger signal. Likewise, if they are out of phase, the signal level is subtracted from the uninterrupted signal, so the net result will be a decrease in signal level.

A relatively new spread spectrum technology using coded modulation is now being applied to bistatic microwave detectors. This technology improves the detector's colocation operation, performance in hostile electromagnetic environment, and immunity to compromise, to which conventional bistatic microwave sensors using continuous wave (CW) amplitude-modulated subcarriers are susceptible. Their modulated signal is uncoded and has a relatively high power spectra density, making the transmitted signal difficult to hide. These characteristics make the amplitude-modulated signal vulnerable to identification and duplication. Spread spectrum modulation improves protection against compromise by using code division multiplexing to address individual receivers. The code can be easily changed in the field on a random schedule. These characteristics make identification and duplication of the coded signal difficult.

Detectors using amplitude-modulated subcarriers rely on using different subcarrier frequencies for each detector when the detectors are used in multiple zone applications. The number of available subcarrier frequencies is, however, limited, which might cause application problems for large multiple zone perimeters. Other systems use transmitter time-sharing to avoid multiple detector interference where only one transmitter is transmitting at any given time. This technique requires control synchronization between a master controller and each transmitter. With spread spectrum coded multiplexing, each detector receiver is assigned an identification code. Selective addressing is achieved by having each transmitter transmit its proper code sequence to its corresponding receiver. Whe the codes are chosen for low cross-correlation, there is minimum interference between the detectors. Number codes are available for large multiple zone perimeters.

Electromagnetic energy interference rejection is also good with spread spectrum modulation because the coded information is spread over a relatively wide frequency band. Therefore, energy at specific frequencies, even within the information band, might not interrupt the code sequence totally. But it would be naive to expect a signal that is easily hidden to operate without interruptions in a harsh electromagnetic environment.

Mr. Ids is shown in Figure 7–1 walking through an invisible microwave energy pattern. In this illustration, the energy pattern is generated by a parabolic antenna array. The wavy lines in front of the transmitter represent the transmitted modulated energy pattern, and the dashed lines forming the cone at the receiver represent the receiver's field of acceptance. The wavy lines reflecting from the ground toward the receiver represent one of many multipath signals arriving at the receiver. As Mr. Ids walks through the

TRANSMITTER

RECEIVER & PROCESSOR

Figure 7-1   Microwave barrier detector.

detection zone, he both distorts the multipath signals and blocks the energy from the receiver. When the signal loss or changes satisfy the detector's alarm criteria, an alarm is initiated.

Applications

Microwave detectors are available with ranges varying from 200 to 1,500 feet. As previously discussed, however, a detection zone length should be limited to about 300 feet to assist the response force in locating an intrusion or identifying the alarm source. The zone length also will depend on the land contour and perimeter configuration. To utilize microwave detectors effectively, the ground should be reasonably level and the perimeter boundaries straight. If portions of the perimeter are hilly or have crooked boundaries, microwave detectors can be used to protect the straight and level sections of the perimeter, and other types of detectors can be used to protect the remaining sections.

The shape of the microwave energy patterns should be considered in their application. Microwave transmitters and receives are point-source arrays, meaning that the energy emanates from a point source and is directed to form a diverging beam. Diverging means that the energy pattern spreads as it leaves the antenna. Again, visualizing a nearly flat football lying on the ground with a transmitter at one point and a receiver at the opposite point, as the energy leaves the transmitter, it spreads, forming one half of the football, while the receiver's field of acceptance forms the other half. Because the arrays are point sources, the triangular area under both the transmitter and receiver are outside the detection zones. These triangular areas can be seen in Figure 7-1. Notice the clear triangular area under the transmitter and the area set off by the dashed line representing the receiver's field of acceptance. Because of these triangular areas outside the detection zone, the transmitters and receivers for adjoining zones must be overlapped to cover these areas. Figure 7-2a shows how the antennas could be overlapped in a corner, and Figure 7-2b shows how they could be overlapped along adjoining straight zones.

The amount of overlap depends on the rate of divergence of the energy pattern and the height of the antenna above the ground. *Rate of divergence* is how fast the energy spreads as it leaves the antenna. When the antennas are mounted about 3 feet above the ground, the smallest overlap required to detect a crawling intruder is about 25 feet. Usually a greater distance is required to detect a low, stealthy intruder. Low-crawling intruders move along on their stomachs to minimize the projected area blocking the microwave energy.

The height of the antenna above ground depends on the ground cover and separation between the transmitter and receiver. If the area is clear of vegetation, the antenna can be mounted closer to the ground than if the ground is covered with grass. To some degree, grass attenuates the microwave energy striking the ground, reducing the energy that would otherwise be reflected toward the receiver. The reflected signals enhance the detection capability of those detectors that monitor multipath signals to detect low-crawling intruders. Grass also reduces the projected area of a low-crawling intruder, thus reducing the detection probability. Longer grass reduces the detection capability even further, as well as complicating the system operations. Moving or blowing grass can create phase distortions that might cause false alarms. Therefore, if microwave detectors are used in grassy areas, they should be mounted higher than if they are operating over bare ground to achieve the same range. The height of the grass in the area between the transmitters and receivers should not exceed about 4 inches.

Another consideration in the application of multiple detector zones is mutual interference. Mutual interference occurs when two or more detectors, operating at the same modulation frequency, electrically interfere with each other's performance. It exists when a receiver in one detection zone receives and operates with the transmitted energy from a detector in another zone, along with the energy from its own corresponding transmitter. This type of interference can cause multiple alarms when someone penetrates the barrier. This in itself is not bad, but variations in the transmitted energy from the two different transmitters might cause false alarm. To eliminate mutual interference, detectors with amplitude-modulated energy patterns have several different modulation frequencies. Each detector can operate at a modulation frequency different from the modulation frequency of the adjoining detectors. If a detector generates a narrow energy pattern, the mutual interference problem is minimized. There should, however, be an adequate

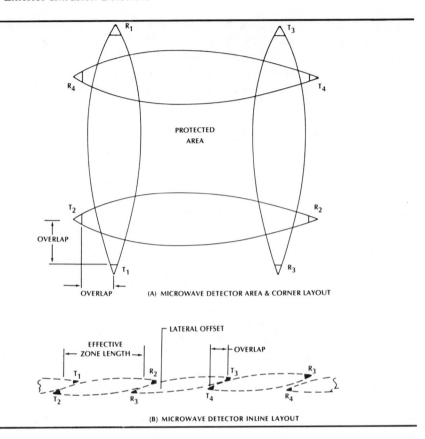

Figure 7-2 Microwave detector layouts.

amount of lateral separation between the detectors in adjoining zones, as shown in Figure 7-2b.

Quite often there is a building wall or some large object in the perimeter zone that interrupts the standard installation of bistatic microwave detectors. If the transmitter or receiver is installed next to the building or wall, an intruder can crawl through the unprotected volume under the transmitter or receiver. Since microwave energy is totally reflected by metal, a flat metal reflector about 2 to 3 feet wide and 3 to 4 feet high can be secured to the building. Then the microwave transmitter and receiver can be colocated on a pole at least 50 feet from the building or in a line perpendicular to the reflector and pointed toward the reflector, as shown in Figure 7-3. In operation, the transmitter illuminates the metal, which reflects the energy back to the corresponding receiver. Anyone crawling next to the building, trying to avoid detection, will be detected by the colocated transmitter and receiver just as if he were crawling through the middle of the detection zone.

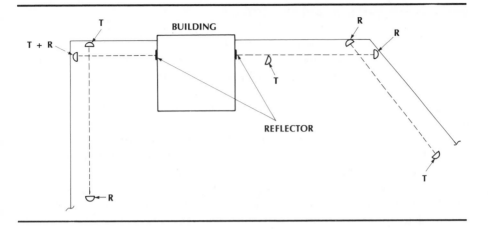

Figure 7-3   Microwave reflector configuration.

This technique also has been used to provide protection around small buildings by installing metal reflectors on posts away from the building at 45-degree angles, with respect to the building sides, to reflect the energy around the building. In this application the transmitter illuminates the first reflector, which redirects the energy to the second reflector. The second reflector then redirects it to the third reflector, and this reflector directs it back to the colocated receiver. In this case the receiver is mounted at a 90-degree angle to the transmitter, in a position to receive the energy from the third reflector. Again, anyone crossing through the reflected energy pattern will be detected just as if they had crossed through the middle of a normal installation. The primary concern with this type of application is that the reflectors must be rigidly mounted to prevent even minute movements (such as blowing grass or rippling water) that could cause false alarms.

Microwave detectors can provide perimeter detection for industrial and commercial installations that are reasonably level and have boundaries straight enough to accommodate detection zone lengths of about 300 feet. Microwave detectors have a high probability of detecting anyone walking or running through the detection zone; however, the probability of detecting crawling intruders is reduced somewhat if the site is leveled and substantially reduced if it is not. If the site can be leveled between the transmitter and receiver, and the vegetation removed or controlled, the probability of detecting low-crawling intruders can be very good.

The application of microwave detectors, like all other detectors, depends on the skill level of the threat. If the threat is expected to run or walk through the barrier, microwave detectors will be very effective. If the threat is skilled, effectiveness will depend on the user's willingness to level and maintain the perimeter grounds.

MONOSTATIC MICROWAVE DETECTORS

Monostatic microwave detectors, unlike bistatic microwave detectors, which have a separate transmitter and receiver, have a self-contained transceiver that both transmits and receives the electromagnetic energy. Microwave transceivers have been widely accepted for interior applications but not for exterior applications because ordinary microwave transceivers are limited by poorly defined detection patterns; false alarms from large moving metal objects outside the normal zone of detection, rain dripping down the face of the radome, and wind vibrating the transceiver; electromagnetic susceptibility; and broad range temperature stability.

Monostatic microwave detectors avoid or minimize these shortcomings by using a unique signal processing technique made possible by operating the detector at two different transmitting frequencies. The dual frequencies provide a means of using a range cutoff circuit that allows a maximum detection range to be established independently of object size, thereby eliminating alarms caused by large moving objects beyond the desired detection range. The dual frequencies also allow a means of employing a unique zero range suppression circuit, which reduces sensitivity to small objects very close to the transceiver so that alarms from raindrops and minor detector vibrations are minimized.

Operationally, the microwave transceiver transmits an electromagnetic energy pattern in the microwave frequency range to form the detection zone. The transmitted energy is reflected from objects in the field of detection back to the receiver. Moving objects in the detection zone cause a Doppler frequency shift in the reflected energy. When the magnitude of the reflected energy's frequency shift satisfies the signal processor's alarm criteria, an alarm is generated. The size of the frequency-shift reflection that will cause an alarm is varied by the sensivity control. At any fixed sensitivity setting, the detection zone for large objects such as trucks would be larger than for smaller objects such as a crawling person.

In the dual frequency signal processing technique, the transmitter is periodically and rapidly turned on and off, first at one frequency and then at the other. The receiver is then switched on for a very short period immediately after transmission begins at each of the two microwave frequencies. Because microwave energy travels at a constant speed near the speed of light, elapsed time between transmission and reception provides an accurate measurement of range from the monostatic detector to the moving object being illuminated. By turning the receiver off after a short period of time corresponding to the maximum desired detection range, reflections from moving objects beyond this range are ignored because they arrive back at the receiver too late to be received even for larger reflections.

Reflections from small moving objects, such as raindrops, very near the transceiver are frequently as large as reflections from someone moving in the detection zone. This problem also is overcome by operating at a dual frequency. Reflections from the first frequency pulse are directed into one signal processor channel, returns from the second pulse are directed into another channel, and the outputs from the two channels are combined. Because the reflected microwave energy is at different frequencies, the resulting reflected Doppler signals from any moving object in the detection zone arrive at the receiver out of phase. Reflections from moving objects at very close ranges, such as raindrops on the radome, arrive almost in phase. Therefore, when the outputs from the two channels are subtracted, there is a resulting signal from out-of-phase reflections and consequently a detection, but there is no resulting signal from the in-phase reflections and consequently no alarm.

The monostatic transceiver uses a circular polarized high-gain, low-sidelobe parabolic antenna system that provides a detection range of about 200 feet. Because the reflected signals from a long detection range are small, the detector has a very sensitive receiver. Also, because of the sensitivity, all the microwave and electronic circuits are housed in a radio-frequency (RF) tight enclosure, and all incoming signals are filtered to reduce interference from external electromagnetic sources.

Mr. Ids is shown in Figure 7–4 walking through the microwave energy pattern generated by the detector's parabolic antenna system. The detection zone length can be extended by adding detectors at the end of each detection zone. For uninterrupted detection, the detectors' energy patterns must be overlapped. The required overlap to detect a man crawling on his hands and knees varies somewhat with the detector's sensitivity setting. Detecting a low-crawling "commando-style" intruder might require additional overlap. As Mr. Ids walks through the detection zone, he produces a Doppler frequency shift in the reflected microwave energy. When the magnitude of the frequency shift satisfies the detector alarm criteria, an alarm is generated.

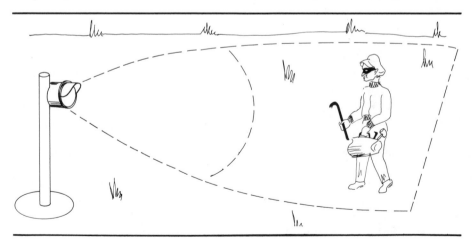

Figure 7–4 Monostatic microwave detector.

Applications

The monostatic microwave detector is available with field-selected ranges of 100, 150, or 200 feet when mounted about 30 inches above the ground. It produces a 24-foot-wide teardrop-shaped energy pattern when the range is 200 feet. With this detection pattern, the detectors can be arranged with sufficient overlap to form a continuous detection barrier around a perimeter similar to that of bistatic detectors. Monostatic detectors are not as cost-effective as bistatic detectors in this type of application. They are more effectively used as traps inside a compound to detect anyone approaching a specific item or area. They also are affective when used in conjunction with bistatic detectors to minimize bistatic detector overlap in corners and to provide detection where fences butt against buildings. Normally, bistatic microwave detectors are overlapped about 25 feet at corners to detect low-crawling intruders. In this application, the bistatic sensor zones can terminate in the corner, and the monostatic detector can be directed across the corner to fill in the vulnerable area under the adjoining bistatic detectors. In applications where bistatic detectors butt against buildings or other obstacles, monostatic detectors can be used to detect penetrations in the area under the bistatic energy pattern at the transmitter and receiver.

Sensitivity should be adjusted to the lowest setting that will satisfy the application requirements. Excessively high sensitivity might cause nuisance alarms from grass, small birds, or windblown debris in the detection zone.

Finally, the monostatic detector has an interference/tamper detection circuit to detect anyone attempting to compromise the detector by placing a metal container over the transceiver in an attempt to eliminate the microwave energy pattern.

INFRARED DETECTORS

Exterior infrared detectors generate a multiple beam fencelike pattern of infrared energy and initiate an alarm when one beam or, in some systems, a combination of beams is interrupted. Since the infrared energy frequency band lies in just below the color red in the visible light spectrum, infrared energy is too low in frequency to be visible to the naked eye. The infrared energy is generated in the detector transmitter by a solid-state infrared source. A commonly used light source is the gallium arsenide light emitting diode (LED). In operation, the light source should be modulated, pulsed at a specific frequency to reduce the possibility of an intruder substituting another infrared source in an attempt to compromise the detector. Modulating the beam also reduces the susceptibility of the detector to false alarms from sunlight or other light sources.

Energy radiating from the infrared light source passes through a collimating beam-forming lens in the transmitter and is directed toward the receivers at the opposite end of the zone. Energy reaching the receiver passes through a collecting lens that focuses the radiant energy onto a photo-electric cell. The photoelectric cell is a semiconductor device that converts the radiant infrared energy into electrical signals proportional to the radiant energy. The receiver monitors the electrical signal and initiates an alarm when its magnitude drops below a preset threshold for a specific period of time. The alarm threshold should correspond to at least a 90 percent block-age for a period of about 75 milliseconds. This reduces the probability of false alarms from birds flying or debris blowing through the beams. Some detectors require a loss of signal from at least two receivers to initiate an alarm. This technique further reduces the detectors susceptibility to birds and debris. The bottom receiver alone, however, should initiate an alarm if it is interrupted. Otherwise, low-crawling intruders will not be detected.

The infrared fence beam patterns are formed between two separate detector columns. One column is located at one end of the protected zone, and the other column is located at the opposite end. Since the exterior infra-red detectors are line-of-sight devices, the area between the columns must be level and clear of any obstacles that might interfere with the transmitted energy. The separation between the two detector columns ranges from a few feet to protect entrance gates to zones as long as 1,000 feet. Weather condi-tions, such as heavy rain, fog, snow, or even blowing dust particles, attenu-ate infrared energy and can affect the operating range. In areas where these weather conditions occur, the detector range might have to be reduced to 100 or 200 feet, depending on the density of the particles.

Two basic infrared detector configurations are available. One configu-ration has a single transmitter along with several receivers on each column. The second configuration has all the transmitters on one column and all the corresponding receivers on the second column. In the first configuration, the transmitter is mounted at the top of one column and at the bottom of the second column. In operation, the transmitted energy from the single trans-mitter usually is adequate to illuminate all the corresponding receivers in the opposite column. There might be applications, however, where either the detector columns are too close together or too high to illuminate all the receivers. In these applications, additional transmitters will be required to illuminate the receivers.

The separation between the individual beams is about 12 inches, with the bottom beam about 6 inches from the ground. The actual number of transmitters and receivers forming a column depends on the desired height of the infrared fence. The normal infrared fence is between 4 and 6 feet high but the columns can be made higher for special applications. If the infrared beams are lower than 4 feet, an intruder might be able to jump over the bar-rier without being detected. If the bottom beam is higher than 6 inches from the ground, a low-crawling intruder might be successful in crawling under the barrier.

In the second detector configuration, one detector column contains four or five transmitters, and the corresponding detector column contains a corresponding number of receivers. Again, the number of transmitters and receivers forming each column depends on the desired height of the infrared fence. As with the first detector configuration, the fence height can be made higher for special applications. In operation, the transmitted energy from the individual transmitters illuminates all or some combination of the receivers in the corresponding columns.

Figure 7–5 illustrates the first detector column configuration. The transmitter on the bottom of the detector column on the right side of the illustration illuminates the three receivers in the column on the left side and vice versa. This receiver/transmitter arrangement gives a crossed pattern of infrared energy so that an intruder walking or crawling through any portion of the beams will be detected. As Mr. Ids walks through the infrared barrier, he interrupts the transmitted energy from both columns. When the electrical signal from the photoelectric cell in the receivers drops below the alarm threshold level, the detector initiates an alarm.

Besides the two-detector configuration, there are at least two different transmitter/receiver enclosures. In one enclosure type, the one shown in Figure 7–5, each infrared receiver and transmitter is enclosed in its own housing. These housings are then stacked end on end to form the desired receiver/ transmitter column configuration and height. In application, the detector zones should be overlapped at adjoining zones to protect the adjoining detectors, or the top of the detector column should be protected with a pressure switch to detect anyone vaulting over the detector. If the detectors are not overlapped or protected by pressure switches, an intruder could vault over the infrared barrier using the detector column as an aid. But even with the top of the detector protected, the pressure switch will detect only the intruder who applies pressure on the detector.

In the second enclosure type, the individual receivers and transmitters are mounted on a 4- to 6-foot-high supporting column covered by a separate enclosure. The enclosure is constructed primarily from opaque plastic panels that are transparent to infrared energy. The opaque panels not only protect the transmitters and receivers, but also hide the transmitters and

Figure 7–5   Infrared barrier detector.

receivers from view. The enclosures are large enough to house the necessary transmitters and receivers required for two adjoining detector zones. For in-line zones, the two sets of transmitters and receivers are mounted on the same supporting column and aligned in the opposite direction to cover their respective zones. For corner adjoining zones, the transmitters are directed at 90-degree angles. Again, the top of the enclosures should be protected with pressure switches to prevent an intruder from vaulting or climbing over the enclosure column without being detected.

Condensation collecting on the infrared transmitter and receiver lenses, and on the inside of the enclosure's optical windows, will affect system performance. Condensation will obstruct the infrared energy and thereby reduce the corresponding received signal level in the same way the presence of snow or fog between the detector columns does. For this reason, thermostatically controlled heaters should be installed in the transmitter and receiver optics, and perhaps inside the enclosure housing, if there are optical windows in front of the transmitter and receiver lenses.

Applications

Infrared barrier detectors are available with operating ranges up to 1,000 feet when operated in clear weather. But as previously mentioned, if the detectors are operated in adverse environments where there is heavy fog, rain, snow, or blowing dust particles, the range might have to be reduced to compensate for the resulting reduction in the energy level at the receivers. For such applications, the detector manufacturer should be consulted before establishing the detector zone lengths.

Infrared detectors, like microwave detectors, are line-of-sight devices. They should be installed over level ground. Therefore, the operating range also depends on the levelness of the ground and the straightness of the perimeter boundary. Since the detectors are line-of-sight, any dips or gullies in the area between the detector columns that pass under the infrared beams should be filled in. Although infrared detectors can operate in clear weather over distances of 1,000 feet between the detector columns if the ground is level enough to accommodate such ranges, it is recommended that the detection range be limited to about 300 feet to assist the response force in locating an intrusion or cause of an alarm.

Alignment between corresponding infrared detector columns is critical because the infrared transmitter beam and the receivers' field of acceptance are very narrow. Any angular movement or deflection of the detector column will cause misalignment between the transmitters and receivers. Since the transmitted energy beam is narrow and the distance between the detector columns is long in comparison, any angular movement of the detector column might redirect the infrared beam away from the receiver. Depending on the amount of movement, the results could be either an inoperable or marginally operable system. Movement of the receiver will reduce the receiver's effective field of acceptance and consequently cause a reduction in the received energy.

Detector misalignment could be caused by movements in the ground from freezing and thawing or something hitting a column. In areas where freezing ground could cause alignment problems, the detector column foundation should be installed deep enough to prevent excessive movement. If the detector columns are in locations where they might be hit, physical barriers should be installed to minimize their vulnerability. If the detectors are installed in grassy areas or where there is excessive snow, care must be exercised during the maintenance of the areas. In the case of grass, the detector foundation could be extended far enough away from the detector column so that a mower could be maneuvered around the column with little chance of hitting it. Snow removal from around the detector column should be done by hand.

Infrared detectors can provide perimeter penetration detection for industrial and commercial installations with level grounds that can accommodate detection zone lengths of at least 300 feet. Infrared detectors have a high probability of detecting anyone running, walking, or attempting to jump over the infrared beams if the detector columns are at least 4 to 6 feet high. They also have a high probability of detecting anyone crawling through the energy barrier if the ground is level between the detector columns and the lowest beam is no greater than 6 inches above the ground.

Chapter 8

Electric-Field
Sensors

Electric-field sensors generate an electrostatic field between an array of wire conductors and an electrical ground and detect changes in the field caused by anyone approaching or touching the array. Two types of electric-field sensors are available: E-field and capacitance sense wire.

E-FIELD SENSORS

E-field sensors generate the electrostatic field between either a three-wire or four-wire fence-mounted or freestanding array. Each array consists of one or two field wires and two or four sense wires. An oscillator generates a non-lethal alternating current on the field wire or wires, which generates the electrostatic field. The radiated field induces an electrical signal on the adjacent sense wires that is proportional to the radiated field strength. As long as there is no one or nothing moving in the radiated field, the sense wire signal is constant. But when someone approaches the sensor array, he distorts the electrostatic field, causing a corresponding change in the sense wire signal. When the characteristics of the signal change satisfy the alarm criteria, an alarm is initiated.

Three-wire array configurations are available to accommodate different applications and environmental conditions. This array has one center-field wire and two sense wires. The sense wires are installed directly above and below the field wire. The four-wire array has two two-wire arrays configured for balanced quadrature detection. That is, the arrays are physically and electrically configured so that far-field lighting will affect each array identically to minimize false alarms.

The signal processor is part of the control unit located on or near the E-field sensor. Signals from the sense wires enter the signal processor and are passed through a bandpass filter. The filter rejects the high-frequency signals that might be caused by wind vibrating the field and sense wires and the low-frequency signals that might be caused by foreign objects striking the fence wires. The signals also must simultaneously satisfy several signal processing criteria before an alarm will be initiated. The first criterion is that the amplitude of the signal must exceed a certain preset level that is a function of the intruder's size and proximity to the fence. This criterion is imposed to discriminate against small animals that might otherwise cause false or nuisance alarms. A second criterion is that the movements of the intruder approaching the sensor must be in the frequency range of the bandpass filter to be accepted by the signal processor. As already mentioned, this criterion is imposed to alleviate alarms from wind and blowing debris. The third and final criterion is that the signal must be present at the processor for a preset period of time. This minimizes false alarms caused by electromagnetic fields generated by lightning and also provides additional protection against nuisance alarms caused by objects blowing or birds flying through the sensor wires.

Another feature of the signal processor is that it has a self-adjusting circuit that automatically adjusts the detector's sensitivity to compensate for objects moved close to the sensor. This means that cars, buses, or other metal equipment could be located near the E-field sensor for protection. Anyone who attempts to move the object will initiate an alarm.

The wire conductors for the field and sense wires are plastic-coated steel. Steel has the necessary high-tensile strength to withstand the mechanical loads, and the plastic coating prevents the conductor from conducting to earth ground in rain or other precipitation. The wire can be secured either to insulators mounted on stand-alone fence posts or on 18-inch dielectric standoffs mounted on existing chain-link fence posts. Springs are installed at the termination of each wire to maintain tension on the wire conductor. The spring tension causes wind-induced wire vibrations to be outside the filter's passband.

Excessive movement between the wire conductors or between the conductors and the fence fabric would induce low-frequency signals on the sense wire that might be interpreted by the signal processor as valid intrusion alarm signals. For the same reason, the chain-link fence fabric should be tight to reduce the relative motion between the fence and sensor. Line supervision for the wire conductors is provided by a terminator installed between the sense and field wire at the end of the E-field sensor. Two terminators are required for three-wire sensor configurations.

Mr. Ids is shown in Figure 8–1 approaching a three-wire fence-mounted E-field sensor. The dashed lines emanating from the top field wire and terminating on the ground represent the electric-field lines in the electrostatic field. As previously indicated, these electric-field lines result from the induced alternating currents. These electric-field lines are symmetrical about the field wire and continuous along the entire length of the wire, not just in the two representative locations shown in the illustration. In the area where Mr. Ids approaches the sensor, more and more of the electric-field lines pass through him to reach earth ground. This phenomenon exists

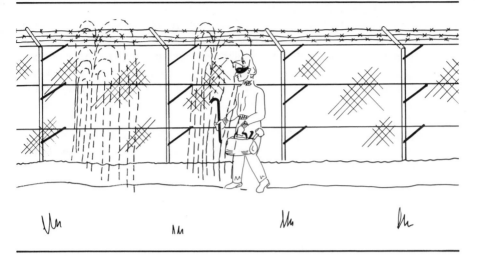

Figure 8-1 Electric-field detector.

because Mr. Ids's body is far less resistant to the electric field reaching the ground than is air. The unbalance in the electric field caused by Mr. Ids's presence distorts the electric field. Changes in the electric field induce changes in the electrical signal on the sense wire. The induced signals keep changing as Mr. Ids approaches the sensor, until their characteristics simultaneously satisfy all the signal processor's alarm criteria. At this time the processor initiates an alarm.

Applications

E-field sensors are available for protecting 1,000- and 1,500-foot zones, and they can be installed in several different configurations. The orientation of the sensor is not critical as long as the sense and field wires are relatively parallel. The sensor can be installed along the ground or vertically up the side of a building. The most popular configurations are the three-wire and four-wire arrays installed on either freestanding fence posts or on standoffs mounted on the posts of a chain-link fence. The two-wire freestanding sensor configuration is shown in Figure 8-1. The field wire is the top wire, which generates the electrostatic field, and the sense wire is the bottom wire, which carries the induced signals to the signal processor. The sense wire is about 14 to 18 inches above the ground, the sense wire and field wire are separated by about 3½ to 4 feet. In the three-wire configuration, the central wire is the field wire, and the sense wires are located above and below the field wire. Again, the bottom sense wire is about 18 inches above the ground, the field wire is about 3½ feet above the sense wire, and the second sense wire is 3½ feet above the field wire. When the sensor is mounted on a chain-link fence, it can detect an intruder trying to gain entrance by climbing over or crawling under the fence or after he has cut the chain link fence and attempts to crawl through. The four-wire array consists of two sense and two field wires arrayed to generate a balanced system that is less sensitive to far-field electromagnetic interference than the three- or two-wire configuration. Other configurations of the E-field sensor can be constructed for specific applications.

E-field sensor gate kits are available to protect gate openings of 25 feet or less. The kit consists of two spring-loaded reels, handles, and insulators. In application, the reels are installed on one side of the gate, and the conductor wires are pulled from the reels across the gate and fastened to the insulators on the opposite side of the opening. To open the gate, the wires are disconnected from the insulators. They are then automatically retracted by the spring-loaded reels. This type of application is fine if the gate is seldom used or can be opened in the morning and closed at night. If the gate requires frequent use, however, disconnecting and connecting the electric-field gate every time would become a nuisance. For this type of application, it is suggested that a microwave or infrared barrier be installed across the opening, as shown in Figure 8–2.

Several important operating requirements should be considered in the application of E-field fences. One requirement is that if the area requiring detection is large and several sensors are used, the adjacent sensors should be operated at different frequencies to reduce mutual electrical interference. If the electrostatic fields are generated by oscillators of the same frequency, there is a good possibility of interference between the sensors, which might cause false alarms. Crystal-controlled generators are available at several different frequencies in the 10,000 Hz frequency range. Having several different frequency generators to choose from, the E-field sensors can be arranged so that no two adjacent sensors are operating at the same frequency.

Another consideration in the installation of an E-field sensor is that the area under the sensor must be clear of vegetation. If grass and weeds are allowed to grow under the sensor, any weed coming in contact with the bottom sense wire will initiate an alarm. Vegetation coming in contact with the sense wire will produce changes in the electrical signal. Since the signal processor cannot differentiate between signal changes caused by the vegetation and the signal from an intruder, it will generate an alarm. Therefore, the vegetation under and around the E-field sensor must be short or better yet, removed from these areas.

The last consideration for an E-field sensor is that the sensitivity should be adjusted to satisfy the facility's protection requirements based on the anticipated threat. If the sensor sensitivity is too high, the sensor is more susceptible to detecting small animals; if the sensitivity is too low, it might not detect a very slowly walking or crawling intruder. Therefore, the sensor's sensitivity should be adjusted to detect a normally walking person within

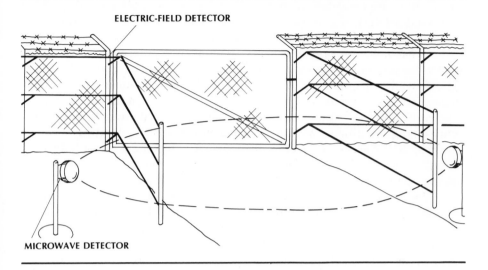

Figure 8-2 Electric-field gate configuration.

approximately 1 to 2 feet of the sensor and a slowly moving person at the sensor.

E-field sensors can provide perimeter protection for many industrial and commercial installations. An application feature is that the sensors will follow the ground contour and perimeter configuration. And if they are mounted on the perimeter fence, the sensors do not occupy a lot of space inside the fence. When the E-field sensor is mounted on the perimeter fence, it has a high probability of detecting anyone climbing over or cutting through the fence and a fair probability of detecting a low-crawling intruder attempting to crawl under the fence and detector. Therefore, if the threat can be expected to lift the fence fabric and crawl under, the bottom of the fence fabric should be secured either to the ground or to a bottom rail to prevent it from being easily lifted. This will increase the difficulty of entering under the fence, forcing the intruder to climb over or cut through the fence fabric.

CAPACITANCE SENSE WIRE SENSORS

Capacitance sensors generate an electric field between an array of fence or barrier top-mounted wire conductors and the electrically grounded fence and monitor the resulting capacitance to detect changes indicating someone touching the array. In application, the capacitance sensor is divided into dual right and left arrays of equal length to allow differential mode detection. In operation, the sensor monitors the capacitance in each array segment. Common changes in capacitance in each segment produced by rain, wind, or lightning are canceled. Changed caused by an intruder are not common and will be detected, and the right or left segment where the intrusion took place is identified for the central monitor.

Capacitance sense wire sensors are dual zone differential sensors that detect the presence of anyone touching the sense wires installed on top of fences, walls, or buildings. In operation the sensor induces a 3 kHz low-voltage signal on three closely spaced sense wire arrays and measures the electrical capacitance between the arrays and electrical ground. The capacitance change to initiate an alarm depends on the sensitivity setting. It can be adjusted to detect a 10-picofarad change for maximum sensitivity or a 150-picofarad change for minimum sensitivity. At the minimum sensitivity setting, the sensor wires must be deliberately touched to initiate an alarm.

The sensor processor operates in a differential mode, where it monitors the capacitance separately from adjacent and equal-length sense wire segments to detect unique changes in a single zone or segment indicating that someone is crossing the sensor. The total length of each sense wire segment must be the same length within 10 percent to achieve proper common-mode rejection. Operating in the differential mode minimizes alarms caused by rain, wind, or far-field lightning and other electromagnetic energy sources. Signal changes produced by these sources should affect both sense wire segments approximately the same, and consequently the resulting signals will be canceled. All input and output signal lines to the processor are filtered and transient protected to reduce electromagnetic interference. Although the signal processor monitors and compares the capacitance in both sense wire arrays, it identifies separately the specific segment or zone where the capacitance change indicates an intrusion.

Figure 8-3 shows Mr. Ids about to grab the capacitance sense wires to pull himself over the fence. His physical act of touching the wires will cause a change in the capacitance in the segment where he is penetrating the fence. This change results in an imbalance in the comparator signal. When the magnitude and duration of the capacitance change satisfies the sensor alarm criteria, an alarm is initiated.

Applications

A distinct application advantage of the capacitance sense wire sensor, as with any fence- or barrier-mounted sensor, is that it follows the barrier contour and occupies very little space inside the protected area. The sense wires can be secured to a fence top or wall by using the manufacturer's supplied dielectric standoff brackets. The brackets support three strands of 16-gauge steel copper-clad wire that forms the sensor array. The brackets can be adapted to any barrier. When the sensor is used on chain-link fences topped with outriggers supporting barbed wire strands, the brackets can be secured to the outriggers with steel clamps. In this configuration, the brackets extend

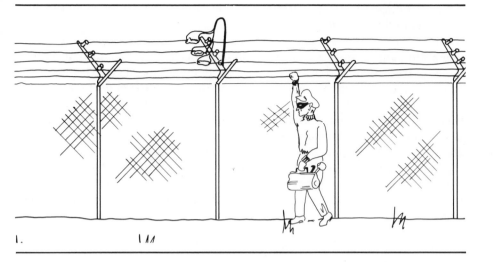

Figure 8–3 Capacitance sense wire sensor.

in the opposite direction from the outriggers, forming a Y-shaped barrier on top of fences using single-arm outriggers to support the barbed wire. On fences with double-arm outriggers, the sense wires will form a third barrier in the center of the V formed by the outriggers. On fences without outriggers, the brackets can be secured directly to the chain-link fence posts with metal clamps, like the fence configuration Mr. Ids is shown penetrating in Figure 8–3. For walls and other barriers, the standoffs can be bolted to the structure using the appropriate mounting hardware. The sensors also can be adapted to double-vehicle gates.

The dual sensor segment can cover 1,000 feet (500 feet per segment), provided the total capacitance per segment does not exceed 2,500 picofarads when the sensor is set for maximum sensitivity or 10,000 picofarads per segment when it is set for minimum sensitivity. In keeping with all exterior sensor applications, it is recommended that a single segment be limited to about 330 feet to maintain a manageable detection zone for the security response force.

The three sense wires forming a sensor segment or zone electrically act as a single sense wire or array. Therefore, the processor monitors the capacitance between the three sense wire arrays and electrical ground. In applications where the sensor is used on top of a fence, the processor monitors the capacitance between the sense wire array and the fence fabric. Therefore, it is essential to have the fence well grounded along the entire length where the sensor is installed. Otherwise, there could be a variation in the sensitivity along the individual segments. This capacitance imbalance could result in an increase in false alarms from wind, rain, and electromagnetic energy sources. The induced energy would affect each segment differently, which would produce an imbalance in the comparator signal. If the signal magnitude satisfied the alarm criteria, a false alarm would result.

Each dual sensor sense wire is held in 50 pounds of tension by an in-line spring and terminated at each end by a dielectric insulator that isolates the wire from electrical ground. To adjust the wire tension, a wire tightener is installed in-line with each sense wire at the opposite end of the wire from the spring. If the proper spring tension is not maintained and the wires become loose, they will move in the wind, causing vibrations in the capacitance between the wires and electrical ground, which could result in false alarms. A dielectric insulator also is used to separate electrically each wire segment forming the dual sensor. The sense wire for each sensor segment is connected to the signal processor with 12-gauge insulated solid copper wire where the two sensor zones interface. The interconnect wires are routed from the processor, mounted adjacent to the sensor zone interface, to the sense wire through metal conduit and then through the manufacturer's plastic gooseneck tubing. The plastic tubing insulates the interconnecting wires from the metal conduit. Otherwise, because the interconnecting wires form part of the capacitance sensor, moisture between the wires and metal conduit would cause a change in the dielectric medium that could result in false alarms.

Chapter 9

Buried Line Sensors

Buried line sensors protect an area along the ground just above the sensor transducers or cables by detecting anyone crossing the protected zone. There are both passive and active buried sensors. Passive sensors detect strain or seismic energy induced in the ground. They also detect the presence of ferrous metals being carried or worn by a person crossing the transducer cable. Active sensors generate an electric field between a ported transmitter cable and a ported receiver cable. These sensors generate a detection zone, and when anyone enters the zone, he distorts the energy pattern, causing changes in the received signals, which initiates an alarm.

Piezoelectric transducers are used primarily to detect short-range pressure disturbances in the ground, and geophones are used primarily to detect longer-range seismic waves. These are basically the same devices as those used for fence disturbance sensor transducers, and in some cases they are the same devices. The difference in the application is the frequency response. Seismic energy is lower in frequency than the mechanical vibrations induced in the fence during a forced penetration. The piezoelectric transducer is capable of responding to the frequency response for both fence disturbance sensors and buried sensors. Although the same basic geophone is usually used for either application, the form of the geophone assembly is different for the two applications. The difference in the frequency response required for fence sensors and seismic sensors is compensated for in the signal processor. The frequency acceptance of the bandpass filter for the fence disturbance sensor's signal processor is higher than the bandpass frequency for the buried sensor.

The spacing between geophones or piezoelectric transducers, and the depth at which they are buried, are primarily functions of the density of the medium in which they are buried. Piezoelectric sensors are usually buried at a depth of about 16 inches in soil and about 3 inches in asphalt. Geophones are buried at shallower depths. The distance between the buried piezoelectric transducers is about 18 inches, and the distance between the geophones is 6 to 12 feet.

Buried line sensors that detect both strain and ferrous materials use a passive ferromagnetic core transducer line. Strain induced in the transducer distorts the residual flux density of the ferromagnetic core material, thus generating an electric signal in the line transducer. Ferrous material moving across the transducer distorts the earth's magnetic force, causing a change in the flux density of the transducer, which also generates an electrical signal in the line transducer. These combined signals are monitored by the signal processor, and when their characteristics satisfy the processor alarm criteria, an alarm is activated.

Several operational characteristics of buried sensors should be considered. Seismic energy and strain are induced in the ground by wind overpressures, animals, moving tree roots, and other naturally occurring phenomen, as well as by human-caused seismic energy sources, such as rotating machinery or moving vehicles. It is sometimes difficult for the detectors to differentiate between these types of stimuli and the energies generated by an intruder. If the area where the buried sensors are being considered is subject to natural or man-made seismic energy sources, detectors with the ability to reduce or compensate for these sources should be evaluated.

Several techniques are used to reduce the detectors' susceptibility to nuisance or false alarm stimuli. Using selected bandpass filters for the input signals is the most common method of reducing false alarms. Other techniques also are used. In one buried sensor system, discriminators are positioned outside the primary zone of detection to eliminate the effect of far-field seismic energy sources. Another system uses several different bandpass filters, and the signals from each filter are processed separately, with the output signals gated together in an AND logic circuit. In this configuration, output signals are required from each bandpass circuit before an alarm is initiated.

Buried line sensors become less sensitive to sources of strain in frozen ground. Reduced sensitivity jeopardizes their ability to detect intrusions. Other ground conditions, such as baked clay and mud, also can affect sensor response. These performance deviations can be compensated for somewhat by seasonally adjusting the detector's signal controls as climatic and ground conditions change.

Active sensors generate the electric field between a ported transmit coaxial cable and a ported receive coaxial cable. Depending on the sensor type and application, cables are deployed on top of the ground or, more popularly, buried in the ground. The electric-field patterns range in width from about 8 to 18 feet and in height from about 4 to 6 feet, again depending on the sensor type and application. An advantage of the active sensor over the passive seismic and pressure-type sensors is that they are not affected by induced seismic energy and the sensitivity is not affected as much by seasonal ground changes. Unlike passive sensors, however, ported coaxial sensors are affected by moving ground water, such as rain runoff or wind-induced ripples on standing water in the detection zone.

The basic principles of operation and application of the individual buried line sensors, and their limitations, will be discussed in the following paragraphs.

GEOPHONE TRANSDUCERS

Buried geophones detect the low-frequency seismic energy induced in the ground by someone crossing the protected area above the sensors and convert this energy into electrical signals. The electrical signals correspond to the frequency of the induced seismic energy, and they are proportional in amplitude to the magnitude of the energy. These induces signals are sent to the signal processor, where they are filtered before entering the processor. The bandpass of the filter corresponds to the seismic energies with frequencies or signatures typical of someone crossing the geophone sensors. When the characteristics of the induced signals satisfy the processor alarm criteria, an alarm is initiated.

A geophone consists of a movable spring-balanced coil of fine wire suspended around a permanent magnet. The coil is cylindrical to slide over the magnetic rod fixed to the geophone housing. When the geophone is acted upon by the seismic energy, the permanent magnet vibrates with the geophone housing at the frequency of the induced energy. The vibrating magnet moves in line with the coil, which tends to stay near rest. It stays near rest because the fine spring holding the coil in suspension around the magnet offers very little resistance to the moving geophone housing. As the magnet vibrates the coil, the magnetic lines of force associated with the permanent magnet induce an EMF in the coil. This EMF, or electrical signal, is the signal that is monitored by the signal processor.

Three techniques used for reducing nuisance alarms from natural or man-made seismic energy are discriminator sensors, dual channel signal processing, and bandpass frequency selection. The discriminator sensors in this case are geophones that are installed about 30 feet ouside the primary zone of detection. These geophones detect seismic energy from sources outside the protected area, such as passing cars, trucks, or trains on nearby highways or tracks, and stationary sources of seismic energy, such as rotating machinery. In some applications, the discriminators might have to be used only in areas between the protected area and the seismic energy source and not all around the protected area. In operation, seismic signals from these outside sources are received by the discriminator geophones. These signals, along with the signals from the geophones in the primary zone of detection, are combined in the signal processor. The processor combines the signals in such a way that signals from the far-field seismic sensor sources are canceled from the primary geophone signals. This cancellation process reduces nuisance alarms while maintaining the ability to detect someone crossing the protected area.

A dual channel signal processor processes the geophone signal in two separate frequency processing channels and logically combines the output from each channel to initiate an alarm. The seismic energy pattern generated by someone running, walking, or crawling is very broadband with respect to the bandpass of the input filter. However, the pattern sometimes has several unique narrow bands of frequencies or signature patterns that have characteristics for each mode of crossing. This is the ideal case. Most of the time it is difficult to isolate any frequency pattern unique to each mode of intrusion. But there is usually a difference between the seismic signature pattern generated by someone crossing the geophone barrier and the seismic energy generated by outside man-made or natural sources. In this case, the bandpass of the two different input filters is selected to differentiate between valid signals and signals from far-field seismic sources. When the signals in both signal processor channels satisfy their respective alarm criteria, then outputs are combined in a logic circuit that initiates an alarm.

Bandpass filter selection is not a signal processing technique. It is simply the selection of the bandpass frequency in the seimic energy pattern with the optimum signal-to-noise ratio. This is accomplished by recording the seismic energy in the area where the system will be installed and comparing the ambient seismic energy with the energy induced by someone crossing the perimeter. The bandpass of the filter is selected for the frequency where valid signatures are predominant in the measured ambient seismic energy pattern.

All these signal processing techniques reduce nuisance alarms to some degree. Like any other sensor signal processing technique for reducing nuisance alarms, however, the design criteria are a compromise between excellent detection and high false alarm or nuisance alarm rates, and poor detection and low nuisance alarm rates.

Another technique being used to differentiate between nuisance alarms and valid intrusions is an audio listen-in feature. The listen-in feature allows the central station operator to listen to the audible seismic signals from the geophones. A trained operator can usually differentiate between stimuli causing nuisance alarms and seismic signals from someone crossing the perimeter zone of detection.

Mr. Ids is shown in Figure 9–1 crossing a line of buried geophones connected by a single multiconductor cable designed for direct burial. Signals from the individual geophones are collectively processed in the signal processor, which is sometimes buried in-line with the sensor cables. As Mr. Ids walks across the geophones, each step generates a seismic signature that travels radially away from the step along the surface and into the ground. As the seismic energy passes the geophone, it forces the geophone housing to vibrate and the permanent magnet to move axially within the suspended coil of fine wire. As the magnetic lines of force intercept the coil of wire, an EMF

TERMINATION   PROCESSOR

Figure 9–1 Geophone sensor.

induced in the wire is sent to the signal processor. When the characteristics of this seismic energy satisfy the alarm criteria, an alarm is initiated.

Applications

Geophone sensor systems are available with twenty and fifty geophones per sensor line. The geophones can be buried about 6 feet apart in a fifty-geophone sensor line and 10 to 12 feet apart in a twenty-geophone sensor line. The fifty-geophone line will protect a 300-foot zone, and the twenty-geophone line will protect 200 to 240 feet of perimeter. The twenty-geophone sensor string capacity can be increased by using preamplifiers with the sensors. Therefore, both geophone sensor systems can protect a zone up to the recommended maximum zone length of 300 feet.

Depending on the system, the manufacturers' recommended burial depth ranges from about 6 to 14 inches in soil and about 3 inches in asphalt. One of the primary precautions when installing geophones is that the soil must be compacted around the case so that the seismic energy is effectively coupled to the sensor. If there is a gap between the sensor and the surrounding soil, the seismic energy will have little effect on the geophones. To help ensure good transmission of the seismic energy to the geophones, manufacturers usually recommended that the geophone be installed between layers of sand. In this case, after the trench is dug for the geophones, several inches of sand are poured into the trench. The geophones are positioned in the sand, and another layer of sand is poured over the geophones. The trench should then be backfilled, and the soil watered and tamped to compact the dirt.

The method of installing the geophones depends somewhat on the geophone construction. Some geophones have a tapered spike as part of the housing. In this case the trench is dug to the desired depth, and the geophones are pressed into the soil in the bottom of the trench. The tapered spike compacts the soil as it is pressed into the soil. After the geophones are installed, the trench is again backfilled, watered, and tamped.

One way of improving the signal-to-noise ratio without filtering the processor's input signal is to add gravel or some other loose material over the geophone sensor line. At least one manufacturer recommends installing a layer of gravel on the ground. The gravel layer should be wide enough so that an intruder cannot conveniently step over or bridge over it. Anyone crossing the gravel covering will generate a distinct, easy-to-detect seismic signature. The primary consideration is that the gravel will identify the buried line sensor location, and the intruder might be able to bridge over the area. In this case the gravel will nullify its effectiveness in improving the signal-to-noise ratio.

Geophones are very sensitive to detecting even low-level seismic energy generated by moving objects anchored in the ground, such as trees, fences, light poles, or telephone poles. When these objects are subjected to wind loads, the overturning forces are absorbed by the ground. As the winds vary, the objects move, inducing seismic energy in the ground. To help reduce the need for the signal processor to differentiate between these energies and valid intrusion signals, the geophones should be installed a reasonable distance from this type of object. A reasonable distance is difficult to define because of all the varying parameters in any given installation, but the following minimum distances can be used as guides: about 30 feet from tree-drip line; 10 feet from fences; and a distance about equal to the height of the light pole or telephone pole.

PIEZOELECTRIC TRANSDUCERS

Piezoelectric transducers detect the stresses or pressure induced in the ground by anyone crossing the protected area above the sensor line. The transducer consists of a quartz crystal that is secured to the transducer case so that when an external pressure is applied to it, the crystal generates a voltage. In operation, when someone steps on the ground above the transducer, as Mr. Ids is doing in Figure 9–1, the pressure from his weight stresses the piezoelectric crystal. The stressed crystal generates an electrical signal that is proportional to the applied pressure. This signal is amplified, filtered, and processed through the signal processor. When the characteristics of the signal satisfy the processor alarm criteria, an alarm is initiated.

Far-field seismic energy is compensated for by one manufacturer in the orientation of the transducers in the sensor line assembly. Each transducer is electrically connected to the sensor line so that the crystal output signal is in opposite polarity to the preceding transducer. This installation technique reduces the far-field seismic signals by cancellation. Any far-field seismic energy should stress each transducer along the sensor line about equally. This is because the wave front of the seismic energy should be almost flat. Since the individual transducers are stressed about equally and the transducers are electrically connected in alternate polarity output signals, the resulting signal at the processor should be, theoretically, zero. In reality, it will probably not be equal because of the discontinuities in the seismic energy pattern caused by the ground anomalies. This cancellation technique should not affect detecting someone crossing the sensor line. Anyone crossing the sensor line would induce a series of localized stresses that would be detected by only one or perhaps two transducers.

Applications

One detector model consists of two separate sensor lines that can be connected to a single signal processor. Each sensor line can operate with between two and one hundred transducers. The transducers can be buried in soil or in hard surfaces. In soil, the transducers are buried about 18 inches deep between two 4-inch layers of sand on about 18-inch centers. In this installation configuration, two 100-transducer sensor lines will protect a perimeter 300 feet long.

For optimum performance, the piezoelectric transducer must be in contact with the surrounding soil. As with the geophones, if the soil is not compacted around the transducer, there will be poor transmission of the local stresses to the transducer. A poor installation will result in poor detection. Therefore, after the trench is dug for the sensors, about 4 inches of moist sand should be placed in the bottom of the trench. Each transducer should be carefully positioned in the sand, exercising care not to damage the sensor cable. Any fractures in the cable or between the cable and transducer will allow moisture to enter the cable, which will eventually cause unit failure. After the transducers have been carefully installed, another 4 inches of moist sand should be poured into the trench. The moist sand should be well packed before the trench is backfilled.

The signal processor is designed for direct burial, but it is recommended that the processor be buried in an enclosure. The enclosure should prevent dirt from collecting around the connectors, as minerals in the soil might corrode the exposed connectors. The enclosure should be waterproof, or, more simply, it should have openings in the bottom to allow moisture to drain out. The enclosure should be buried within the buried transducers' sensitive zone so that anyone attempting to uncover the processor for tampering will be detected.

STRAIN/MAGNETIC LINE SENSORS

The combined strain and magnetic line sensors detect both the pressure or strain induced in the ground by someone crossing the sensor line and the presence of ferrous materials carried or worn by the person. The sensor consists of a passive transducer cable and an alarm electronics module. The passive transducer cable uses a magnetic material wound with a pair of sense coil windings. This assembly is wrapped with a stainless steel jacket and covered with an outer plastic jacket. The two sense windings are wound on the magnetic core and connected together in a manner to cancel far-field seismic and magnetic disturbances.

In operation, the residual flux density of the ferromagnetic core material and the flux density of the earth's magnetic field remain constant during normal circumstances. But the weight of anyone crossing the sensitive area above the transducer cable stresses the ferromagnetic core material. The induced stress alters the magnetic flux, which generates a voltage in the sense winding overlay around the coil. A voltage also is induced in the sense winding when someone crosses the transducer cable carrying or wearing ferrous materials. In this case, the ferrous materials distort the earth's magnetic field. The changing magnetic field alters the coil's magnetic flux density, generating a voltage in the sense winding. Signals resulting from mechanical stress, the presence of ferrous materials, or these combined are processed and analyzed by the signal processor in the alarm electronics module. But before the signal is analyzed, it is amplified, prefiltered, divided, and routed through two separate bandpass filters. Signals from the two bandpass filters are separately analyzed, and when their characteristics satisfy the established alarm criteria, an alarm is initiated. The purpose of dual channel signal processing is to reduce false alarms from wind and electrical interference.

Mr. Ids is shown in Figure 9–2 walking over a buried strain/magnetic detector, carrying the tools of his trade. As Mr. Ids walks on the sensitive area over the transducer cable, his weight moves or deforms the ferromagnetic core material. Deforming the core changes the corresponding magnetic lines of force. As the magnetic lines of force intercept the sense coil windings around the core material, they induce a voltage in the windings. This signal is analyzed by the signal processor, and because the signal is generated by a valid intrusion, an alarm is initiated.

Mr. Ids is also carrying a steel wrecking bar over the transducer cable. The ferrous material in the bar will distort the earth's magnetic field in the area of the bar. As the bar is carried over the cable, the earth's magnetic field lines continue changing. These moving field lines will also induce voltages

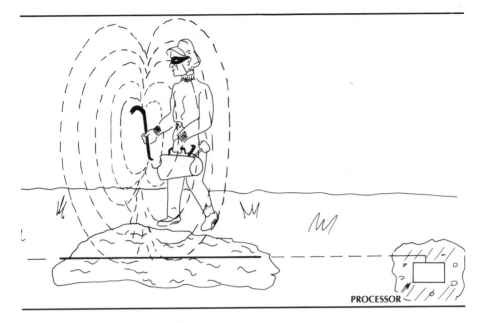

Figure 9-2   Buried line magnetic sensor.

on the core sense windings. Again, because the induced signals represent a valid intrusion, they will initiate an alarm.

Applications

One strain/magnetic sensor model consists of a passive transducer cable and an alarm electronics module. Transducer cables are available in standard lengths of 100 and 500 feet, and they can be buried in soil, asphalt, or concrete. The cable is usually buried about 10 inches deep in soil and 3½ inches deep in asphalt or concrete. The buried depth does depend on the soil characteristics, however. The trench should be dug about 4 inches wide and 12 inches deep. About 2 inches of sand or pulverized soil should be poured into the trench before installing the cable. Another 2 inches of sand or pulverized soil should be installed over the cable. Sandwiching the cable between the two layers of sand or loose soil will help protect it from potential damage from rocks that might be in the fill dirt. The sand or loose soil will be easier to pack around the cable when tamped. Like any other buried seismic or pressure cable, the soil must be compacted around the transducers to minimize attenuation in the induced seismic energy or pressure.

The transducer cable detects perturbations in the earth's magnetic field caused by ferrous material crossing the cable, and it detects pressure or strain induced in the ground by someone crossing the sensitive area.

Because the transducer cable is sensitive to these energies, natural or man-made sources of seismic and electrical interference, the perimeter of an installation where strain/magnetic line sensors are planned should be surveyed to identify these energy sources.

False alarms can be generated by EMI caused by transients in power lines. If possible, utility lines should be avoided; especially avoid routing the transducer near and parallel to utility lines. If the transducer cable must pass under or over utility cables, it should be positioned perpendicular to the cables to reduce the electrical interference. Orthogonal electrical fields will not interfere. After the trench is dug and the transducer cable is deployed, the cable should be moved back and forth in the trench and rotated to minimize the signal output. This installation technique will help reduce false alarms that might be generated by unbalanced currents in the power lines.

Other sources of electrical interference, such as switching substations, electric welders, and radar, also should be identified and avoided in the transducer cable layout, with the maximum possible separation.

Sources of seismic energy should be identified during the survey and avoided if possible. Some suggested minimum separation distances from seismic sources are 15 feet from chain-link fences; 30 feet from the tree drip line; a distance equal to the height of utility poles; 20 feet from utility pole guy-wire terminations; and about 300 feet from highways. Maintaining these minimum distances in the installation of the transducer cables should yield a low rate of false alarms, even in high winds.

The alarm electronics module should be installed in the ground near the input to the transducer cable. The module can be buried in the ground, but it is recommended that the unit be installed in an underground enclosure to prevent dirt from collecting around the connectors. The enclosure does not have to be watertight. In fact, it can be constructed with tile or concrete slab sides with a slab cover, leaving a dirt floor. Installing the electronics module in an enclosure will also facilitate maintenance.

In an installation requiring a number of transducer cables to protect the perimeter, the cables should be installed with the input connector ends together. Installing two modules in each enclosure will reduce the number of enclosures. It also will reduce the number of interconnecting signal line trenches between the enclosures and the primary signal line trench.

Alarm signal, power, and test cables must not be installed in the same trench with the transducer cables. If the signal cables are installed in the same trench, electrical signals on these cables might induce signals in the transducer cable. Because of the proximity of the signal cables and transducer cables in the same trench, the magnitude of the induced signals will probably be adequate to generate false alarms. For this reason, the signal cables should be installed in a separate trench at least 3 feet from the transducer cable. The interconnecting trench between the electronics module enclosure and the primary signal trench should be dug perpendicular to the transducer cable to reduce electrical interference.

PORTED COAX CABLE SENSORS

Ported coax sensors are field disturbance intrusion detection sensors normally used as buried line sensors. There is, however, a portable sensor available that can be deployed on top of the ground to provide temporary perimeter protection around assets such as parked aircraft and vehicles. These sensors generate an electromagnetic field between a pair of ported coaxial transducer cables, sometimes called "leaky" cables, and detect perturbations in the field resulting from someone entering the zone of detection.

In operation, a transmitter is connected to one of the pair of ported cables, and a receiver is connected to the second cable. Because the outer conductor is ported (contains closely spaced small openings in the outer shield), electromagnetic energy propagating along the transmit cable radiates into the surrounding medium, establishing a static field of coupling between the cable pair. The cross-section of the field of detection is somewhat elliptical, with most of the field above the cable pair but some of the energy below. Some of the radiated energy is coupled into the ported receive transducer cable and monitored by the receiver looking for changes in the signal pattern, which would indicate that someone was entering the field of detection. The field is about 3 to 4 feet above the ground and 9 to 12 feet wide, depending on the transducer cable separation and the dielectric characteristics of the burial medium. The dielectric characteristics also affect the field depth below the cables. With this energy pattern, the sensor will detect anyone crossing over or tunneling under the sensor.

Pulsed and CW ported coax sensors are available. In principle, pulsed sensors operate as a guided radar. They transmit a pulse of RF energy into the transmit cable and look at the received signal to detect and locate (using time domain analysis) the intruder's position along the ported cable. Continuous wave sensors use either codirectional or contradirectional coupling. In codirectional coupling, the transmitter transmits RF energy along one cable, and the received signal is monitored by the receiver connected to the opposite end of the adjacent cable. A contradirectionally coupled leaky cable sensor transmits RF energy along one cable, and the received signal is monitored by the receiver connected to the same end of the adjacent cable. Continuous wave ported coaxial sensors, regardless of whether they use codirectional or contradirectional coupling, detect the intruder's presence and identify the sensor zone affected, but they do not identify the intruder's position along the cable length. The individual zone lengths can be up to 400 feet for one manufacturer and 500 feet for another, but the nominal 330 feet zone length is recommended. Others have longer zone lengths, usually for short perimeters or specific protection applications.

The ported transceiver cables are normal coaxial cables that have small apertures formed or milled in the outer conductor shield to allow a controlled amount of electromagnetic energy to radiate from the transmit cable and to couple into the receive transducer cable. Since both pulsed and contradirectionally coupled CW sensors have their transmitter and receiver located at the same end of the transducer cable pair, the cable apertures increase in size as the distance from the transmitter to the receiver increases, to compensate for signal losses along the cable length. Because codirectionally coupled CW sensors have their transmitter and receiver located at opposite ends of the cable pair, the cable port size is constant along the entire cable length.

Selecting the operating frequency is very important in designing a ported coax sensor. The most important factor in selecting the operating frequency is the effective radar cross-section of a human target. The human cross-section is relatively constant from 40 MHz to 100 MHz, but the lower frequencies within this range provide better discrimination between humans and small animals and birds. The usable frequency range is between 30 MHz and 100 MHz for most cable designs. The lower the operating frequency, the less the cable attenuation, but coupling in the typical buried transducer cables increases with frequency. Currently available ported coax sensors operate at the lower 40 MHz and 66 MHz frequencies as a trade-off among coupling, target definition, and lower attenuation.

The RF energy coupled through the cable apertures creates a surface wave that propagates along the outside of the transducer cables. The velocity and attenuation of the surface wave is a function of the dielectric properties of the medium surrounding the cable. If the cables are buried in dry, low-loss soil, the wave velocity is greater and the attenuation lower than if they are buried in a conductive or wet soil. Permittivity and conductivity of soil also vary dramatically with soil types and water content, which subsequently affects the coupling between the cables. For instance, the relative permittivity of water decreases from 80 to 4 when it freezes. Therefore, when wet ground freezes, the coupling and surface wave velocity increase and the attenuation decreases. Since the height and width of the field is a function of the cable separation and also the permittivity and conductivity of the surrounding medium, the sensitivity of the sensor might have to be seasonally adjusted to compensate for the changing ground conditions.

A distinct advantage of any buried sensor is that the precise location of the sensor cables, and hence the detection zone, can be concealed, and the sensor cables can be installed to follow the terrain and perimeter shape. Another advantage is that ported coax sensors are sensitive only to changes in dielectric properties or conductivity in the area of the buried cables caused by someone entering the detection zone and are insensitive to seismic energy, which is a source of false alarms with seismic and pressure-type buried sensors.

As with all sensors, potential sources of nuisance alarms should be recognized. Heavy rainfall, water runoff, wind disturbance of standing water over the cables, and lightning can cause alarms. Movement of closely located loose metallic fence fabric or vehicles, as well as dielectric objects such as animals, people, or plants in the vicinity of the sensor cables, can cause alarms. Small animals (less than 9 pounds) generally do not cause alarms, but groups of small animals congregating over the sensor cables can. Careful planning during the design phase and installation can significantly reduce these nuisance alarm sources. Results from operational sites and from testing indicate that ported coax sensors can provide detection with reasonably low nuisance alarm rates.

One pulsed sensor consists of a processor/display unit, cable transducer segments, and line amplifiers. The processor/display unit processes the received signal and annunciates and displays the alarm information for the operator. Alarm information also is available as an option in both serial and parallel format for integration with other equipment, as well as the display. The processor also supplies power to the transducer cable amplifiers, which are required when the perimeter is greater than about a mile.

In operation, the sensor processor monitors the time-varying amplitude of the received signal generated by the transmitted pulse. The transmitted pulse travels along the cable at a constant velocity approximately 80 percent of the speed of light. As the pulse traverses the transmit cable, it generates a continuous time-varying RF signal in the receive cable. The profile of the varying amplitude or signature is stored in processor memory for continual comparison. Variations in the amplitude of the received signal are caused by variations in the dielectric characteristics of the soil or medium surrounding the buried cables. As long as the dielectric medium characteristics remain constant, variations in the profile of the energy pattern or signature remain constant. But because the ported coax sensors are buried out-of-doors, where the environment and soil conditions are usually changing slowly, the memory storing the received signal signature is continuously updated to capture these slow changes for each transmitted pulse. Then the resulting signature of each energy pulse is compared with the previous pulse signature to look for changes in the signal characteristics of an intruder.

Since the velocity of the transmitted pulse is constant, the received signal is processed by time domain analysis to identify the disturbance location along the sensor cable. This is accomplished by analyzing each signal in time increments that correspond to specific sensor zones or cells along the length of the transducer cables. When there is a signal change, the processor can determine and identify on the map display where the intrusion occurred along the sensor zone. The pulse and sampling characteristics correspond to a detection cell size of 110 feet, where three cells can be combined to form a 330 feet sensor zone.

An algorithm has been recently developed by the manufacturer that uses the received pulse shape to improve cell resolution. With the algorithm, the detection zone boundaries are programmable and can be tailored to fit the perimeter configuration or aligned with closed circuit camera coverage or other sensors. The zones can be reprogrammed without changing any cables to accommodate site changes.

Once a pulse is transmitted, another pulse is not transmitted until the first pulse is terminated with a passive matched load at the cable terminator. If a second signal was transmitted before the first signal terminated, it would interfere with the first pulse profile. The transmit pulse rate is a function of the surface wave velocity and the transducer cable length of about a mile, which is one-half of the maximum 2-mile cable length. Since the surface wave velocity is 80 percent of the speed of light, the pulse rate is fast enough that intrusions are detected almost instantaneously when anyone enters the sensor's zone of detection.

To illustrate the basic principles of operation of the ported coax sensor, Figure 9–3 shows Mr. Ids entering the pulsed sensor's zone of detection. His presence causes a change in the electric field, which produces a corresponding change in the profile of the received signal. The signal processor compares this signal profile with the previous profile in the time window corresponding to the detection zone along the transducer where Mr. Ids intruded. When the intrusion criteria are met, the resulting alarm is annunciated at the monitoring console, and the intrusion location is identified on the map display for the console operator.

One CW ported coax sensor consists of multiple transceiver modules with cable sets, a control module, an interface unit, and an auxiliary printer and color graphics operator display. Each transceiver module transmits a CW signal to either one or two cable sets attached to the transceiver and receives and processes the return signal to identify characteristics indicating an intrusion. Each cable set can operate at one of a number of different frequencies to avoid interference. To achieve this objective, each transceiver frequency is crystal controlled. In one application, even-numbered trans-

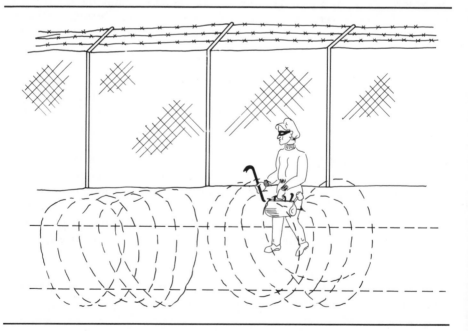

Figure 9–3   Ported coax cable sensor.

ceivers operate at one frequency, and odd-numbered ones operate at a sec-
interference from adjoining cable sets. Radio-frequency decouplers are used
to interconnect adjacent cable sets. They block the RF transmitted energy
but pass the power and communication signals.

The transceiver transmit and receive circuits switch at a low rate from
one cable set to the other. This technique enables the transceiver module processor to determine whether an intruder is in one or the other sensor zone.
The processed information is reported to the control module on command
from the module. The control module then reports any alarm through an
interface unit, which is compatible with most monitoring systems, to an
existing monitoring console; or it can report the alarm information directly
to a compatible color operator terminal display and printer. The transceiver
can be remotely activated to perform other functions such as a self-test or to
activate a deterrent. In addition, the transceivers can supply limited 12 VDC
power to other sensors. Remote activation and 12 VDC power features are
available as options.

Unlike the pulsed ported coax sensor, which uses only two sets of transmit and receive transducer cables for a 1-mile zone and divides the sensor
into smaller zones electronically, the CW sensor uses multiple transceiver
modules with either single or dual cable sets cascaded together to form the
perimeter zones.

Each cable set can be extended to cover a single 500-foot zone. A maximum of thirty-two 500-foot sections can be connected to a single control
module to cover 3 miles. A second control module must be added to provide
detection for longer perimeters.

A unique time and frequency domain multiplexing technique is used by
the control module to distribute power and collect data from each transceiver module. An additional feature of the transceiver module is that other
sensor information, such as the alarm status of exterior microwave sensors
or fence disturbance sensors, can be collected by the transceiver module and
reported to the control module along with the ported sensor alarm information. The control module polls each transceiver at a rate of approximately
two times per second so that the detection and alarm annunciation are
almost instantaneous. The control module stores the information in nonvola-
tile memory and communicates it to the operator's terminal.

A self-contained portable ported coaxial sensor can provide temporary
perimeter detection for assets such as aircraft parked on jetways, parked
vehicles, and the like. Like buried pulsed and CW ported sensors, this sensor
consists of a separate transmit and receive ported transducer cable. Unlike
the buried sensor, the portable sensor is deployed on top of the ground.

In operation, the transmitter generates a continuous 60 MHz signal on
the transmit cable that is codirectionally coupled into the receiver cable. Disturbances in the field caused by someone entering the detection zone must
simultaneously satisfy the following alarm criteria. Changes in the amplitude
and phase of the received signal must exceed a preset threshold. These

changes are a function of the mass and movements of the person and his proximity to the electromagnetic field. The disturbance also must exist for a period typical of the length of time an intruder would take to traverse the sensor zone of detection.

In application, the portable transmit and receive transducer cables are deployed approximately 50 inches apart on top of the ground to form up to a 900-foot-long perimeter around the assets requiring perimeter protection. The 900-foot zone is formed by two 450-foot cable sets. Smaller perimeters can be protected by a single 450-foot cable set. When deployed, the transmit transducer cable is positioned toward the inside of the cable loop, and the receive cable is outside. This arrangement forms a detection pattern width of about 8 feet and a height of 5 feet.

Applications

The pulsed ported coax sensor's processor/display unit is normally installed in the control monitoring station, but the station cannot be located more than 660 feet from the perimeter because of cable losses. The sensor cables that interface with the processor have 660 feet of nonradiating lead-in cables. The processor will fit into a standard 19-inch desktop or short equipment rack. Access to the display's control panel on the front of the processor unit is required during installation and maintenance. The display panel can be used as an optional operator display or primary display in the absence of another display. The displayed perimeter is described by a mimic display of lamps, where each lamp represents a perimeter zone of user-programmable size. Other displays can be interfaced with the ported coax sensor's processor to display the alarm information. In this case only the sensor processor must be installed less than 660 feet from the perimeter. The display can then be any distance from the processor, but the processor must be installed indoors for protection from the elements and to reduce its vulnerability to tampering.

A cable transducer segment consists of both the nonradiating lead-in cable and the active leaky section from a single continuous cable. There are no buried connectors. Two cable sections can be connected directly to the processor display unit to protect up to a mile. The protection can be expanded to 2 miles by adding a line amplifier in the two additional transmit cable segments. The line amplifier is designed for above-ground installations up to 73 feet inside the perimeter sensor. Power for the amplifier is supplied from the processor unit over the transmit transducer cables for ease of installation.

Calibration is accomplished on the pulsed ported coax sensor by placing the processor in the calibration mode and having a person walk between the sensor cables from the beginning to the end of the transducer cables. The processor calculates an alarm threshold level for each detection cell based on the minimum signal return during the calibration walk multiplied by the threshold scale factor stored in the processor memory. Alarm levels for each cell are those signals exceeding the individual cell threshold. The alarm threshold also can be manually adjusted if necessary.

One CW ported coax sensor operator terminal that displays alarm information from the control module consists of a color graphics display and printer. These units are available for either rack or desktop mounting. The control module, which provides power to and collects data from the transceiver modules, is designed for rack or wall mounting in an indoor environment. It is desirable to install the control module in the control center near the operator to take advantage of its control panel. While the control module panel's primary function is to support maintenance and installation, the liquid crystal display (LCD) can be used to operate the system independently of the operator terminal.

A single transducer cable consists of a 66-foot nonradiating lead-in and either a 165-, 330-, or 495-foot section of leaky or ported cable. The ported cable sections can be shortened for site-specific applications by cutting the cable at the RF decoupler and installing the decoupler on-site. Two cable sets can be connected to a single transceiver, and sixteen transceiver modules can be monitored by a single control module. Additional control modules are required for longer perimeters. The transceiver is designed to be installed above ground in an exterior environment up to 66 feet inside the detection zone. The transceiver enclosure has a tamper switch to initiate a tamper alarm at the operator terminal when the enclosure is opened.

Calibration is accomplished on the CW ported coax sensor by placing the transducer module in the calibration mode and manually adjusting the alarm threshold while monitoring the analog output from the processor when someone walks between the sensor cables. The alarm threshold is established based on the signal response. As with any sensor system, the detection level must be defined at each site based on the perceived threat and the required security level. Periodic performance testing is required to maintain the established detection level.

There are some common application considerations for both pulsed and CW ported coax sensors. Routing the transducer cables under chain-link fences or over metallic objects should be avoided where possible. Close metallic objects can distort the electric field, causing local variations in sensitivity. Where metallic pipes or cables must be routed under the sensor, they should be buried at least 3 feet below the sensor cable. When the sensor cables are routed along or between chain-link fences, the transducer cables must be installed at between 6 and 10 feet from the fence to avoid field distortions and to reduce potential false alarms from motion of the fence fabric during windy weather.

Regardless of which ported coax sensor is used, install it in accordance with the manufacturer's recommendations. The transducer cable burial depth and cable separation must be maintained throughout the perimeter to achieve uniform sensor response. When installing the transducer cables, avoid making sharp corners that will cause the electromagnetic field to extend farther from the cables than desired. If the cables are installed in rocky ground, they should be installed between layers of sand to prevent damage by the rocks.

Some potential sources of false alarms should be considered when using ported coax sensors. Heavy rainfall, water runoff, and water puddling over the transducer cables can cause alarms. It is not the actual presence of the water that causes the alarms but the motion of the water. Heavy rains penetrating porous ground in close proximity to the cables, water runoff over the cables, or wind causing ripples on the surface of the standing water cause reflections in the field that can couple onto the receive cable and be interpreted by the processor as valid intrusion. If the perimeter is properly graded, many of the water problems can be eliminated.

Large animals and people in the detection zone will, of course, cause alarms. Small animals and birds less than 9 pounds should not cause alarms, but groups of small animals or birds in the detection zone can be a problem. Installing fences outside the sensor zone will keep out most larger animals and people, but usually not small animals and birds. Removing vegetation and minimizing accumulation of standing water might discourage small animals from gathering in the vicinity.

Vehicular traffic in the vicinity of the sensor detection zones can reflect the radiated energy into the receive transducer cable and be interpreted by the signal processor as an intruder. Like all sensors, electromagnetic fields associated with lightning and other near sources of electromagnetic energy, such as heavy-duty electrical equipment and electric substations, also might interfere with sensor performance and cause false alarms. As with any sensor, concern about the applications of the ported coax sensors in areas where there may be small animals, a harsh electromagnetic environment, or any other concern should be discussed with the sensor manufacturer.

In application, the ported coax sensors are stand-alone perimeter intrusion detection systems. They generate an electromagnetic field above the ground 3 to 4 feet high and 10 to 12 feet wide, depending on the transmit and receive cable separation and ground characteristics, and they provide some detection in the ground. There might, however, be applications where the above-ground electromagnetic field may not be adequate because of the threat or because snow accumulation will reduce the effective height of the radiated field. In these applications, bistatic microwave detectors can be installed above the ported coax sensors to increase the overall height of the detection zone. Because of vast differences in operating frequency, the ported coax sensors will improve detection in areas where the ground surface is not flat enough to use bistatic microwave sensors alone to detect stealthy commando crawlers penetrating the detection zone. Under these conditions, the ported coax sensor will easily detect the crawlers, and the bistatic microwave detectors will improve the detection zone height.

BALANCED PRESSURE SENSORS

The balanced pressure sensor detects personnel and vehicles by sensing the pressure waves generated as they move across the earth's surface toward the buried sensor line. The sensor line is generated along a perimeter by cascading the required number of 330-foot sensor tube segments connected by dual sensor units. The dual sensor unit monitors the pressure in the two single-segment sensor tubes and produces an analog signal that is proportional to the differential pressure in the two tubes. This signal is transmitted to an analyzer looking for characteristics indicating that someone or something is approaching the sensor line.

The balanced pressure sensor consists of dual sensor tube lines, a dual sensor unit, compensating valves, and an analyzer. Each sensor line is comprised of two 330-foot long (maximum) sensor tubes or hoses separated by about 3 feet. The sensor tubes are filled with water or a water/glycol solution for cold climate applications and are pressurized to about 2.5 atmospheres. A separate pressure sensor switch in the dual sensor monitors the fluid pressure and initiates an alarm if the pressure drops below about 1.6 atmospheres.

The tubes are made of a pliable synthetic compound that will adjust to changes in pressure in the medium surrounding the tubes. When someone approaches the sensor line, the medium around the tube nearest the intruder is compressed, causing an increase in the fluid pressure in that tube, followed by an increase in pressure in the farthest tube. The resulting increase in fluid pressure is sensed in each sensor tube by a pressure transducer in the dual sensor unit. The pressure transducer converts the fluid pressure into an electrical signal that is proportional to the fluid pressure. In operation, the electrical signal from the nearest sensor tube transducer is compared to the signal from the farthest tube transducer, and the differential signal is transmitted to the analyzer.

The analyzer amplifies the incoming signal and passes it through a bandpass filter that passes only those signals in the frequency range that have been determined to be representative of those signals generated by someone passing through the sensor zone. The resulting signal is then analyzed for specific signal changes or characteristics representing an intrusion. When the intrusion criteria are satisfied, the analyzer initiates an alarm at the central station monitor.

A self-compensating valve, located at the end of the two sensor tubes opposite the dual sensor unit that form one of the dual sensor zones, provides a slow leakage path between the tubes. Under quiescent conditions, the valve maintains a perfect balance in the fluid pressure in the two tubes, and consequently no differential signal results at the dual sensor unit. Gradual pressure differences between the two tubes caused by changing ground conditions is slowly equalized through the compensating valve. Anyone approaching the sensor line will produce an increase in ground pressure faster than the compensating valve can accommodate it, which will result in a greater increase in pressure in the sensor tube nearest the intruder than in the tube farthest from the intruder. This compensating feature allows the system to reset automatically following an alarm.

When Mr. Ids, shown in Figure 9–4, approaches the dual sensor line, he induces pressure in the ground that is proportional to the force he exerts as he approaches the sensor. The force is not only a function of Mr. Ids's weight, but it also depends on whether he is walking or running. Of course, if he is walking, the force will be less than if he is running. As Mr. Ids approaches the sensor, the resulting pressure in the nearest sensor tube will be greater than the pressure in the farthest tube, resulting in an increase in the differential signal from the dual sensor tranducers. When the differential signal amplitude exceeds the analyzer alarm threshold, an alarm initiated by the analyzer will identify the sensor zone in alarm to the console.

Applications

A single dual sensor unit monitors the pressure from two separate sensor zones. Each zone can be up to 330 feet long, but the four sensor tubes must be the same length within 2 percent of the total length. If any one tube is longer than the others, a disproportionate noise level will be accumulated over its length, which will diminish the noise rejection feature. The sensor tubes are normally buried 10 inches deep and 4 feet apart. In this configuration, the detection zone is between 10 and 13 feet wide. The most sensitive

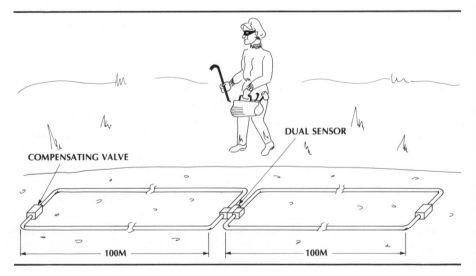

Figure 9–4   Balanced pressure system.

point in the detection zone is right over the sensor tube, with a progressive reduction away from it. Therefore, maintaining the manufacturer's recommended separation between the sensor tubes is an important factor in maintaining the level of detection. Separating the tubes beyond the recommended limits will reduce the sensitivity in the center of the zone between the sensor tubes, until eventually a dead area is created.

Variations in the burial medium will affect the sensor tube's installation dimensions. In gravel the standard burial dimensions should be maintained, but in fine sand the tubes should be closer together, about 4 feet apart. Under asphalt the sensor tubes should be buried between 4 and 8 inches deep. Balanced pressure sensors should be used under concrete only to detect vehicles. Forces exerted by someone crossing the sensor line under concrete are not adequate to be reliably detected.

In installations where sharp stones are present and could damage the tubes during backfilling of the trench, the tubes should be installed between layers of sand to protect the tubes. Once the tubes have been buried, the backfilled material will not be as compact initially as the surrounding ground. Because the sensor sensitivity is a function of the pressure transmission properties of the ground, the detection zone will not be as wide as it will be when the ground returns to its original compactness. Artificial means can be used to compact the ground, but normally 4 to 6 weeks of settling time is required before a noticeable improvement will be obtained in the system's performance.

In installations where the sensor lines are installed under paved areas, no settling time is required, provided there is good contact between the soil medium and asphalt. Care should be exercised to ensure that an air gap does not exist or form between the burial medium and asphalt. The air gap will prevent the exerted force from reaching the sensor tubes. Ideally, the sensor tubes should be buried some time prior to commissioning the system to allow for settlement.

The dual sensor unit and compensating valves should be placed inside an enclosure buried with the sensor tubes. The enclosure should be of adequate size and structure to prevent dirt from filling in around the equipment and have adequate drainage to prevent water accumulation. This installation concept will allow easy access to the dual sensor and valves for inspection and maintenance.

The differential pressure transducer signal is transmitted from the dual sensor unit to the analyzer over a multiple screened, multiple core, reinforced direct burial cable. Due to cable losses, the maximum cable length between the dual sensor and analyzer is 3,300 feet. A standard analyzer monitors one dual sensor unit or two detection zones. The analyzer should be located out of the detection zone in a weather-resistant enclosure mounted above the ground for maintenance and for easy access to the calibration controls located on the front panel. The enclosure should be locked and equipped with a tamper switch that will initiate an alarm when the door is opened or the cover removed. The analyzer output and tamper switches are monitored by a separate signal transmission system that carries the information to the central monitor.

Because of the differential principle of operation, the balanced pressure system has a high degree of immunity to environmental noise and consequently has a slow false alarm rate. Ground vibrations induced by vehicles, falling rain, aircraft, and wind level produce equal pressure in both sensor tubes due to the proximity of the tubes to the energy source. Wind and rain produce a nearly uniform overpressure on the ground.

Vehicles produce pressure waves that propagate from the point where the vehicle touches the ground. As the waves propagate through the ground, the wave front spreads until it reaches the sensor tubes, provided the traffic is at least 16 feet from the sensor line. It then produces a nearly equal pressure in both tubes.

Balanced pressure sensors are not disturbed by vegetation. In installations where the sensor line passes close to trees, however, they should not be installed less than 10 feet from any tree. Any roots crossing the sensor tubes should be cut to eliminate unbalanced pressure caused by root movement when the wind blows. If the tubes must be closer than 10 feet to a tree, they can be installed closer together in the vicinity of the tree. The manufacturer should be consulted for these and other unique applications.

Chapter 10

Application Guidelines

Many false alarms can be prevented by selecting the proper sensor for the application and by using good installation practices. The points listed below should be considered in the intrusion detection system design, along with guidelines recommended in the manufacturer's installation manual for the specific equipment being installed.

Before listing guidelines for specific exterior detectors, some general guidelines applicable to all detectors are listed. These are not given in any order of priority.

GENERAL

1. Check all equipment for shipping damage prior to installation.
2. Check the equipment after installation for damage.
3. Check that all electrical connections are secure.
4. Mount detector transducers, especially active motion detector transducers, rigidly on vibration-free surfaces.
5. Adjust the detector's sensitivity level for adequate detection in the worst case operating environment.
6. Areas containing sources of electromagnetic energy (radio transmitters, radar, electrical switches, large motors, generators, etc.) could cause severe operational problems.
7. Avoid adjusting any detector sensitivity so high that it will be susceptible to false alarms.
8. Detector enclosures should be tamper-protected and the tamper alarms monitored continuously.
9. Detector processor units installed out-of-doors should be in weatherproof enclosures, and the circuit boards should be conformal coated.
10. All interconnecting cables should be installed in sealed conduit and, where applicable, buried in the ground.
11. Exterior detection zone lengths should be limited to about 300 linear feet.

FENCE DISTURBANCE SENSORS

1. The fence fabric should be reasonably tight and the fence posts well anchored.
2. All fence signs should be removed or secured so they will not rattle.
3. Gates should be well secured so they will not rattle.
4. The bottom of the fence fabric should be in close proximity to the ground or, better yet, anchored down.
5. All brush and tree branches should be cut or removed so they will not rub against the fence.

MICROWAVE DETECTORS

1. The ground should be level, with no dips or obstructions between the transmitter and receiver.
2. Zones of detection should be overlapped (approximately twice the distance from the transmitter to where the beam touches the ground).
3. Grass should be removed or maintained at a length of no greater than 4 inches between the transmitter and receiver.
4. Snow should not accumulate more than about 4 inches.
5. Detectors should be located far enough from the fence that the fence will not interfere with the microwave beam.

INFRARED DETECTORS

1. The ground should be level, with no dips or obstructions between the detector columns.
2. The bottom beam should be no greater than 6 inches above the ground.
3. The top infrared beam should be at least 4 feet above the ground.
4. Zones of detection should be overlapped or the top of the detector columns protected with a pressure switch.

ELECTRIC-FIELD DETECTORS

1. When a detector is installed on chain-link fences, the fence fabric should be reasonably tight.
2. Wires forming the electric-field arrays must be kept tight.
3. All electric-field detectors must be installed on dielectric supports to insulate the wire arrays from the fence or barrier on which they are mounted.
4. All vegetation must be removed from under E-field sensor arrays.

5.   Fences protected with capacitance sensors must be well grounded along with capacitance sensors to minimize variations in capacitance between the fence and sensor arrays.

GEOPHONE SENSORS

1.   Sensors should be positioned to avoid objects anchored in the ground that could move in the wind.
2.   Backfill dirt for the geophone trench should be well tamped.

STRAIN/MAGNETIC LINE SENSORS

1.   Sensor cables should be positioned to avoid objects anchored in the ground.
2.   When crossing over or under power lines cannot be avoided, the sensor line should cross perpendicular to them.
3.   Routing signal and power cables in the same trench with the transducer cable should be avoided.
4.   Backfill dirt should be well compacted.

PORTED COAX SENSORS

1.   Sensors should not be buried under areas where there is surface water drainage a high percentage of the time or under standing water.
2.   Sensors should not be installed in highly conductive media.
3.   Vegetation over sensor cables should be removed to lessen the likelihood of small animals congregating in the vicinity of the cables.
4.   Cables should not be buried where they can be damaged by sharp rocks, either in the trench or in the backfill material.
5.   Routing sensor cables under chain-link fences or other metallic objects that can cause local sensitivity variations should be avoided.
6.   When installing sensor cables, sharp corners that can cause the field to extend farther than described should be avoided.
7.   Sensor cables should be installed at the recommended burial depth and separation, with reasonable tolerance to promote uniform sensor responses.

BALANCED PRESSURE SENSORS

1.   Pressure tubes must be the same length within 2 percent of the total length.

2. Burial depth of pressure tubes varies with the burial medium, so the manufacturer's installation instructions should be consulted for the proper depth.
3. Tubes should not be buried where they can be damaged by sharp objects.
4. Tree roots should be removed from areas where pressure tubes are buried.

PART III

INTERIOR INTRUSION DETECTORS

Interior intrusion detectors are classified here as active and passive, and combination active and passive, volumetric motion detectors, barrier penetration detectors, operable opening switches, proximity detectors, and barrier detectors. These detectors, as the title implies, are designed for interior applications and should never be used outside without extensive testing to determine whether the detector will function in the intended application. The primary reason for not using interior detectors outside is that they are not weatherproof or rugged enough to survive the environment. Another reason is that some detectors are very susceptible to false alarms, especially volumetric motion detectors. Their detection techniques are influenced by things such as moving grass and trees.

VOLUMETRIC MOTION DETECTORS

The whole volume or just a portion of the volume of a room or building can be protected using volumetric motion detectors. Whether the whole volume or just part of the volume is protected depends on the facility's detection requirements. Again, depending on the requirements, motion detectors can be used to provide the primary intrusion detection for a building, or they can be used in conjunction with other interior detectors, such as barrier and proximity detectors, to satisfy the detection requirements. An advantage of volumetric motion detectors is that they will detect an intruder moving in the zone of detection independently of his point of entry into the zone. For example, a store could use volumetric motion detectors to detect motion in the interior of the store, along with magnetic door switches to detect anyone opening the entrance doors and glass breakage detectors to detect breaking the showcase glass. In this type of application, an intruder coming into the store through a hole in the wall or ceiling will be detected by the volumetric

147

motion detector just as though he had entered the store through a protected door.

The amount of volumetric coverage and the configuration of the volume requiring protection dictate the number of detector transducers required to detect motion in the volume. A transducer, sometimes referred to as a sensor head, is the device that responds to an event or stimulus within the detection zone and produces an electrical signal for processing. The detector processor analyzes the electrical signal and activates an alarm circuit when the signal characteristics satisfy the alarm criteria.

Volumetric motion detectors consist of either a single transducer with a self-contained signal processor or multiple transducers connected to a common signal processor. While some of the single transducer detectors have a large zone of detection, detectors with multiple transducers usually rely on several transducers to cover the same volume. An advantage of the multiple transducers is that the individual transducers can be positioned to form a patterned zone of detection. This pattern can be configured to protect a specific commodity or the most probable entrance route of an intruder. The decision to use a large-volume single transducer detector or detectors with multiple transducers is only one of many trade-offs that should be considered when selecting volumetric motion detectors.

There are two basic types of volumetric motion detectors—active and passive. Active motion detectors include ultrasonic, microwave, and sonic. Active detectors fill the protected volume with an energy pattern and recognize a disturbance in that pattern when an intruder moves within the zone of detection. Ultrasonic detectors fill the volume with inaudible acoustical energy, microwave with electromagnetic energy, and sonic with audible acoustical energy. While active detectors generate their own energy pattern to detect an intruder, passive detectors detect the energy generated by the intruder. Passive detectors include infrared and audio. Infrared detectors detect the presence of an intruder either by sensing the body heat or thermal energy in the infrared frequency range emanating from the intruder or by sensing changes in the thermal energy background as a result of the intruder's shadowing the background while moving through the protected zones. Audio detectors detect the presence of an intruder by simply listening for the noises generated by a forced entry into the protected facilities or the noises generated as the intruder carries out his objective inside the protected area.

Combination active microwave or ultrasonic and passive infrared detectors also are available. These detectors take advantage of the difference in false alarm stimuli of active and passive sensors to minimize false alarms.

BARRIER PENETRATION DETECTORS

Forcible entry through perimeter barriers, walls, ceilings, and windows can be detected by barrier penetration detectors. There are several types of penetration detectors, including vibration, heat, breakwire grids, foil tape, and security screens. Vibration detectors detect low-frequency vibrations generated by a physical attack on a structural wall or ceiling and high-frequency vibrations generated by breaking glass. High-frequency vibration detectors are often referred to as glass breakage detectors. As the name implies, they are used to protect display or showcase windows.

Heat sensors are sometimes used as intrusion detectors to detect unusual thermal activity. An example of such activity would be a torch cutting through a metal barrier such as a safe or vault. Foil tape has been used for many years to protect glass windows, but it also can be installed around perimeter walls and ceilings to detect penetration. Breakwire grids are constructed with slotted wooden dowel rods lined with a fine wire that breaks if the frame is cut or broken. They are used to detect penetrations through windows or any other man-size openings, such as heating and ventilating ducts, leading into a protected area. Breakwires also can be installed in a grid pattern directly on the perimeter barrier to detect penetration. Since the foil tape and breakwire installed directly on the perimeter barriers break easily, they should be protected against day-to-day abuse. Foil tape on windows can be protected with a clear, hard plastic coating, while sheet materials, such as plywood or gypsum board, installed directly over the breakwire patterns will provide lasting protection. Security screens can be used as barriers to detect penetration through windows. Foil tape, breakwire grids, and security screens are connected directly to a control unit or signal transmitter that recognizes an open circuit as an alarm. An intruder who penetrates the protected barrier breaks the foil tape or wire and thereby initiates an alarm.

OPERABLE OPENING SWITCHES

Several types of switches are available to detect entrance through operable openings such as doors and windows. These include balanced magnetic, magnetic, mechanical contact, and tilt switches. In a typical door installation, a switch detects movement between the door and the door frame. The switch is usually mounted on the door frame, and the activating device, if required, is mounted on the door. When the door is opened, the activating device either opens or closes the switch contacts, thereby initiating an alarm. Operable opening switches can be connected directly to a control unit that recognizes either an open or closed circuit as an alarm condition, depending on whether the switch is normally open or normally closed.

INTERIOR BARRIER DETECTORS

The entrance or the most probable avenue an intruder would take when entering or moving through a protected area can be protected by interior barrier detectors. The actual barrier can be either an invisible infrared beam or a trip-wire device. The infrared beam, generated by an infrared source in the transmitter, is projected onto a photoelectric cell in the receiver. When the beam is interrupted, the incident infrared radiation projected onto the photoelectric cell is interrupted, and the detector initiates an alarm. A trip wire, as the name implies, consists of a thin wire or cord and a spring switch for terminating the wire. In an actual application, the trip wire is stretched across the entrance to the protected area and fastened to the termination switch. An intruder who comes in contact with the wire trips the termination switch and initiates an alarm.

PROXIMITY DETECTORS

Anyone coming in close proximity to, touching, or lifting a protected item can be detected by proximity detectors. They are used for protecting metal safes, art objects, and so on. Probably the most popular proximity device is the capacitance detector used to protect metal devices such as safes and file cabinets. They detect changes in the electrical capacitance between the protected metal objects and the ground plane formed by the surrounding surfaces and floor. Pressure mats and tilt switches also can be used as proximity detectors. Pressure mats detect an intruder who steps on the mat installed in the vicinity of the protected item. They are also used as barrier detectors to protect entrances and the probable route through the protected facility. Although tilt switches are primarily used to protect operable openings, they can also be used as proximity detectors. In such applications, the tilt switches are fastened to valuable movable items such as paintings and other art objects. Thereafter, if a protected item is tilted, the switch initiates an alarm. This is another example of how detection devices can be used for alternate protection applications.

The following chapters describe the basic principle of operation of interior detectors, with an emphasis on application features that should be considered in a system design.

Chapter 11

Active Volumetric Motion Detectors

Active volumetric motion detectors generate their own energy pattern and analyze the disturbance in that pattern for that portion of the energy reflected back to the receiver from a moving intruder. The disturbance in the energy pattern is referred to as a frequency shift or, in particular, a Doppler frequency shift. A Doppler frequency shift can best be explained by the classic example found in most elementary physics books. A person standing near a railroad track observing an approaching train and hearing the blowing whistle will first hear an increase in the pitch of the whistle and then hear a distinct lowering in the pitch as the train passes. Pitch increase is a result of the compression of the whistle sound waves as the train approaches, and the decrease in the pitch is a result of the expansion of the sound wave as the train moves away from the observer. The change in the whistle pitch illustrates a wave principle that was discovered by the Austrian physicist Christian Doppler (1803–1853), and it is applicable to all wave motion.

The Doppler principle can be used to measure the velocity and determine the direction of a moving target. Velocity is determined by continually measuring the time required for coded transmitted signals to return to the measuring device from a moving target. Target direction is determined by monitoring the frequency shift of the reflected signal. A target moving toward the measuring device produces an increase in the frequency of the signal, and, conversely, a target moving away from the measuring device produces a decrease in the frequency. Active volumetric detectors use the Doppler principle to detect an intruder's motion in the detector zone. Some manufacturers monitor just the magnitude of the Doppler frequency shift regardless of the direction. Other manufacturers use the additional directional phenomenon in their signal processing to reduce nuisance alarms caused by oscillatory motion in the zone of detection. Another measuring device, with which we are all becoming familiar and that relies on the Doppler principle to determine target velocity, is the traffic radar device used by the police to detect speeders.

The most popular active volumetric detectors using the Doppler principle are ultrasonic and microwave motion detectors. As already mentioned, ultrasonic motion detectors generate an inaudible acoustic energy pattern and process the Doppler frequency shift caused by an intruder moving in the detection zone. Microwave motion detectors basically operate on the same principle, except that they generate a pattern of electromagnetic energy. Because they do transmit electromagnetic energy, the detector's operating frequencies and power output are regulated by the FCC. The FCC has allocated five operating frequencies for microwave motion detectors. The lowest frequency is 915 MHz, and the highest is 22,125 MHz; most microwave detectors operate at 10,525 MHz.

Another, but to date less popular, active volumetric motion detector is the sonic detector. Unlike ultrasonic detectors, sonic detectors generate an audible instead of an inaudible acoustic energy pattern and detect phase changes in the energy pattern, as well as Doppler frequency shifts caused by someone moving in the zone of detection. Audibility of the sonic energy is probably the reason for the limited application of sonic motion detectors, but there are applications where the sound is not a problem, and in fact it could be a deterrent against an intruder who might otherwise consider entering the protected area.

The signal processing technique used for analyzing an intruder's reflected signal characteristics varies between detectors. Signal processor designs are based on the manufacturer's opinion as to what the detection parameters should be to detect a specific threat in a particular environment. Because of all the varying signal processing techniques, if there is any doubt about the performance ability of a specific manufacturer's detector, the detector should be installed in its intended environment and operated for at least a week to evaluate its performance.

In this type of evaluation, it would be desirable first to measure the output signal level in the detector processor caused by the most severe ambient or background energies that might cause the detector to alarm. This background signal should be compared with the signal generated by someone moving in the detection zone, again in the most severe environment. To minimize nuisance alarms, the intruder alarm signal should be much greater than the background energy signal level. If it is impossible to make these measurements, the detector alarm output should be recorded for about a week, hopefully to reveal any possible nuisance alarm problems.

There are a number of active volumetric motion detector application features that should be considered when designing an alarm system. One important feature is that the coverage from a single detector is limited to a specific range. For instance, a single ultrasonic detector with a single transceiver or with a separate transmitter and receiver can detect motion in an area approximately 20 feet wide by 30 feet long. A microwave detector can detect motion in an area approximately 25 to 100 feet wide by 50 to 300 feet long, depending on the detector's antenna configuration.

Objects moving within any active motion detector zone can cause severe false alarm problems, especially if the motion is near the detector transducers. The severity of the problem is a function of the size, displacement, direction, and frequency of oscillation or velocity of the moving object relative to the transducer position. These object functions affect both the magnitude and frequency of the Doppler frequency shift. Under the right circumstances, the moving object can produce a Doppler frequency shift just like that produced by someone moving in the energy pattern.

Size of the moving object becomes critical as it moves closer to the transducers. Even small moving objects such as birds flying near the transducer can produce Doppler signals similar to a moving intruder. Displacement is the distance the object can move, and in this context it relates more to hanging objects that are free to swing or oscillate, such as hanging signs, decorations, or drapes. The greater the displacement, the higher the probability of the swinging object producing false alarms. Of course, the closer the swinging object is to the transducer, the greater the chance of false alarms.

Direction is important because motion directly toward or away from a motion detector transducer produces a larger Doppler shift than motion perpendicular to the detector. If the hanging signs are swinging in the direction of the transducer or the bird is flying toward it, they will produce larger frequency shifts and are more likely to produce false alarms. Velocity of the moving object influences both the amplitude and frequency distribution of the Doppler frequency shift. In general, the faster the object is moving, the greater the frequency shift. If the object is moving too fast, however, it might not cause an alarm. The object might be moving so fast that the resulting frequency shift would be out of the bandpass of the input filter. Another reason the fast-moving object might not produce an alarm is that it does not move in the zone of detection long enough to be interpreted as a valid alarm. For instance, a bird might fly past a detector too fast to initiate an alarm.

Birds flying in areas protected by motion detectors are a problem for any type of motion detector. In areas where volumetric motion detectors are used, birds and the like should be removed and their access to the area eliminated. Moving signs, banners, decorations, etc., suspended from wires, such as the advertisements and decorations found in retail stores and schools, can cause false alarms. The only way to eliminate these problems is for the security system designer or the installer to emphasize the importance of eliminating any moving objects in the area of the detectors to the user or individuals responsible for the operation. A demonstration of how the moving signs generate alarms might be helpful.

Any type of moving displays and decorations affect the operation of ultrasonic and sonic motion detectors; however, only metal or metallized displays or decorations affect the operation of microwave detectors. Microwave energy passes through cardboard and paper objects as if they are not there, but metal or metalized objects reflect microwave energy. If the metal objects are moving, and they reflect the microwave energy toward the detector transducers, they could cause false alarms. A good example of metallized objects that can affect the performance of any active motion detector is Christmas decorations. The metallized tinsel, icicles, or ornaments, although beautiful, can cause severe false alarm problems. Christmas season can be a trying time for the security industry.

Small objects, such as birds flying unrestricted, or medium-sized objects, such as poster-size advertisements oscillating back and forth in the zone of detection, can cause severe false alarm problems. Larger objects, such as roll-up garage doors, portable room dividers, or thin flexing walls, moving with only minor displacements, also can cause false alarms. Large objects can reflect more energy than small objects; therefore, minor displacements can produce Doppler frequency shifts similar to those produced by someone moving in the area. In any installation being protected by active motion detectors, all moving objects within the protected area should be removed or secured, if possible, so that they will not interfere with detector performance. The transducers should never be pointed toward moving objects, even larger objects that move just slightly.

An application feature of microwave detectors is the containment of the microwave energy within the areas being protected. Ultrasonic energy is easily contained by the walls of a room, but microwave energy is very difficult to contain because it penetrates to some degree into most walls, windows, and internal partitions. If the microwave energy outside the area is reflected back to the receiver inside the building, the reflected signal might cause a false alarm. Even though ultrasonic energy is contained by physical barriers, it can leak through cracks around doors and windows and might interfere with other ultrasonic detectors' operation. For this reason, if the transmitter frequency stability is not controlled, synchronization might be required between adjacent ultrasonic detectors, even though they might be in separate but adjoining rooms, to prevent mutual interference.

An operational feature available on many ultrasonic, microwave, and infrared motion detectors is individual transducer alarm indicator lights. Indicator lights simplify detector installation and maintenance by indicating when a transducer initiates an alarm. With this feature, during installation the sensitivity of each detector or detector transducer can be adjusted and walk-tested without monitoring the control unit's alarm output. Operational tests can be performed by simply walking in the zone of detection and observing the indicator light to determine when the detector initiates an alarm. Some detectors have provisions for latching the alarm indicator on until they are reset. This provision provides immediate identification of the detector or transducer that initated the alarm. Knowing which transducer initiated the alarm expedites the search for the response force and identifies the malfunctioning unit in case of a false alarm. This information reduces the time required to identify and correct any malfunctioning detectors.

Alarm indicator lights certainly simplify adjusting the transducer's sensitivity and operationally testing individual transducers. But for security purposes, consideration might be given to incorporating a switch in the circuit inside the control unit so that the lights can be deactivated until they are needed. This change would remove the possibility of an inside adversary studying alarm occurrences in the protected areas to establish the boundaries of any dead zones in which he might escape detection. The change also would remove the possibility of alerting intruders to the fact that they have been detected. Activating the indicator light switch would make available the benefit of the indicator lights for the maintenance personnel.

These features, along with other application and operation features, will be discussed for the individual active motion detectors in the following paragraphs.

ULTRASONIC MOTION DETECTORS

A basic ultrasonic motion detector consists of a transmitter, receiver, and control unit. The control unit contains the signal processor, power supply, and standby battery. In operation the detector transmitter generates an acoustical energy pattern that fills the zone of detection. Energy reflecting from the walls, ceiling, floor, and objects within the energy pattern and entering the receiver's field of acceptance is processed and analyzed by the signal processor. As long as the reflected energy is at the same frequency as the transmitted energy, there is no alarm; but anyone moving in the energy pattern produces a Doppler frequency shift that changes the reflected signal. When the signal characteristics satisfy the processor's alarm criteria, the detector initiates an alarm.

Most ultrasonic detectors operate at a specific frequency in the range between 19 and 40 kHz. Acoustical energy generated at frequencies above 19 kHz is considered inaudible to the average human ear and is defined as ultrasonic energy. A feature of ultrasonic energy is that it will not penetrate physical barriers such as walls; therefore, it can be easily contained in closed rooms. Since acoustical energy will not penetrate physical barriers, the walls of the protected room either absorb or reflect the energy. Since most walls absorb very little ultrasonic energy unless they are covered with a very soft material, such as heavy drapes, most of the energy is reflected. This reflected energy helps fill the zone of detection, making it more difficult for an intruder to escape detection.

There are two basic ultrasonic motion detector configurations. The first consists of a number of transceivers connected to one common control unit. A transceiver is a single unit that has a transmitter and receiver in one housing. In case of an ultrasonic transceiver, it has a separate transducer that transmits and receives ultrasonic energy. The second detector configu-

ration consists of a number of separate transmitters and receivers also connected to one common control unit. The number of individual transceivers
or separate transmitters and receivers in a specific installation depends primarily on the size and configuration of the area requiring protection. The
limiting factor on the number of transceivers or receivers and transmitters
connected to a single control unit is the maximum allowable number of units
designated by the manufacturer. Other application features that should be
considered will be discussed in the applications section later in this chapter.

Ultrasonic motion detector transceivers are considered directional
devices because the transmitter generates an oval energy pattern that can be
directed toward the areas requiring protection. A baffle can be installed on
the front of the transceiver to broaden the energy pattern for applications
where a broader pattern is required. The transceivers can be wall or ceiling
mounted and pointed in the direction of desired coverage. In an area with
10- to 12-foot ceilings, a single transceiver can in general protect an area
approximately 20 feet wide by 30 feet long.

Figure 11–1 shows a single ultrasonic transceiver mounted on the wall
opposite the entrance door and pointed in the direction of the door. This
mounting configuration takes advantage of the larger Doppler frequency
shift produced when someone is walking toward or away from the transceiver rather than tangential or perpendicular to it. There are installations
where the physical configuration of the room is such that the energy will be
reflected from an object back to the receiver, giving the appearance that the

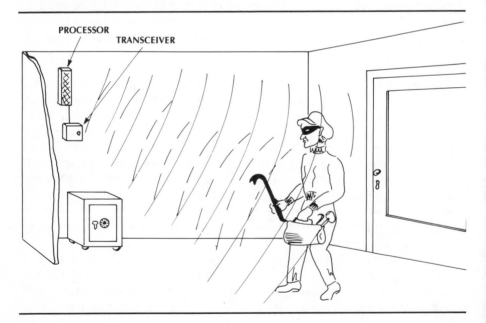

Figure 11–1   Ultrasonic motion detector with transceiver.

detection is the same or even better in the tangential direction than in the radial direction. In this illustration the transceiver transmits an acoustical energy pattern, depicted by the solid lines, that fills the room, reflecting from the floor, walls, and ceiling. As long as no one is moving in the room, the reflected energy returning to the receiver is the same frequency as the transmitted energy, and there is no alarm. When Mr. Ids enters and moves through the room, the transmitted energy is reflected from his body back to the transceiver. The reflected energy, depicted by the broken lines, contains frequency components of both the transmitted frequency and the Doppler frequency shift caused by Mr. Ids' motion. This frequency shift is analyzed in the signal processor, and when the signal characteristics satisfy the alarm criteria, the processor initiates the alarm.

The second ultrasonic motion detector configuration uses separately located transmitters and receivers to transmit and receive the ultrasonic energy. The most popular transmitter and receiver transducers are omnidirectional; directional or semidirectional transducers also are available. Omnidirectional transducer transmit and receive energy in a hemispheric rather than an oval pattern, the pattern produced by transceivers or directional transducers. Figure 11–2 shows separate omnidirectional transmit and receive transducers mounted approximately 20 feet apart on the ceiling along the middle of the room. In this mounting configuration the transmitted energy, depicted by the solid lines, reflects from the walls, ceiling, and floor, completely filling the room. As Mr. Ids moves through the room, he produces a Doppler frequency shift, depicted by the broken lines, that is received and analyzed by the signal processor. When the signal characteristics satisfy the alarm criteria, an alarm is initiated.

Piezoelectric and magnetostrictive transducers are used in ultrasonic motion detectors to convert electrical energy into acoustical energy and vice versa. In the piezoelectric transducer, the crystal is mounted in the center of a circular diaphragm mounted in the front of the transducer housing. When an alternating current is applied to the crystal, it physically expands and contracts at the frequency of the alternating current. This expansion and contraction causes the mounting diaphragm to vibrate, which in turn causes the air in front of the diaphragm to vibrate. This vibrating air is the acoustical energy. Conversely, reflected acoustical energy exerts an external force on the receive transducer, causing the crystal mounting diaphragm to vibrate. These vibrations stress the crystal, which generates an output signal for the signal processor. The signal is proportional to the strength of the reflected energy.

Piezoelectric transducer crystals are optimized to operate over a rather narrow frequency band. Although they operate very well at these frequencies, their ability to transmit and especially to receive energy at frequencies much above or below their design frequency is marginal. Although the piezoelectric transducer's frequency response is considered narrow, the transducers are quite capable of receiving an ample signal to detect a moving

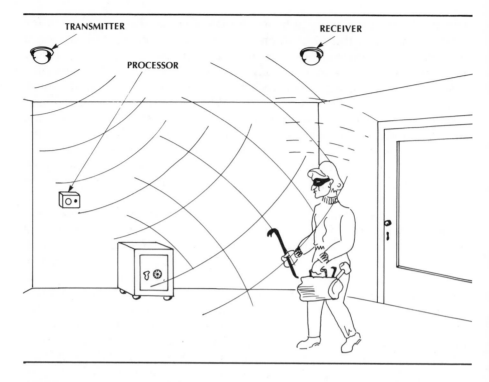

TRANSMITTER

RECEIVER

PROCESSOR

Figure 11-2 Ultrasonic motion detector with separate transmitter and receiver.

intruder. A moving intruder produces a Doppler frequency shift containing frequency components that range from 20 to 800 Hz on either side of the primary operating frequency. The amplitude and range of the frequency shift depend on the moving intruder's size, speed, and direction. The speed is not just the velocity of the intruder's body; it also includes the velocities of his swinging arms and legs. For instance, a classic Texas cowboy, walking in the acoustical energy pattern swinging his arms and legs, will generate greater Doppler frequency shifts than the same size smooth-walking person.

Magnetostrictive transducers perform the same functions as piezoelectric transducers, but instead of a vibrating crystal the magnetostrictive transducer uses a laminated nickel rod wound with a wire coil. When the coil around the nickel rod is excited by an alternating current, the resulting magnetic field expands and contracts the rod at twice the frequency of the impressed field—twice the frequency because it expands and contracts the rod on both halves of the alternating electromagnetic field. A permanent magnet is used to bias the coil and cancel out the flux generated on one half cycle of the impressed electromagnetic field. Removing one half cycle of the impressed field, or halving the frequency, reduces the transducer frequency to the original alternating current frequency.

In the piezoelectric transducer, the crystal mounting diaphragm excites the air medium, but in the magnetostrictive transducer, the nickel rod is connected to the base of a hemispherical aluminimum shell or to some other shaped diaphragm that excites the air medium. When the nickel rod expands and contracts, it vibrates the hemispherical shell or diaphragm that generates the acoustical energy pattern. The receive transducer is identical in configuration to the transmitting transducer. Reflected acoustical energy impinging on the hemispherical shell or diaphragm stresses the nickel rod in compression and expansion at the frequency of the reflected energy. The compression and expansion of the nickel rod generates a signal for the processor that is proportional to the strength of the reflected energy.

Most ultrasonic motion detectors are designed to operate at lower ultrasonic frequencies because low-frequency acoustical energy is less affected by air currents. The lower operating frequencies, approximately 19.6 kHz for the magnetostrictive-type transducers and 25 kHz for the piezoelectric transducers, are also compatible with the construction characteristics of the individual transducers. Although the detector's operating frequencies have been described as low frequencies, the acoustical energy at these frequencies is still out of the audible frequency range for most human ears. The frequencies are high enough, however, that the detector's operation is not affected by common audible noises occurring in the protected areas. Resorting to higher operating frequencies above 25 kHz to further isolate the detector from common noises would result in a loss of coverage due to the resistance air imposes on the propagation of ultrasonic energy.

To review briefly the ultrasonic motion detector's basic principle's of operation discussed thus far, the detector's transmitter generates a pattern of acoustical energy. This acoustical energy pattern fills the detector's specific volume of detection by reflecting from the various objects and walls within the volume. A good way to visualize the acoustical energy pattern is to observe the surface waves on the water in a bathtub. After the tub is full, turn the water down to a constant drip or drop pebbles into the water at a constant rate. Observe the wave pattern of the surface of the water and how the waves are reflected by the sides of the tub. If there is no other disturbance, the wave pattern will appear to be stationary. These stationary waves are referred to as standing waves. If you put your finger or hand in the water and move it around, the waves generated by your moving hand will be similar to the energy reflected by an intruder moving in an acoustical energy pattern.

The primary difference between various ultrasonic motion detectors is the signal processing techniques used to interpret and identify "valid" Doppler frequency shifts. A valid Doppler frequency shift is generated by someone moving in the zone of detection and not by some mechanically produced stimuli such as air turbulence or miscellaneous acoustic energy sources within the protected zone. Air turbulence from heating or air-conditioning ducts, drafts, and so on, can reduce the effectiveness by limiting the coverage of ultrasonic motion detectors and, at the same time, can cause false alarms. Acoustic energy generated by ringing bells and hissing noises, such as the noises produced by leading radiators or compressed air, contains frequency components in the operating frequency band of ultrasonic motion detectors. These sources of ultrasonic energy sometimes produce signals similar to an intruder that can confuse the signal processor, resulting in false alarms. Because of these various operating limitations, the performance of the ultrasonic motion detector depends on the worst case environment selected for designing the signal processor.

One basic signal processing technique used to reduce the susceptibility of ultrasonic detectors to false alarms caused by mechanically produced signals is to filter the acoustic energies with frequencies above and below the signals with frequencies characteristic of a moving intruder. Usually the energies associated with most noise sources are lower in frequency than the operating frequency of the ultrasonic motion detector and can be easily filtered. But the frequency of the acoustic energy from ringing bells and hissing noises is very broadband, extending from low audible frequencies up to 60 kHz. While much of the energy from these sources is at frequencies above and below operating frequency of the motion detector's bandpass filter, some of the energy still has frequency components within the detector's operating frequency band. Therefore, if only the input signals to the processor are filtered, a large amount of acoustic energy can still enter the signal processor, and it might be interpreted as a valid signal.

Another signal processing technique capitalizes on the fact that signals from mechanically generated acoustic energy usually fluctuate considerably in both amplitude and frequency, while the Doppler signal produced by a moving intruder tends to be more constant, particularly when the intruder moves along a straight line. This processing technique senses the presence of the fluctuating energy and automatically adjusts the alarm threshold to a higher level to compensate for the externally generated acoustic energy. But with automatic adjustment, referred to as automatic gain control (AGC), the detection range sometimes decreases as background acoustic energy increases until the detection of some detectors becomes ineffective. Under such circumstances, an intruder might be able to defeat the detector by mechanically generating acoustic energy while slowly but successfully carrying out his mission.

Still another signal processing technique capitalizes on the fact that an intruder moving in a straight line toward the detector receiver produces a Doppler frequency above the detector transmit frequency, while the converse is true for an intruder moving away from the receiver. Operating on this phenomenon, the processor is designed to ignore noise signals that do not collectively represent a *net change in range* characteristic of a signal from a moving intruder. Mechanically generated acoustic energy or noise, as discussed earlier, usually has frequency components throughout the bandpass of the detector; therefore, it might not produce a net change or imbalance in the energy in the side bands on either side of the detector's transmit frequency. This processing technique also minimizes the number of alarms caused by swaying objects such as drapes or mobiles. Normally drapes and mobiles move in a slow oscillatory or back-and-forth motion when they are exposed to air drafts. Since the motion is oscillatory, there is no net change in the frequency and therefore no alarm. In other words, when the drapes move forward, they produce a Doppler frequency shift above the operating frequency, which is assigned a positive value, and then, when the drapes move back, they produce a Doppler shift of equal magnitude below the operating frequency, which is assigned a negative value. Since there is no net motion of the moving drapes, the net Doppler frequency shift is zero, and there is no false alarm. But an intruder moving in the protected area generates either a net positive or negative signal and thereby activates an alarm.

Other compensation schemes are often used as part of the primary signal processing circuit. One such compensation circuit requires the intrusion signal to be present for at least 2 to 3 seconds before an alarm is generated in order to eliminate possible alarms from short-duration noises such as telephone rings. Of course, this means an intruder must be continuously moving in the protected area for at least 3 seconds before he is detected. Walking at a normal pace of one step per second, the detector requires approximately three steps by the intruder before initiating an alarm. Circuits requiring motion to be present for several seconds before an alarm is activated are time delay circuits.

These are some of the basic ultrasonic motion detector signal processing techniques used to analyze a valid intruder signal. Detector selection should be based on the applicability of the detector to perform in the specific environment. For instance, if the detector must function in an environment with moving drapes or other oscillatory motion, then the signal processing technique should reject oscillatory motion; however, if the area requiring protection has no moving object, the oscillatory requirement is not necessary. Anyone who must select a motion detector for a specific requirement and is not familiar with the detector's operation should obtain and install one of the proposed detectors in the most difficult area requiring protection and evaluate its performance for at least one week.

Those individuals having meager knowledge of ultrasonic detectors and other intrusion detection devices should consider selecting Underwriters Laboratories (UL), Inc., listed equipment. But just because a detector is UL listed does not mean it will provide 100 percent detection with zero false alarms; it does mean that the unit has been evaluated and determined satisfactory in terms of safety and that the detection characteristics have been checked. Above all, the UL listing indicates that the detector is safe to operate in terms of health, fire hazards, and electrical safety.

Applications

Two basic configurations of ultrasonic motion detectors are available, as previously described. One configuration consists of multiple transceivers connected to a single control unit. The second configuration consists of multiple transmitters and receivers connected to a common control unit. Whether a detector with transceivers or one with separate receivers and transmitters is selected for a specific application depends on the physical size of the area requiring intrusion detection, including the ceiling height.

Another important consideration in selecting a detector configuration is the arrangement of the equipment, furniture, supplies, etc., located inside the area being protected. Arrangement is important because ultrasonic energy cannot penetrate physical objects. If objects are located between the transceiver and the area requiring protection, they will block the energy, creating areas with poor or no detection. In many applications either detector configuration will quite adequately satisfy the protection requirements. For these applications the motion detector selection is based primarily on the designer's or user's preference.

Transceivers are available for both wall and ceiling mounting; however, wall-mounted versions are probably the most popular because they can be directed to cover the area of interest. A single wall-mounted transceiver mounted approximately 6 feet above the floor generates an oval energy pattern that can protect an area about 20 feet wide by 30 feet long with a 10- to 12-foot ceiling. A plan view of this energy pattern is shown in Figure 11–3b. The oval energy pattern can be broadened by installing an energy director on the face of the transceiver in front of the transducer.

Ceiling-mounted transceivers generate a cone-shaped energy pattern that can cover a circular area about 30 feet in diameter when the transceiver is mounted 10 to 15 feet above the floor. This energy pattern also can be reshaped to cover an oval area by installing deflectors on the front of the transceiver. A feature of ceiling-mounted transceivers is that they can be mounted directly over the area requiring protection. This feature is especially valuable in areas where it is difficult to protect with wall-mounted transceivers.

Long-range ultrasonic transceivers are available with long, narrow energy patterns for protecting aisles and hallways. A single detector can protect a hallway about 70 feet long. A plan view of the energy pattern is shown in Figure 11–3c. Multiple wall-mounted transceiver arrangements are shown in Figures 11–3a and 11–3d.

As mentioned, an ultrasonic transceiver generates an oval energy pattern, similar to the shape of a teardrop. This shape is the result of the piezoelectric transducer configuration. When the circular diaphragm in the transducer is excited by the vibrating crystal, it compresses and expands the air medium in front of the diaphragm, thus generating the acoustical energy pattern. In operation, the transmit transducer generates an energy pattern that fills the zone of detection in the protected area, reflecting from the walls and other objects in the area. Reflected energy falling in the receive transducer's acceptance field of view strikes the transducer diaphragm, forcing it to vibrate at the frequency of the reflected energy. The vibrating diaphragm stresses the piezoelectric crystal that converts the reflected energy into an

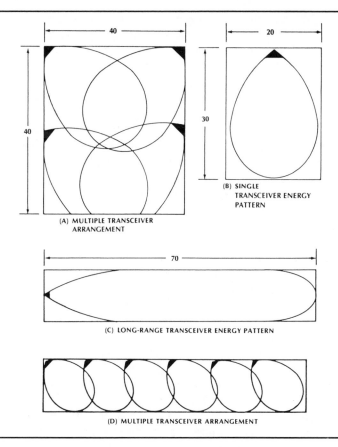

Figure 11-3   Ultrasonic transceivers.

electrical signal for the signal processor. As long as the reflected energy is at the same frequency as the transmitted energy, there is no alarm. But someone who enters the pattern produces a Doppler frequency shift that is recognized as a valid signal, and the processor initiates an alarm.

Multiple transceivers are required to protect both large and irregularly shaped areas. Figure 11-3a shows an arrangement of wall-mounted transceivers for protecting a large rectangular area. Figure 11-3d shows a transceiver arrangement for protecting a long hallway. Furniture and equipment arrangement within a protected area not only affects the detector configuration selection, but also influences the number and mounting location of the individual wall- and ceiling-mounted transceivers. Additional application factors should be considered for multiple transceiver installations.

To eliminate unprotected areas, ultrasonic transceivers, whether in a single or multiple transceiver installation, should be positioned in locations where the transmitted energy is not blocked. The transceivers should be pointed so that the transmitted energy is directed toward the most probable intruder entry point or route through the protected area, such as entrance doors and aisles. Directing the energy toward the intruder takes advantage of the larger Doppler frequency shift produced when walking toward the transceiver.

In multiple transceiver installations the energy patterns of the individual transceivers should be overlapped to eliminate unprotected areas. The transceivers should never be pointed toward each other, however, unless they are separated by at least 60 feet or obscured by some physical barrier. If they are located too close together, energy from one transceiver could affect the detection capability of the other transceivers connected to the same control unit. Energy interference can reduce the individual transceiver detection range and even cause false alarms.

Individual transmitters and receivers in the second detector configurations shown in Figure 11-2 are available as omnidirectional and semidirectional transducers. Omnidirectional transducers generate a hemispherical energy pattern, and semidirectional transducers generate a conical pattern. Individual ultrasonic omnidirectional transmitters and receivers are usually ceiling mounted; however, semidirectional transducers can be either ceiling or wall mounted. Like the transceiver installations, the individual transmitters and receivers should be positioned to minimize shadowing and to protect the areas of interest, especially those areas where an intruder would enter.

A basic detector consisting of one each omnidirectional transmitter and receiver mounted to the ceiling about 25 feet apart can protect an area about 40 feet long and 30 feet wide with ceiling heights between 15 and 20 feet. A plan view of the basic detector coverage is shown in Figure 11-4a. Figures 11-4b and 11-4c show multiple transmitter and receiver arrangements for protecting a large, irregularly shaped area. In typical installations, the separation between the individual transmitters and receivers ranges from about 15 to 35 feet, depending on the acoustics and operating environment in the area requiring protection.

Transceiver-type detectors can accommodate about twenty transceivers per control unit. Detectors with separate transmitters and receivers can, on the average, accommodate about twenty pairs of transducers; however, there are detectors capable of operating with up to one hundred transducer pairs. The actual number of individual transceivers or transducer pairs connected to a single control unit can be affected by the acoustics and environment within the protected area. In a multiple transceiver installation, each receiver, whether it is part of a transceiver or a separate receiver, receives not only the reflected energy from its own transmitter but also energy from the other transmitters in the area. Along with these energies, the receivers receive the energies generated by other sources of ultrasonic energy and respond to disturbances in the energy patterns. These extraneous energies can affect the detector's signal-to-noise ratio and limit the number

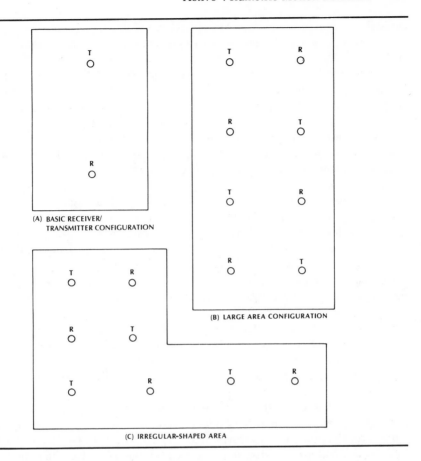

Figure 11–4 Ultrasonic receiver/transmitter arrangement.

of transducers. In areas where there is marginal signal-to-noise, microwave motion detectors should be considered or additional ultrasonic control units should be used to improve the detection; the transceivers should be divided between at least two processor units.

Other sources of ultrasonic energy include hissing noises, such as those from escaping air or steam leaks, and ringing bells. Both hissing noises and ringing bells are very rich in ultrasonic energy at frequencies up to and even exceeding 40 kHz. Because these energies are so broadband, some of the energy falls within the bandpass of the signal processor. These signals certainly contribute to the background energy level reducing the detector's signal-to-noise ratios. Depending on the amplitude and amplitude variation of these energies, they can be interpreted by the signal processor as valid signals and can cause false alarms.

Some detectors reduce their susceptibility to false alarms from extraneous ultrasonic energies by filtering all energies except those with frequencies typical of a moving intruder. Susceptibility is further reduced in some detectors by compensating for some extraneous energies with automatic gain control, especially those energies with more uniform amplitudes such as hissing noises. Energies associated with some ringing bells vary appreciably between frequencies within the bandpass of the filter. These energy variations are difficult to accommodate in the signal processor and consequently can cause false alarms. Because of the randomness of the amplitude variations of some ringing bells, it is difficult to determine if a specific bell in an area will cause false alarms. Therefore, it is recommended that all bells within a protected area be replaced with buzzers.

Other stimuli that can affect the performance of ultrasonic motion detectors are moving air, such as forced air from heating and air-conditioning ducts; drafts from open windows, doors, and vents; and thermal air currents from heat sources. Moving air can distort the energy pattern, appreciably reducing the effectiveness of the detection range and, depending on the air velocity, can cause false alarms. Low-velocity air currents sometimes produce Doppler frequency shifts similar to those signals generated by a slow-moving intruder. These signals can be interpreted by the signal processor as valid signals, resulting in false alarms. Therefore, regardless of whether the energy sources generate hissing noises or ringing sounds or produce moving air, the transceivers and separate receivers should be positioned as fas as possible from these energy sources to still provide the desired coverage.

Heating and air-conditioning drafts can usually be avoided by mounting the receiver at least 15 feet from the register. The transmitter location is not as critical, and if either the transmitter or receiver must be located near the register, let the transmitter be located there. Because of the effect of these stimuli on the detector's performance, the sensitivity of the detectors should be adjusted when these stimuli are activated to ensure that the detectors will provide the desired detection in the most severe environment.

Another environmental condition that can affect ultrasonic detector performance is the climate within the protected area. Since ultrasonic energy uses air as the transmission medium, the sensitivity of a detector can be affected by changes in the relative humidity in the protected areas. Attenuation of ultrasonic energy at the most popular operating frequencies is greatest when the relative humidity is between 20 and 30 percent. Therefore, the detectors are less sensitive when the relative humidity is within these percentages.

Appreciable changes in the relative humidity can change the detector's sensitivity until, in some installations, a detector can become very sensitive to the environment, which could result in false alarms. For instance, if an ultrasonic motion detector is protecting a heated room, and the detector's sensitivity is adjusted during the day when the weather is mild and the relative humidity is between 20 and 30 percent, the detector will become more sensitive at night when the heater comes on and dries the air. Depending on how much the humidity is lowered, the increase in sensitivity could result in false alarms. Therefore, in areas where the relative humidity is subject to such changes, the sensitivity of the detector should be adjusted during the time of day when the detector will be operating in the secure mode. Another consideration is to reduce the detector's sensitivity if it is adjusted when the relative humidity is between 20 and 30 percent to compensate for the increase in sensitivity when the humidity deviates appreciably from this range.

Ultrasonic motion detectors can be used to protect areas such as schoolrooms, offices, retail stores, department stores, or any area where there are no large sources of ultrasonic energy that might cause false alarms or large volumes of moving air that might reduce the performance by distorting the transmitted energy pattern. When the detectors are installed in accordance with the manufacturer's installation instructions, they can provide many hours of reliable operation with few, if any, false alarms.

MICROWAVE MOTION DETECTORS

While ultrasonic motion detectors generate inaudible acoustic energy patterns and recognize a disturbance in those patterns caused by a moving intruder, microwave motion detectors generate an electromagnetic energy pattern that serves the same function. Also, ultrasonic motion detectors consist of a single control unit with multiple transducers. Most microwave detectors are self-contained units, however—that is, the detector's antenna, signal processor, and power supply are contained in a single unit. Microwave detectors are available with multiple transceivers connected to a common control unit. Even though each of the multiple transceivers contains its own signal processing circuit, they share the same power supply and alarm relay in the control unit. With multiple transceiver detectors, each transceiver usually generates a smaller energy pattern than the single unit detectors. In application of the multiple transceiver detectors, additional transceivers are required to protect large volumes, but each detector can be directed to cover a specific area.

Microwave energy has the distinct ability to penetrate glass, wood, and even cinder block walls to some extent, depending on the frequency and antenna direction. Therefore, microwave motion detectors can be used where the volume of the facility to be protected is large and when it is advantageous to detect intruders through internal partitions and walls. Microwave detectors also can be used for volumetric detection when air turbulence in the area requiring protection might cause false alarms with ultrasonic detectors.

Mr. Ids illustrates the principles of operation of a microwave motion detector in Figure 11–5. In this illustration, a single low-frequency microwave detector is protecting two separate rooms partitioned by standard Sheetrock. The transmitted microwave energy, depicted by the solid lines, protects the room containing the detector, then penetrates the interior wall

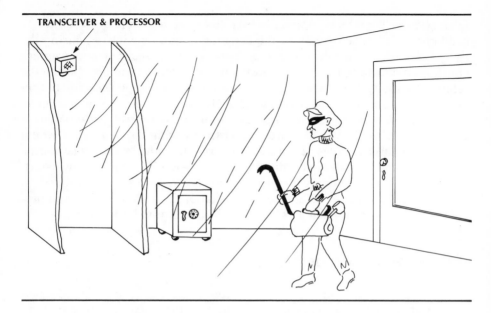

Figure 11-5   Microwave motion detector.

to protect the room containing the safe. As Mr. Ids enters the room and moves toward the safe, he reflects the detector-transmitted energy back to the transceiver, where it is received and processed. When the characteristic of the signal satisfies the detector's alarm criteria, an alarm is initiated.

The microwave motion detectors described in this chapter are for indoor applications only. Indoor microwave detectors should never be used outdoors unless they are designated for outside use by the manufacturer; outdoor microwave detectors can be used indoors. The reason indoor detectors should never be used outdoors is that indoor units recognize a Doppler frequency shift produced by a moving target to detect intruders. Moving trees and waving grass can produce Doppler frequency shifts similar to those produced by a moving intruder. This type of motion can cause serious false alarm problems.

Microwave motion detector operating frequencies, unlike ultrasonic motion detector operating frequencies, are assigned and regulated by the FCC. The FCC regulations governing unlicensed use of field disturbance sensors are in Part 15, Subpart F appended to OCE 11 under the category "Field Disturbance Sensors." The FCC has assigned five operating frequency bands for microwave motion detectors as follows: 915 ± 13 MHz; $2{,}450 \pm 15$ MHz; $5{,}800 \pm 15$ MHz; $10{,}525 \pm 25$ MHz; and $22{,}125 \pm 50$ MHz. The FCC also limits the maximum allowable field strength of the transmitted energy. In the first three bands, the maximum field strength level at a range of 100 feet is 50,000 microvolts per meter. The two higher frequency bands are allowed field strengths up to 250,000 microvolts per meter. In addition to limiting the field strengths, the FCC requires that all out-of-band spurious signals be held to – 50 dB relative to the fundamental frequency.

The most popular operating frequencies for microwave detectors are 915 MHz, 2,450 MHz, and 10,525 MHz. Detectors operating at 915 MHz and 2,450 MHz are more effective than higher-frequency detectors in protecting areas with internal partitions. Microwave energy at these frequencies can penetrate through wood and Sheetrock with little or no attenuation and can even penetrate brick and cinder block walls to some degree. Conversely, the attenuation of higher-frequency energy is greater, and detectors operating at the higher 10,525 MHz frequency can be used to protect areas where it is desirable to contain the microwave energy.

Although the resistance to higher-frequency microwave energy passing through wood, Sheetrock, and brick is greater than for lower-frequency energy, the energy can penetrate the walls. The fact that it can penetrate walls has both advantages and disadvantages. An advantage occurs when an intruder is detected by the microwave energy penetrating partitions within a protected volume. But if it detects someone or something moving outside the protected area, or even outside the building, that is a definite disadvantage. The fact that microwave energy is difficult to contain should be considered in locating and directing the detector-transmitted energy within the area requiring protection.

The shape of the transmitted energy pattern is a function of the antenna configuration. Detectors are available with antennas that generate both omnidirectional and directional energy patterns. Omnidirectional antennas generate a circular donut-shaped, hemispheric or ellipsoid energy pattern, while directional antennas generate broad teardrop-shaped patterns to protect large rooms or long, narrow teardrop-shaped patterns to protect long corridors. Figure 11–6 shows some typical directional antenna patterns available from most manufacturers of microwave detectors.

The omnidirectional donut-shaped energy pattern is generated by a quarterwave monopole antenna mounted on a small metal disc ground plane. The donut pattern is approximately 60 feet in diameter. Both the detector transmitter and receiver share the same monopole antenna. Detectors generating directional teardrop-shaped patterns have either dual or single waveguide horns or flat array antennas. Detectors using monopole, single horn, or flat array antennas rely on the same antenna for transmitting and receiving the reflected microwave energy. Detectors using dual horns rely on one horn for transmitting and the other horn for receiving the reflected microwave energy. About the only difference between detectors using dual horns and the ones using single horns is the physical size of the detectors and the signal receiving and processing circuitry.

The signal processing techniques used by most microwave motion detector manufacturers are similar to the techniques used by ultrasonic motion detector manufacturers. These techniques include comparing the transmitted microwave signal with the reflected signal, and as long as there

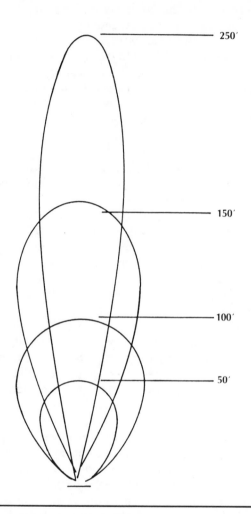

Figure 11-6 Typical microwave antenna patterns.

is no movement in the protected zone, the transmitted and received frequencies are equal and there is no alarm. But someone moving in the area generates a Doppler frequency shift in the reflected signal, and if the signal exists long enough to satisfy the detector's alarm criteria, an alarm is initiated.

As with ultrasonic detectors, microwave processors include circuits to reduce the incidence of false alarms. One such design uses counting logic in the processor to reduce nuisance alarms caused by random short-duration disturbances in background motion, such as flying birds or insects. This is assuming the birds or insects fly through the pattern and do not dwell there.

The counter is adjusted to set the number of motion cycles ignored before the detector interprets the disturbance as a valid alarm. To prevent the counts from accumulating, the counter returns to zero after a fixed time interval, usually about 10 minutes, following each counted motion.

Another technique for reducing false alarms is to use noise compensation circuits to cancel the effects of minor but constant background motion. The objective of this design is to permit the operation of the detector in electrically noisy areas where there is rotating machinery. Microwave motion detectors are susceptible to false alarms if they are installed near flourescent lamps; therefore, in these applications it is desirable that the signal processor have a 120 Hz narrowband filter to reject the interference from the on/off ionization cycle of the flourescent lamps.

As with the ultrasonic motion detector, the recommended signal processing depends primarily on the application. For those not familiar with a specific manufacturer's microwave motion detector, either from firsthand experience or observation, a unit should be installed in the most difficult area requiring protection and monitored for at least a week. During this time, any operational deficiencies should be discovered. UL listed units also are recommended, especially if the user is not familiar with either the manufacturer or the equipment.

Applications

Microwave motion detectors generate omnidirectional or directional energy patterns. Detectors that generate omnidirectional energy patterns should be mounted on the ceiling over the area requiring protection. The omnidirectional pattern is symmetrical in the shape of a donut or semisymmetrical in the shape of an ellipsoid. An ellipsoid pattern resembles one half of a football that is cut through the center from point to point. Ellipsoid patterns are about 20 to 30 feet wide by 40 to 60 feet long. The symmetrical donut-shaped patterns are about 40 to 60 feet in diameter. The actual shape of the energy pattern, whether it is omnidirectional or directional, depends on the antenna configuration.

Microwave detectors that generate teardrop-shaped energy patterns are very popular because their energy can be directed toward the areas requiring protection. Likewise, it can be pointed away from any possible false alarm stimuli. The size of the teardrop-shaped pattern ranges from broad short-range to narrow long-range patterns, as shown in Figure 11–6. Broad energy patterns range from a small pattern about 15 feet wide and 20 feet long to a large pattern about 40 feet wide and 50 feet long. Long, narrow energy patterns extend as far as 250 feet. Directional antennas with broad patterns are used to protect large areas, while long, narrow patterns are used to protect long corridors.

The fact that microwave energy can penetrate most construction material should be considered in the application of microwave detectors. Directional detectors should never be pointed directly toward any exterior wall, especially if there are large, moving metal objects outside that could reflect the energy back through the wall, where it might be received by the detector. For instance, if automobiles or trucks pass near the exterior wall when the detector is operating, they could reflect enough energy back through the wall to cause false alarm problems.

Walls constructed of dense building materials, such as brick, cinder block, and especially concrete, attenuate more energy than glass, wood, or Sheetrock, but the problem could still exist. The severity of the problem depends on the size of the moving object and the direction of the transmitted energy. In terms of size of the moving object, the larger it is, the higher the probability of the object outside the area causing problems. As previously mentioned, the detectors should never be pointed directly at the exterior wall; however, they can be directed so that their energy is transmitted parallel to the wall, with little or no penetration. The angle at which the transmitted energy strikes the wall is very important with respect to the amount of energy that actually penetrates it.

As with the application of ultrasonic motion detectors, the size and configuration of the facility requiring protection, as well as the arrangement of the equipment, furniture, etc., inside the area, influences the number of detectors required to protect the facility. Determining the number of detectors required to protect a specific size or configured area can be accomplished simply by installing an adequate number of detectors to cover the area. However, the total area inside the facility usually does not require total detection throughout the facility. In most applications only the valuable items or vital areas or the avenues leading to these areas need protecting. Limiting the detection to cover only the vital areas reduces the number of detectors and thus reduces the possibility of false alarms. For example, department stores have areas where high-value items such as furs, jewelry, or appliances are displayed or stored. Detectors can be positioned to detect anyone entering only those areas of interest. Protecting the whole store is usually not necessary.

The arrangement of the objects within the area requiring protection influences the number of detectors because the detectors must be located and positioned either to avoid the objects or to protect around them. Microwave energy penetrates wooden furniture, wooden or Sheetrock partitions, wooden shelving, etc., but it does not penetrate metal furniture, safes, file cabinets, metal partitions, etc. Metal objects or surfaces can reflect microwave energy as mirrors reflect light. Metal objects within the energy pattern of microwave detectors can cause false alarm problems that are sometimes difficult to identify unless the installers are familiar with the characteristics of microwave energy.

There are several interesting stories about false alarm problems created by someone relocating or adding metal objects into the energy pattern of microwave detectors. Synopses of several stories are related here to illustrate some of the peculiar problems that can occur. The stories all start about the same way. The microwave detectors have been installed and operating satisfactorily for a long time without any problem. Then, for no apparent reason, an installation starts having false alarms. Of course, the first thing the user does is call the alarm company.

In the first instance, a large office area with a desk, chairs, file cabinets, etc., was protected by a single directional microwave detector. The detector was in the corner of the room pointing away from the windows in the adjoining wall. The secretary of this office decided to rearrange the furniture. The desk was not moved enough to affect detector performance, but the file cabinets were moved from along the wall underneath the detector to the wall opposite the detector. Then the false alarms started, and the alarm company was notified.

The installer arrived and checked the performance of the detector and found it operating satisfactorily. Understanding the characteristics of microwave energy, he started looking around the room for possible causes and immediately noticed the file cabinets. Now instead of the energy pattern being directed over the cabinets to detect anyone approaching the files, the energy was directed at the metal cabinets. The installer then noticed the relative position of the cabinets with respect to the detector. The way they were positioned, they could reflect the energy out of the office windows toward the street. He then asked the secretary if the file cabinets were always located along that wall. She replied, "No, they were over there, but last week the office was rearranged." He then asked if they started having false alarms after the rearrangement and the answer was yes.

The alarm installer explained what he believed had happened and asked if he could move the files to another mutually agreed upon location out in the detector's energy pattern. The secretary did not believe that the file cabinets were causing the problem but agreed to move them under the condition that he would move them back after a couple of weeks if the false alarms continued. He agreed and relocated the files, which did alleviate the problem.

A similar circumstance arose when a secretary decided to redecorate her office. Along with the new drapes, rug, etc., she had two of the walls wallpapered and two paneled. Several days after the decorating was completed, the company started having false alarms. The alarm company was notified, and the installer arrived and checked the detector. The detector was all right, but as the installer was trying to identify what might have caused the alarm, he noticed the shiny wallpaper. On close examination, he found that it was metallized paper. The metallized paper had been installed on the wall opposite and adjacent to the detector. The way the microwave detector was pointed, the energy could be reflected from the wallpapered walls toward the office windows overlooking the parking lot. The parking lot was hardly used at night, which probably accounted for the fact that several days passed before the first alarm. In his case the installer was not going to suggest changing the wallpaper. He relocated the detector to the adjacent corner so that the energy was pointed toward the interior paneled walls. Relocating the detector solved the problem.

Another example of how unexpected objects can reflect microwave energy to cause mind-boggling problems follows. In this case two directional microwave detectors were installed in front of a large drugstore. They were mounted close to the ceiling near the corner of the store and pointed toward the middle and back of the store to cover the front area and aisles. In this position the energy was directed away from the front windows. After several months of successful operation, the detectors started to generate false alarms. This problem was not so easy to solve. After several trips by the installer to check detector operation, he noticed several shoplifting-type mirrors installed near the center of the store. The installer asked the proprietor how long the mirrors had been there. Sure enough, they had been installed about the time the detectors started false alarming.

The installer explained how the metallized paint on the reflective surface of the mirrors might be reflecting the microwave energy out into the parking lot. Then at night, when a car came close to the front of the store, it could reflect enough of the energy back to the mirror and on to the detector. This reflected signal, depending on the size and speed of the car, could be similar to a moving intruder inside the store. The result would be a false alarm. After some doubtful looks, the proprietor allowed the installer to remove the mirrors if he agreed to replace them if the problem continued. The installer agreed, but removing the mirrors solved the false alarm problem.

These examples show the type of peculiar problems that can happen when microwave motion detectors are pointed toward metal objects. The objects can cause false alarm problems, especially if the energy is reflected toward construction material that offers very little resistance to the microwave energy, such as glass, wood, and Sheetrock. Microwave detectors should be mounted high, near the ceiling of the area being protected, and pointed in the direction of desired coverage but away from metal objects that might reflect the energy toward areas that might be sources of false alarms. Mounting the detectors high and pointing them down directs the energy toward the floor and reduces the possibility of the energy being reflected out of the area.

Microwave detectors should never be pointed toward any moving metal objects such as rotating machinery, thin metal walls, metal garage doors, Christmas ornaments, or rotating fan blades. As previously discussed, the amount of motion required to cause the detector to false alarm is a function of the size of the moving object, its distance from the detector, and the velocity or frequency of the object. For instance, the thin metal walls of a metal warehouse can cause severe false alarm problems for microwave detectors close to the walls when the wind blows. The wind causes the walls to vibrate, and because the walls are so large, the small amount of motion produces signals similar to valid signals. Even vibrating metal pipes located near and in the field of the energy pattern can cause false alarms. In this case the objects are small, but they are near the detector.

Microwave detectors are suited for protecting industrial areas because they are not affected by large volumes of moving air. In such applications, however, they should never be directed toward rotating or reciprocating equipment. Care also should be taken to ensure that equipment such as overhead chain hoists is moved out of the energy pattern and, if practical, tied down. Any large fans, especially fans with metal blades, also should be moved away from the detectors. Even if the fans are turned off, a draft might cause the fan blade to turn. A slowly turning fan blade can produce a Doppler frequency shift in the reflected signal similar to a moving person. Moving fan blades also can cause false alarms with ultrasonic motion detectors.

Microwave motion detectors can be used to protect facilities such as industrial plants, office buildings, schools, department stores, or any area where metal objects will not reflect the energy or move to cause false alarms. Always install the detectors in accordance with the manufacturer's installation instructions for the most reliable operation.

SONIC MOTION DETECTORS

Sonic motion detectors are similar to ultrasonic motion detectors inasmuch as they both use air as their signal transmission medium. The primary difference between the two is that sonic detectors fill the volume requiring protection with energy in the audible frequency range (typically 800 Hz) instead of with ultrasonic energy (above 20 kHz). Since the audible energy is lower in frequency than inaudible ultrasonic energy, the audible energy has longer wavelengths and, consequently, is less sensitive to air currents that might distort ultrasonic energy patterns. It is also less sensitive than that of ultrasonic motion detectors to small moving objects such as insects, cats, or rodents in the zone of detection. This sensitivity difference results from the fact that the wavelength of sonic energy is much longer than that of ultrasonic energy. Therefore, the distortions generated by small animals are not as significant as they are with the ultrasonic detector.

Sonic detectors consist basically of a control unit that contains the power supply and signal processor. The central unit can operate from one to eight transceivers. The transmitter section of these units fills the area requiring protection with acoustical energy, while the receiver section collects the reflected acoustical signals for the signal processor. The transmitted acoustical energy is reflected by the walls and other objects within the protected area, thus generating standing wave patterns of acoustical energy. Any disturbance in these energy patterns that satisfies the detector alarm criteria initiates an alarm, as is the case with the ultrasonic and microwave motion detectors.

Sonic motion detectors monitor the received acoustical energy for both a change in the amplitude of the received energy and a Doppler frequency shift in the standing wave pattern. These changes can be detected by comparing the frequency spectrum of the reflected signal with that of the transmitted signal. When both the standing wave amplitude change and the frequency shift satisfy the detector's alarm criteria, an alarm is initiated.

Applications

Electromagnetic speaker transducers are used as the detector transceiver. A single transceiver can protect a volume about 40 by 40 feet square with 10- to 12-foot ceilings. Seven additional transceivers can be connected to the control unit for protecting larger volumes. If additional transceivers are needed, another control unit must be installed.

A precaution necessary when protecting large areas or separate rooms that are near each other is that the transmit oscillators must be synchronized to prevent one detector from causing the other detector to false alarm. There might be a variation in the oscillator's output frequency between the detectors that could otherwise change the amplitude of this signal at the receiver. Depending on the magnitude of the signal change, the results could be a false alarm. In other words, the detectors must either be separated far enough so that one detector cannot "hear" the other, or they should be synchronized.

Remember that the high-intensity sound of sonic detectors can be heard outside the protected area unless the area is soundproof. The 800 Hz sound will be annoying to anyone who would have to be in the area for an extended period of time. The fact that the audible energy can probably be heard outside the protected area has the potential advantage of discouraging intruders by virtue of its irritating sound.

Sound can escape through cracks around doors and windows and through vents or any opening through which air can pass. Sound also can be regenerated by thin partitions, metal buildings, or glass windows. In this case, the acoustical energy inside the building forces the thin walls or glass to vibrate. The vibrating walls and glass regenerate the sound outside the building but at a lower sound level. The walls and glass do reduce the sound level somewhat.

Sonic detectors can be used to protect areas such as warehouses, industrial plants, schools, or any remote area where the sound will be a deterrent and not a nuisance.

Chapter 12

Passive Volumetric Motion Detectors

Active motion detectors, such as ultrasonic, sonic, and microwave detectors, generate their own energy patterns and recognize a disturbance in that pattern to detect an intruder, while passive motion detectors detect the energy generated by the intruder. In other words, passive detectors do not generate their own energy patterns. They detect the presence or change in the energy as a result of the intruder's presence, or they detect the energy generated during the intrusion. Two types of passive volumetric motion detectors are currently available. One type is an infrared motion detector, and the other is an audio detector.

Infrared motion detectors detect a change in the thermal energy pattern resulting from a moving intruder and initiate an alarm when the change in energy satisfies the detector's alarm criteria. Audio detectors are not motion detectors per se. They depend on the intruder to generate noises, either breaking in or moving within the protected area. When the noise level reaches the detector's alarm threshold, an alarm is activated.

The principles of operation, limitations, and precautions applicable to both infrared and audio detectors are discussed in the following paragraphs.

INFRARED MOTION DETECTORS

Infrared motion detectors detect the body heat of thermal energy at the frequencies corresponding to the body temperature of 98°F. They also detect changes in the background thermal energy caused by someone moving through the detector field of view and shadowing the energy emanating from the objects in the background. The field of view of an infrared detector is similar to the acceptance field of view of active motion detectors. With active detectors, energy within the acceptance field of view of the receiver or transceiver is received and sent to the signal processor. The field of view for infrared detectors is the area or areas in front of the detector that are in view of the detector's thermal sensor element.

Detecting changes in the background, radiant energy is usually the more sensitive mode of detection, depending on the radiation characteristics of the objects in the detector's field of view. All objects with temperatures above absolute zero degrees Kelvin (– 273°C) radiate thermal energy; therefore, regardless of the temperature of the protected room, each object in the room emanates energy. The magnitude and frequency of the radiated energy depends on the absolute temperature and surface finish of the objects. The characteristics of the background energy pattern depend on whether the objects in the detector's field of view are dark or shiny, assuming they are all at the same temperature. Dark objects are more efficient radiators than shiny objects; therefore, a background of objects with different surface finishes will create a greater variation in the radiated thermal energy reaching the sensor when someone passes through the sensor field of view. In general, the probability of detecting someone moving through a varying background will be higher than detecting the same person moving through a constant background. This is especially true in areas where the temperature is about 98°F.

Thermal sensors are responsive to thermal energy with wavelengths between about 1 and 1,000 microns; however, the most popular detection range for infrared detectors is between 8 and 14 microns. The peak radiation for most objects at room temperature occurs at wavelengths of about 10 microns. In an indoor environment, the radiant energy of the exposed skin is also within the 8 to 14 micron wavelength. Clothing reduces the energy incident on the thermal sensor; however, in most applications the magnitude of the radiant energy is adequate for detection.

Thermistor bolometers and thermopile sensors are used to detect thermal energy in the infrared frequency range. Thermistor bolometers can detect radiant energy with wavelengths from the longest infrared to the shortest ultraviolet. Radiant energy impinging on the sensor raises its temperature, causing a change in resistance in the semiconductor oxide material. Infrared detectors using thermistor bolometers monitor the resistance to detect changes characteristic of someone entering the detector's field of view.

Thermopiles are multijunction thermocouples. Each thermocouple consists of a pair of thermoelectric junctions of dissimilar metals. One junction is shielded from the incident radiation, and the second junction is blackened to improve absorption. The difference in the junction temperature between the two dissimilar metals produces an electromotive force (EMF). Detectors using thermopile sensors monitor this EMF to detect radiant energy changes in the detector's field of view.

Two basic signal processing techniques are used to monitor the electrical signals or changes in the signals produced by thermal changes in the sensor. Since the thermal background is constantly changing because of air movement, temperature fluctuations, etc., the signal processor must be able to discriminate between thermal variations in the environment and changes produced by someone in the detector's field of view. One technique is to monitor the rate of change or the speed the signal changes when anyone enters the detector's field of view. The second technique monitors the signals from separate thermal sensing elements to produce signals of opposite polarity. Anyone who enters the sensor's field of view produces multiple signals of the same or opposite polarity. The signal processor analyzes these signals, and when it detects at least two signals of opposite polarity, or even two distinct signals of the same polarity, an alarm is initiated. Both the rate of change and the multiple signal processing techniques require the signal or signals to meet the minimum detection threshold level and to be present within a time window for several seconds before an alarm is initiated.

Mr. Ids illustrates the principles of operation of a multiple beam detector in Figure 12-1. The multiple fields of view are represented by the five conical beams. The wavy lines represent the thermal energy emanating from Mr. Ids in the direction of the detector. As he moves through the sensor beam, his presence is detected either by the detector's sensing a change in the thermal energy caused by his presence or by its sensing a change in the background energy that he is blocking. When the signal changes and acquisition time satisfy the alarm criteria, an alarm is initiated.

A detector's operating frequency band is determined by the characteristics of the filter or combination of filters positioned in front of the thermal sensor. The most popular filter material probably is germanium. Whatever the filter material, it should have qualities to filter thermal energy with wavelengths longer than 2.7 microns to reduce false alarms from sunlight or bright headlights that might shine through a window into the field of view. Infrared energy with wavelengths shorter than 2.7 microns is attenuated by most glass.

Power supplies for infrared detectors are basically identical to those used for active motion detectors, except for the power requirements. Since infrared detectors are passive—that is, they do not generate an energy pattern—their power requirements are less than the requirements for active detectors. As a result, they can operate from batteries like those required to operate active detectors for an extended period of time when AC power is not available. Because of their reduced power requirements, infrared detectors could be used to protect areas where AC power is not available. Of course, the batteries would have to be replaced and recharged on a periodic schedule; however, replacing the batteries might be a minor inconvenience worth the added protection offered by the infrared detectors.

Applications

Infrared detectors are self-contained units—that is, the thermal sensor, signal processor, and power supply are contained in a single unit. Detectors are available with a single long conical field of view or with a multiple beam field of view. Long single beam detectors are used to protect corridors, and

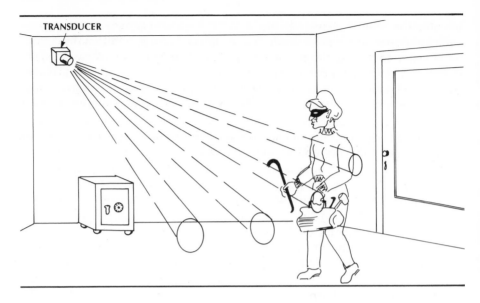

TRANSDUCER

Figure 12–1 Infrared motion detector.

those with multiple beams, like the one shown in Figure 12–1, are used to protect larger open areas. The range of the multiple beam detectors is about 20 to 30 feet with a 70- to 120-degree beam width. The range of single narrow beam detectors is about 50 to 60 feet.

Birds and small flying insects can cause false alarms with infrared detectors, just as they can with active ultrasonic or microwave detectors. With infrared detectors, birds flying near the detector can block the background energy from the thermal sensor, and if the bird is in front of the detector long enough to satisfy the alarm criteria, the result is a false alarm. Because the infrared detector's lens is small, an insect crawling on the lens can shadow the field of view. Again, if the insect is present on the lens long enough, it will cause a false alarm. To reduce the possibility of false alarms, birds and large flying insects should be eliminated from the area where infrared detectors are used.

Another important consideration is to locate infrared detectors away from any heat sources that could produce thermal gradients in front of the detector's lens. Also remove or direct the detector away from any intermittent hot spots in the detector's field of view. For instance, an infrared detectors should never be mounted over or near radiators, heaters, hot pipes, etc. Radiant energy from these sources can produce thermal gradients in the view of the detector's lens that might change the background energy pattern. Depending on the intensity of the heat source, the thermal gradients might cause false alarms.

Hot spots in the detector's field of view also can cause false alarms. For instance, if an unshielded incandescent light is left on within 10 to 15 feet of the detector, it might cause a false alarm if it burns out or goes out as a result of loss of power. The sudden reduction in thermal energy when the light goes off might cause a false alarm. Another source of heat that can cause hot spots is the sun. Sunlight filtered by glass windows is usually not a problem because the glass filters out most infrared energy with wavelengths longer than 2.7 microns. The problem is that the sunlight or radiant energy can heat up a dark object in the field of view enough to cause a thermal change that results in a false alarm. Both the heat sources and hot spots can usually be compensated for if they are considered during system design.

Infrared detectors can be used in rooms or areas in industrial plants, office buildings, schools, retail stores, or where there are no heat sources that might affect the thermal field of view.

PASSIVE AUDIO DETECTORS

Audio detectors are not motion detectors in the same sense that active or infrared detectors are. They do not generate an energy pattern to detect motion, nor do they detect thermal energy emanating from someone in the protected area as do infrared detectors. Audio detectors listen for audible noises generated by an intruder's forced entry into the protected area or for noises from destructive activities within the area. Since they can be used to detect forced entry, audio detectors could be classified as penetration detectors, but they are classified here as motion detectors because any noise that satisfies the detector's alarm criteria, whether it is associated with penetration or movement, will initiate an alarm.

Audio detectors consist of a number of microphones strategically located within the protected area to listen for sounds in the audio frequency range. These sounds are sent to the signal processor in the control unit. The signal processor includes a manual sound level adjustment for setting the sound level alarm threshold above the normal audible background sounds in the protected area. In certain applications it is difficult to adjust the sound level threshold satisfactorily for the prevailing background sound levels. If the threshold is set too high above the normal sounds in the protected area, actual intrusion sounds might not be detected. If the threshold is set just above the normal background sounds, exterior noises might exceed the alarm threshold and cause false alarms.

Two signal processing techniques are used to minimize false alarms caused by exterior noises. One technique is to use an adjustable pulse counting circuit; the second is to use cancellation microphones. Pulse count circuits can be set to initiate an alarm only after counting a selected number of noise bursts or pulses within a specific time period. If there are not a sufficient number of noise pulses within the designated time period to satisfy the alarm criteria, the accumulated pulses will be canceled after about ten minutes. The count circuit will then be ready to start counting the next series of noise pulses. This feature reduces false alarms from noises that exist for only a short time, such as thunder or backfiring vehicles.

The second technique to reduce false alarms from exterior noises or common interior noises is to use cancellation microphones. Cancellation microphones are installed outside the protected facility or near any interior noise sources to listen for sounds that could be received by the microphones. Signals received by the cancellation microphones are used to cancel the corresponding signals received by the detection microphones. This signal cancellation is accomplished in the signal processor. Typical outside noises that could be canceled are those from trucks, airplanes, trains, etc., while inside noises might be from compressors, generators, and fans.

Although pulse count circuits and cancellation microphones do not appreciably affect the detector's effectiveness against a low-skill intruder, they do reduce the probability of detecting an intruder with a higher skill level. A low-skill intruder, such as someone entering a facility for vandalism, usually generates sufficient noise while breaking and entering or while accomplishing his task to satisfy the signal processing alarm criteria. However, higher-level threats might be made by someone who will exercise patience and caution and be extremely quiet. In such a case the intruder might escape detection. This is especially true if cancellation microphones are used and the intruder strikes when there are loud outside noises, such as during an electrical storm.

Some audio detectors detect only high-frequency sounds generated during forced penetration through masonry construction materials such as cinder block, brick, and concrete. They also can detect torch cutting or hacksawing through expanded steel grilles and bars. These materials generate energy over a broad frequency range when they are subjected to forced penetration or cutting. The frequencies generated during these attacks extend well into the ultrasonic frequency range.

As indicated before, one of the limitations in the application of audio detectors is that they are susceptible to alarming by audible energy or noise. To reduce this vulnerability, these audio detectors use bandpass filters that pass only high-frequency signals above 20 kHz to the signal processor. Because these detectors will not detect low-frequency energy, they should not be used to detect penetrations through soft materials such as Sheetrock and wood. Forced penetrations through these soft materials might not generate a sufficient quantity of high-frequency energy to be detected.

Mr. Ids demonstrates the application of an audio detector, used to protect a high school, in Figure 12–2. In this demonstration Mr. Ids is shown breaking the glass of a showcase. The audible sounds are received by the school speaker, which also serves as a microphone for the audio detector. When the magnitude and duration of the sounds satisfy the processor's alarm criteria, an alarm is initiated.

Figure 12-2   Audio detector.

Applications

Audio detectors can be very cost-effective intrusion detection systems when they are used to detect intrusions in facilities such as schools that already have public address systems. In this type of application, the existing speakers can usually be used as microphones for the audio detection system during the hours when the building is secured. In these facilities, however, some of the speakers might be in undesirable locations where they receive exterior sounds. These speakers would have to be disconnected from the audio detection system. Sometimes additional sensors might be required to provide adequate protection in out-of-the-way locations.

A possible limitation of public address speakers is that they might not have the frequency response required to detect breaking glass, especially if the breaking of the glass is far from the speaker. For this reason, many audio detector manufacturers recommend that more sensitive microphones be used with their detectors instead of using the public address microphone. Public address speakers should be used only after their compatibility with the audio detector has been determined.

An application consideration when using audio detectors is that the microphones can provide a means for the central station operator to listen to noises that initiate alarms. For instance, when there is an alarm, the signal transmission line can be connected to the audio detector microphones so that the operator can listen to the noises over a common signal transmission line. If the operator can identify the noises, he can more effectively decide whether a response force is needed. Moreover, the listen-in capability, properly used, can reduce false alarms.

A necessary precaution when relying solely on the alarm station operator to decide whether or not an alarm is valid is to be certain that the operator is familiar with the normal noise environment for each audio detection system in use. The operator must be familiar with these sounds to differentiate between valid intrusion sounds and normal background sounds in the protected facility. Nevertheless, if the number of systems with which one operator must become familiar becomes unmanageable, a valid alarm could be misinterpreted by the operator. In such a case the audio listen-in feature is ineffective. Generally, however, it is a desirable feature that should be considered in the application of audio detectors. Its effectiveness will depend on the proficiency of the central station operator to recognize the normal sounds from each facility.

Audio detectors alone have limited effectiveness and should be depended on only to detect low-skill intruders—intruders who will make a lot of noise while entering or moving within the protected facility. Schools and some retail stores, warehouses, or any interior area with a low-level threat and where the normal background noises are not so loud that they will overwhelm the intrusion noises can be protected with audio devices.

Audio detectors can be combined with other intrusion detectors to improve the level of detection. In this type of application the listen-in feature of the audio detectors can still be used to assist the central station operator in determining the possible cause of the alarm. However, if the combination of detectors is to be used to detect higher-skill intruders, do not count on the intruders to make much noise. In fact, they will probably be very quiet. In a combined system, audio detectors should be used only to verify, not to discount, intrusions.

Chapter 13

Dual Technology Motion Detectors

The previous two chapters have described active and passive volumetric motion detectors separately, but several manufacturers have recently combined these two technologies to form single unit dual channel detectors. These detectors attempt to achieve absolute alarm confirmation while maintaining a high probability of detection. Absolute alarm confirmation ideally is achieved by combining two technologies that individually have a high probability of detection and do not have common false alarm–producing stimuli. If the false alarm suppression of each sensor is poor, the combination performance will probably be poor. This chapter will discuss the basic principles of operation and application of dual technology sensors.

Currently available dual channel motion detectors combine either an active ultrasonic or microwave detector with a passive infrared detector. As previously discussed, ultrasonic and microwave detectors generate their own energy patterns and analyze disturbances in that portion of the energy reflected back to the receiver to determine whether they were caused by someone moving in the protected area. Passive infrared detectors detect thermal changes produced by someone moving through the detector's field of view. The thermal changes can be produced by the presence of a person's body moving through the field or by his blocking the thermal background normally sensed by the detector as he moves in the area. When used in combination, alarms from either the active ultrasonic or microwave detector, depending on the manufacturer's preference, are logically combined with the alarms from the infrared detector in an AND gate logic configuration. The AND gate logic requires nearly simultaneous alarms from both the active and passive sensors to produce a valid alarm.

MICROWAVE/INFRARED DETECTORS

One manufacturer combines one twenty-five zone dual element infrared detector with a primary microwave detector in a single unit for normal applications. It also has a secondary microwave detector that operates independently of the primary microwave for applications in which detection is required under extreme environmental conditions when the background temperature nearly equals the body temperature. This is when the infrared probability of detection might be reduced.

The twenty-five segment multifaceted mirror array is patterned to form a field of view to match the pattern of the wide-angle primary microwave detector. This pattern is teardrop shaped and covers an area about 65 feet deep and 50 feet wide. Thirteen segments of the twenty-five zones are arrayed uniformally to conform to the outer boundary of the microwave pattern. The remaining twelve segments fill in the volume near the detector and under the thirteen segments.

The segmented or zonal field of view creates a pattern of sensitive and insensitive areas. Thermal energy from the twenty-five sensitive segments is focused on dual element pyroelectric transducer. The transducer produces two vertical sensitive areas in each sensor zone or segment. Thermal changes in one segment produce a positive-going electrical signal from one element of the dual element transducer and a corresponding negative-going signal from the second element. In operation, when anyone crosses a sensitive area, he produces a change in the infrared energy at the transducer.

Because of the opposite polarities produced by the dual element transducer, the resulting electrical signal change is significant. When the signal change satisfies the alarm criteria, an alarm signal is generated and is registered at the logic AND gate. The AND gate is a logic circuit that performs one of the fundamental operations of digital technology. If a corresponding alarm signal is registered at the AND gate from the microwave and infrared detectors, the combined alarm signal is allowed to pass to the monitor console.

The microwave detector detects Doppler changes in the reflected microwave energy pattern produced by someone moving in the area with some radial velocity relative to the detector. A gallium arsenide field effect transistor (GaAs FET) microwave source is used to generate the energy pattern. When no one is moving in the energy pattern, the reflected signal is basically zero because there is no Doppler change. When someone moves, he produces phase and, to a lesser degree, magnitude changes in the reflected signal.

When these changes satisfy the alarm criteria for the primary microwave detector, a signal is registered at the logic AND gate. When the secondary detector is used, it operates independently of the combined primary microwave detector and infrared detector. When its alarm criteria are satisfied, it produces an alarm signal directly to the central monitor.

The major difference between the primary and secondary microwave detector is the energy pattern size and detection criteria. The secondary detector generates a smaller but similar teardrop-shaped energy pattern inside the primary pattern. Its size is selectable between being approximately one-half and one-quarter of the primary detector pattern. As with the primary detector, the detection criteria are related to a preset distance the intruder must move in a radial direction in a specified time with respect to the detector.

Another manufacturer of microwave and infrared dual channel detectors has four detector models, which have different pattern sizes and configurations to satisfy a wider range of applications. Like the previous detector, the detection pattern is defined by the teardrop-shaped microwave energy pattern and the passive infrared field of view segments as configured to complement the microwave coverage. Two detector models are designed for applications in open areas. Their patterns are about 40 feet deep and 25 feet wide, and 75 feet deep and 45 feet wide, respectively. The third and fourth models have long, narrow teardrop-shaped patterns of 120 feet and 200 feet for applications in long corridors or narrow areas. An advantage of combining microwave and infrared technologies is that they are complementary in providing long, narrow fields of detection. These units do not, however, have a second microwave detector for applications in high-temperature environments.

ULTRASONIC/INFRARED DETECTORS

Several manufacturers combine active ultrasonic detectors with passive infrared detectors for dual detection. Ultrasonic detectors generate a teardrop-shaped pattern of acoustical energy at frequencies well above those audible to humans. The patterns are typically about 30 feet deep and 25 feet wide. They detect perturbations in the reflected energy from anyone moving in a radial direction in the energy pattern. The infrared detector's field of view segments conform to the ultrasonic energy pattern configuration, including filling in the volume near and under the detector. Anyone moving in the protected area creates a common alarm from the ultrasonic and infrared sensors to the AND gate, which allows the alarm to be transmitted to the monitor console.

Another manufacturer of passive infrared and ultrasonic sensors does not combine its sensors in a common unit. Instead, the alarms from the two separate detectors are wired to a common AND gate. The reason for separate sensors is that ultrasonic detectors are more sensitive to radial motion—someone moving directly toward or away from the detector—than tangential motion—someone moving across the field of view. Conversely, the infrared detector is more sensitive to tangential motion than radial motion. Therefore, to optimize the probability of detection, this manufacturer recommends mounting the two detectors at a right angle to each other with intersecting patterns directed toward the intruder's likely direction of approach.

This manufacturer produces an AND gate module that will accept inputs from any two closed-loop devices. An open-circuit alarm from one sensor for more than ½ second initiates a timer that counts down a preselected time. If, during this countdown, the second sensor initiates an alarm, the AND gate module allows the combined alarm to continue to the monitor console. The AND gate module offers selectable countdown times from 8 to 60 seconds. Selectable countdowns give the user flexibility in configurating two sensors to optimize their performance. The module is particularly useful in upgrading existing systems to take advantage of dual technology using sensors already installed.

Mr. Ids illustrates the principles of operation of dual technology motion detectors in Figures 13–1 and 13–2. Figure 13–1 shows Mr. Ids moving through the combined active energy patterns and passive infrared field of view from a common unit. Figure 13–2 shows Mr. Ids moving through the overlapping active and passive detection zones from separately mounted active ultrasonic and passive infrared motion detectors. In both configurations, when Mr. Ids is detected by both sensor technologies, their individual alarms are combined at the AND gate. When the individual alarms are registered at the AND gate within the preset time window, the combined alarm registers at the monitor console as a system output alarm.

Applications

Combined microwave and infrared detectors cover open areas from 40 feet deep and 25 feet wide up to 75 feet deep and 45 feet wide as well as long,

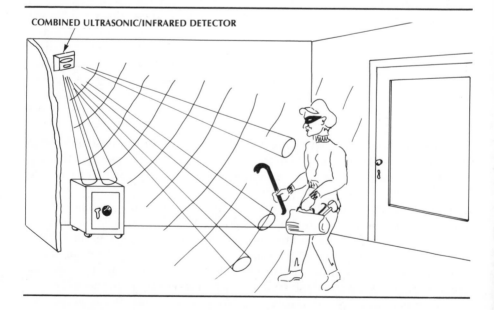

COMBINED ULTRASONIC/INFRARED DETECTOR

Figure 13–1   Combined ultrasonic/infrared motion sensor.

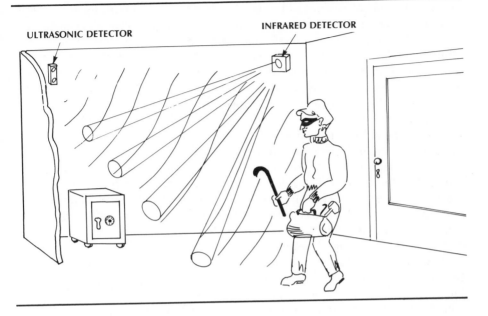

ULTRASONIC DETECTOR

INFRARED DETECTOR

Figure 13-2   Overlapping ultrasonic/infrared motion sensor.

narrow areas up to 200 feet long. Some combined ultrasonic and infrared detectors can cover open areas 25 feet by 25 feet. Separate ultrasonic and infrared detectors can be logically combined through a separate AND gate that can cover the same size open areas.

Separate microwave detectors can be combined with infrared detectors by using the separate AND gate. The primary concern when combining separate microwave and infrared detectors is to remember that a microwave detector's detection zone is usually much larger than an infrared detector's field of view. To achieve maximum area protection, two or more infrared detectors might have to be combined to cover the same detection zone as the microwave detector. In fact, any combination of sensors can be combined using an AND gate, but the sensors must be physically combined so that any act of penetration affects both sensors simultaneously or within the preset combining time window.

Although, in theory, combined technology detectors are more immune to false alarms than single technology detectors, it is important to avoid environments where either detector type would be prone to false alarms. If either detector is exposed to an environment where it experiences a high number of false alarms, then the probability of one of these false alarms being present at the logic AND gate when a false alarm arrives from the second, and perhaps more stable, sensor is high.

For instance, if a combined ultrasonic and infrared detector was installed in a drafty area where the ultrasonic detector could experience a high number of false alarms due to the distortions in its projected energy pattern and the infrared detector might experience a few alarms due to background temperature changes caused by the drafts, the probability of a coincident alarm from both sensors would be increased. A combination microwave and infrared detector would be a far better choice for such an application because the microwave detector would not be affected by this environment. The drafts would still cause temperature changes that could affect the infrared detector, but since it would be combined with the microwave detector, the probability of coincident alarms would be low, and consequently the false alarm rate would be lower.

Combined technology detectors usually have a lower false alarm rate than single technology detectors when the detectors are properly applied and assuming each detector has a low false alarm rate. But it is important to know that when two sensors are logically combined, the probability of detection of the combined detectors will be less than the probability of detection of the individual detectors. For instance, if an ultrasonic motion detector has a probability of detection of 0.95 and it is combined with an infrared detector that also has a probability of detection of 0.95, the combined probability of detection is the product of the individual probabilities of detection, or only 0.90. Also, ultrasonic and microwave detectors have the highest probability of detecting motion directly toward or away from the detector, while infrared detectors have the highest probability of detecting someone moving across the field of view. Therefore, the probability of detection of the combined detectors in a single unit will be less than if the individual detectors are mounted perpendicular to each other with overlapping energy patterns and fields of view. Of course, the cost of the individual detectors will be higher, but if a higher probability of detection is needed for the application, separately mounted logically combined detectors are recommended. To achieve the highest probability of detection, the individual detectors should be separately annunciated.

Chapter 14

Barrier Penetration Detectors

Barrier penetration detectors detect cutting and breaking types of forced entry through walls, ceilings, windows, doors, vaults, etc. They detect penetrations either by sensing the physical phenomena caused by the physical attack on the barrier or by detecting the actual penetration. Vibration detectors and heat sensors detect physical disturbance phenomena; foil tape, breakwire, and grid wire screens detect actual barrier penetrations. Audio detectors, especially those detectors designed to detect actual penetrations, can certainly be used as barrier penetration detectors.

Two types of vibration detectors are available to detect the phenomena generated by physical attacks on barriers. One type detects low-frequency structural vibrations; the second type detects high-frequency breaking glass vibrations. Structural vibration detectors, used for detecting physical attacks on walls and ceilings, detect the low-frequency energy generated by penetration attacks. Glass breakage detectors, used for protecting glass windows or showcase glass, detect the high-frequency energy generated as the glass is broken. Heat sensors detect the heat generated by a torch cutting through metal walls or doors.

Foil tape, breakwire, and grid wire screens detect the actual penetration through walls, ceilings, windows, etc. These devices depend on the forced entry breaking the foil tape or wire. Foil tape and grid wire screens are used primarily to protect windows, but they also can be used on the inside of walls to detect penetrations.

The principles of operation and application of the individual detectors are discussed in the following paragraphs.

STRUCTURAL VIBRATION DETECTORS

Structural vibration detectors detect the low-frequency energy or vibrations generated by a forced attack on the physical barrier in which they are installed. Although vibration detectors can be used to detect penetrations through barriers constructed from any rigid construction material, caution should be exercised before using them to protect walls of lesser structural integrity, such as Sheetrock or thin metal. These types of barriers are more prone to vibrate from external forces that might cause false alarms. In general, if the valuables are worthy of barrier penetration detection, they should be stored behind masonry walls.

In Figure 14–1 Mr. Ids demonstrates the application of a structural vibration detector used to protect physical barriers around an area. In this demonstration Mr. Ids is shown striking a masonry wall with a sledgehammer. Every time he hits the wall, the energy is dissipated, causing the wall to vibrate. The higher-frequency energy is usually attenuated very quickly, but the higher-amplitude lower-frequency energy travels several feet from the point of impact, depending on the construction materials. These vibrations excite the vibration detector's transducers; these in turn send corresponding electrical signals to the detector's signal processor, where they are analyzed. When the signals satisfy the detector's alarm criteria, an alarm is initiated.

The low-frequency energy generated in a forced attack on a barrier is sensed by transducers that are secured directly to the barrier being protected. Two basic types of transducers are used to detect forced entries. One type is the piezoelectric transducer; the other is the mechanical contact switch. Piezoelectric transducers sense the mechanical energy and convert it into electrical signals that are proportional in magnitude to the mechanical vibrations. The piezoelectric transducers used to detect forced entries are basically the same as the transducers used in accelerometers to convert accelerations into electric signals.

Electric signals from the piezoelectric transducers are amplified and sent to the signal processor over shielded or coaxial cables. Shielded cables are required to shield the piezoelectric low-voltage signals from outside electrical interference. Otherwise, electrical interference could totally mask valid signals and probably cause the detector to false alarm. With shielded cables, only valid signals are received and analyzed by the signal processor. To reduce false alarms from single accidental impacts on the protected barrier, most vibration detectors use an adjustable pulse counting accumulator in conjunction with a manual sensitivity adjustment. The count circuit can be set to count a specific number of pulses having a specified magnitude before it will initiate an alarm. Then, when the number of pulses with amplitudes equal to or exceeding the preset threshold is accumulated, an alarm is initiated.

The second type of transducer, the mechanical contact switch, uses a seismic mass that makes the electrical connection between the switch contacts, or it uses a seismic mass to open a switch contact. A seismic mass is simply a small weight that responds to an externally applied force that causes the weight to accelerate. For instance, if you place a small object on a table and strike the table with your fist, the object will bounce. The height of the bounce depends on how hard you hit the table. This is basically how the

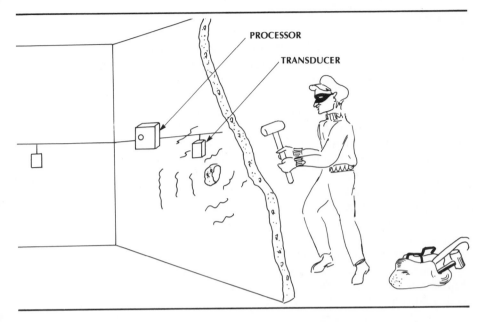

Figure 14–1   Structural vibration detector.

mechanical contact switch functions. When the force of the impact on the protected barrier is adequate to bounce the seismic mass, the contact is opened, generating a momentary open circuit.

In the mechanical switch that used a seismic mass to make electrical contact, the seismic mass is free to vibrate along a vertical axis, returning to rest on the contacts under its own weight. Every time the mass is accelerated or bounced from the contacts, it causes a momentary open circuit. In the unrestricted seismic mass switch, the size of the seismic mass and the spacing between the electrical contacts are designed so that the detector can differentiate between small impacts from normal activity and large impacts from a forced entry. When the seismic mass forms part of the movable switch's contact arm, the force impacts accelerate the seismic mass, which then opens the switch contacts.

The difference between mechanical switches that use a spring-loaded seismic mass and those that use an unrestricted mass is that the spring-loaded mechanical switches rely on the force of the spring to close the contacts, and the unrestricted switch relies on the weight of the seismic mass to make the contact. Since the spring-loaded switches rely on a spring to make the contacts, they can be mounted in any orientation on the wall or ceiling. They usually have an adjustment screw for varying the force on the contact to satisfy the particular application requirement. The switch with the unrestricted seismic mass must always be mounted in a vertical position so that the seismic mass will return to rest on the electrical contacts.

Applications

The primary application advantage of structural vibration detectors is that they provide early warning of a forced entry. Vibration transducers can be installed 8 to 10 feet apart along a wall where a penetration might be expected. The ideal separation of the sensors depends primarily on how well the wall will transmit the impact energy. To ensure that the impact energy is sensed by the transducers, the transducers must be securely fastened to the surface they are protecting. If the vibration detectors are not firmly secured to the walls, it is very unlikely they will sense the vibrations. Furthermore, if possible, each transducer should be protected by a tamper switch located between the transducer case and the mounting surface, to prevent it from being pried from the surface when the area is not monitored.

A primary consideration when applying vibration detectors is that the detector's transducers might generate false alarms if mounted on the walls that are exposed to external vibrations. If the walls are subject to severe vibrations caused by rotating machinery, vibration detectors definitely should not be used. However, there are applications where the protected walls might be subject to an occasional impact. In these applications, vibration detectors with a pulse accumulator or count circuit might be effective. The basic pulse count circuit was described with the signal processor circuit used for piezoelectric transducers. Pulse count circuits that can count contact openings also are available. This type of counter can be beneficially used with mechanical transducers when it is not already part of the basic detector.

Vibration detectors are sometimes connected directly into a control unit that recognizes a momentary open circuit as an alarm, such as the circuit used to monitor door contact switches. In this type of application an alarm will be activated on the first impact at the protected barrier, regardless of whether the impact is accidental or deliberate. Consideration should be given to connecting mechanical vibration detectors to a pulse count circuit that can be adjusted to activate an alarm after the preset number of contact openings have been received. The number of counts should be selected based on the number of impacts required to penetrate the protected barrier. Also, the pulse count accumulator circuit should cancel accumulated counts after a period of about 10 minutes if an insufficient number are not accumulated to initiate an alarm.

One difference between piezoelectric vibration detectors and the mechanical detectors is that the piezoelectric detectors allow greater flexibility in adjusting the sensitivity of the transducers and in presetting the alarm criteria. The sensitivity of the transducers can be adjusted over a range to detect the impacts from whatever forces are required to penetrate a concrete or cinderblock wall. The sensitivity setting also is a function of the actual transducer separation on the protected barrier. Spring-loaded mechanical vibration detectors normally have a screw adjustment to vary the force of impact required to open the contacts. However, the adjustment is often coarse and difficult to make over a broad range of responses. Adjustments on vibration devices should be adequate to compensate for differences in the vibrational characteristics of various protected barriers.

Vibration detectors can be used to protect walls and ceilings, and thereby provide early warnings when the assets being protected attract threats who attempt forced entry.

GLASS BREAKAGE DETECTORS

Glass breakage detectors are similar to structural vibration detectors. The difference is that piezoelectric and mechanical transducers are designed to respond to the higher-frequency energies generated by breaking glass and not the low-frequency structural vibrations. In fact, one of the cautions about selecting glass breakage detectors is their response to low-frequency vibrations. If they are sensitive to low frequencies, they will be prone to false alarms caused by someone knocking on the protected glass.

Another difference is that the signal processor should initiate an alarm on the first high-frequency signal from the piezoelectric transducer or series of pulses from the mechanical transducers. Glass breakage detectors should not be connected into a pulse count circuit, as are structural vibration detectors. They should respond to the first impact on the window because most often only one impact is required to break the window.

Mr. Ids is shown in Figure 14–2 breaking a plate glass window protected with glass breakage detectors. As Mr. Ids's hammer hits the glass, it starts vibrating at frequencies much higher than structural-type material. These high frequencies cause the glass to break as they travel away from the point of impact toward the outer edges of the window. These vibrations excite the glass breakage transducers, which generate electrical signals monitored by the signal processor. When these signals satisfy the short-duration alarm criteria, an alarm is initiated.

Applications

A single glass breakage transducer can protect about 100 square feet of plate glass. Larger glass windows might require two or more detectors. The detectors are usually mounted in the corner of the window approximately 2 inches from the edge of the frame.

Like the structural vibration transducers, the glass breakage transducers must be securely fastened to the glass in order to respond to the high-frequency vibrations. If the transducers are loose, they cannot respond to the breaking glass, and they might cause false alarms if they should come loose and strike something hard. Therefore, the adhesive used to bond the trans-

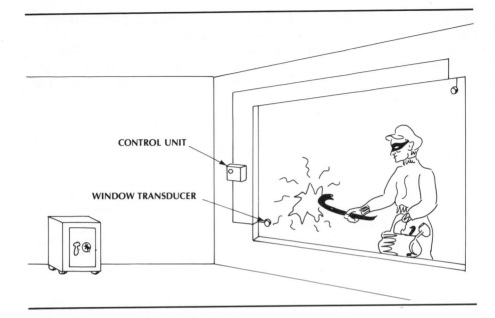

Figure 14–2   Glass breakage detector.

ducers or the adhesive pads should be in compliance with the detector manufacturer's specifications. The adhesive should be able to withstand long exposures to summer heat, winter cold, and condensation that might collect on the window. The glass can get as hot as 150°F in the summer and as cold as – 30°F in the winter. These temperatures can be even more severe in some environments. The bonding adhesive should hold even in these extreme environments.

Glass breakage detectors can be used to detect breakage of any type or size plate glass window. A feature of these detectors is that they can provide this detection without being as conspicuous as foil tape.

HEAT SENSORS

Heat sensors respond to the physical phenomena of an intrusion by detecting the heat generated by a cutting torch or burn bar while cutting through a metal barrier such as a safe or vault door. The sensor consists of a thermostat that opens an electrical contact when the temperature of the mounting surface reaches a preset temperature. The detection temperature for heat detectors used to protect metal barriers is between 135°F and 165°F.

A thermostatic heat sensor uses a mechanically restricted bimetallic strip that distorts with increasing temperature until the preset temperature is reached. At this time the bimetallic strip has distorted to its limit and snaps open. When it opens, the electrical contacts open, and an alarm is activated.

Applications

Heat sensors can be used to detect thermal attacks on vault doors, safes, or any metal surface. A precaution applicable to heat detectors is that the temperature of the protected surface must reach the preset temperature before an alarm can be activated. If the intruder should use a cutting technique that does not generate enough heat to raise the temperature of the protected surface to 135°F, an access hole might be cut through the protected barrier without being detected.

FOIL TAPE

Foil tape is a metallized conductive tape used to protect window glass and other barriers against forcible entry. In the case of windows, the tape should be secured around the perimeter of the glass within 2 to 4 inches of the window frame. When the glass is broken, as demonstrated by Mr. Ids in Figure 14–3, the glass severs the foil tape, thus initiating an alarm.

Often foil tape is installed on a glass window in a closed-loop pattern. A closed loop is formed when the installer starts applying the tape in one corner of the glass and continues around the periphery of the glass until he returns to the starting point, connecting the tape to the terminal strip where he started. This type of installation can be surreptitiously compromised dur-

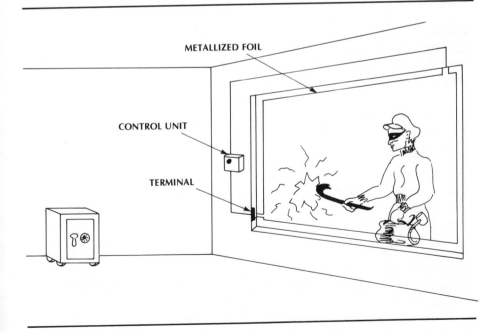

Figure 14–3   Foil tape detector.

ing open hours by electrically shorting or bridging between either the ends of the foil tape or the terminal connections with a piece of conductive material. The intruder can then return after closing and knock out the window to gain entry without being detected.

To eliminate this type of compromise, the tape should be installed so that it can be electrically supervised at the alarm's signal transmitter with either double-circuit protection or end-of-line impedance terminations. Double-circuit protection supervises one section of the foil when one electrical polarity is provided by an electrical DC source, which could be a battery, connected across the ends of the foil tape. If the foil tape is cut, there is an open circuit, and if the circuit is electrically shorted, there is a loss of signal. Either attempted compromise initiates an alarm. An end-of-line impedance termination, either a resistor or a resistor/capacitor network, is connected across the end of the foil tape. The end-of-line impedance is monitored by a balanced bridge network in the alarm signal transmitter. If the foil is cut or shorted, the bridge becomes unbalanced, initiating an alarm. Regardless of the type of circuit supervision, an alarm should be initiated if the foil tape is cut, broken, or electrically shorted. Normally the foil circuit should be supervised 24 hours a day, whether the area is open or closed. Continually supervising the circuit will reduce the possibility of someone compromising the protection.

Applications

Foil tape can be used to detect breaking glass windows. In this application the tape is installed around the window about 2 to 4 inches from the frame. After the tape is installed on the glass, an adhesive or protective coating should be applied over the tape to protect it from splitting. The coating material should be resistant to aging, moisture, and temperature changes.

Foil tape also can be used to detect penetrations through walls and other barriers. It should be installed directly on the wall. The tape should be installed in a continuous strip along the wall, parallel to the floor at a level that is below that convenient for penetration. The strips should be continuously installed in parallel rows spaced approximately 5 to 6 inches apart until the wall is protected to a height above the anticipated level of penetration. Of course, electrical splices might have to be made in the tape to maintain electrical continuity.

After the tape is installed on the walls, it should be covered with a material to conceal it from view and protect it from day-to-day abuse. The tape could be covered with Sheetrock, plywood paneling, or wallpaper. The disadvantage of such an installation is that if the tape breaks, it will be difficult to repair.

A consideration in using foil tape to detect breaking window glass is that the tape is very visible and the intruder may choose to avoid the window and enter at another location. Depending on the size of the glass, he might choose to make a hole in the center of the glass and enter undetected. A feature of foil tape is that it could be a psychological deterrent to some would-be intruders.

BREAKWIRE GRIDS

A breakwire grid is a closely spaced grid pattern created by a continuous electrical wire forming a closed electrical circuit. The breakwire can be installed directly on the barrier requiring protection, or it can be installed in a grille or screen that is, in turn, installed on the barrier or over an opening requiring protection. Breakwire grids should be continually supervised, and when a forcible entry penetrates the protected surface and breaks the wire, the electrical continuity is interrupted and an alarm is initiated.

Applications

The wire used to form the breakwire grid should be solid hard-drawn insulated wire with a tensile strength of less than 4 pounds. The wire size should be no longer than No. 24 American Wire Gauge (AWG) and should be capable of carrying an electrical current of 60 milliamperes at 60 volts with a temperature rise of no more than 1°C. If the breakwire grid is installed directly on the surface requiring protection, it should be covered with Masonite, plywood, or Sheetrock to conceal the wire from possible compromise and to protect it from day-to-day abuse. The breakwire grid should be connected to an electrically supervised circuit and continuously monitored.

Breakwire grids and screens can be used to detect forcible penetrations through vent openings, floors, walls, ceilings, locked storage cabinets, vaults, and skylights. They also can be used to detect penetrations through doors, but the electrical connection between the door's grid wire and the signal wire must be able to withstand the continuous opening and closing of the door.

Chapter 15

Operable Opening Switches

Operable openings are doors, windows, gates, hatches, or other movable objects that can be opened to gain access to closed areas. Therefore, operable opening switches are devices used to detect anyone moving or opening protected doors, windows, etc. The types of devices used to detect anyone using these openings are balanced magnetic, magnetic, mechanical contact, and tilt switches.

An important consideration in protecting doors, before selecting any type of door switch, is to evaluate the durability of the door itself. Doors range in durability from vault doors to hollow-core doors often used in homes. The durability of the door is an important consideration because an intruder can simply cut or knock a hole through the door to gain access. He does not have to open the door. Remember, an operable opening switch will detect only an intruder who is polite enough to open the door when entering the protected area. Of course, durability considerations apply to any type of opening requiring protection.

Another consideration in protecting doors or windows is that the doors or windows should be securely fastened to prevent movement caused by wind or some other force. Excessive movement might cause an operable opening switch to false alarm. Therefore, loose doors and windows should be fixed so that they can be securely fastened before any contact switches are installed.

Regardless of the type of switch used to protect a door, it should be installed along the top of the door near the leading edge, if possible. In this position there is greater displacement between the door and door frame than at any other position along the top of the door, with respect to the angular displacement. Because the door displacement is greater at the leading edge, the sensitivity of the switch is not as critical in terms of alarm position, and the switch will not be as sensitive to small displacements if the door is slightly loose.

BALANCED MAGNETIC SWITCHES

Balanced magnetic switches consist of a switch assembly that is usually mounted on the door or window frame and a balancing magnet mounted on the movable door or window. The electric contact switch is a three-position reed switch mounted adjacent to an adjustable biasing magnet in the switch assembly. The reed switch is held in the balanced or center no alarm position by two interacting magnetic fields. The primary field is generated by the balancing magnet and the secondary field by a small biasing magnet. As long as the magnetic field remains balanced around the reed switch, the contacts remain in contact in the center position. If the balancing magnet is moved or the magnetic field is unbalanced by an external magnet, the switch becomes unbalanced and initiates an alarm.

A typical application of a balanced magnetic switch is illustrated in Figure 15–1, where Mr. Ids is shown coming through a protected entrance door. The balanced magnetic switch assembly is mounted on the door frame, and the balancing magnet is mounted on the door. When the door is closed, the magnetic field generated by the balancing magnet interacts with the field from the biasing magnet so that the net magnetic force acting on the reed switch is zero. Since the net force is zero, the contact remains closed. When Mr. Ids opens the door, the balancing magnet is moved away from the switch

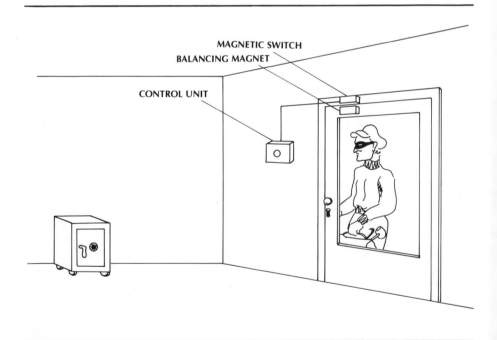

Figure 15–1 Balanced magnetic switch detector.

assembly, and the field is no longer balanced. The force from the biasing magnet displaces the reed switch contact arm, thereby initiating an alarm.

Applications

The balanced magnet switch assembly should be mounted on the door frame near the leading edge of the door and the activating magnet mounted on the door directly under the switch assembly, as shown in Figure 15–1. The position where the displacement of the door initiates an alarm can be controlled by adjusting the biasing magnet in the switch assembly. The switch should be adjusted to initiate an alarm when the door is opened between ½ and 1 inch.

Balanced magnetic switches provide a higher level of protection for doors than either magnetically and mechanically activated contacts or tilt switches. But the protection is only as good as the penetration resistance of the door, and it is adequate only if the intruder opens the door to enter.

CONTACT SWITCHES

Both magnetically and mechanically activated contact switches are available to detect anyone opening a protected door or window. Magnetic contact switches are similar to balanced magnetic switches only inasmuch as they are both magnetically activated. A magnetic contact switch is a two-position reed switch rather than a three-position switch. Therefore, instead of the reed contact switch being held in a balanced magnetic field, the two-position switch is held either in an open or closed position when the door or window is closed. The no-alarm contact position depends on whether the signal monitoring circuit recognizes an open or closed contact to initiate an alarm. In a circuit where the monitor recognizes an open circuit as an alarm condition, the switch would be installed so that when the door is opened, moving the magnetic field, the switch opens and initiates an alarm. In general, the contact switch is mounted on the door frame, with the activating magnet mounted on the door.

Mechanically actived contact switches are available with either push-button or level actuators. Push-button switches are normally mounted on the hinge side of the door frame. When a door is opened, the switch contacts open and initiate an alarm. Since the push-button switch is mounted on the hinge side of the door frame, the position at which the door is opened far enough to initiate an alarm is critical. If the door can be opened far enough to slide a thin piece of metal over the push-button, the switch can be defeated. Lever-type switches are usually installed on a door frame along the top of the door so that when the door is closed, it holds the switch closed.

When the door is opened, the lever opens, allowing the switch contacts to open.

Applications

Magnetically and mechanically activated switches can be used to protect doors and windows, but they should be used only to protect against a low-skill threat. Even then, caution should be exercised in their application and installation.

Mechanical contact switches are vulnerable to compromise, especially if there is a crack between the door and door frame that will allow an intruder to slide a thin piece of plastic or metal through the crack and hold the switch closed while opening the door. To prevent this type of compromise, install molding around the edge of the door to cover the crack.

Mechanical contact switches also are vulnerable to someone installing tape over the push-button or activating lever during the day when the door is not monitored. The intruder can then return after closing and open the door undetected.

Chapter 16

Active Barrier Detectors

Barrier detectors are used in intrusion detection systems across entrances leading into protected areas and across probable routes an intruder would take inside the protected areas. Photoelectric detectors are the most popular inside-barrier detectors. The newer active infrared detectors form an invisible beam of light in the infrared frequency range between a transmitter located on one side of the area requiring protection and a receiver located on the opposite side. When anyone interrupts or breaks the beam, the infrared energy is blocked from the receiver, thus initiating an alarm.

Trip-wire devices also are used as barrier detectors, but they are becoming unpopular because they must be set up and taken down at closing and opening. This task quickly becomes a nuisance, especially if the protected area has more than one or two trip-wire devices.

Barrier detectors can be easily avoided, especially if they are visible or the intruder is aware of their existence, because the barrier usually consists only of a single beam or trip wire. The beam or trip wire is installed about 30 inches from the floor. At this level, if the intruder can see it, he can simply crawl under the beam undetected. If the beam is lower than 30 inches, the intruder can probably step over it. Therefore, any barrier detector should be concealed or disguised to minimize its vulnerability to defeat, and at least two beams should be used to reduce the vulnerability to an intruder crawling under the barrier.

PHOTOELECTRIC DETECTORS

Photoelectric beam detectors consist basically of a light transmitter and a separate receiver. The light transmitter is located on one side of the entrance or area requiring protection, and the receiver is positioned on the opposite side of the entrance to receive the radiant energy from the transmitter. In earlier photoelectric detectors an incandescent lamp was the light source in the transmitter. The light, radiating from the lamp, passed through a lens that collimated the light source. The light then passed through a red filter to reduce its visibility. The collimated beam was projected onto a photoelectric cell in the receiver. The photoelectric cell converted radiant energy into an electrical signal that was amplified for the detector's processor. In actual applications, the photoelectric detector initiated an alarm when interruption of the radiant energy incident on the photocell satisfied the alarm criteria. The red beam of light, formed by the incandescent lamp, was visible and therefore easy to bypass.

Photoelectric detectors are used for many applications other than as intrusion detection devices. Some of these applications include automatic door openers, automatic feed packaging systems, safety barriers, and many other automatic systems. In these types of applications, the visible light beam does not affect the function of the device. But for the photoelectric device to be an effective intrusion detection barrier, the light beam should be virtually invisible to the naked eye. Gallium arsenide LEDs are now being used because they generate a beam of light in the infrared frequency range that is virtually invisible to the naked eye. Thick fog and smoke in the area of the beam will scatter the light particles, making the beam visible, especially near the transmitter. Gallium LEDs are solid-state devices that are highly shock and vibration resistant and have about a 10-year life expectancy.

Photoelectric detector light beams should be modulated to minimize the possibility of an intruder defeating the detector with another light source. Modulating the light beam requires only that it be pulsed at a specific frequency. The result of the modulation is that the intensity of the light source changes as many as one thousand times a second. The frequency of the modulated light source is recognized by the detector processor. This feature makes it very difficult for an intruder to substitute another light source, even a pulsed light source, to compromise the detector. An added benefit of modulation is that detectors using modulated light beams are less susceptible to false alarms from sunlight or other light sources.

Both constant beam and modulated beam photoelectric detectors should initiate an alarm when 90 percent or more of the beam is interrupted for a period of no more than 75 milliseconds. The detector's obscuration time (the time the light beam is obscured from the receiver) should respond to a momentary interruption caused by an intruder running through the light beam.

In Figure 16–1, Mr. Ids demonstrates the application of a photoelectric detector used to protect across a number of aisle entrances in a warehouse. The detector is mounted in the wall on the side of the warehouse, approximately 30 inches from the floor. It is concealed in the wall in such a manner that it is difficult to detect. When Mr. Ids interrupts the modulated beam of invisible light, the infrared energy focused on the photoelectric cell is momentarily blocked, resulting in a loss of signal. The loss of signal is detected by the signal processor initiating an alarm.

Figure 16–1 Photoelectric detector.

Applications

Photoelectric detectors are available with beam ranges between the transmitter and receiver from 75 to 1,000 feet. The detectors can be installed with the transmitter and receiver in the line of sight, as illustrated in Figure 16–1, or mirrors can be used to redirect the beam. With mirrors the photoelectric beam can be reflected around corners, increasing the protected barrier from a single detector. For instance, in the case of the warehouse in Figure 16–1, the aisle entrances at both ends of the warehouse could be protected by installing the transmitter in one corner, then redirecting the infrared beam in three corners to form a square or rectangle around the area with the shelves. The third mirror then reflects the beam to the receiver located adjacent to the transmitter.

Several application limitations associated with the use of mirrors to redirect the photoelectric beam should be considered. One is that the range of a photoelectric detector is reduced when mirrors are used. The photoelectric beam strikes the mirror, and only part of the incident energy is reflected. The remaining part is refracted and scattered. Each mirror added to the system reduces the beam's intensity. If the area being protected is dusty, dust accumulating on the mirrors and detector lenses will contribute to scattering of the photoelectric beam and reduce the intensity even further. Alignment is another consideration when using mirrors. If a mirror becomes misaligned for any reason, the photoelectric beam's continuity will be interrupted, resulting in an alarm. The misaligned mirror will have to be realigned before the detector is operational. Therefore, to prevent misalignment, the detectors and mirrors should be securely mounted on a surface that does not vibrate. Caution should be exercised when using mirrors with photoelectric detectors, especially for covering long ranges. Mirrors are not recommended for long-range applications.

Another consideration to reduce the vulnerability of an intruder bypassing the photoelectric beam is to install at least two detectors to form a barrier. One detector can be installed approximately 12 inches, and the second detector 30 inches, from the floor. This type of barrier configuration will increase the level of detection. Mirrors also can be installed to reflect the photoelectric beam back and forth to form a fencelike pattern across the entrance. One fence configuration can be formed by installing the transmitter approximately 30 inches from the floor and the receiver 12 inches from the floor on the opposite wall. A mirror is installed on the wall opposite the transmitter to reflect the light beam back to a spot about 18 inches under the transmitter. Another mirror is installed at that spot to reflect the light beam onto the photoelectric cell in the detector receiver. The resulting fence pattern looks like a z. This is only one fence configuration, and others can be formed.

Photoelectric detectors are not susceptible to many of the stimuli affecting active ultrasonic or microwave detectors or passive infrared detectors; however, there are conditions that can affect their performance. Smoke and dust in the air (fog for outside detectors) scatter the photoelectric light beam until, depending on the density of the particles, the incident energy on the photoelectric cell is reduced to a level that causes the detector to initiate an alarm. Falling objects, birds, small animals, or anything that could interrupt the photoelectric beam long enough can initiate an alarm. Variations in the background light levels or sunlight might cause false alarms. Detectors using modulated light beams are less susceptible to alarming caused by illumination variations.

Photoelectric detectors can be used to protect entrances and to form a square or rectangular barrier to protect an open or enclosed area. If the threat can be expected to enter the area through the roof or locations that bypass the barrier, however, the detector will be ineffective. Like any other detector, the application of photoelectric detectors depends on the sophistication of the threat.

TRIP-WIRE DEVICES

A trip-wire device consists of a spring-loaded switch and a spring-loaded wire that can be stretched across the entrance to a protected area or across any path an intruder might take after entering the area. The trip wire is connected to the switch, which initiates an alarm if the wire is bumped, stretched, or retracted. When anyone comes in contact with the wire, the wire stretches, disconnecting the switch that initiates an alarm. The wire is also part of a supervised circuit to detect cutting. Some trip-wire devices have the wire attached to a retractable spool for storing when the area is open. An advantage of a trip wire is that it will not initiate an alarm unless someone or something comes in contact with the wire. Therefore, false alarms from trip-wire devices are minimal.

Applications

Trip-wire devices are becoming unpopular, especially in industrial applications, because they require resetting each night; however, they can be used for low-threat applications where resetting is not a nuisance.

Chapter 17

Proximity and Point Sensors

Proximity and point sensors detect anyone approaching, touching, or attempting to remove valuable items, or attempting to penetrate high-value storage areas. These sensors are discussed together in this chapter because they provide the innermost level of protection. They give the response force the least amount of time to respond to an alarm once the intruder is detected, but the amount of response time depends on whether the item is openly displaced and physically unprotected or physically protected in a safe. If the items requiring protection are readily accessible, such as art objects in a museum, the guards should be in the immediate area so that they can respond quickly to any alarms. Even though proximity and point sensors provide the innermost level of protection, they are essential in many intrusion detection system applications.

Capacitance proximity detectors protect metal items such as safes and file cabinets. They detect changes in the electrical capacitance between the item being protected and an electrical ground plane under the item. Capacitance detectors also can be used to protect valuable items such as artifacts or oil paintings by mounting the detectors on a metal surface isolated from the ground plane. Pressure mats can be used as proximity detectors if they can be concealed, for instance, under a carpet. Anyone approaching the protected item will initiate an alarm when stepping on the mat.

Pressure switches and mechanical vibration transducers can be used as point sensors. In such applications the point sensors initiate an alarm when the protected item is picked up or moved. To ensure that an alarm will be initiated, the protected item should be well secured to its mounting surface so that it is impossible to remove the item without initiating an alarm.

A caution about using pressure switches and mats is that they can often be easily defeated or bypassed if the intruder is aware of their existence. Other point sensor and proximity detector application considerations, along with the sensors' principles of operation, will be discussed in the following paragraphs.

CAPACITANCE PROXIMITY SENSORS

Capacitance proximity sensors can detect anyone either approaching or touching metal items or containers that the sensors are protecting. Capacitance detectors operate on the same principle as electrical capacitors. A capacitor is an electronic component that consists of two conductor plates separated by a dielectric medium. A change in the electrical charge or dielectric medium results in a change in the capacitance between the two plates. In the case of the capitance proximity detector, one plate is the metal item being protected, and the second plate is an electrical reference ground plane under and around the protected item. The metal object is isolated from the ground plane by insulating blocks. This leaves only air around and between the metal object and ground. Therefore, air is the dielectric medium.

In operation, the metal object is electrically charged to a potential that creates an electrostatic field between the object and reference ground. The strength of the field is nonlethal, but it is adequate to cause a detectable change in the capacitance if anyone approaches or touches the object. The electrical conductivity of the intruder's body alters the dielectric characteristics. The dielectric changes result in a change in the capacitance between the protected item and the reference ground. When the net capacitance change satisfies the alarm criteria, an alarm is activated.

The detector's sensitivity can be increased to detect an intruder approaching a protected item or lowered to require the intruder to touch the item. Although some detectors can be adjusted to detect an intruder at a distance up to 5 feet from the protected object, this level of sensitivity is not recommended unless it is required for some specific application. The level of sensitivity should be limited to detect the intruder at a distance of about 6 inches or even require him to touch the item to initiate an alarm.

A lower sensitivity will not affect the response time but will help reduce false alarms. If the detector's sensitivity is adjusted to detect an intruder 4 feet from the protected item, the electrostatic field close to the item would be very sensitive, perhaps sensitive enough to cause false alarms.

The sensitivity of capacitance detectors is affected by changes in relative humidity and the relocation of other metal objects closer to or away from the protected item. Changes in the relative humidity vary the dielectric characteristics. An increase in the relative humidity causes the conductivity to increase and reduces the capacitance. Conversely, a decrease in humidity or a drying of the air reduces the conductivity. When a metal object is moved close to a protected object, it is electrically coupled to the object by the electrostatic field. The object basically increases the size of the capacitor plate and reduces the capacitance monitored by the detector.

The capacitance detector's signal processor is basically a balanced bridge circuit with the protected metal object as part of the circuit. Anyone approaching or touching the object changes the capacitance, thus unbalancing the circuit and initiating an alarm. Initially, the circuit must be adjusted either automatically or manually to balance the bridge. If the circuit is adjusted manually, then every time metal objects are moved closer to or away from the object, the circuit must be rebalanced. Sometimes manually adjusted sensors need readjusting when the seasons change to compensate for changing humidity. For instance, if the detector is adjusted in the summer when the relative humidity is high, it must be readjusted when winter comes and the heating system dries the air.

Capacitance detectors using a self-balancing circuit adjust automatically to the changes in relative humidity and relocation of metal objects close to the protected item. Detectors with an automatic or self-balancing circuit should be considered when selecting a capacitance detector.

Applications

A typical application of a capacitance proximity detector protecting a safe and two file cabinets is shown in Figure 17–1, where Mr. Ids is attempting to open the safe. Although the sensitivity is set to detect someone within about 6 inches of the protected items, it is still adequate to detect Mr. Ids, even though he is wearing heavy gloves in an attempt to defeat the detector. When Mr. Ids reaches the safe, his presence alters the capacitance of the balanced or tuned circuit and initiates an alarm.

Notice that the safe and file cabinets in Figure 17–1 are set on blocks to isolate them from the ground plane. These blocks should be made of a nonconductive plastic or nonhydroscopic material. Wooden blocks should not be used because they are hydroscopic and might absorb enough moisture over a period of time to change the dielectric enough that the protected objects become insensitive. Wooden locks are very susceptible to absorbing moisture when used to isolate objects from tile floors, especially if the floor is wet-mopped. Every time the floor is mopped, water coming in contact with the blocks is absorbed until the blocks become so conductive that the object is no longer isolated from the ground plane, resulting in an alarm.

Sometimes safes or items requiring protection are located in areas with poor grounding conditions. In such places a reference or ground plane can be established by installing a metal sheet or screen under the item. The metal can be grounded by connecting it to a cold water pipe or to a reference ground that is part of the signal processor. For instance, if the safe and file cabinets in Figure 17–1 were sitting on a carpeted wooden floor, a wire screen could be installed under the carpet and electrically grounded to a cold water pipe. This type of installation usually increases the detector's sensitivity because it provides better electrical coupling between the protected items and the reference ground plane.

Capacitance proximity detectors also can be used to protect paintings, tapestries, and other art objects by installing a relatively large copper foil sheet or metal screen under the objects requiring protection. In this type of

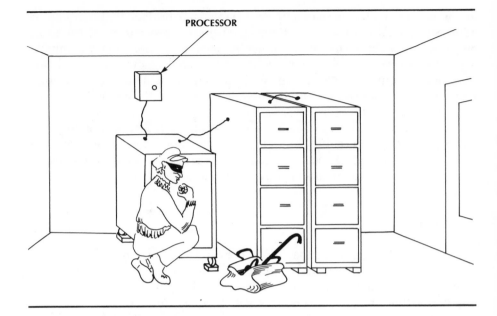

Figure 17-1　Capacitance proximity detector.

application the metal screen becomes part of the protected circuit, as is the safe or any other metal object. The metal sheet should be large enough to provide an adequate capacitance change to detect anyone approaching or attempting to remove the item or items of value.

The primary consideration in using capacitance proximity detectors is that the intruder is at the protected item when he is detected. Therefore, the item of value should have adequate physical protection to protect it until the response force can arrive, or the guards should be close enough to respond immediately. Like any other sensor application, the value of the assets, the threat, and the response force should be carefully considered.

PRESSURE MATS

Pressure mats can be used as proximity detectors to detect anyone approaching valuable objects, or they can be used as barrier detectors to protect entrances leading to areas requiring protection. Pressure mats are available as individual mats for multiple application purposes and as continuous runners that can be cut to any length. Individual mats are usually used for protecting small areas, such as at entrances, under windows, or on steps. Runners are installed under carpets to cover larger areas, such as in the area of a safe or other valuable objects.

Pressure mats consist of a series of ribbon switches positioned parallel to each other approximately 3 inches apart along the length of the mat. Ribbon switches are constructed from two strips of metal in the form of a ribbon separated by an insulating material. They are constructed so that when an adequate amount of pressure, depending on the application, is exerted anywhere along the ribbon, the metal strips make electrical contact. Individual ribbon switches are available in lengths up to 20 feet, but the switches used in pressure mats or runners are about 2 to 3 feet long. The series of switches forming the mat are electrically wired in parallel, and the assembly is sealed between two plastic sheets or molded in rubber to form a durable, weatherproof mat.

Applications

Pressure mats have many industrial and commercial applications, as well as security applications. In security applications they can be used a doormats, under windows, on steps, along probable intruder routes, or around valuable objects. When using pressure mats in security applications, the mats should be well concealed under carpets or even under tile or linoleum floor coverings. If the intruder is aware of their existence, however, he can just step or bridge over the mat.

Pressure mats alone should be used only to detect low-skill intruders. An intruder who would enter the protected area without prior planning gives little consideration to the fact that the area is protected. Pressure mats can be used along with other sensors in a system designed to provide a higher level of protection.

POINT SENSORS

Pressure switches and mechanical vibration transducers can be used as point sensors. Pressure switches can be mechanically activated contact switches or single ribbon switches used in pressure mats. Normally open switches are used as point sensors; then, when the item requiring protection is placed on the switch, it closes the contacts. Anyone removing the item relieves the mechanical actuator and allows the switch to open and initiate an alarm. The switch should be well concealed. Also, the interface between the switch and protected item should be offset or secured together so that a thin piece of material cannot be slid under the object to override the switch while the object is being removed.

Vibration transducers are secured to the item being protected rather than to the mounting surface, as is the case with most mechanical contact switches. When the protected object is removed, the forces required in the act of removing the object will cause the vibration transducer to initiate a series of open-circuit pulses. These pulses are detected by the supervisory circuit and initiate an alarm. Items being protected by vibration switches or transducers should be physically secured to their mounting surfaces to ensure that adequate force is required to initiate an alarm as the item is being removed. Signal wires to the transducer should be kept short and well secured.

Applications

Point sensors can be used to protect art objects or any similar items that can be easily carried away. The primary consideration when using point sensors is that the response guard should be close to the protected item.

Chapter 18

Application Guidelines

The intent of this summary is to present a list of basic guidelines that should be considered in the selection, design, installation, and operation of interior intrusion detectors.

ULTRASONIC MOTION DETECTORS

1. Avoid using ultrasonic detectors in areas with large volumes of moving air caused by open windows, doors, vents, etc.
2. Avoid directing the transceivers at large glass windows, nonrigid partitions, warehouse doors, etc., that might vibrate and cause false alarms.
3. Avoid pointing transceivers directly at each other unless they are separated by an adequate distance (usually about 60 feet) to prevent interference.
4. Avoid locating individual receivers or transceivers close to air-conditioning and heating registers.
5. Position the transceivers and separate receivers at least 10 feet from telephone bells or other types of bells (unless otherwise indicated by the manufacturer).

MICROWAVE MOTION DETECTORS

1. Avoid locating detectors closer than 10 feet to bare fluorescent lamps, especially if the detectors will be pointed toward the lamp, without first determining that the fluorescent lamps will not affect the detectors.
2. Avoid directing the transmitted energy toward nonrigid metal partitions, thin metal walls, or large metal doors that might be vibrated by wind, passing trucks, airplanes, etc.
3. Avoid directing the transmitted energy toward windows, wooden walls, or any wall that the energy can penetrate and perhaps detect outside movement through.
4. Avoid directing the transceivers toward rotating or moving machinery.

5.   After an installation is complete, check movement outside the protected area that might cause alarms. (Remember, cars and trucks are
larger targets and can cause alarms when at greater distances than
humans.)

SONIC MOTION DETECTORS

Consider the fact that sonic detectors generate an audible high-frequency
tone that might be heard several hundred feet from the area being protected,
depending on the building's construction.

INFRARED MOTION DETECTORS

1.   Avoid directing the detectors toward heat sources that cycle on and off.
2.   Avoid directing the detectors toward burning incandescent lamps.
3.   Avoid mounting the detectors over heat sources such as radiators or hot
pipe lines.
4.   Avoid directing the detectors toward windows where sunlight enters.

DUAL TECHNOLOGY DETECTORS

All the basic guidelines that apply to each individual detector forming the
dual technology detector apply to dual technology detectors.

AUDIBLE DETECTORS

Avoid locating the receivers close to inside noise sources or near outside
walls or doors where exterior noises could be a problem.

VIBRATION DETECTORS

1.   Both structural and glass breakage detectors should be well secured to
the surface where they are detecting penetrations.
2.   Structural vibration detectors should be connected to a pulse
accumulating supervisory circuit that can be adjusted for the specific
application and not alarm on a single impact.

OPERABLE OPENING SWITCHES

Doors and windows should be well secured to prevent excessive motion that might cause false alarms.

PHOTOELECTRIC DETECTORS

1. Mount transmitters and receivers, along with any mirror, securely on vibration-free surfaces.
2. Avoid using mirrors with detectors covering ranges more than 100 feet.
3. Conceal transmitters and receivers to reduce compromise.

CAPACITANCE PROXIMITY DETECTORS

1. Avoid using wooden blocks to isolate the protected metal object from the ground plane.
2. The reference ground plane should be well grounded to provide an adequate electrical potential differential between the metal object and ground.

PRESSURE MATS

Conceal pressure mats to reduce compromise.

PART IV

ALARM STATION MONITORING SYSTEM

The alarm monitoring system is one of the three primary components of an effective intrusion detection system, along with the intrusion detection sensors and the alarm response force. It is important because if no one receives the alarm signal initiated by the sensors, the response force or other key personnel will not be alerted to the emergency. In fact, this is the primary reason for using a central alarm station. Trained monitoring operators should always be available to monitor the alarm display panels and to alert the proper authorities in case of an emergency.

An alarm station is the control center where the alarm, access/secure status, and other status signals from the protected areas are received and the information is displayed for the alarm station operators. This information can be manually recorded by the station operator, but most central alarm stations have event recorders or line printers to perform this function. Automatic recording devices are almost a necessity, especially in large central stations. They relieve the station operators of the tedious task of recording the status information and thereby allow them to devote full attention to their primary duties of monitoring the displays.

Many functions can be performed by a central alarm station besides monitoring intrusion alarms. They can be used to monitor fire alarms, duress or panic alarms, and equipment sensing devices such as thermometers, flow indicators, and pressure. Some monitoring systems have the capability of initiating commands to operate equipment in the protected areas. This function is accomplished by using the same transmission system used to transmit the alarms and status signals. Closed circuit television monitors are often used in central stations for intrusion alarm assessment and surveillance of the protected areas. Alarm stations can monitor personnel access to controlled areas by means of access control devices such as card readers, voice analysis, or fingerprints. Even though all these monitoring, control, and surveillance features might not be necessary, they should be considered for immediate and future needs when selecting or designing a central station.

A central alarm station can be either commercial or proprietary. The primary difference between the two, other than the fact that commercial stations are operated for a profit, is that commercial stations are usually remotely located from the facility they are monitoring, while proprietary stations are usually located within or near the protected facility. Although most proprietary stations are located on-site, there are some that monitor remote facilities. For instance, many cities use a single proprietary station to monitor both intrusion and fire alarms, and in some cases environmental controls, for all their schools and school facilities.

Proprietary stations are owned and operated to provide an integrated security system designed specifically to satisfy the security requirements of the owner's facility. Whether you choose a commercial central station or design a station to suit your particular requirements, the monitoring system should be compatible with the facility's overall operation.

A basic intrusion detection monitoring system consists of an alarm signal transmission device and an alarm annunciating/display panel. Alarm transmission devices transmit the alarm signals from a protected area to the monitoring station, where they are annunciated and displayed for the station operator. Depending on the particular alarm transmission device, the alarm signals are transmitted over either dedicated or undedicated communication channels.

A dedicated transmission line, as the word implies, is dedicated to the sole purpose of carrying alarm and other status signals from the protected area to the central station. For example, DC transmission devices require separate dedicated transmission lines, while other devices, such as McCulloh circuits and multiplexed systems, use a single dedicated transmission line for carrying the alarm signals from a number of transmitters. Still other alarm signal transmitting devices do not require dedicated transmission lines. These devices, such as digital dialers, dial the monitoring station through the telephone exchange network and transmit their messages when the dialed number is received and verified at the central station. Radio transmission is also becoming a popular method for communicating alarm signals. It is especially popular in areas where dedicated telephone lines are difficult to acquire or nonexistent.

SIGNAL LINE VULNERABILITY

The transmision lines between the protected area and the monitoring station are usually the most vulnerable part of any physical security system. This is especially true when a central or proprietary station monitors remote facilities. In these instances, the transmission lines leave the protected area and travel through public areas to the monitoring station. In unprotected areas, a transmission line might be vulnerable to compromise, if it can be identified and isolated. Therefore, it is very important that the signal lines between the protected area and central station are, if possible, inaccessible, and certainly not easily identified outside the protected facilities. Many cases have been cited where either alarm installers or telephone repairmen have marked terminals in the telephone junction boxes outside the protected area for maintenance convenience. In these areas, if the intruder is planning to circumvent the alarm transmission system, he does not even have to search out the proper transmission lines because they are plainly marked.

In most proprietary systems the transmission lines lie entirely within the protected facilities. But even in these applications, if the signal lines are accessible outside the protected areas, they could still be vulnerable to compromise, especially to an inside threat. The security of such lines can be improved by installing them in sealed conduit, especially if the conduit is buried in the ground or walls.

Because of the vulnerability of the signal transmission lines, considerable attention should be devoted to selecting a monitoring system with an effective line supervisory system. A line supervisory system should ensure the authentication of the alarm signals at the monitoring station in spite of any overt or clandestine attempts to compromise the security system. Therefore, the adequacy of the line supervisory system should be commensurate with the sophistication of the anticipated threat. If the threat possesses the technical knowledge and has the time and resources, it should be assumed that he can compromise any transmission system.

ALARM MONITOR

Alarm signals from the protected areas are received at the alarm station by a monitoring system that displays the information in a manner that permits alarm sources to be quickly identified. Alarms can be displayed separately on individual display panels, or they can be monitored collectively by a common receiver and displayed individually by numeric displays. Ancillary devices such as map displays and event records also can be added to the basic monitoring system to improve its overall operating effectiveness.

Map displays are visual displays of the protected areas and are used to assist the operator in locating the origin of alarms. They identify individual sensors or sensor zones, along with the boundaries of the interior and exterior protected areas. The primary function of a map is to assist the monitoring operator in identifying alarm locations and giving directions to the response force. Therefore, the size of the display should be adequate to show the layout of the facility clearly. An event recorder improves the effectiveness of the monitoring system by relieving the monitoring operator of the task of recording all the alarms and status changes of the protected areas. It also provides a valuable hard copy record of this information for future reference.

Computers are becoming very popular for managing monitoring functions in central alarm stations. They are used primarily in security applications to monitor the access, secure, and alarm status of all the protected areas; however, they also can be used to monitor and provide response instructions for fire alarms, duress alarms, power status, guard tours, access control terminals, and equipment operating sensors. Along with the monitoring function, computers can perform command functions such as operating environmental controls, electric door strikes, CCTV camera controls, CCTV monitors, or about any equipment control function. Another application of the command function might be to activate deterrent devices located in the protected area. These are just some of the more popular monitoring and command functions that can be performed by computers.

Computers have the capacity to perform many functions, but they are not fully utilized in most alarm monitoring applications, especially in proprietary central station applications. Economically speaking, in most cases it is advisable to utilize the full computer capacity. But consideration should be given to the fact that each time the computer is used to perform a function other than a security function, personnel associated with the added function will need access to the computer. The additional personnel access could increase the vulnerability of the computer to compromise and require additional safeguards.

Computerized monitoring systems use CRT displays, lighted indicator panels, slide projectors, map displays, line printers, or a combination of these devices to display alarm and status information. In security applications, the displays identify the types of alarms and their locations, the access and secure status, the power status of the protected areas, and, where applicable, personnel access information. Some displays also provide alarm response instructions for the station operator. In case of the CRT, this information is displayed in English text on a televisionlike display screen. Some computers are programmed to give a simple graphic presentation on the CRT screen showing the layout of the specific protected area that is in the alarm state, along with information describing the alarm location and the guard response instructions.

Other computer-managed monitoring systems use lighted indicator panels to display the alarm and status information of all protected areas. Carousel slide projectors are sometimes used with these displays to assist the operator in identifying the alarm location and to describe the response actions. The slide projector presentation is prerecorded on the slides. When an alarm occurs, it is indicated on the lighted display panel, and the computer simultaneously calls up on the slide projector the corresponding slide that depicts the layout of the protected area, along with the proper response instructions.

The following chapters describe the basic principles of operation and application for the various types of signal transmission devices, monitoring systems, and computer-managed monitoring systems.

Chapter 19

Signal Transmission Systems

A signal transmission system communicates the protected area's status information to the central alarm station. It should be capable of communicating this information under adverse environmental conditions and during any attempts to compromise the transmission system. An adverse environment is one in which conditions exist, either man-made or natural, that could affect the performance of the signal transmitting equipment or even be detrimental to its operation. False alarms are usually the result of systems operating in an adverse environment, but in some environments, especially lightning storms, the equipment could be partially or even severely damaged.

One of the worst operating environments for any electronic equipment, especially signal transmitting systems, is near large sources of electromagnetic energy. Electric motors, electric welders, radio transmitters, radar, electrical substations, and high-tension power lines are some of the man-made sources of electromagnetic energy; however, the strongest source of electromagnetic energy is lightning. Lightning storms produce intense electric and magnetic fields. The electric fields near a cloud charge area just before a lightning discharge can be as high as 500,000 volts per meter. Current in the lightning strikes to ground usually exceeds 20,000 amperes, and in some isolated cases 200,000 amperes. The large magnetic fields associated with the high-current discharges or lightning strikes couples to the transmission system power and signal lines, producing high-voltage spikes or transients on the lines. These transients can cause false alarms in the signal transmitting system. And depending on the nearness and the magnitude of the lightning strike, it can actually destroy or damage the equipment, especially if the signal and power transmission lines entering the equipment are not protected by lightning suppression circuits.

Man-made sources of electromagnetic energy can cause electromagnetic interference problems, especially with the more sophisticated digital transmission systems. But these sources of interference are normally lower in magnitude than the interference from lightning, and they exist at a fixed frequency, such as the 60 Hz interference associated with electrical power sources. These types of interference can usually be eliminated by electromagnetic shielding and filtering on the power and signal lines. When selecting an alarm transmission system to operate in an electromagnetic environment, especially lightning, consideration should be given to the equipment's lightning suppression, shielding, and input filtering.

A high-moisture environment also can affect the operation of signal transmitting systems using metallic transmission lines. Moisture between the metallic conductors and ground will alter the transmission line's electrical characteristics, and depending on the length of the line and the sensitivity of the transmitting system, these electrical changes could cause false alarms. For instance, if the metallic signal line for a dedicated balanced current system becomes wet, the resulting changes in the line resistance to ground can alter the associated current flow until it exceeds the system's allowable deviation limits and initiates an alarm. Similar problems exist with analog and digital systems. In these systems, a wet transmission line increases the leakage conductance, affecting the transmission qualities of the line. Regardless of the type of transmitter, wet transmission lines can result in false alarms. Therefore, the physical condition of the transmission lines is an important consideration when selecting a signal transmitting system. For reliable communication in a moist environment over metallic transmission lines, especially long lines, the cables should be in good condition.

An alarm signal transmitting system should have some form of line supervision or signal authentication to detect line faults, as well as any attempts to compromise the system. Compromising ranges from simple attempts to cut or short the transmission line to more sophisticated clandestine attempts to deceive or spoof the monitoring system. Spoofing is the act of defeating or compromising an alarm system by substituting bogus signaling devices for a real transmitter or line supervision device located in the protected area.

A transmitting system's line supervision is basically accomplished by sending a continuous or coded signal through the signal transmission circuit and then monitoring the signal for changes characteristic of line faults and tampering. When selecting an alarm transmitting system, the level of line supervision should be selected based on the sophistication of the anticipated threat and the required safeguards. It also should be assumed that any transmission system can be successfully analyzed and defeated by a sophisticated threat, given adequate time and resources.

Good security measures should be exercised when designing and installing an alarm transmission system, especially the signal lines, to limit access and delay any attempted penetrations. Signal transmitters should be installed in enclosures that will protect the electronic components from any normal abuse and provide some physical protection against forced penetration. Enclosures supplied by the transmitter manufacturer might provide this protection, but depending on the anticipated threat and safeguards, additional protection might be required. In this case, the transmitter could be installed inside another separate enclosure. This enclosure also could house other control circuitry or intrusion detection equipment.

The enclosure construction should be commensurate with the application. Any ventilating openings, such as louvers or perforated holes large enough to allow probing, should be protected by expanded metal. The enclosure should have a hinged cover or one that is fixed to the enclosure in some manner to prevent easy removal. Locking provisions should be included so that the enclosure can be locked for limited access. The door also should have tamper protection to detect openings. Tamper protection, which is usually a mechanical switch, should be continually monitored, even when the security system is in the access mode, to alert the central alarm station operator when anyone opens the enclosure. But the switch should have an override position so that it can be deactivated once it has performed its function, to allow authorized access for maintenance.

As previously mentioned, additional signal tansmission line protection can be achieved by using conduit on the signal cables between the transmitter enclosure and the telephone junction box or the central station monitor. Conduit provides physical protection and electromagnetic shielding for the signal cables. Of course, if the cables are connected to the telephone system and travel to a remote central station, the conduit will provide very little EMI shielding.

Signal cable junction boxes between the protected area and the central station monitor located within the facility should be locked and tamper protected, even when they are located inside the protected area. If possible, telephone junction boxes also should be locked and tamper protected. This type of protection will limit access to the most vulnerable point of the signal transmission line, the terminals. In many installations the signal cable junction boxes, especially the telephone junction, are located in some out-of-the-way corner, closet, or utility room, completely unprotected. In this type of installation, the signal cables are very vulnerable to compromise. An intruder would have unlimited access to analyze the transmitted signals in an attempt to defeat the alarm transmission system.

There are numerous stories in the alarm industry about both successful and unsuccessful attempts to compromise an alarm transmission system. In many of the attempts, bogus signaling devices, commonly referred to as black boxes, were found connected across the signal transmission line terminals in the junction boxes. In some of the compromises, the appropriate terminals were even marked to identify the area protected by the alarm system. Terminals should never be marked identifying the area where the signal originates, even when the junction box is locked and tamper protected. Numbers can be assigned to the terminals, and these numbers can be identified on a cross-index card for maintenance purposes; however, this card should be kept in a safe, secure location and released only to authorized personnel. The primary thing to remember is that the signal transmission lines are in most cases the most vulnerable part of any signal transmission system, and they should be protected accordingly.

Several types of alarm signal transmitting devices are used in both commercial and proprietary central alarm stations. The basic principles of their operation and application will be discussed in the following paragraphs. Line supervision for the various transmitting techniques will be emphasized, but only in a qualitative manner. Quantifying the line supervision techniques would be impossible without a complete analysis of all the available systems.

Before discussing the individual alarm transmitting techniques, the available transmission media will be discussed. The most common alarm signal carrier, especially for proprietary systems where the alarm signal does not have to leave the site, is 22 or 24 gauge stranded copper wire. Stranded wire is more popular than solid wire because it is more flexible and consequently easier to pull and less likely to break.

Commercially available transmission media consist of twisted pairs, microwave, and fiber-optic cable, or any combination of these carriers. Telephone companies describe the quality of their transmission system as voice-grade in accordance with standard Bell 3002. Commercially available hardwired transmission systems that will provide continuous metallic paths from a protected facility to a remote central station are almost impossible to obtain. This limits the applications of signal transmission systems that require continuous metallic lines from the transmitters to the receivers. Alarm information is transmitted on metallic lines as direct current, alternating current, or digital signals.

Microwave transmission alarm information is carried to the transmitter on a metallic or fiber-optic carrier as analog or digital signals. At the transmitter, the signals are converted to high-frequency microwave signals that are transmitted either directly or indirectly through repeaters to a line-of-sight receiver. At this point, the information is converted back to an alternating or digital signal and continues along the voice-grade communication path.

Fiber-optic transmission systems also can transmit analog and digital information, which not only includes voice and digital data, but also real-time video signals. Fiber optics has several advantages over metal cables. One distinct advantage is that the cable is dielectric, which eliminates electromagnetic interference. Another advantage is that the cable is much smaller in diameter and lighter than metal cables. Still another advantage, which is important in security applications, is that the cable is more resistant to clandestine tapping than metal cable, but it is not immune to tapping. Because fiber-optic transmission has distinct advantages for security applications, it is discussed in greater detail in the following paragraphs.

FIBER-OPTIC TRANSMISSION

A typical fiber-optic system consists of a transmitter, receiver, and fiber-optic cable. The transmitter converts the information-carrying electrical signal to an optical signal generated by a high-intensity light source or light emitter. The light is formed into a collimated beam and directed into the core of the cable. Information is optically transmitted by varying the light intensity or waveform proportional to the electrical signal. The optical signal travels along the cable to the receiver, where a photodetector, which is highly sensitive to the emitted light, converts the optical signal back to an electrical signal. This signal is amplified to a level compatible with the interfacing equipment.

Fiber-optic cables are constructed of single or multiple optical fibers. The fiber is a thin filament of very pure glass or plastic about the diameter of a human hair. Glass fiber cables are normally used for transceiving long transmission distances or when high data rates are required. Plastic fibers do not have the dimensional stability and environmental durability of glass, but they are less expensive and are suitable for many industrial applications.

The fiber cores are covered with plastic and sheathed in a protective jacket. Polyurethane, polyvinyl chloride (PVC), and steel alloys are used in the jackets to improve puncture resistance and mechanical strength. Fiberglass or metal strands can be added in the jacket to improve the tensile strength needed for cable pulling. Sometimes the outer jackets are larger than the fiber bundle and filled with a soft buffer material to permit slight movement of the fibers when the cable is physically stressed or thermally stressed by temperature changes. The additional space and buffer material also help prevent microbending and consequent signal attenuation. The cable construction depends on the application. Cables used indoors usually do not require the same mechanical strength and physical protection as cables used outdoors, especially direct burial cables.

Fiber-optic cables do require special care and attention when splicing or installing connectors and couplers onto the cable. Reliable splices can produce a permanent connection with very low loss, but they require someone with reasonable skill and special tools. Splicing generally involves melting and fusing the fibers, then covering the splice with a shield. Standard connectors are available that have integral means for aligning and securing the fibers, but the fiber ends require special cutting and polishing. These connectors have attenuation values ranging from 1 to 5 dB, depending on the connector type, fiber size, and finish on the mating surfaces. Couplers are used along the fiber-optic cable where the fibers are joined or split. They are similar to connectors and exhibit comparable attenuation characteristics.

Fiber-optic cables offer a number of advantages over conventional metallic cables used for signal transmission. Probably the most important advantage is that since the optical fibers are dielectric, they cannot conduct or radiate electromagnetic energy. Therefore, the cables are immune to electromagnetic interference and cable cross-talk. Also, because they are dielectric, fiber-optic cables eliminate ground loop and common grounding problems associated with metallic signal cables and coaxial cables used for video transmission. For the same reason, fiber-optic cables permit safe operation in hazardous environments by providing high-voltage isolation.

Since fiber optics does not radiate electromagnetic energy, there is a very low probability of intercepting the transmitted message. Because the cables do not radiate and the fibers have such a small diameter, they are more resistant to clandestine tapping and false signal injection than metallic cables. But they are not totally resistant to tapping and signal injection. A highly skilled adversary can, given access to the cable, extract information from and inject signals into it.

Applications

Fiber-optic transmission systems can be used to transmit security alarm information and television video signals from protected areas to a central monitoring area. The decision to use fiber optics for alarm signal transmission in proprietary installations depends on the electromagnetic interference problems associated with using metallic cable and whether electrical isolation is required. It is usually not cost-effective to use fiber-optic transmission for alarm signal transmission unless the environment dictates it because a separate transmitter and receiver and a corresponding power supply are required for each transmission link. If all the alarm points can be combined at a central point before being transmitted to a central monitoring area, then it might be cost-effective to use a fiber-optic multiplex system to transmit the alarm signal from the central point to the monitoring area.

Fiber-optic cable provides significant advantages over coaxial cable for television applications. Besides eliminating electromagnetic interference and ground loop problems, which will be discussed in Chapter 24 on CCTV, fiber-optic cables provide low-loss, high-resolution transmission without amplifiers over significantly longer distances than coaxial cables.

Fiber-optic transmission is extremely attractive for Tempest applications to prevent unauthorized interception of electromagnetic signals in sensitive installations. In this or similar types of screen rooms or shielded enclosure applications, fiber-optic cable is required where the data or signal cables exit the shielded area.

Both glass and plastic fiber tend to cloud in radiation environments. Therefore, caution must be used when applying fiber-optic cables in radiation environments, such as those that might exist in a nuclear power plant. Normal nuclear plant environments have little effect on fiber-optic cables, but radiation release during an accident might affect the cables' transmission capabilities. This might be a time when alarm signal transmission is critical, so copper cables should be used for data transmission in such areas.

McCULLOH CIRCUITS

McCulloh circuits are similar to the old telephone party lines. Each system uses a single transmission line to service the communication needs of a number of different customers who are usually located in the same neighborhood or along the same route. The techniques used to alert the operator are also somewhat similar. In the telephone system, the operator was alerted by a series of rings initiated by the customer, who turned a crank on his telephone. But in the McCulloh circuit, instead of the customer alerting the central station operator, a transmitter, located on the customer's premises, sends an identification code that identifies the customer, along with the alarm message. Both the identification and message are sent as a series of coded pulses. The pulses are received at the central station, where they are decoded and recorded on a punched paper tape recorder to alert the station operator.

The pulses that form the identification number are transmitted as a series of grounds and breaks or breaks and grounds, depending on the particular McCulloh circuit. A ground pulse is generated by momentarily connecting the transmission line to the ground. A break pulse is generated by momentarily opening the transmission line. In the original and most common version of the McCulloh circuit, the electrical pulses are generated by gearlike teeth on one or more code wheels, which activate corresponding electrical switches. The teeth on the signal wheel are spaced in unique increments around the perimeter of the wheel so as to generate a predetermined code. As the wheel or wheels rotate, the gearlike teeth activate the electrical switches as the teeth pass over the switch contacts. The switches are connected in series to the signal transmission line. Therefore, as the code wheels rotate, their teeth activate the electrical switches and initiate a corresponding series of ground and break pulses. In this version of the McCulloh circuit, the code wheels are rotated by either an electrical or a mechanical spring windup motor. In some newer versions of the McCulloh circuit, the ground and break pulses are generated electronically, thus eliminating the need for a motor.

The coded pulses are transmitted from the protected facility to the central station over a single metallic conductor relying on a good earth ground for the return signal. A cold water pipe is usually recommended for connecting the ground return. The metallic conductor is routed from the central station to a code transmitter located in each of the customers' facilities and back to the central station. It can be visualized as forming a large loop that connects a number of customers' facilities with the central station, similar to a series of Christmas tree lights. For this reason, the McCulloh circuit is also referred to as the McCulloh loop.

The maximum number of customers that can be connected to a single McCulloh loop ranges from about fifteen to forty-five. One limiting factor in determining the number of customers is the electrical resistance in the transmission line. This resistance is a function of the size and length of the conductor, including the code transmitters. The longer the conductor, the greater the resistance. Generally speaking, the closer the customers are located to the central station, the shorter the transmission line, and consequently the more customers that can be connected to the loop. The converse also is true: The farther the customers are from the central station, the longer the transmission line, and the fewer customers that can be served by the loop.

When selecting a central station that uses the McCulloh circuit or when designing a McCulloh circuit monitoring system, another factor that should be considered is clash. Clash results when two or more code transmitters are activated and simultaneously attempt to transmit their messages over the same transmission line. The resulting signal is similar to that on a telephone party line when several persons talk at the same time. To a person trying to listen, the conversation would sound very garbled. In the McCulloh circuit, the central station receiver is comparable to the listener, and if the coded pulses are too garbled, the receiver might not be able to decode and interpret the signals. Clash might not be a problem if only a few code transmitters are connected to a single loop or if the probability of several alarms occuring simultaneously is low. Clash also can be eliminated in a proprietary system by using code transmitters that have positive noninterfering circuits. With this feature, if simultaneous operation of several transmitters occurs, one transmitter takes control of the signal line, transmits its full message, and then releases the transmission line for successive transmission by the other transmitters, which are held inoperative until they, in turn, gain control.

McCulloh transmission loops are usually supervised in the central station to the extent that the circuits can be conditioned to continue to receive signals even though a line fault occurs along the conductor at a single distant location. A line fault can be an open circuit, a grounded line, or a combination of the two. Such faults are monitored by a current meter in the receiver. When a fault occurs, it is annunciated by an audible sound and indicated by the appropriate light, either ground or open. A single fault can be controlled so that the system will continue to function by rotating the line-conditioning selection switch to the appropriate position.

Even though the circuit is supervised to detect such line faults, protection against compromise may be only minimal or nonexistent. For instance, if both the transmission lines of a code transmitter are cut, the transmitted pulses will not leave the customer's premises. When the lines are cut, a line fault condition will be indicated at the central station, but it will take time to locate the open circuit. During this time an intruder might be able to complete his mission. This vulnerability can be reduced if the transmission line enters the protected facility underground. The transmission line vulnerability may be further reduced if alternate lines are routed to the facility along a path remote from that of the primary line. A common mistake is to assume an alternate line in the same telephone cable, as the primary line will provide the desired redundancy. In actual fact, when lines are accidentally or intentionally cut, usually the entire cable is affected.

Another method of supervising the transmission lines is to program the code transmitters to send a test signal hourly (or more often) to the central station during periods when the facility is secured. This signal would verify the integrity of the entire McCulloh circuit, including the code transmitter and the signal transmission line, between the central station and the protected facility. After this test, the circuit is still vulnerable until another check test is performed; however, the intruder will probably not know when the test will occur and will be at risk.

Applications

The block diagram in Figure 19–1 shows a McCulloh circuit with N number of transmitters connected in series by a signal conductor to a receiver located in the central alarm station. As previously mentioned, the maximum

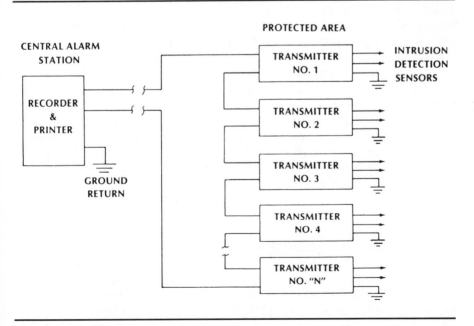

Figure 19–1 McCulloh circuit block diagram.

number of transmitters connected to a single loop ranges from fifteen to forty-five. In the block diagram, the Nth transmitter could be any number from the five shown to forty-five. Aside from need, the actual number of subscribers on a single loop depends on the loop resistance and the possibility of a clash occurring between transmissions.

The transmitter in each protected area monitors the series-connected intrusion detection sensors and transmits an alarm signal to the central station when an intrusion occurs. In this type of installation, when the sensors are connected in series to the transmitter, the transmitter initiates an alarm signal when any sensor detects an intrusion. The transmitter does not identify the sensor initiating the alarm. Therefore, the number of sensors connected to a McCulloh transmitter should be limited to those in a single area or adjoining areas to assist the response force in assessing the alarm. If the protected area is large or there are numerous rooms that require protection, the protection circuits should be subdivided and additional transmitters used to monitor these areas.

A primary consideration for selecting a McCulloh transmission system is the anticipated sophistication of the threat. The question is: Will the threat have the ability to defeat or compromise the transmission system? Another consideration is that the would-be intruder might defeat or compromise the system if he has free access to the signal cables. But if the transmission cables are well secured, attempts to compromise the system will be complicated. An example would be a complex that has its own proprietary central station where the signal transmission cables between the protected areas and the central station are installed in conduit. For additional protection all the conduit joints are secured and the junction boxes locked and tamper protected.

The obvious advantage of using McCulloh circuit transmission systems is that they require fewer signal lines between the central station and the protected areas than do dedicated systems. This is an important feature because in many areas metallic telephone lines are difficult or impossible to obtain. And even when they are available, they are expensive to lease. Multiple signal lines also can be expensive to install, depending on the size of the installation and the required number of lines. Therefore, in certain applications the McCulloh circuit can be a useful and effective alarm transmission system.

DIRECT CURRENT TRANSMISSION

Direct current signal transmission devices have been used for many years in the alarm industry to transmit alarm signals. These transmitting devices, unlike McCulloh circuits, require a dedicated pair of metallic conductors between the central station monitor and each protected area. That is, a metallic wire conductor is required to complete the circuit between the transmitter and central station receiver. In the earliest versions of the DC systems, there was normally no current flow in the signal lines. Current flow occurred only when an intrusion detection sensor activated the alarm circuit. The induced current was detected and annunciated by the monitor located at the central station. The problem with this system was that it could be easily compromised by simply cutting the signal line to prevent the alarm signal transmission.

These DC systems were replaced by systems that supplied supervisory current on the signal lines at all times and then interrupted the signal for an alarm. This type of line supervision would detect anyone cutting the signal line; however, the systems were still vulnerable to compromise. For example, the normal line current supplied by a battery at the protected area could be replaced by connecting another comparable battery across the signal lines outside the protected area. Then the signal line between the battery and protected area could be cut without initiating an alarm. As the vulnerability of this type of line supervision became better known, new DC signal transmission devices were designed, again to improve the line supervision.

One design improvement consisted of adding circuitry for detecting changes in the normal line current that exceeded preset levels. This technique was discussed in Part II as a method of improving line security between the detectors and the alarm signal transmitters. It is repeated here because this same technique is used to provide signal line supervision for the DC transmission systems used to transmit alarm signals from the protected area to the central alarm station. In the DC system the normal line current ranges from as low as 300 microamperes to as high as 10 milliamperes. A variation from about 2 to 30 percent of the normal line current will initiate an alarm. As previously mentioned, a system requiring a 2 percent current variation might appear to offer much more line security than a system using a 30 percent variation; in reality, the 2 percent system is only slightly more difficult to defeat than one using a 30 percent variation. Also, the more sensitive (2 percent variation) systems tend to exhibit a higher false alarm rate, especially when the signal lines are exposed to inclement weather.

Another improvement to the DC system consists of superimposing several AC signals on the basic DC carrier for additional line supervision. These signals are imposed on the signal lines at the protected area and monitored at the central alarm station. Any variation in the combined outputs of the AC signals that is greater than the preset level initiates an alarm. With this type of line supervision, anyone trying to defeat the transmission system would not only have to compromise the balanced current supervision, but he also would have to successfully duplicate and superimpose the multiple AC signal.

A typical DC transmission system using the balanced current type of line supervision consists of an access/secure control module located in the protected area and a monitor module located in the central station. These two devices are interconnected by a dedicated pair of metallic conductors. A

A switch, usually key activated for selecting the system operating mode, is located on the front panel of the access/secure module. The control module also contains an alarm relay and two different value end-of-line resistors. One resistor is inserted into the circuit when the control panel switch is in the access position; the second one is inserted when the switch is in the secure position. These resistors, along with a potentiometer used to balance the resistive bridge, are part of a bridge network located in the monitor module. The front panel of the monitor module has an access/secure switch, a reset switch, an alarm indicator lamp, and a separate access and secure lamp.

The basic principle of operation of the DC balanced current system can be described by first assuming that a nominal 300 microampere current is supplied across the resistive bridge network. The current flow through the two legs of the resistive bridge, including the resistors located in the access/secure module at the protected area, is balanced with the potentiometer. The resistive bridge is first balanced with the resistor inserted in the circuit that corresponds to the secure mode. That is, the access/secure switch on both the control panel in the protected area and the switch monitor module panel are positioned in the secure mode. The potentiometer is then adjusted until the current flow through the resistive bridge is balanced. The same procedure is followed to adjust the resistive bridge for the access mode of operation. Thereafter, if the current in the balanced bridge varies beyond the preset level, usually ± 10 or ± 20 percent, because of a sensor alarm or someone tampering with the transmission line, an alarm is indicated on the monitor panel. The alarm is annunciated by an audible tone and indicated by a red lamp. Acknowledging the alarm by activating the acknowledge switch silences the audible tone, but the red alarm light remains illuminated until the system is reset.

Direct current balanced current transmission systems provide a higher level of line supervision than McCulloh circuits, but they are also vulnerable to compromise, since a small range of signal line current variations can occur without initiating an alarm. Additional line supervision superimposed on the DC balanced curcuit supervision, such as the superimposed AC signal previously described, certainly enhances signal line supervision.

Applications

The block diagram in Figure 19–2 shows one DC transmission system concept. This is probably the most common concept used by both commercial and proprietary central alarm stations. In this concept, an access/secure control module is located in the protected area for connecting the alarm outputs from all the sensors. Usually two sets of alarm terminals are available in the module. One set is used for connecting the sensors required when the area is

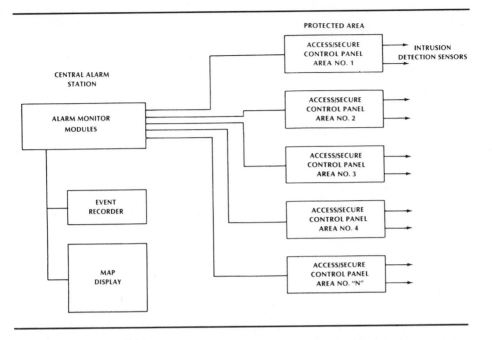

Figure 19-2   Direct current transmission concept 1 block diagram.

secured. The second set is for those sensors or tamper switches requiring continuous monitoring, regardless of whether the area is in access or secure mode.

Two limiting factors on the number of access/secure control modules that can be monitored in the central station are the number of available monitor modules and the availability of dedicated transmission lines. Each monitor module is dedicated to monitor a single control module over a pair of dedicated conductors. The monitor modules in the central station should be mounted in a configuration that is compatible with their collective functions. An event recorder also is recommended for recording all alarms and access/secure status changes. A map display might be helpful, especially in a proprietary installation, where it will help identify quickly alarm locations for the response guard.

Another DC transmission concept is shown in Figure 19-3. In this concept, the alarm signals from individual detectors or sensors are separately monitored and displayed on an alarm indicator panel located in the central station. This type of system can be used effectively in proprietary installations to monitor detectors that normally require continuous monitoring. Examples are door contacts that protect external doors, window protection devices, and exterior perimeter or area detectors. An end-of-line resistor is installed in each detector component of the resistive bridge network in the alarm indicator module. As with the previously described balanced current

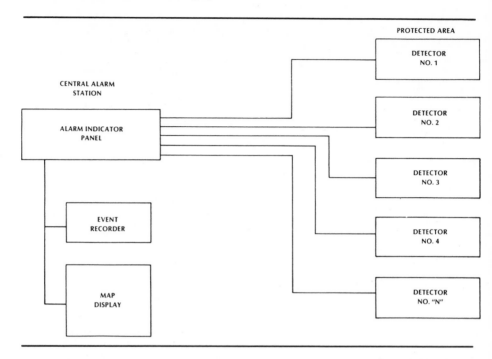

Figure 19-3   Direct current transmission concept 2 block diagram.

system, a supervisory current flows through the protected loop and the end-of-line resistor; if the protected loop is interrupted, the balanced bridge network becomes unbalanced and initiates an alarm. The alarm is annunciated and displayed on both the indicator panel and map display, then recorded on the event recorder.

One application of this type of alarm transmission system is that it can be used to monitor the exterior intrusion detection sensors around a facility having a proprietary central alarm station. The balanced current line supervision for the signal cables between the alarm indicator module and each detector will detect signal line interruptions such as open circuits and shorted signal lines. For additional security, even with the balanced current line supervision, the signal line to the individual exterior detectors should be installed in conduit and buried where possible. A map display is especially desirable in this type of installation because it quickly identifies the perimeter zone where detection has occurred. Event recorders are always recommended to record the sequence and incidence of alarms.

Direct current transmission systems are being used less and less in commercial central alarm stations because the metallic or direct copper transmission lines required for these systems are becoming more difficult to obtain from telephone companies. But DC systems are being used successfully in proprietary installations where the signal cables are available or can be conveniently installed.

An advantage of a DC transmission system is that if a monitor module fails, only the monitoring function of a single protected area is lost. In monitoring systems that use a common receiver, if the receiver fails, the total monitoring capability is lost until the unit can be repaired or a spare installed.

ALTERNATING CURRENT TRANSMISSION

Alternating current signal transmission systems are very similar to DC systems. The primary difference between the two is that the AC signals are usually transmitted as audible tones, while DC is a direct current. Consequently, the DC resistor bridge network in the monitor module is replaced with an AC bridge network for an AC system. Also, the resistive termination in the control module in the protected area is replaced with a complex end-of-line impedance termination. In AC systems, the frequency and amplitude or phase of the AC signals are monitored, and an alarm is initiated when the signal characteristics change by some preset level. A major advantage of AC systems is that they do not require dedicated metallic signal lines. When the AC signals are audible tones, the protected area status information can be transmitted over voice-grade telephone lines.

Other AC signal transmission techniques are used to improve line supervision while maintaining reliable signal transmission. Several techniques are used, including that of superimposing multiple tones on the signal lines and monitoring those tones either separately or collectively to obtain the protected area status information and to detect possible line tampering. Another system superimposes two carrier frequencies on the signal line. One carrier frequency verifies line integrity, and the other is digitally encoded to communicate the status information. Still another signal transmission technique superimposes randomly modulated signals on the transmission line and monitors the phase of both the transmitted and returned signals. Deviations in these signals exceeding a preset level initiate an alarm.

The level of line supervision provided by the more complex AC systems using multiple signal superimposition is about equivalent to the DC transmission systems that impose multiple AC signals on the DC balanced current signal for added line security. The difference between these two transmission techniques is that systems using both AC and DC signals require continuous or dedicated metallic signal lines between the central station and the protected area, while systems using only AC audible tone signals can transmit their information over voice-grade telephone lines.

Alternating current signal transmission systems generally provide a higher level of line supervision than do DC balanced current systems, but these systems are also vulnerable to compromise. Systems using only AC balanced bridge signal transmission can be compromised in a manner similar to the DC systems. Even systems using multiple tones for signal transmission and line supervision can be compromised. As previously stated, the difference in the level of supervision offered by the various types of signal transmission can be measured only in the delay they provide against compromise by the anticipated threat.

Applications

Alternating current transmission systems are used in applications similar to those using DC systems. But unlike DC systems, AC systems are becoming very popular with commercial central alarm stations because they do not require continuous metallic lines; they can communicate over voice-grade telephone lines.

MULTIPLEX TRANSMISSION

Multiplex systems can simultaneously or sequentially communicate a facility's alarm and status information, as well as command functions for a number of protected facilities, over a single communication channel. The communication channel can be a twisted wire pair, coaxial cable, voice-grade telephone line, microwave link, radio, or any combination of these signal transmission paths. The most popular method of communication, however, is over voice-grade telephone lines for commercial central stations and twisted pair (wires) or coaxial cable for proprietary stations.

A major advantage of multiplexing is that it can be very cost-effective in terms of cabling in layouts, where a single transmission line can replace several separate signal lines. This is especially true for layouts where the distance between the protected facilities and the central station is in terms of miles. For instance, some multiplex systems can monitor the functions of as many as one hundred protected areas on a single communication channel. This means that one transmission line can replace one hundred pairs of dedicated metallic wires required for the same number of DC transmission systems, one hundred voice-grade telephone lines for AC systems, or perhaps three or four McCulloh circuit loops. The savings in transmission line costs can be appreciable, especially for long transmission distances. Communicating the information for one hundred protected facilities over a single transmission line might be impractical in some instances. But with the increasing difficulty in obtaining telephone lines, especially dedicated lines, the reduction in the transmission line requirement offered by the multiplex systems can certainly help relieve the telephone line leasing problem.

There are two basic multiplexing techniques. One is called frequency division multiplexing (FDM) and the other time division multiplexing (TDM). In FDM the signal communication channel is subdivided into a number of separate frequency subchannels. Each subchannel is assigned to a separate protected facility for communicating with the central station. The number of subchannels on any one communication channel or transmission path is a function of the type of transmission path, whether it is a telephone line or microwave. If the transmission path is a voice-grade telephone line, it can be divided into approximately five subchannels. The actual number depends on the stability of the signal generator oscillator and the selectivity and stability of the tone filters. An advantage of an FDM system, since each protected facility is assigned a dedicated subchannel for communications, is that each protected facility has continuous communication with the central station.

In TDM an interval of time or time cycle is divided into subintervals called time slots. Each protected facility is then assigned a time slot in the time cycle to communicate its status information to the central alarm station. For instance, if a TDM system is capable of monitoring one hundred protected facilities and has a 1-second transmission slot for each, the total time cycle for communicating the status information of all the facilities will be 100 seconds. If each protected facility communicates its status information sequentially, it will transmit and then wait 99 seconds before transmitting the next response. The waiting time is the elapsed time between transmissions. In this example, if an alarm occurs, it might be as long as 99 seconds before the alarm is transmitted to the central station, depending on when the alarm occurred in the sequence. This waiting time is referred to as the system response time.

Time division multiplexing techniques will be discussed in more detail than FDM because TDM is the most popular transmission method in the alarm industry, as well as in communications and computer technology in general. It is particularly applicable to a digital format, which consists of data words constructed from a series of binary bits called logic ones and logic zeros. The bits of logic ones and zeros are initially generated as two separate low-level DC voltages that represent each logic state. One voltage represents a logic one and the second lower voltage a logic zero. The length of each bit, or the data rate, varies between systems, but typical data rates are 1,200 and 2,400 bits per second. This means that an 8-bit word (8 bits is a popular word length) requires about 6.6 milliseconds to be generated and transmitted.

The data words constructed from the binary logic states can be transmitted over twisted wire pairs. But if they are transmitted over any other transmission path, such as voice-grade telephone lines, the words must be converted to AC signals or tones. This conversion is accomplished by a modulator/demodulator called a modem. A modem transmits the digital information using frequency shift keyed (FSK), phase shift keyed (PSK), or on/off keyed (OOK) signal transmission. Although PSK and OOK can be used for signal transmission, FSK is the most popular, especially when the information must be transmitted over long distances.

If FSK modems, the module coverts the DC binary logic states into separate AC tones. One tone represents a logic one, and a second tone represents a logic zero. A demodulator at the opposite end of the transmission path converts the FSK signals back to the original logic states. Depending on the type of digital multiplexer, both a modulator and demodulator might be required at each end of the transmission path.

Digital multiplex systems can transmit information either one way on a transmission line or both ways, depending on the system response. One-way transmission is called simplex; two-way nonsimultaneous transmission is called half duplex; and two-way simultaneous transmission is called full duplex. Time division multiplexing transmission time slots must be synchronized to ensure that the protected facility's communications do not interfere. If they did, signal interference or clash would result, as when two or more McCulloh circuits are activated simultaneously.

Several synchronization techniques are used. In a simplex digital multiplexer, the time slots are synchronized between the transmitter and receiver by a pair of synchronized clocks. One clock is located in the transmitter, and the second one is in the receiver. These clocks synchronize the communication times between the transmitter and receiver. In a half-duplex system, a synchronization pulse is transmitted from the central station at the beginning of each time cycle. This simultaneously synchronizes the clocks in the transponders in all the protected facilities. Status information is then sequentially transmitted from each protected facility in its respective time slot to the receiver located in the central station.

The third transmission technique used by digital multiplexers to communicate with the protected facilities is interrogate/response. An interrogate/response multiplexing system consists of an interrogator located in the central station and a transponder located in the protected facility. The transponder receives the interrogate signal from the central station and then transmits the facility's security status information back to the interrogator. Interrogate/response systems can be either half duplex or full duplex. In general, full-duplex systems have faster system response to alarms, and they can execute command functions simultaneously with the interrogate and response function.

The interrogate/response systems initiate a separate address word for each protected facility transponder. On receipt of the address word, the transponder in the protected facility responds with the security status of the facility. To help reduce false alarms in the signal transmission cycle, the status information message is transmitted at least twice by the transponder to the interrogator, where the messages are received and compared. If the messages compare, then the next transponder is interrogated. If they do not compare, then the same facility transponder is interrogated a second time. A single facility is usually interrogated about three times, and if the signals do not compare, an alarm occurs. Of course, if both signals indicate an alarm or change of status on the first interrogation, the new status is immediately displayed on the monitor.

Two-way communication in half-duplex and full-duplex systems operating through the telephone network can become very complex. This is especially true when information must be multiplexed between the central station and many remote facilities that are not operating on the same transmission line. In this case the transmission lines entering the telephone exchange must be bridged together for the central station. Basically, the bridges provide isolation between the protected facilities on the separate transmission lines and amplification to the AC tones as required. Installation of the bridging circuits is not a common service provided by the telephone company; as a result, there can be system start-up problems. Most multiplex manufacturers are familiar with these problems, however, and can assist in generating specifications for the bridging circuits.

Digital multiplex systems have several desirable features. One feature that has already been discussed is that multiplexing can reduce the signal line requirements by accommodating the signal transmission from many protected facilities on a single communication channel.

Another feature is that more detailed information can be transmitted in the digital message than in the normal alarm and access/secure status information. For instance, a transponder in a multiplex system has between eight and sixteen separate alarm terminals identified in the transmitted message. Therefore, an alarm signal can be communicated with sufficient detail to identify the particular detector or area that is in the alarm state. By identifying the separate alarm terminals, the detectors can be more effectively zoned so that the response force will be able to locate quickly the detector or area that is in alarm. This information also can assist maintenance personnel in locating malfunctioning detectors.

Another desirable feature of digital multiplex systems is that they provide a high degree of line security when some form of random or pseudorandom binary sequence encoding is used for the signal transmission. Encoding or encrypting techniques basically scramble the message, making it unintelligible so it cannot be read without knowing the key or code. Encryptors encode data through the implementation of a mathematical algorithm. Most encryption devices used in computer communications use the NBS Data Encryption Standard (DES), established in 1978. This is they only encryption method sanctioned by the U.S. government. It is being used for encrypting data ranging from transferring bank funds to intrusion detection system transmission.

With random encoding, the binary bits of logic states in words describing the security status of a protected facility and the sequence of interrogation or transmission are randomly changing during the signal transmission. Random encoding provides the highest level of line security, but it requires storing large quantities of random keys for encoding the data words. With pseudorandom encoding, the data words are randomly encoded, but only for a specific number of words or period of time. The data sequence is then repeated. Pseudorandom encoded digital multiplex systems offer a high level of line supervision, provided that the encoding sequences are sufficiently long to protect against compromise. The DES algorithm uses a 56-bit key to encrypt the message. The message is decoded at the receiver with the proper decryption key and presented to the monitor operator as an intelligible message. The number of possible codes that exist when using the DES algorithm is 2^{56}, or more than 72 quadrillion codes.

Because of this coding capability, there is a feeling that any system using some form of encoding, especially DES encoding, is extremely secure. This is not necessarily true because there are different ways to implement the DES. The simplest is the codebook mode, which is inappropriate for intrusion detection systems because a sophisticated intruder can infer by observation or experiment what constitutes the all clear and alarm messages. At best, this allows an intruder to determine when he has tripped a sensor. At worst, it allows him to overwrite response with what he determines must be the all clear code. This particular problem can be corrected by employing an NBS-suggested feedback mode, in which the next response depends not only on the clear text, but on the last cipher text response.

It is unlikely that any intrusion detection system manufacturer would be so naive as to use the codebook mode. But more subtle implementation weaknesses may be found in actual intrusion detection systems. One easily explained example is that the DES uses an encryption key, a binary word used to "unlock" the DES algorithm. This binary word can be any sequence of logic ones and zeros. But suppose that for convenience, an implementation restricts it to words translatable to alphabet letters. This is analogous to our deciding to ease the memory burden at our office by making all safe combinations conform to some restricted format. Just as this will reduce the number of real combinations on our three-number, thirty-position lock from twenty-seven thousand to twenty-seven, it will make it possible for a burglar to open our safe in a matter of minutes if he discovers the general format. As with this lock example, it might allow an intruder to determine the key to the signal transmission system in a few hours through exhaustive trial and error using high-speed computers.

There are more subtle implementation flaws that might allow a sophisticated challenger to gain control of the encrypted signal transmission system. Such flaws must generally be found by persons in that select community of mathematicians and engineers who really understand cryptography. This is perhaps fortunate in that it reduces the number of potential adversaries able to discover such implementation flaws. It is unfortunate in that it makes it difficult to certify that a given implementation is safe. The point is that simply specifying use of the DES, or any other accepted tool, might not guarantee adequate security.

The most important single element of an encryptor device is the encryption key, which tells the machine how to encrypt the data. Both the information transmitted and that received must have identical keys to encrypt and decrypt the communicated message. The key is programmed into the machine either automatically or by a security manager for hardware encryption systems. The key should be changed frequently, depending on the technical sophistication of the perceived threat, to ensure maximum security. Also, only a few responsible individuals should have access to the key and control when and how the key is changed.

The most secure multiplex alarm transmission system is one that encrypts both the interrogate and response message using the DES or an equivalent key-changeable encryption technique.

Applications

The basic block diagram in Figure 19–4 shows an interrogate/response multiplex system that operates over voice-grade telephone lines. This system is representative of a commercial or proprietary central alarm station that must rely on telephone lines for signal transmission. As previously mentioned, signal transmission can also be by coaxial cable, twisted pair wire conductors, microwave link, or radio. Coaxial cable and twisted wire pairs are primarily used in proprietary installations where the interconnecting cables can be

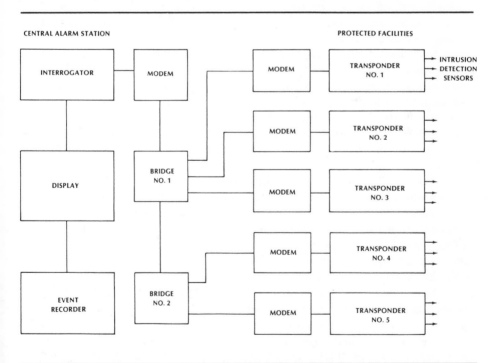

Figure 19–4 Interrogate/response multiplex system.

conveniently installed within its premises, while microwave links and radios are used for long-range transmission or for areas where telephone lines do not exist or are difficult to obtain or install.

The basic interrogate/response system diagram shown in Figure 19–4 consists of an interrogator, a display, an event recorder, and a number of transponders. The interrogator is a combined transmitter and receiver with a sequence generator and data processor. In a typical transmission, an address data word is generated in the interrogator and transmitted over the telephone lines to all the transponders. The properly addressed transponder receives its address word, then transmits the security status of all associated sensors in the protected facility back to the interrogator, where it is received and analyzed. If the status of the protected area has not changed since the previous transmission, the interrogator then signals the next transponder. But if there is a change in the security status, the new status information is annunciated and displayed at the interrogator. A map display can be incorporated in the system along with an event recorder to facilitate alarm identification and guard response.

In the system shown in Figure 19–4, an FSK modem is required at both the central station and at each transponder to convert the data word logic states into AC signals or tones and vice versa for transmission over the voice-grade telephone lines. The transponder address is converted into two discrete frequencies that correspond to the logic states in the address by the modem modulator at the interrogator. These frequencies are then converted back into their original logic states by the modem demodulator located at the transponder. When the transponder responds with its status information, the transmission process is reversed. The modulator at the transponder converts the data word into the corresponding frequencies, and the demodulator at the interrogator converts the frequencies back to their original logic states. As previously mentioned, the combined modulator/demodulator is called a modem, and the frequency-modulated AC signal transmission is called frequency shift key (FSK).

The distribution of the FSK signals from the interrogator modem to the corresponding transponder modems requires one or more bridges to interconnect all the transponders with the single transmission line from the interrogator modem. Bridges provide isolation and signal line balance on the signal lines between the individual transponders, as well as between the transponders and the interrogator. Both active and passive bridges are available, but active bridges predominate in the communications industry.

In commercial central alarm stations and proprietary stations that use telephone lines for signal transmission, bridging is usually required at telephone exchanges where several separate transponder signal lines terminate. The same is sometimes true at protected facilities requiring two or more transponders. In the block diagram in Figure 19–4, bridge 1, which connects transponders 1 and 2, could be located in a telephone exchange, while bridge 2, connecting transponders 4 and 5, could be located in a protected facility or in another telephone exchange. The multiplex system manufacturers should be helpful in generating the bridging specifications and providing assistance during system design and installation.

When evaluating applications of multiplex systems, consideration should be given to operational contingencies in case of a major component failure. For instance, if an interrogator fails, the entire monitoring function could be out of order. A contingency possibility would be to have a spare interrogator available to assume the monitoring function. Another possibility would be to repair the interrogator. This contingency would be practical only if the major interrogator components are plug-in modules with convenient test points or methods to check their function. With these maintenance features, along with a readily available maintenance person and spare modules, a repair contingency might be acceptable.

When a transponder fails, other contingencies besides replacing or repairing the unit could be exercised, such as sending a guard to the area or increasing the guard tour patrolling rate. These are the types of measures that must be considered when selecting any monitoring system; however, contingency measures are extremely important when one major component failure could compromise the entire central station's monitoring functions.

There are several desirable features of multiplex systems that should be considered when selecting a monitoring system. One valuable feature is that there are no limitations on the distance over which multiplex systems can communicate using voice-grade telephone lines, including microwave links. Another feature is that with the present state-of-the-art devices in signal line supervision, digital systems have the highest immunity to compromise when random encoding is used for the signal transmission. Pseudorandom encoding offers a high degree of immunity to compromise, especially when the encoding sequences are sufficiently long. Still another feature is that multiplex systems are operationally compatible with computers. This is a very desirable feature if a computer is used or if consideration is being given to future expansion of the multiplex system into a computer-managed monitoring system.

Multiplex systems are capable of accommodating a large number of transmission lines. Because of this and other related features, multiplex systems are being used in commercial central alarm stations and have many applications in proprietary central stations that have a large monitoring requirement and in instances where the protected areas are widely distributed.

Multiplex systems in proprietary central stations can be used for monitoring security functions in office buildings, apartment and condominium complexes, learning institutions, industrial installations, and individual schools in a single city or district. Although multiplex systems have many desirable application features, as in any system selection, these features should be evaluated with respect to specific application requirements and the anticipated threat.

DIGITAL DIALERS

Digital dialers can monitor and communicate the security status of the various intrusion detection sensors in a protected facility to an associated transceiver in the central station. Besides reporting intrusion alarms, digital dialers can transmit holdup or duress and fire alarms and identify the alarm zone. They also can be used to report facility openings and closings and to monitor equipment sensors such as temperature sensing devices and flow or pressure gauges.

Digital dialers, as the name implies, communicate the protected facility's security status to the central station transceiver in a digitally encoded message. They should not be mistaken for tape dialers. Tape dialers communicate a recorded voice message to several preprogrammed telephone numbers where someone must be available to respond. Digital dialers construct the message in binary logic and transmit it over voice-grade telephone lines. The message is transmitted by FSK, similar to digital muliplex systems. Because the message is digitally encoded, digital dialers can communicate only with compatible transceivers that can interpret the digital message and display the information in a meaningful format for the central station operator.

Digital dialers offer two-way communication between the dialers and transceiver in the central station. In fact, some manufacturers refer to their dialers as digital communicators. Two-way communication allows acknowledge and reset commands to be transmitted from the receiver for verifying the reporting dialer's identification and for resetting the dialer after its message is received and cross-checked. Cross-checking is accomplished by requiring the dialer to transmit status information twice for each message. The two messages are compared for repeatability before the message is accepted as being valid. This verification minimizes the possibility of errors caused by noisy telephone lines. After verification, a reset command is transmitted from the receiver to shut down the dialer in order to minimize transceiver tie-up. A complete message transmission should take only about 3 to 5 seconds. If the listen-in feature, available with most digital dialers, is used, the transceiver could be tied up for longer periods of time.

To prevent someone from deliberately jamming the telephone lines, dialers should have a telephone line release circuit or line seizure relay. The line seizure relay will capture a telephone line whether it is in use or not and will allow the intrusion message to be transmitted. Without a seizure relay, someone could conceivably call the protected facility and tie up the telephone line, assuming only one outgoing line, while he accomplishes his mission.

For a similar reason, the transceiver at the central station should have the capability to hang up on invalid calls such as wrong numbers or someone attempting to call and tie up the transceiver. Without this feature, someone who knows the telephone number of the transceiver could call and tie up the transceiver, preventing other calls from being answered. The hang-up feature disconnects the incoming call and accepts the next call. Even though the invalid calls can be disconnected, anyone using this jamming technique might be effective in compromising the system long enough for the intended purpose. For this reason, the telephone number of the transceiver should be one that has been out of use for a while to minimize wrong number calls. The number also should be given only to those persons who have an absolute need to know.

Applications

The block diagram in Figure 19–5 shows a basic digital dialer signal transmission system operating through a telephone exchange network. This system is representative of a commercial or proprietary central alarm system that relies on the telephone network for signal transmission. The transceiver is located in the central alarm station, and the digital dialers are distributed throughout the area serviced by the station. This area could be a single city or multiple cities throughout the United States, since there is no limit on the distance a telephone message can be communicated.

In a typical application, a dialer is connected to a single telephone exchange convenient to the protected facility. When the message reaches the

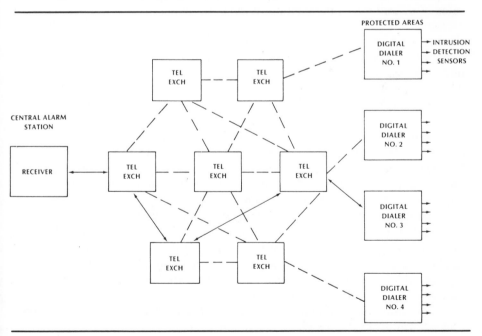

Figure 19–5 Digital dialer transmission concept.

first exchange, it is automatically switched in or out through the various telephone exchanges to the central alarm station receiver. The broken lines between the individual telephone exchanges shown in Figure 19–5 represent the alternate signal paths. Any route along these broken lines between the digital dialer and the receiver is a possible transmission path. The solid line represents the signal path to the receiver from digital dialer 3. The arrows on both ends of the solid lines indicate two-way communication between the dialer and receiver.

Digital dialer transceivers are capable of handling several hundred dialers and, in some systems, as many as a thousand dialers. The actual number of dialers communicating with a single transceiver depends a lot on the type of message. For instance, if routine messages such as openings and closings are communicated in addition to alarms, additional transceivers might be required, especially during normal opening and closing times. To reduce the number of messages being transmitted, the need for transmitting openings and closings should be considered.

Opening and closing messages do, however, provide a daily operational check of the transmission system, as well as reporting the contents of the message. If opeing and closing reports are not required and additional system checking is desired, dialers can be programmed to transmit a test report periodically to the central station. The reports can be transmitted every 12 or 24 hours, or at some other periodic increment, depending on the required safeguards and the sophistication of the anticipated threat. An advantage of periodic test reports is that the tests can be programmed so that all the reports are not transmitted at approximately the same time every day, as with opening and closing reports. Programming the test reports to be transmitted during periods of moderate message communication will reduce peak demands on the transceiver.

When evaluating the application of digital dialers, consideration should be given to the fact that telephone lines are not constantly supervised. If the telephone line between a dialer and the initial telephone exchange is cut, there is no way the dialer can transmit a message to the central station. Therefore, the physical integrity of the telephone line is important. It can be improved by installing a dedicated cable in conduit, and even further improved by burying it in the ground.

Another technique for improving the signal transmission is to install dual digital dialers. These dialers can be used to monitor separate areas of the protected facility and yet be connected so that they both transmit all alarm messages. With a dual system, each dialer should be connected to a separate telephone line, and the lines should exit the building in different directions. Dual digital dialers certainly improve the safety and the probability of communicating the alarm message when the telephone cables follow separate routes to the telephone exchange.

Another evaluation consideration of digital dialers, as with multiplex systems, is the operational contingencies when there is a major component failure. If a major transceiver component fails, the entire monitoring function could be out of order. As with multiplex systems, a contingency possibility is to have a spare transceiver available to assume the monitoring function. Another possibility is to repair the receiver immediately. Because of the downtime, however, repair is practical only if major receiver modules are convenient to test and replace or are of the plug-in type.

A feature of many digital dialers that should be considered in the application evaluation is the listen-in capability. Since dialers communicate over voice-grade telephone lines, the listen-in feature is very practical. It provides a means for a trained operator to listen in at the protected facility for uncommon noises or sounds when there is an alarm. It must be emphasized, however, that the absence of noises does not necessarily mean that there has not been an intrusion.

In summary, digital dialers have many applications in both commercial and proprietary central alarm stations. They can be used to communicate intrusion, fire, and holdup or duress alarms from retail and wholesale stores, offices, filling stations, private homes, and schools. As in any security system or monitoring system design, the equipment should be selected based on the required safeguards.

RADIO-FREQUENCY TRANSMISSION

Radio-frequency transmission systems used in central stations consist of radio transmitters that on command can report alarm messages from the facility they are monitoring to the central station receiver. Radio systems can be used for monitoring facilities in remote areas where telephone lines are not available or are difficult to obtain. The FCC has five dual frequency channels available for central station applications between the frequencies of 460.9 MHz and 466.0 MHz, with a maximum power output of 110 watts. The FCC regulations governing the central station applications of radio transmission systems appear in Part 91, Industrial Radio Services of the Commission Rules. The FCC also has lower-frequency channels available for general communication purposes that are licensed for central station applications.

Radio-frequency systems operating at these frequencies are basically line-of-sight transmission systems. This implies that the transmit and receive antennas are essentially in view of each other. They are line-of-sight because the transmitted energy at these frequencies essentially travels in a straight line, not following the earth's curvature. Any large object between the transmitter and receiver, such as a large hill or building, will block or scatter the energy away from the receiver. This line-of-sight distance or range between the transmitter and receiver depends basically on the transmitter output power, antenna gain, and antenna mounting height. If the transmit antenna is approximately 30 feet from the ground and the receive antenna is 50 feet from the ground, the line-of-sight range is about 12 miles. The range can be increased, assuming adequate power and antenna gain, by increasing the antenna mounting height. Increasing the antenna height increases the distance the antennas can transmit. If the line-of-sight range is limited by transmitter output power, the range can be increased by using directional transmitting antennas to direct the energy at the receiver.

Radio transmitters communicate their alarm messages to the central station receiver in a coded message. Each radio transmitter is assigned an identification number, and the identification code is transmitted along with the coded message that describes the nature of the alarm. Prior to sending its alarm message, the radio transmitter sends a preamble to alert the receiver. The receiver then locks in on the alarm transmission, receives and decodes the alarm message, and displays the information for the central station operator. The protected facility's identification code is displayed on a numeric readout, and the information is printed by an event recorder. Receivers can accommodate up to a thousand different transmitters. The actual number of transmitters reporting to a single receiver can be limited to a lower number based on the need for signal transmissions.

Radio-frequency transmission systems are susceptible to electromagnetic interference. In the case of systems used in central station applications, the ambient electromagnetic energy can distort or mask the transmitted coded message until it is unrecognizable by the receiver. The energy also can introduce signals that could be interpreted by the receiver as a valid alarm message. Several signal transmission techniques are used to minimize the interference problem. The most common technique is simply to transmit the alarm message repeatedly for several minutes to improve the probability of accurate communication. Repeating the message transmission eliminates most interference from momentary electromagnetic fields, such as those associated with lightning.

Another transmission technique to reduce interference is to transmit the alarm information using dual frequency channels. One method is to transmit the coded message first at one frequency for several seconds, then a short time after the first message has been transmitted, transmit the message again at the second frequency. This alternating transmission continues for several minutes. A second transmission method is to transmit the coded message at one frequency and require the presence of a second frequency along with the first frequency to validate the alarm message. Dual frequency transmission certainly improves the probability of completing and validating the alarm message.

Crystal-controlled oscillators are used in RF transmission systems to maintain the frequency stability of the transmitted signals. With this type of stability, the receiver can use narrowband filters that pass only the signals within their bandpass. Filtering reduces the interference from extraneous signals, thereby improving the signal-to-noise ratio of the received signal and consequently the probability of accurately communicating the alarm message. Improving the signal-to-noise ratio also reduces the vulnerability of the receiver to deliberate jamming from an external RF source. A jamming attack could mask the transmitted signal and prevent the receiver from receiving a valid alarm message.

Other vulnerabilities of an RF transmission system are the transmit and receive antennas and the interconnecting transmission cable. In an actual radio transmission, the transmitted energy is radiated from the transmit antenna to the receive antenna. The energy is picked up by the receive antenna and routed through an RF transmission cable to the receiver. The transmitter relies on the transmit antenna to radiate the energy, and the receiver relies on the receive antenna, along with the transmission cable, to carry the signal to the receiver. If any of these components are destroyed, the alarm message will not be communicated. Therefore, particular attention should be given to the location and protection of the antennas and their interconnecting transmission lines.

Applications

The block diagram in Figure 19–6 shows a basic RF transmission system. The system consists of N radio transmitters that report the security status of their respective protected facility intrusion detection sensors to the receiver in the central station. N is the total number of transmitters reporting to the

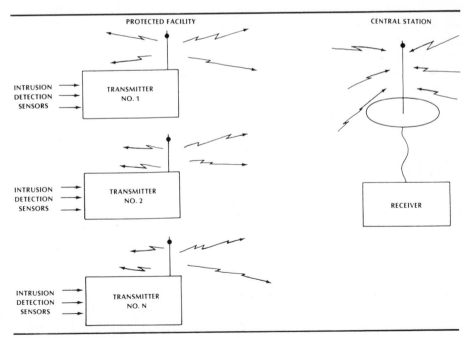

Figure 19–6   Radio-frequency transmission system.

receiver. The number can range from one to the maximum allowable number of transmitters that can be accommodated by the receiver, or it can be fewer based on the estimated rate of radio transmissions. *Rate of transmissions* is the number of security status reports transmitted to the receiver during a given period of time.

The rate of transmissions is important to know because each radio transmission usually lasts several minutes. If there should be several simultaneous transmissions or several transmissions within a short period of time, one or more of the radio transmissions might be missed by the receiver. Therefore, the transmission rate should be estimated for the anticipated busiest reporting period. To reduce the transmission rate, less-vital information, such as facility openings and closings, should be transmitted for a shorter period. In fact, if the opening and closing reports might jeopardize the receiver's ability to receive valid alarm transmissions, consideration should be given to eliminating or at least minimizing the number of nonvital reports.

Opening and closing reports, if they are transmitted to the central station, serve an additional function other than reporting the action. Receiving these reports proves that the RF transmission system is operational, although this is not necessary because a daily operational test can be initiated by a 24-hour clock in the transmitter. The clock can be set to initiate a daily test or even multiple operational tests at the same time or times when the radio transmission rate is low. To maintain a reasonably low transmission rate for any given period, each transmitter clock can be set to initiate an operational test at a different time, thereby staggering the radio transmissions.

A potential vulnerability that should be considered in the system design is the location of the antennas and their respective transmission lines. As previously mentioned, the radio transmitters and receivers rely on their antennas to radiate and receive the transmitted security messages. If the antennas are destroyed, the system will not operate. Of the two antennas, the transmit antenna is usually the most vulnerable, as in cases where the protected facility is vacated after working hours. The antenna will be especially vulnerable if it is installed outside the protected area, unless it is installed in some inconspicuous or difficult-to-reach location. If the protected facility is an all-metal building, the antenna will have to be mounted outside the building because RF energy will not penetrate metal. In this situation, the exterior antenna should be carefully located for its physical protection. If possible, it should be installed inside the protected facility, where it is protected by the intrusion detection sensors.

There should be very little attenuation of the transmitted signal by most building materials at the assigned operating frequencies. This includes materials such as wood, glass, cinder block, brick, and fiberglass. But thick concrete walls will attenuate the transmitted signal to some degree. Depending on the operating range, this could affect the performance of the system. In this type of application, the system performance should be evaluated with the antenna in its anticipated location before finalizing the design. In fact, it is good practice to evaluate the performance of any radio transmission system prior to installation because there are often unanticipated anomalies that can be remedied.

The receive antenna should be mounted as high as possible at the central station in a difficult-to-reach location. A high antenna will improve the overall system transmission range. If the location is difficult to reach, the antenna will be less vulnerable to damage. The RF transmission line between the antenna and receiver also should be well protected. If the transmission line must be routed along some accessible portion of the building, it should be physically protected to reduce its vulnerability.

Radio-frequency transmission systems have applications in both commercial and proprietary central stations. Other than their applications in monitoring commercial establishments, radio transmitters can be used for monitoring remote assets such as sailboats, yachts, and cabin cruisers. They also can be used in a nonsecurity role to monitor remote industrial control functions such as valve positions, flow, and temperature. As with any signal transmission system, the application should be evaluated based on the anticipated threat.

Chapter 20

Alarm Signal
Display

The function of a central station monitoring system is to monitor the security
status of a protected facility, transmit any changes in its status to the central
alarm station, and display this information in a meaningful manner for the
station operators. The type of display depends primarily on the signal transmission system. For instance, if the transmitters are dedicated to communicating the security status of each protected area separately over dedicated
signal lines, as are DC and AC transmission systems, the status information
is usually displayed on separate dedicated annunciator panels. If the monitoring system transmitters communicate with a single recorder or receiver,
such as McCulloh circuits, digital dialers, or radio transmitters, the status
information is collectively displayed on a single numeric readout. In this
type of display the protected area is identified by a preassigned identification
number. Depending on the display, the identification number is either
printed by the recording device or displayed on a numeric readout and
recorded by an event recorder, along with the security status information.
Multiplex transmission displays will be discussed with computer-managed
monitoring systems.

Although the basic type of display depends on the signal transmission
system, the alarm monitoring function can be improved for some installations by including a map display as part of the monitoring system. Map displays depict the physical layout of the protected areas and identify each sensor location or zone of detection with a separate indicator light. They are
especially effective in proprietary systems that have interior detectors at
various locations inside the facility and exterior detectors located around the
perimeter. In this type of application, the pictorial representation of the protected areas can assist the central station operator in identifying the area or
zone in alarm and expedite dispatching the response force.

Event recorders also can improve the effectiveness of any monitoring
system that does not already have a recorder as part of the basic display.
Event recorders print all alarms and changes in status, along with the date
and time the event occurred, on paper tape, thereby relieving the operator of

this tedious task. The access/secure status changes are printed in black or blue, and the alarms are printed in red. Printing the alarms in red makes them easily distinguishable from the routine status changes. With an event recorder, the printed status information is immediately available for the central station operator. The paper tapes can serve as a record of the day's events.

Once the monitoring system signal transmission and display equipment have been selected, the layout and presentation of the equipment should be human-engineered to ensure an effective system/operator interface. Alarm station operators usually have tasks other than their monitoring duties to perform in their normal day-to-day function. Therefore, the monitoring system should be laid out and the displays arranged in a manner to accommodate the operators in performing these tasks. The first phase of the alarm station design is to position the monitoring equipment within the station. The second phase is to arrange the display in an effective configuration for the central station operators to perform their monitoring functions effectively.

The physical layout or positioning of the monitoring equipment depends on the physical configuration of the area allocated for the alarm station, unless it is a new facility. Even though designing a new central station certainly has advantages over trying to utilize an existing area, the basic design parameters remain the same. These parameters include providing adequate visibility, mobility, and accessibility for the central station operators.

Visibility is important in central stations in terms of both positioning the monitoring displays and illuminating the area around the display and the work area. Displays should be positioned so that they are always in view of the alarm station operators, even when they are performing their routine tasks around the station. Perhaps visibility is not as critical for installations using displays with audible annunciators, assuming the operators can always hear the annunciator, but visibility is important in central stations using television monitors. Even if the monitors are observed only to assess an area after an alarm occurs, they should always be positioned so they are visible to the operator.

The illumination level in most central stations should be adequate for the central station operator to read the display panels and activate the appropriate controls or switches. There are installations, however, where this level of illumination would be incompatible with the operators' monitoring functions. For instance, in a proprietary installation where the operator performs visual surveillance of the grounds outside the monitoring station, the work area should not be lighted, or only dimly lighted, to accommodate the operator. The display panels should be only dimly lighted to provide visibility to the operator in identifying the alarm.

Central stations with television monitors are another example of installations where standard laboratory lighting, especially around the monitors, might be too bright and undesirable for the operator. Provision should be made for adjusting the illumination level in the monitoring areas to improve the television picture contrast. Having variable light levels, the operator can adjust the level for his own viewing comfort.

Operator mobility is an important consideration when laying out the equipment in a central station. The work area should have adequate space for the required number of operators. They should be able to move freely between rows of equipment, around anyone performing a full-time monitoring function at a display console, or around a maintenance man working on the equipment. Conflict between operators performing their monitoring function can be very distracting, especially if it exists when one is acknowledging an intrusion or emergency alarm.

Accessibility is another important consideration. The monitoring equipment should be positioned so that it is accessible for repair. Accessibility is especially important when major monitoring equipment items malfunction and must be repaired to continue monitoring the protected facilities. If the monitoring equipment is accessible from the back, then it should be positioned far enough away from the wall or other equipment so that any faulty module can be conveniently removed or repaired. In areas where there is not an adequate work area to leave space behind the equipment, alternative methods of providing access must be considered. Perhaps provision could be made to pull the equipment away from the wall to perform the repair. All these parameters are important and should be considered when designing a central station.

The second phase in laying out the monitoring equipment is to arrange the displays and other ancillary equipment in an effective operator/display configuration. Both the display configuration and the operator's method of monitoring the displays depends primarily on the type of alarm monitoring system, and to some degree on the number of facilities or zones being monitored.

For instance, if DC or AC transmission systems are used for monitoring the alarms from several hundred facilities, the display area required for all the individual annunciator panels would be too large for a console arrangement. The operators would have to patrol the monitoring panels and acknowledge all alarms and change-of-status conditions from a standing position. Since the operators are standing, the annunciator panels should be rack mounted in rows in an area between 36 inches and 68 inches from the floor. The area under the annunciator panels can be used for mounting power supplies and storing other equipment not essential to the monitoring function. In this type of installation, the event recorders, radio microphone, and telephones should be centrally located at a desk usually occupied by the shift supervisor. If a map display is used, it should be mounted in front of the operator's desk or in full view from the desk so that he will not have to leave the radio or telephone to observe the map.

If multiplexers, digital dialers, or radio signal transmission systems are used for communicating security status information, the displays can usually be configured in a console arrangement for a single operator. In this case the operator will probably be seated in front of the console. Therefore, the receivers should be close enough to the operator so that he can conveniently actuate the acknowledge and reset switches and read the printed status information on the event recorder from his seated position. The radio microphone and telephones also should be within reach. Again, if a map display is part of the monitoring system, it should be mounted in full view of the operator, preferably over or at least near the operator's console.

In applications where television cameras are used for visual alarm assessment or area surveillance, the monitors should be located in view of the central station operator. Whether they are located directly in front of the operator or off to one side depends primarily on the television application.

In an alarm assessment application, the operator might occasionally observe the monitors for general surveillance. But when there is an alarm, his full attention is directed toward observing the monitor to determine the cause of the alarm. Since the operator is alerted to the alarm by the alarm monitoring system, the monitors do not have to be located directly in front of him. When articulated cameras are used for visual assessment, however, the monitor and controls should be located in a position of easy access for the operator. Accessibility will enhance the operator's ability to operate the camera pan, tilt, and zoom controls and observe the corresponding scene on the television monitors.

Although there might be applications where television cameras are needed for constant visual surveillance of an area, it should be realized that constant monitoring is very fatiguing for the operator. The maximum number of monitors he can effectively watch, sitting at a console, is six when they are arranged in an area about 20 inches high and 24 inches wide. Tests have indicated that an operator can effectively monitor television screens for only about 30 minutes. Then he should be relieved for 1 to 2 hours. Constant surveillance applications should be limited only to those areas where the required safeguards justify such an application.

Not only must the central alarm station display and operator interface be designed to accommodate the monitoring functions, but the operating instructions and response procedures also should be well documented for the operators. Even though the operators are, or should be, well trained in the operation of the monitoring equipment, detailed instructions should be available if a question should arise. Operating instructions should include the basic step-by-step procedures for acknowledging status changes and alarm responses and for making CCTV alarm assessment, access control responses, or emergency alarm responses. Telephone numbers of whom to call in case of an equipment failure should be available. Response instructions, such as whom to contact in case of an alarm or emergency, should be documented, along with their telephone numbers. Contingency plans should be documented for any emergencies that might arise at the central station or at any one of the protected areas. Special instructions or procedures that might pertain to certain protected areas should be documented. For instance, if the area contains hazardous materials, this information should be available to anyone responding to an alarm. These types of instructions might appear very basic and unnecessary, but sometimes in an emergency the basics might be forgotten.

The following paragraphs will describe the types of displays and their applications.

ANNUNCIATOR PANELS

Annunciator panels display the alarm and access/secure status of individually protected facilities or sensors for the central station operator. Mechanical drops and current meters have been used to indicate alarms, but newer annunciators use indicator lights to identify alarm and status changes. Alarms are indicated by red lights, access by amber lights, and secure by green lights. Sometimes other status information also is displayed, such as power at the protected facility. The auxiliary information is usually indicated by white lights.

The AC and DC balanced current systems, newer McCulloh systems, and some multiplex systems use annunciator panels. These panels can be separate rack-mounted modules, or they can be single-panel displays with multiple sets of status indicator lights. Each set of lights is dedicated to annunciating the security status of a single protected area or sensor. Single panel displays are often used to annunciate the status of individual sensors in proprietary installations. They also are used with some multiplex systems. Most DC and AC balanced current systems use separate annunciator panels. An advantage of separate modules is that the monitoring system can be easily expanded and configured to satisfy new requirements.

A major advantage of any annunciator panel is that the status of each protected area or sensor is constantly displayed. Any changes in the status of a protected area or sensor is instantly identified for the central station operator. Individual alarms or status changes can be easily acknowledged and reset by operating the corresponding switches on the annunciator panel.

Applications

An important application consideration of annunciator panels is that if an annunciator module fails, only the corresponding protected area is affected. In installations using many annunciator panels, it would be economical to have spare modules available. Having spare modules will minimize the downtime because the station operator should be able to replace any malfunctioning unit. Each individual module component, such as lights, circuit boards, and relays, can be interchanged between units, if necesssary.

Annunciator panels have several disadvantages when used to monitor large numbers of protected areas. Because separate modules are required for each area, it might be impractical for one or even several operators to monitor, acknowledge, and reset all the individual annunciators. This could present operating problems during times such as facility openings and closings. During such times, it would probably be difficult for the operators to absorb and assess all the information displayed.

NUMERIC DISPLAYS

Numeric readout displays use Nixie tubes or LED displays to identify the detection zones or protected areas reporting to the monitor. Indicator lights are used with the numeric display to indicate the appropriate alarm or access/secure event being reported. This information, along with the identification number and the date and time the event occurred, are recorded on the display's event recorder.

Numeric displays are used to display information being communicated by digital dialers and some multiplex systems. In these types of communication systems, each protected facility or zone is assigned an identification number. When there is an alarm or change of status in the protected area, the identification number, along with the event, is transmitted to the central station. The identification number is displayed on the numeric readout, and the corresponding event, alarm, or access/secure notification is identified by the appropriate indicator light. On receipt of the event message, an audible annunciator alerts the central station operator, who acknowledges the message and responds accordingly. This information is then recorded by the event recorder.

Applications

An application consideration when using numeric displays is that only one event can be displayed at a time. Emergencies or alarms could be delayed because concurrent events are recognized and processed serially on a first-in/first-out basis. If an emergency or alarm event should occur during a time when openings and closings are being transmitted, the response to the event could be delayed. To minimize such delays, additional displays can be used. Two other possibilities are to limit opening and closing transmissions and to report emergencies and high-risk area alarms on a separate display reserved for such reportings. If the probability of several of these events occurring simultaneously is minimal, there should be minimal delays in reporting.

A disadvantage of a numeric-type reporting system is that if there is an equipment failure, the entire reporting capability is lost. Therefore, consideration should be given to having a spare unit or spare modules available.

MAP DISPLAYS

Map displays are used to identify zones of detection and, in some cases, individual sensors on a pictorial representation of the protected installation. A well-designed display can be useful in identifying individual alarms and directing response personnel. To achieve maximum effectiveness, however, the map must accurately represent the physical relationship between the zones of detection and the layout of the installation. The scale of the map layout should be adequate to depict the individual detection zones clearly. Cluttering the display might be confusing to the central station operator.

Selecting an adequate layout scale that will give an effective presentation of an installation with both perimeter and interior zones of detection might be difficult. For instance, if an installation has a large perimeter with respect to the buildings within the protected area, a scale that would clearly show the zones of detection within the buildings will probably result in an overwhelming display when the perimter is included. In this type of installation, it might be advisable to use two separate presentations of the installation. One presentation could show the perimeter zones of detection with only outlines of the building within the perimeter to show their relative positions with respect to the perimeter. The second presentation could show the interior of the building, identifying the protected areas or sensor locations on a larger-scale layout. This type of display can be descriptive, yet less cluttered and confusing.

Applications

A map display can be a board-mounted drawing with indicator lights to identify the zones of detection, a computer-generated CRT display, or an automatic computer-controlled slide projector display. Map board displays can be made as basic or as detailed as the installation presentation requires. They also can be used effectively as the primary annunciator panel, especially if the display is not cluttered. As a primary display, green and amber lights should be added along with the alarm indicator to indicate whether an area is in access or secure mode. Panels are available for constructing map displays, but large or detail displays would probably have to be custom-made. A consideration is that custom-made displays would be difficult to modify to accommodate changes.

Computer-generated graphic displays are generated on a CRT display, which has limited resolution. Consequently, the presentation might be of poor quality in areas requiring a lot of detail. Slide projections showing actual photographs of the protected area make for the most realistic presentation. A consideration with using slide projectors is that only one slide can be presented at a time.

The application of map displays, as with the application of annunciator panels, depends on the type of signal transmission system, number of areas being protected, and size of the installation. Another consideration, especially in the use of map displays, is whether the central station is commercial or proprietary. Although it would be possible to use map boards in commercial installations, they are more adaptable to proprietary applications. Computer-generated CRT displays and slide projector displays are quite adaptable to any type of computer-managed central station monitoring application.

Chapter 21

Computer-Managed Monitoring Systems

Computerized monitoring systems have the capability to perform many more functions than just monitoring and displaying sensor alarms and access/secure status changes. They can report and log routine events being transmitted from the protected area and initiate command functions at these areas. Having these monitoring and command capabilities, computers can perform a vast number of operations and provide flexibility for system growth and modifications.

A computer is basically a collection of electronic components and elecromechanical devices systematically designed to follow a programmed sequence of instructions for executing the desired operational commands and functions. It is more than just a collection of electronics hardware, however. The hardware can do nothing without programmed instructions or software, but the software needs the hardware to execute the programs. Therefore, a computer is not a collection of hardware or software; it is both.

Computers can be divided into two classes: analog and digital. Analog computers process information in the form of physical analog signals, such as voltages or currents, which represent other quantities, such as angular position, pressure, or mass. They are more suitable for direct solution of complicated equations through simulation of many variable parameters. Analog computers are often used for controlling other machines, such as the autopilot of an airplane. In this application, the computer receives information directly from the airplane's sensing devices and generates the actual control signal for maneuvering the plane.

The most popular digital computers process information in the form of binary numbers. Binary numbers are represented by groups of only two digits, zero and one. These digits, or bits, are represented in the computer by two distinct voltage levels. One voltage represents a logic zero, and a second level represents a logic one. The use of binary numbers greatly simplifies the computer's hardware.

Digital computers have the ability to store vast amounts of data, to retrieve the data quickly, to process the data accurately, and to execute programmed instructions. The programmed instructions can include conditions that direct the computer operations. For these reasons digital computers have many applications, including their use in alarm station computer-managed monitoring systems.

A computerized monitoring system normally consists of a digital computer processor; one or more displays such as a CRT, printer, or slide projector; an operator keyboard input; and a communication processor to communicate with the protected area's transponders. Figure 21–1 shows a block diagram of a computer-managed monitoring system. The digital computer processor is divided into three basic functions: memory, input/output, and central processing. The memory stores both the data to be processed and the processing instructions. This information is stored in the form of binary numbers. Each binary number, or *word*, is stored in a specific location in the memory. This location has an identifying number called an *address*.

The memory is used to recall or store data in read or write functions. In a *read function*, the data at a specific address is retrieved to instruct or command an event. The event could be to display instructions for the alarm station operator or to initiate a command at a particular protected area. In a *write function*, new data is placed in memory at a specific location for later retrieval. The memory is used to program the computer and to store information such as area openings and closings. The storage capacity of the memory is one limiting factor of a computer's application capability.

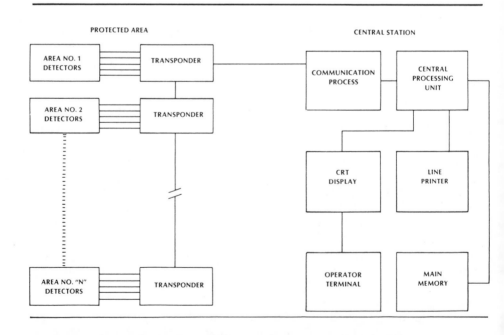

Figure 21–1   Computer-managed system block diagram.

The computer's central processing unit (CPU) interprets the programmed instructions and controls the sequence and manner in which the data are transferred between the computer registers. Since both the instructions and data being processed are stored in memory, the CPU must first retrieve the instruction data from memory. Then it decodes the data and executes the commands in accordance with the programmed instructions. This sequence of events is executed with registers that carry out these operations. An arithmetic logic unit within the CPU performs the calculations and manipulates the data so that they may be displayed or recorded. It enables the CPU to combine data in the registers with data coming from memory.

The input/output unit, as the name implies, controls the transfer of data into and out of the CPU. Inputs to the computer may come from punched cards, magnetic or paper tape, or, in the case of central station computers shown in the block diagram in Figure 21–1, the communication processor. Data also can be entered into the computer through the operator keyboard. The computer output section can send data to magnetic tape or disks, a CRT, a random access slide projector, or a line printer. Input and output are the functions by which computers interface with peripheral equipment and talk to the outside world.

The communication processor shown in Figure 21–1 communicates the status of each protected area's transponder to the CPU as they are sequentially polled. The transponder in each protected area continuously monitors the security system's status and reports this information to the alarm station when addressed by the communication processor. The communication between the processor and the individual transponders is by TDM. This is basically the same multiplex transmission system described in Chapter 19, "Signal Transmission System." In this system each transponder is assigned a binary-coded identification number. When the transponder is interrogated by the communication processor, it recognizes the identification number and responds to the interrogate message. The message could simply be to report the security status of the protected area, or it could be to activate a command function. Both the interrogate and response messages are communicated in representative binary numbers.

In operation, the communication processor requests the status of a transponder and reports the status to the computer, where it is compared with the previous status. If there is change in the status from the previous transmission, the CPU recalls from memory the computer instructions for the proper response to the status change. The status change could be an alarm. In this case, the instructions might be to display the alarm on the CRT display along with a message for the central station operator, perhaps to alert the police or call the proprietor. The instructions could include printing the same information on the line printer and recording it in memory. Depending on the security, the instruction might be to activate a deterrent device in the protected area. In this case, the CPU sends the command directions through the communication processor. The processor transmits the identification number of the transponder where the event occurred and relays the command function. The transponder then executes the command. These interrogate, response, display, and command functions are all communicated in binary numbers in thousandths of a second (milliseconds).

The communication processor interrogate/response polling cycle is continued sequentially for each transponder reporting to the alarm station. Any alarm or changes in the access/secure status are reported at this time. Areas of high priority can be polled more than once on each polling cycle to reduce the system's response time.

Applications

Computer-managed monitoring systems used in alarm station applications are normally used to manage intrusion alarms, fire alarms, guard tours, openings and closings, access control television assessment camera controls, and environmental equipment controls. One of the simplest computer tasks is to monitor sensor alarms, either intrusion or fire. The sensors in a particular protected area are continuously monitored by the area transponder, which reports the sensor status to the CPU every time it is polled by the communication processor. When there is an alarm in one of the areas, it is displayed for the alarm station operator, printed on a line printer, and recorded in memory by the CPU.

Routine events such as guard tours, openings and closings, periodic maintenance, or any task that is conducted periodically can be computer managed. To manage these events, each protected area is assigned a time window during the hour, day, week, or even month, depending on the periodicity of the event. The window time and periodicity of the event are programmed in the computer instructions and stored in memory to control the monitoring function. For guard tours a time may be assigned for every hour or every 4 hours for the guard to punch in at a specific location. These times could be staggered in a large installation where the guard must check a number of protected areas. If the guard should fail to punch in within the time window in any one of the protected areas, the alarm station operator is alerted. Otherwise, the fact that the guard did punch in is automatically recorded in memory for future retrieval if required. Routine openings and closings can be handled in a similar manner.

The length of time assigned for the time window should be commensurate with the criticality of the event. For instance, facility openings and closings and guard tours should have a narrower time window than maintenance tasks. Even some opening and closing time windows might require closer control than others. Regardless of the window time interval, the computer monitors the window, and as long as the event occurs within the assigned time, it is recorded in memory. If the event does not occur within the designated time, the computer alerts the alarm station operator.

Although the computer can perform these types of monitoring functions, each function type requires a unique set of programmed instructions in memory and consumes some time. Since the memory capacity and execution time are limiting factors in determining the computer's operating capability, each additional operation or function should be carefully considered before it is added.

Access control systems provide security by controlling who can enter where, and, in some systems, when they can enter. These systems rely on one or a combination of techniques for controlling access. One technique requires the person entering a protected area to enter a memorized code into a keyboard that controls a lock. This technique provides only minimal access control because almost anyone can find out the memorized code. Another technique uses a card reader that can read and identify encoded cards inserted into the reader. Card readers provide a higher level of security, but the cards can be lost or stolen, perhaps without notice. Assessment of personal characteristics for positive identification, such as fingerprints and a voiceprint, is the most secure method of controlling access. Closed circuit television monitoring is another method. Combinations of these access techniques, such as the combination of a voiceprint and coded card reader, can be used to increase the access control security. Any one or combination of these control techniques can be computer managed. Each time an additional access criterion is added, however, it occupies space in the memory and requires time to execute. In fact, in installations where many people are required to enter through controlled areas, the access controls are often handled by a separate computer system.

Television cameras are commonly used in security applications for both exterior perimeter and interior alarm assessment, as well as for general surveillance. Often in these applications, there are too many cameras to have a dedicated television monitor for each camera. In this case several cameras are connected to a single monitor through a coaxial switch. Although this is not related to the computer's monitoring function, the number of cameras connected to a single monitor should be commensurate with the security application. Usually no more than four cameras should be connected to a monitor.

Regardless of the number of cameras, the camera selection can be computer controlled through the switching network. In this application, when a sensor in a zone with television coverage initiates an alarm, it is registered in the corresponding transponder. The transponder reports the alarm to the computer when it is interrogated. The transponder's response message addresses the memory for instructions through the CPU. The camera covering the area in alarm is identified and switched to a television monitor in the alarm station. The computer also can be programmed to articulate a camera with pan/tilt and zoom controls to cover a specific area in alarm. This method of alarm assessment should be carefully considered, however, because it requires additional time for the camera to be properly aimed at the specific area.

Building environmental control systems can be computer managed. The heating and air conditioning can simply be turned on or off at specific times during the day or week to conserve energy. The computer can be programmed to control a building's temperature based on the anticipated daily occupancy or operating schedule and the outside temperature. For instance, in the simplest case, if a building is occupied only five days a week, then the computer can be programmed to operate the environmental system accordingly. In more sophisticated applications the computer can be programmed to control the temperature for an anticipated occupancy size. For instance, a shopping center might anticipate a small crowd during weekdays and a large crowd in the evenings and all day Saturday. The heat or air conditioning is then reduced or increased accordingly to control the comfort level for the anticipated crowd. Both environmental control techniques reduce energy consumption. The effectiveness and savings of the control system depend a lot on the outside temperature extremes. It has been reported that computer-managed environmental control systems have saved enough in energy costs to pay for the total computer monitoring system after only a few years of service.

In the application of computer-managed monitoring systems, as with any other major system component, consideration should be given to keeping the system operational in case of a computer failure. A spare computer could be available to accept the management operation in case of a failure. Switchover between the computers can be either automatic or manual. Another possibility is to have spare modules and the capability available to expedite any repairs.

Computer-managed monitoring systems are a real asset to an alarm station for monitoring and control applications. They can be used to perform many operations and command functions with great speed and accuracy. A real advantage is that the system can be reprogrammed to incorporate changes or modifications without changing the hardware. The flexibility and expandability of computer systems through software changes is a favorable feature in their application.

Chapter 22

Application Guidelines

The intent of this summary is to present a list of basic guidelines for selecting, designing, installing, and operating an alarm signal transmission and monitoring system.

ALARM TRANSMITTERS

1. It should be assumed, when designing an alarm transmission system, that anyone with the technical knowledge, resources, and time can compromise the transmission system or signal line.
2. Never identify the alarm signal lines or signal line terminals in the junction box along the signal line route between the protected facility and monitoring station.
3. Install all signal lines in sealed metal conduit where practical.
4. Only shielded cables should be used for signal transmission in the area of electromagnetic energy sources.
5. Signal cables and junction boxes should be in good condition so that moisture will not affect the electrical characteristics of the transmission line.
6. All signal cable junction boxes should be locked and have tamper protection.
7. Signal line supervision should be commensurate with the sophistication of the anticipated threat.

McCULLOH CIRCUITS

1. Avoid connecting so many transmitters to a single loop that "clash" will be an operational problem.
2. Consider using coded transmitters with positive noninterfering circuits to eliminate clash in proprietary systems.
3. McCulloh circuits provide very little signal line supervision.

DIRECT CURRENT (DC)

1.   Signals are transmitted over a pair of dedicated metallic conductors between the protected area and corresponding monitor.
2.   Each protected area's access/secure and alarm status is monitored and displayed separately.
3.   Direct current transmitters provide a higher level of signal transmission line supervision than McCulloh circuits.
4.   The current variation level in a balanced current system should be between 15 and 25 percent.
5.   Additional signal line supervision is provided by transmission systems that superimpose AC signals on the DC signal.

ALTERNATING CURRENT (AC)

1.   Signals are transmitted over a dedicated voice-grade telephone line between the protected area and monitor.
2.   Each protected area's access/secure and alarm status is monitored and displayed separately.
3.   Signal line supervision is usually better than with balanced current DC systems.

MULTIPLEX

1.   Status information is transmitted from multiple transponders over a single communication channel to the monitoring station.
2.   Multiplex systems can provide more detailed information then the normal access/secure and alarm status.
3.   Signals can be transmitted over any type of communication channel.
4.   Operational contingencies should be considered in case of a major component failure, such as a problem with the interrogator.
5.   There is no limit on the distance that digital information can be transmitted over voice-grade telephone lines.
6.   Other devices such as fire alarms can be communicated by multiplex systems, but there should be provisions to identify their response separately.
7.   Commands can be communicated to activated devices in the protected area.
8.   Multiplex systems provide a high level of line supervision when random or pseudorandom coding is used for the signal transmission.

DIGITAL DIALERS

1. Digital dialers transmit protected area status information over voice-grade telephone lines, even through exchange networks.
2. There is no limit on the distance the information can be transmitted over voice-grade telephone lines.
3. A listen-in feature is available for surveillance.

RADIO TRANSMISSION

1. Consider radio transmitters for areas where telephone lines are not available or are difficult to obtain.
2. The signal transmission range is limited to the line of sight between the transmitter and receiver.

ALARM DISPLAYS

1. Alarms should be annunciated and displayed so that they can be identified quickly by the operator and associated with the exact alarm location.
2. Event recorders should be used to record all access/secure status changes and alarms in protected areas.
3. Map displays should be considered to identify alarm locations for all proprietary alarm monitoring systems.
4. The scale of the map layout should be adequate to depict the detection zones clearly.
5. The illumination level in the monitoring area should be commensurate with the operator's visual tasks.
6. The monitor console and map display's location and arrangement should be human-engineered to optimize the operator's efficiency.

COMPUTER-MANAGED MONITORING SYSTEMS

1. Computer-managed monitors are automated systems with broad capabilities.
2. They can monitor and display status information, log routine events, provide instructional information, and initiate commands.
3. They can manage intrusion detection systems and other related functions such as access control, fire alarms, guard tours, television monitor control, and environmental control.
4. The initial cost of computers is relatively high.
5. Service/maintenance contracts will probably be required.

PART V

VISUAL SURVEILLANCE AND ALARM ASSESSMENT

Visual surveillance and sensor alarm assessment can be accomplished by using guards alone or guards supported by CCTV. The exact method depends on the site application. If the application is just for general surveillance, guards alone might be adequate. But when the application requires sensor alarm assessment, television will probably be required to supplement the security guards.

When properly applied and installed, intrusion detection sensors can adequately detect most intrusions. If sensors detected only valid intrusions and not the stimuli that cause them to false alarm, there would be a reduced need for patrolling and response security guards. Guards would be needed only on those rare occasions when there was an actual intrusion.

Use of microprocessor technology will improve the sensors' signal processor intelligence so that the circuits can discriminate with a higher degree of confidence between valid intrusions and stimuli that would otherwise appear valid. It will certainly improve exterior sensor performance where there are many stimuli that can cause alarms. But regardless of how adequate microprocessor-controlled sensors are, there will always be instances when the sensors will not be able to discriminate between a valid intrusion and an external stimulus that appears valid to the sensor. Therefore, there will always be a need for security guards to support the intrusion detection system by assessing and responding to sensor alarms.

Interior sensors, when properly applied and installed, have a relatively low false alarm rate and can be reasonably well managed by security guards. But employing enough guards to adequately survey, assess, and respond to alarms at sites having large exterior perimeter sensor systems is usually very expensive because of high false alarm rates, especially in inclement weather. In these applications, security guards are often reinforced with CCTV systems. These offer a cost-effective way of assisting guards in alarm assessment and surveillance in both interior and exterior intrusion detection systems. A much higher percentage of CCTV systems is being used to support exterior intrusion detection systems than interior systems. Therefore, this section of the book is devoted primarily to exterior surveillance systems. The basic technology does, however, apply to interior systems.

With a properly designed CCTV system, a single monitor guard can replace or relieve a number of patrolling guards. The exact number depends on the size of the site, the size of the intrusion detection system, and, of course, the adequacy of the existing guard force. At most sites the adequacy of the guard force in terms of size is questioned, CCTV should be used to enhance its effectiveness, not necessarily diminish its size.

Television cameras convert the viewed physical scene into electrical signals suitable for transmission over a variety of media to a monitor in the central monitoring area. Cameras can be installed in a fixed position to provide visual assessment of a single intrusion detection sensor zone or a fixed area, or they can be installed on a pan/tilt pedestal, which the guard can remotely pan and tilt to direct the camera to cover multiple sensor zones or larger areas. Fixed cameras usually have fixed optics to cover the desired area, whereas movable cameras have movable optics so that they can survey large areas and then zoom in and focus on desired targets. The image viewed by the remote camera is transmitted from the camera to the monitor over coaxial cable, fiber-optic cable, or a microwave or optical link, depending on the application and, in particular, on the distance between the camera and monitor. At the monitoring station the camera image is reconverted to a visual image.

To be effective, patrolling guards and television cameras must be supported with artificial lighting for night operations. Guards can function at night in unlighted areas if they are equipped with night vision goggles or night vision devices, but these devices are expensive and difficult to use. Night vision devices are, however, very effective in covert surveillance operations. Low light level cameras and thermal imaging cameras are available for use in unlighted areas, but they also are very expensive to obtain and maintain. As with night vision devices, there are security surveillance applications for which low light level cameras are appropriate, but for most security applications, standard daylight cameras supported with artificial lighting are more cost-effective to obtain, operate, and maintain.

The need for lighting systems depends primarily on the site's surveillance and alarm assessment requirements, but it is also affected by the site's configuration and environmental and climatic conditions. When the security requirements can be satisfied by patrolling guards, the lighting system design is usually not too critical because the guards can move closer to targets of interest for better viewing, and they can carry a flashlight to search poorly lighted areas. When the security requirements can be satisfied only by fixed guards and CCTV, then the lighting system design is much more critical. The luminaires must be located so that they can adequately illuminate the critical areas. They must be positioned or directed so that they will not create glare problems for the guards or television cameras or cause lighting or glare problems for people outside the protected site.

Luminaire lamps must be selected with care to accommodate the guards' and television cameras' spectral response. Otherwise, additional lights will be needed to produce the same camera response as a properly matched camera or human eye and lamp.

There are many different types of lamps. Incandescent lamps are instant-on and have good spectral qualities for both television and human viewing, but they are very inefficient and have a short life. High-intensity discharge lamps have efficiencies that range from very good to excellent, but they require at least 2 to 10 minutes to reach full illumination and must cool before restarting. This means that auxiliary instant-on lights might have to be used during power outages, or perhaps contingency plans would have to be established to increase the number of patrolling guards when there is a power outage.

The lighting system design is relatively easy to determine, compared with the television system design for a site using cameras to assess perimeter sensor zones. The camera tube and lens must be selected to accommodate the lighting, sensor positions, and sensor zone configuration, and they must be adequately protected to accomplish this function in the prevailing climatic conditions. The camera-to-monitor transmission system must be designed to ensure a quality television picture regardless of the transmission distance, electromagnetic environment, and climatic conditions. Finally, the television monitors must be selected to display an adequate picture size and quality to ensure that the operator can effectively perform his surveillance or alarm assessment task. Designing an effective lighting and television system is complex and, in most applications, requires the services of a lighting and television system engineer. While security managers should not be expected to design these systems, they should work closely with the engineer to ensure that all their security requirements are met. To accomplish this task, they should have a basic understanding of lighting and television terminology.

Special recognition is due my primary sources for information in Chapters 23 and 24. The Illuminating Engineering Society's *IES Lighting Handbook* was used as a source for discussing lighting systems in Chapter 23. The *Intrusion Detection Systems Handbook* by Sandia National Laboratories was used as an information source and for preparing tables in Chapter 24.

Chapter 23

Surveillance and Assessment Lighting

Along with their many other security duties, security guards perform general surveillance and respond to intrusion detection alarms. These functions are performed by guards patrolling indoor and outdoor facilities on foot or by vehicle and by their monitoring CCTV. To execute these duties properly, they need adequate lighting or some other means to see in the dark. During daylight hours and for interior applications, adequate lighting is usually not a concern because sufficient natural lighting is available outdoors and adequate artificial lighting is available indoors. The real problem is providing adequate equipment for the guards to perform their surveillance and alarm assessment duties at night. They may be equipped with night vision devices, but this is not recommended, except perhaps for covert surveillance operations and for applications in which it is impossible to have artificial lighting. The range of night vision goggles is limited to about 100 to 200 feet, depending on the ambient light. This range might be adequate for patrolling guards, but probably not for fixed guard posts. Other devices, such as starlight scopes, are limited by their narrow field of view.

Artificial lighting allows the security guards to perform their duties without having to wear night vision goggles or to look through night vision devices. Lighting has the added benefit of being a deterrent to some intruders, usually low-skill opportunistic ones, consequently improving night security in those areas where this type of threat exists. The greater the lighting effectiveness, the more visible the intruders, the greater their apprehension of detection, and the more likely they are to be deterred by the lighting. This relationship assumes that there are security guards or police within the immediate area and these officers endanger the intruders.

The effectiveness of security lighting in reducing urban, industrial, and residential crime has been documented in law enforcement reports. These reports also have documented that approximately 75 percent of all urban burglaries against commercial establishments occur during the night against facilities having either no lighting or inadequate lighting. Similarly, the frequency of urban crime is known to be highly correlated with the total number of hours of darkness during the course of a given 24-hour period. Comparisons of urban crime patterns both before and after new street lights were installed tend to show that increased light levels result in a reduction in crime. It should be noted, however, that the crime reduction observed in these studies frequently occurred in high-crime areas of the cities involved and that crime rates frequently increased in neighboring low-crime areas of the city that did not have street lights. In some cases there was also evidence of a shift to increased crime in the daytime.

Even though various studies on the effectiveness of security lighting, including the evidence from the above studies, indicate that lighting is generally a crime deterrent, it should be noted that the evidence is not conclusive because of the lack of appropriate experimental control. It also should be noted that the crimes were of the type committed by low-skill intruders. Clearly, a highly motivated trained intruder or a group of intruders contemplating a surreptitious or full-scale event attack against a high-value target is not likely to be deterred by the presence of security lights. In fact some security managers responsible for high-value targets do not want additional security lighting because they say it attracts undue attention to the site and will aid the adversary.

The lighting system design depends primarily on the specific site surveillance and alarm assessment requirements, but it is also influenced by site size, configuration, environment, and weather. Besides providing adequate illumination for the guards to perform their visual tasks, other issues must be addressed. First, the luminaires must be of a type and be positioned so that they will not produce glare for the security guards, interfere with off-site traffic, or annoy neighbors. Glare is fine only when it reduces the visual performance of an adversary. Second, the luminaire type and position should provide good light-to-dark uniformity. Ligthing uniformity is not as critical for guards as it is for television cameras because the human eye has a greater dynamic range in which to accommodate the varying light levels. But the lighting uniformity ratio, the ratio of the brightest area to the darkest area, should not exceed 6 to 1 in those areas where surveillance, and especially alarm assessment, are required. Third, if lighting is needed, it should be needed all the time. Therefore, consideration should be given to providing emergency power, or contingency plans to increase guards must be instituted for those times when the power is off. Both emergency power and contingencies will be influenced by the type of lamp used. For instance, high-intensity discharge (HID) lamps require between 2 and 10 minutes, and sometimes longer, to regain full illumination once power is lost, even for a few seconds. These deficiencies will be addressed in greater detail later in the chapter.

In lighting system design, if the requirement is for guards to perform general surveillance on foot or from a patrol vehicle passing outside a protected site or some distance away from a building, then the light sources should be installed away from the area or building requiring surveillance, between the patrol road and site. They should be directed at the site or building to minimize glare. When building illumination is the objective, the lights can be installed at ground level and directed at the building. This technique can enhance the building's architecture and aesthetics, while producing the shadow of anyone approaching the building. This lighting might have to be augmented by area lighting to cover larger open areas. If there are no buildings, area lighting alone might be sufficient.

If the guards are patrolling inside a site looking away from the protected area toward the perimeter, as well as searching within the protected area, the light sources illuminating the perimeter should be located inside the perimeter fence, between the fence and patrol road, and directed toward the fence. The luminaire type and location should be such that there is little backlighting that could cause glare and illuminate the patrolling vehicles, making them an easy target for adversaries.

If the guards are stationed in fixed locations around the site, such as in towers, the lights should be mounted high above the guards or far enough away so that they will not interfere with the guards' visual task. Designing such a system is difficult because the guards are usually observing large areas or several sensor zones for alarm assessment. One way to accomplish this is to use high-masted roadway-type luminaires. These 100-foot and higher mast luminaires are often used to illuminate highway intersections. One advantage of high-mast luminaire arrays is their extended illumination coverage due to the cluster of lamps, so fewer luminaires can illuminate a large area. Another advantage, because of their height, is that they produce very uniform light patterns. If high-mast luminaires cannot be used, care must be taken when locating the lower lights to ensure that they will not interfere with the guards' visual tasks.

Vision

Before discussing the details about designing security lighting systems, let's look at the fundamental relationships between light and vision. Our eyes are our primary gateway to the world, but without light we cannot see. With inadequate light or the wrong kind, seeing can be inefficient, uncomfortable, or even hazardous.

Many factors must be considered when designing a lighting system, and their relative importance can vary widely depending on the visual task. In security applications the most demanding visual task for the guards is trying to detect intruders from patrolling vehicles or fixed stations, or especially by monitoring television screens for a long time. Performing these tasks during daylight hours in good lighting is tedious enough, but performing them at night, especially under marginal lighting conditions, is extremely tiring. Therefore, it is very important that the lighting system provides adequate visibility so that the visual tasks can be performed with the required speed and accuracy and with minimum effort.

Our eyes are our visual sensory receptors. A horizontal cross-section of the human eye is shown in Figure 23–1. Its spherical shape is maintained by the sclera, a tough outer coat that also protects the eyes, and the cornea, the clear front covering of the eye. The optical system consists of the cornea, pupil, and lens, with the cornea supplying about 75 percent of the total dioptric power. The pupil controls the amount of light entering the eye, and the lens focuses this light on the retina. The ciliary muscle controls the lens curvature so that the eye can focus accurately on an object at one distance and then change its focus to another object at a different distance. This focusing process is called accommodation, and it is the control that allows the guards to perform an accurate visual search task.

The retina consists of a mosaic of photoreceptors and several layers of connecting nerve cells, along with supporting cells that line the rear inside part of the eye. Light reaches the photosensitive receptor cells after passing through the various retinal layers. There are two types of photosensitive receptor cells, called rods and cones. These designations are based primarily on their shape. The distribution of the rod and cone receptors varies across the retina. Cones fill the central region of the retina, which is called the fovea. The density of the cones decreases from the fovea to the periphery of the eye, while the density of the rods increases. Fine image detail can be resolved by the cones in the fovea. This is why the process of accommoda-

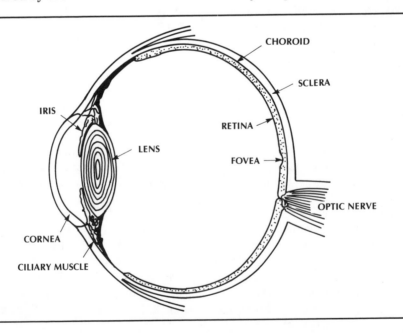

Figure 23–1 Horizontal cross-section of human eye.

tion and fixation attempts to produce a retinal image in sharp focus on the fovea.

The response of any portion of the retina at a given moment depends on the light level on that region of the retina just prior to the moment of interest. Under steady retinal illumination the area of the retina exposed is described as being adapted to that light level. Any change in the illumination level produces a change in the retina, causing it to adapt to a new equilibrium level. Since it takes a finite time for the retina to adapt, there will be a time delay before the retina reaches maximum sensitivity for a given adaptation level. The length of the delay is a function of the difference in the light levels from one moment to the next. The greater this difference, the longer the adaptation process. A loss in visibility is often produced subsequent to a change in luminance level occurring when an individual shifts his point of fixation to surfaces having different luminances. A loss of vision for a security guard searching an area could be critical, which is why it is so important to have uniform lighting without glare.

Rods have a lower threshold to light, or are more light sensitive, than cones. Cones do not respond when the luminance of the visual field is less than about 0.01 foot-lamberts, which means that security guards rely primarily on their rod receptors for night vision surveillance under low lighting conditions. Vision under low levels of field luminance is called scotopic vision. When cone receptors are primarily involved in the visual task at higher luminance levels, it is called photopic vision. Vision at luminance levels between the photopic and scotopic levels is called mesopic vision, which is where both rod and cone receptors are used. Security guards rely primarily on mesopic vision to perform their visual tasks at night, even under adequately designed security lighting systems.

Rods acting alone are insensitive to color, so objects appear gray under low lighting conditions. Mesopic vision yields a gray response from rod stimulation, which must be integrated with the color response from the cones located in the periphery of the retinal field. In the rod-free foveal region of the retina, the color response of the cones is not diluted with the gray response of the rods. For this reason, it is important that security guards performing access control by viewing color-coded badges have adequate illumination so that the visual task can be accomplished primarily by the cone receptors.

TARGET ASSESSMENT

A target's characteristics and its immediate background constitute the visibility level variables that must be considered when designing security lighting systems. The target and background characteristics of greatest importance are target size, target movement, target/background luminance contrast, target/background color contrast, background luminance intensity, background luminance uniformity, and background glare. This discussion relies almost exclusively on an NBS report, "NBS Special Publication 480-27, Security Lighting for Nuclear Weapons Storage Sites: A Literature Review and Bibliography" by Patrick G. Meguire, Joel J. Kramer, and Addie Stewart.

Target size, or the retinal image size of the target, is a very important visibility factor in visual assessment. As would be expected, the larger the target, the easier it is to see. This obviously dictates that security observers should be located as close as possible to high-value assets or to areas with a high probability of intrusions. The observers can be equipped with optical enhancement aids to make closer assessments, but moving the observer closer is preferable.

Moving targets are easier to detect than static ones. This phenomenon is presumably a result of lower movement detection thresholds in peripheral as compared to foveal vision, or perhaps moving targets are detected faster during the visual search process because they are detected more efficiently in peripheral vision. To encourage intruders to keep moving, the illuminated clear zones around the protected site should be a minimum of 30 feet wide, and preferably wider. There should be no obstructions where intruders could hide.

Target background luminance contrast is perhaps the single most important factor in target assessment. Furthermore, it is this factor more than any other that complicates the specification of minimum illumination levels for general visual surveillance tasks. The visibility of a target is far less dependent on the total amount of illumination falling on the target and its background than it is on the relative luminance differences or contrast between the target and its background. High illumination levels might not succeed in making a low-contrast target visible, while extremely low illumination levels might succeed in making a high-contrast target very visible. The amount of luminance contrast between a target and its background depends on the relative reflectance of their respective surfaces. To complicate matters more, the visibility level of a target with a given target/background luminance contrast value will increase as the overall background luminance increases.

That means that if an intruder wears low-reflectance clothing in a low-reflectance background, he will be difficult to detect based on contrast alone. Of course, the ideal background for such an intruder would be one having high-reflectance characteristics. The Belvoir Research and Development Center at Fort Belvoir, Virginia, has conducted tests using retroreflectors to enhance reflectance characteristics. The results of this study will be presented later in this chapter.

Target/background color contrast is an important factor in the determination of target visibility level. In physical security applications, however, light levels are usually adequate to support only scotopic vision, or at best mesopic vision. Therefore, for target/background color contrast to be significant, the overall illumination level would have to be increased to where photopic vision is predominant. To improve detection, the illumination level does not have to be increased to where "true" colors can be identified, but rather to a level where some color contrast will be rendered by the lighting system.

The contrast sensitivity of the human visual information processing system increases a function of increasing background luminance. Also, relative contrast sensitivity is more affected by low-level than by high-level changes in background luminance. In fact, the visibility level increases with an increasing total level of illumination, but the rate of this improvement becomes lower and lower as the background luminance increases. At low initial illumination levels, small illumination increases might result in tremendous improvements in target detection, while at high initial illumination levels, large increases might be required to improve target detection substantially. There is a point of diminishing return at which additional increases in the illumination level will not yield appreciable increases in intruder detection. The precise illumination level to maximize the background luminance intensity is too dependent on other variables to be defined for all lighting systems.

Background luminance influences target visibility in three ways. First, it increases the rate at which the search task can be performed by reducing the number of natural fixation points or dark versus bright areas within the search field. Second, it reduces the harmful effects of transient changes in retinal adaptation level. Third, it causes a drastic constriction of the effective field, probably as a result of narrowing the attention span.

Visual search strategies are of three basic types: (1) random search, where the observer randomly fixates successive points in the field of search; (2) systematic search, where the observer systematically fixates successive points in the field of search according to some preplanned search strategy; (3) adaptive search, where the observer automatically reacts to both the overall character of the field of search and the anticipated target, alternating between random and systematic search patterns in accordance with his perception of moment-to-moment changes in the search requirements. Most observers conducting visual surveillance and alarm assessment tasks use adaptive search. The search task can be improved by decreasing the search area size, decreasing the number of confusing objects or shadows that might be mistaken for intruders, and providing guards with appropriate visual aids or using special lighting.

Transient adaptation is an important factor in determining target visibility levels. A momentary loss in visual contrast sensitivity occurs when the eye momentarily views a bright area and then moves to view a darker area where the visual target is located. Even though the deleterious effects are not extremely serious, a brief period of insensitivity might be sufficient to result in failure to detect an intruder. The time of visibility loss is a function of the extremes of luminous uniformity—that is, the greater the uniformity extremes within the observer's field of view, the greater the potential for deleterious adaptational effects.

Visual target detection performance for peripherally presented targets decreases with increasing foveal luminance levels. This tunnel vision effect presumably results from a constriction of the active area of directed attention. A visual-orienting response to unusually bright areas occurs; therefore, such an area could result in a high degree of distraction and a consequent reduction in the area of effective visual search.

Based on background luminance uniformity, security lighting systems should be designed so that (1) light sources are approximately equal in intensity; (2) light sources are equally spaced around the perimeter areas with sufficient overlap of adjacent ground lighting patterns to ensure luminous uniformity; (3) fewer and brighter wide-angle beam luminaires are used to reduce discontinuous ground luminance patterns.

Background glare is recognized as influencing target visibility in two ways: disability and discomfort glare. The glare might emanate directly from the light sources within the observer's visual field or indirectly from highly reflective objects. Disability glare results when the retina is peripherally exposed to illumination sources that are considerably brighter than the luminous level to which the eye is foveally centered. It reduces foveal visual performance through a process of veiling or masking the visual target. The magnitude of this veiling is a function of both the intensity and angular distance from the glare source's line of sight.

LIGHTING

The Illuminating Engineering Society (IES) defines light as visually evaluated radiant energy. Radiant energy of the proper wavelength makes visible those things that emit or reflect energy in sufficient quantity to activate the eye receptors. From a physical viewpoint, light is that portion of the electromagnetic spectrum between the wavelength limits of 380 nanometers and 780 nanometers. There are individual variations in spectral response and limits, and these response characteristics change with time, age, and the individual's state of health. Therefore, the selection of any individual to act as a standard observer is not scientifically feasible.

From the wealth of data available, however, a spectral luminous efficiency curve has been selected for engineering purposes to represent a typical human observer. A plot of the curve for night scotopic and day photopic vision is shown in Figure 23-2. These curves can be used to compare the spectral luminous of the various light sources to that of the hypothetical observer to evaluate the effectiveness of individual lamp sources.

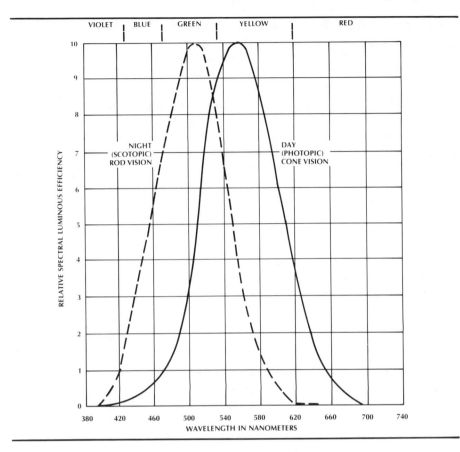

Figure 23-2 Spectral luminous efficiency curve.

Basic Lighting Terms

Following are definitions of some basic lighting taken primarily from the IES handbook:

Candela: (formerly candle) The unit of luminous intensity.
Footcandle: A unit of illumination for light measurement. It is the illumination on a surface 1 square foot in area where there is a uniformly distributed flux of 1 lumen, or the illumination produced on a surface where all points are at a distance of 1 foot from a directionally uniform point source of 1 candela.
Glare: The sensation produced by luminance within the visual field that is sufficiently greater than the luminance to which the eyes are adapted and therefore causes annoyance, discomfort, or loss in visual performance and visibility.

Illuminance: An alternate term for illumination that is receiving world-wide acceptance, especially in science.

Illumination: The density of the luminous flux incident on a surface.

Luminaire: A complete lighting unit consisting of a lamp or lamps, together with the parts designed to distribute the light, to position and protect the lamps, and to connect the lamps to the power supply.

Luminous flux: The time rate of flow of light.

Lux: The international unit of illumination. It is the illumination on a surface 1 square meter in area on which there is a uniformly distributed flux of 1 lumen.

Reflector: A device used to redirect the luminous flux from a source by the process of reflection.

Refractor: A device used to redirect the luminous flux from a source, primarily by the process of refraction.

Retroreflector: A device designed to reflect light in a direction close to that at which it is incident, whatever the angle of incidence.

Photometry

The measurement of light is called photometry, and the basic instrument used to measure the quantity of illumination is a photometer. There are both visual and photoelectic photometers. Visual photometers are luminance comparison devices. The eye can judge brightness only by comparing adjacent brightness in terms of their equality; therefore, the visual photometer relies on the eye to compare the brightness of two surfaces and usually adjusts them to equality for determining illumination devices.

Photoelectric photometers are convenient to use, and they eliminate personal judgment and variations between individual observers. They respond to illumination or radiant energy incident on the photosensitive element and thereby produce an electrical charge that corresponds to the illumination level. To be meaningful, these measurements must relate to the light source in the same way the eye does. Therefore, the sensitivity characteristics of the photometer should be equivalent or as close as possible to an accepted standard observer so that the eye remains the ultimate judge of light both qualitatively and quantitatively. There are two classes of photoelectric photometers: those using solid-state devices such as photovoltaic and photoconductive cells and those using photoemission tubes. The latter type requires considerable additional equipment for operation and is usually not used for lighting system designs.

A photovoltaic cell converts radiant energy into electrical energy. It not only produces a small current that is approximately proportional to the incident illumination, but it also produces a small electromotive force capable of forcing the current through a low-resistance measurement circuit, such as a microammeter or galvanometer. These circuits do, however, require compensation because of their nonlinear response when exposed to higher levels of incident illumination.

Some of the portable illumination meters in use today consist of a photovoltaic cell or cells connected to a meter calibrated in footcandles. Some of these are the multicell meter, case-type hinged-cell meter, pocket-size color and cosine-corrected meter, and illumination meter with color and a cosine-corrected photocell and operational amplifier.

GENERATION OF LIGHT

The most abundant source of light or radiant solar energy is, of course, the sun. About half this energy reaches the earth's surface as sunlight or visible radiation. The other half is divided between invisible ultraviolet and infrared energy. When absorbed, virtually all the radiant energy from the sun is converted to heat, whether it is visible or invisible. Therefore, solar energy, sunlight, and solar heat are just different names for radiant solar energy.

The amount of visible energy varies, depending on the depth of the atmosphere the light traverses, the elevation of the sun above the horizon, and variable atmospheric conditions, such as moisture and dirt. The atmosphere is responsible for scattering a considerable amount of solar energy. The blue color of a clear sky and the reddish appearance of the rising or setting sun are common examples of this scattering effect.

The average luminance of the sun is approximately 160,000 candles per square centimeter viewed through the atmosphere at sea level. The resulting illumination of the earth's surface on a sunny day can exceed 10,000 footcandles, and on a cloudy day it might drop to less than 1,000 footcandles. Solar energy is also reflected from the moon, but the reflectance of the moon's surface is low, and consequently its luminance is only about 0.25 candelas per square centimeter. The resulting illumination level on the earth's surface on a moonlit night is about 0.01 footcandles.

Since reflected lighting from the moon is not adequate, artificial or man-made light sources must be used to support the security guard's visual surveillance and alarm assessment tasks.

Lighting Sources

Lighting sources can be divided into three major categories: incandescents, fluorescents, and HID lamps.

Incandescent Lamps

A primary consideration of any lamp designer is that the lamp will economically produce the spectral radiation needed for the intended application.

The efficacy of light produced by incandescent filament lamps depends on the filament temperature. The higher the filament temperature, the greater the quantity of radiant energy in the visible region. For this reason, the lamps are designed so that the filament temperature can be kept as high as is consistent with satisfactory life. Incandescent filament lamps are filled with inert gases to allow higher filament temperatures and hence higher efficacies without a sacrifice in life. Inert gases are necessary to prevent chemical action between the gas and internal parts of the lamp. The filament temperature for a 200-watt lamp is near 4,700°F. Normal changes in the outdoor ambient temperature will not appreciably affect its light output or life.

Incandescent lamps have several common features. They are a compact and inexpensive lighting source and have good color rendition (no distortion of color) unless modified to project a certain color. But they have a relatively short life (500 to 10,000 hours), project a high-radiant heat level, and do not hold up well when handled roughly. Worst of all, incandescent lamps are the most inefficient light source, with a rating of between 17 and 23 lumens per watt. That means they produce the least amount of visible light for the amount of energy consumed and therefore are the most expensive to operate. One advantage of these lamps is that they illuminate instantly with the application of power. Therefore, they are often used as emergency lights until the more efficient complementary high-intensity discharge lamps reach full illumination after power is restored.

Fluorescent Lamps

The fluorescent is an electric discharge source in which light is produced predominantly by fluorescent powders activated by ultraviolet energy generated by a mercury arc. The lamp, usually a long tubular bulb with an electrode sealed into each end, contains mercury vapor at a low pressure with a small amount of inert gas, principally argon, for starting. The inner walls of the bulb are coated with fluorescent powders called phosphors. When voltage is applied, an arc is produced by current flowing between the electrodes through the mercury vapor. The discharge produces some visible radiation but mostly invisible ultraviolet radiation. The ultraviolet energy excites the phosphors to produce visible light. In general, the phosphors are selected and blended to respond most efficiently to ultraviolet energy at a wavelength of 253.7 nanometers, the primary wavelength generated in a mercury discharge lamp.

Like most electric discharge lamps, fluorescent lamps must be operated in series with a current limiting device commonly called a ballast. The ballast also provides the required starting and operating lamp voltage. Because all fluorescent lamps require an external ballast, they are inefficient in applications where they are frequently turned off and on.

Fluorescent lamps have good color rendition, long life (12,000 to 20,000 hours), and relatively high efficiency (67 to 83 lumens per watt). They are far more cost-effective to operate than incandescents. A disadvantage of normal fluorescent lamps for outdoor operations is that they are adversely affected by low temperatures. The closer the temperature gets to freezing, the less light is produced, until lighting is hardly effective. For outdoor applications, the lamp must be equipped with low-temperature lamp operation ballasts.

High-Intensity Discharge Lamps

These lamps produce visible light by direct interaction of an arc with a gas. This category includes mercury vapor, metal halide, high-pressure sodium vapor, and low-pressure sodium vapor lamps. These lamp types consist of a compact lighting source containing a small arc tube within a large outer glass bulb. The lamps vary from having little color distortion to distorting all colors except yellow, as in the case of low-pressure sodium lamps. Their efficiency ranges from very good to the highest available. They produce the greatest amount of light for the least cost and have very long lives. The primary disadvantage of all HID lamps is that they require an auxiliary ballast for operation, so they need time to reach full light output.

Mercury Vapor Lamps.   In mercury lamps, light is produced by the passage of an electric current through mercury vapor. Mercury has a low vapor pressure at room temperature and an even lower pressure at cold temperatures. A small amount of more readily ionized argon gas is introduced to improve starting. The original arc is struck through the ionization of the argon gas. Once the arc strikes, its heat begins to vaporize the mercury, and this process continues until all the mercury is evaporated and the lamp reaches full brightness.

Most mercury lamps are constructed with two envelopes: an inner arc tube and an outer envelope that shields the arc tube from outside drafts and temperature changes. The outer envelope contains an inert gas to prevent oxidation of the internal parts and to maintain a relatively high breakdown voltage across the outer bulb parts. The envelope provides an inner surface for coating phosphors and in some cases acts as a filter to remove certain wavelengths of arc radiation.

The pressure at which a mercury lamp operates accounts in a large measure for its characteristic spectral power distribution. In general, a higher operating pressure tends to shift a larger proportion of emitted radiation into longer wavelengths. Within the visible region, the mercury spectrum consists of five principal lines: 404.7, 435.8, 546.1, 557, and 559 nanometers. This spectrum results in greenish blue light, emphasizing the blue, green, and yellow in objects; orange and red appear brownish.

Mercury lamps require a starting circuit. The more common three-electrode lamps have an auxiliary starting electrode placed close to one of the main electrodes, making it possible to start the lamp at a lower voltage. An electric field is generated between the starting electrode and the adjacent main electrode, causing an emission of electrons, which ionizes the starting gas. The arc then starts between the main electrodes, gradually vaporizing the mercury vapor. During the warm-up period of several minutes, the light changes in color from a bluish glow to the normal blue-green of the mercury. If the arc is extinguished, the lamp will not relight until it cools sufficiently to lower the vapor pressure to a point where the arc will restrike. The time for initial starting to full brightness and the restriking times varies between 3 and 7 minutes.

Metal Halide Lamps.   These lamps are similar in construction to mercury lamps. The primary difference is that the metal halide arc tube contains various metal halides in addition to mercury. Three typical combinations of halide used in metal halide lamps are (1) sodium, thallium, and indium iodides; (2) sodium and scandium iodides; (3) dysprosium and thallium iodides. When the lamp attains its full operating temperature, the metal halides in the arc tube are partially vaporized, producing a white and more intense light than mercury lamps. The resulting spectral power distribution from these metals produces multiline spectra across the fill visible region. Because of their spectral power distribution, metal halide lamps have excellent color rendition and should be considered where this characteristic is of primary importance.

The luminous efficacy of metal halide lamps is greatly improved over that of mercury lamps. Some metal halide lamps have efficacies 1.5 to almost 2 times that of mercury lamps. More specifically, mercury lamps have efficiency ratings between 45 and 63 lumens per watt, while metal halide lamps have ratings between 80 and 100 lumens per watt. But metal halide lamps should not be used where longevity is a factor because their burning hours per year are lower than those of other HID lamps. Therefore, even though their operating costs will be lower than those for mercury vapor lamps, the shorter lamp life will result in a higher maintenance cost. If the lighting system is not maintained regularly and burns out, the system is useless.

The method of starting metal halide lamps is the same as that for mercury lamps. Because of the presence of halide in the lamps, however, the starting voltage is sometimes higher than that for mercury lamps. As the lamp warms up, it might exhibit several color changes as the various halides begin to vaporize. Several minutes are required for it to reach its equilibrium color and operating characteristics. Restrike time might be up to 15 minutes because the halide arc tube operates at a higher temperature than the mercury tube, and it takes longer to cool and to lower the vapor pressure to a point where it will restrike.

High-Pressure Sodium Vapor Lamps.   These lamps produce light by passing an electric current through sodium vapor. Like mercury lamps, the sodium lamp is constructed with two envelopes. The inner envelope is polycrystalline alumina, which has properties to resist sodium attacks at high temperatures, a high melting point, and good light transmission. The arc tube contains xenon as a starting gas and a small quantity of sodium-mercury amalgam, which is partially vaporized when the lamp attains its operating temperature. The outer envelope is evacuated and serves to prevent chemical attack on the arc tube's metal parts and to isolate the arc tube from ambient temperature effects and drafts.

High-pressure sodium vapor lamps radiate energy across the visible spectrum, producing a warm, golden white color. All visible frequencies are present in the spectral power distribution, but because of the predominance of energy at some wavelengths, however, there is some color distortion. The distortion is minimal, however, and consequently allows an observer to distinguish color. These lamps have efficacies of about 110 lumens per watt and have a very long operating life (approximately 24,000 hours).

Because of the small diameter of the lamp arc tube, no starting electrode is built into the tube as in the mercury lamp. A high-voltage, high-frequency pulse is used to ionize the xenon starting gas. Once started, the lamp warms up in approximately 15 minutes. During this time the color rendition changes from poor when the lamp first starts to its normal golden white color when stable operating conditions are achieved. If extinguished, it will restrike in 1½ to 2 minutes.

Low-Pressure Sodium Vapor Lamps. These lamps produce light by passing an arc through vaporized sodium. The starting gas is neon, with small additions of argon, xenon, or helium. To obtain the maximum efficacy, an arc tube bulb wall temperature of approximately 500°F must be maintained. Any appreciable deviation from this temperature will result in undesirable efficacy losses. To maintain the proper operating temperature, the arc tube is enclosed in a vacuum flask or in an outer bulb at high vacuum. The low-pressure sodium lamps rank high on the efficiency scale by producing between 135 and 183 lumens per watt. They also have a fairly long operating life of between 18,000 and 20,000 hours.

Light produced by the low-pressure sodium arc is almost monochromatic (a single color), consisting of a double spectral line in the yellow region of the visible spectrum at wavelengths of 589 and 589.6 nanometers. This yellow distorts all colors, except yellow, making reds look brown and flesh tones look gray. This distortion would make it impossible for a guard to interpret any type of color-coded access control badge.

The starting time to full light output is 7 to 15 minutes. When first started, the light output is the characteristic red of the neon discharge. The red graudally changes to the characteristic yellow as the sodium vaporizes. The lamp will restart immediately after a power interruption. This is an operational advantage where emergency generators will almost immediately assume the electrical load.

Lighting Luminaires

In general there are four types of lighting units used for exterior security lighting systems: floodlights, streetlights, Fresnel lens units, and searchlights. The type of unit selected for any given application depends on the required illumination level, illumination distribution, glare, and convenience in servicing.

Floodlights

These are used to illuminate specific areas or where it is desirable to locate the lighting unit in an inaccessible or protected location and project the light onto the critical area. Floodlighting also is used to illuminate boundaries, fences, and buildings and for local emphasis of vital areas or buildings. Reflectorized lamps with suitable holders are applicable for lighting small areas and irregular spaces, such as around buildings, setbacks, piles of materials, and tanks, and for boundary lighting where the light must be confined to the immediate fence area.

Streetlights

Proper distribution of the light is one of the essential factors in efficient streetlights. The light emanating from the luminaire is controlled and proportioned in accordance with the visibility requirements. Light distributions are generally designed for a typical range of conditions that include luminaire mounting height, overhang location of the luminaires, width of the clear zone being lighted, arrangement of the luminaires, percentage of the lamp light directed toward the ground and adjacent areas, and maintenance efficiency of the system.

   For practical operating reasons, the range in luminaire mounting heights is often kept constant. Therefore, it becomes necessary to have several different light distributions to effectively light different clear area widths, using various luminaire spacings at a particular luminaire mounting height. All luminaires can be classified according to their lateral and vertical distribution patterns. Different vertical distributions are available for different spacing-to-mounting-height ratios. To achieve specific illumination results, it is necessary to consider and to check the magnitude and uniformity of the illumination distribution by checking the ratio of maximum footcandles to minimum footcandles in the clear area. This ratio should be an average of 3 to 1, not to exceed 6 to 1 for any position in the clear zone.

   There are four basic streetlight or roadway luminaires: Type I, Type II, Type III, and Type IV. There are also four beam versions of Type I and Type II. Type I luminaires generate two symmetrically opposed narrow beam patterns. This luminaire is used to illuminate large areas where the luminaire can be located centrally with respect to the area to be lighted. Type II, III, and IV luminaires have asymmetric patterns, with Type IV being more asymmetric than Type III and so forth. These luminaires are used where the position of the lighting unit is inside the clear zone to be lighted. The particular luminaire used depends on the unit's mounting height and spacing and the illumination requirements.

Fresnel Lens

Fresnel lens units used for protective lighting produce a fan-shaped beam of light approximately 180 degrees in the horizontal and from 15 to 30 degrees in the vertical. It directs the light outward to illuminate approaches without illuminating inside areas, affording guards comparative concealment in darkness. Its application is limited to locations that can take advantage of its unique characteristics without causing objectionable glare.

Searchlights

These lights have limited application in general surveillance and alarm assessment applications. Searchlights used in protective lighting systems are usually of the incandescent type because of the small amount of attention required for their operation and because of their instant-on capability. They are rated in diameter of reflector and lamp wattage. For most security applications a diameter of 12 to 29 inches and a wattage of 250 to 3,000 watts, with a beam angle of between 3 and 8 degrees, should be adequate.

MAINTENANCE OF LIGHTING

Proper maintenance is the only way to ensure the effectiveness of any lighting system. Maintenance must be planned and executed on a regular schedule. It includes all the measures necessary to keep the lighting output as near to its initial level as practical.

Light loss factors must be included when designing a lighting system, which is a basic admission that even proper maintenance cannot keep the lighting output to its initial level. The value of the light loss factors used indicates the uncontrollable depreciation, assuming a good maintenance program.

Trained maintenance people are recommended to implement the maintenance plans. Large installations can usually afford to equip and train their own people, but many companies find it advantageous to hire outside specialists. In medium and small installations, the lighting maintenance contractor can supply planning sources, equipment, and manpower, which might be more cost-effective.

The following paragraphs discuss basic causes of light loss; advantages of planned relamping and cleaning; operating programs, methods, materials, and equipment; and remedies for mechanical and electrical difficulties that can develop in lighting systems.

Causes of Light Loss

The following factors contribute to the depreciation of light at both interior and exterior installations: luminaire ambient temperature, voltage to luminaire, ballast factor, luminaire surface depreciation, room surface dirt depreciation, burnouts, lamp lumen depreciation, and luminaire dirt depreciation. The effect of each factor varies with the environment. Exterior installations are usually exposed to more severe operating conditions than indoor systems.

Lamp Lumen Depreciation

Dirt accumulation on luminaire surfaces is usually the most significant contributor to light loss. The amount of light loss also depends on the luminaire design and finish, along with the lamp type and shape.

Ventilated lighting units used indoors tend to collect less dirt than closed units because the temperature difference between the lamp and the surrounding air causes convection currents that help prevent dirt from accumulating on its reflector. Outdoor luminaires minimize dirt accumulation on the reflector by sealing the luminaire from air.

Accumulation of dust also might change the light distribution in some luminaires. For example, dirt accumulation on a specular aluminum reflector in a high-bay luminaire can change the beam shape from narrow to wide. The loss in utility in this example is much greater than the loss in efficiency.

Burnouts

Certainly lamp burnouts contribute to loss of light. If lamps are not replaced promptly after burnout, the illumination level will be reduced.

Luminaire Surface Depreciation

Luminaire construction materials differ in their resistance to deterioration. Processed aluminum finishes, while not as high in initial reflectance as enamel finishes, tend to have a slower depreciation rate. Enamels are, however, usually easier to clean.

Temperature and Voltage

Utility power voltage variations can cause variations in light output from day to day. Fluorescent lamps in particular are affected by temperature changes. For specific information about how temperature might affect the luminaire, as well as for answers to any other questions, consult the manufacturer.

Planned Relamping and Cleaning

A properly planned relamping program will maintain illumination levels by limiting lumen depreciation and preventing many lamp burnouts. Reduction of burnouts gives an added advantage in saving the time and expense involved with individual burnout replacement. A relamping and cleaning schedule should be established with the lamp manufacturer.

When a lighting system is periodically relamped and cleaned according to a schedule, it provides more light than when lamps are replaced only after burnout and when luminaires remain dirty. If the lighting system designer is ensured that a maintenance program will be performed, he can design for a given average level of illumination using fewer luminaires, thus reducing the capital investment and operating costs.

VISUAL SURVEILLANCE AND ASSESSMENT ENHANCEMENT

Target/background luminance intensity and contrast are probably the most important controllable factors that influence visual surveillance and assessment performance. Both intensity and contrast can be enhanced by using artificial ground covers. White and light-colored crushed stone has been used to reduce vegetation growth and soil erosion, and it also improves the visual environment. What has not been extensively evaluated is the use of retroreflective materials to enhance visibility.

The Physical Security Equipment Division at the Belvoir Research Development and Engineering Center in Fort Belvoir, Virginia, made a brief evaluation of these reflective effects. Retroreflective arrays were installed in a clear zone colocated with the security lighting at their perimeter security test site. The test contains two parallel chain-link fences, which are 900 feet long, 7 feet high, and separated by 35 feet. A 25-foot-high observation tower is located at one end of the clear zone between the fences. The clear area is illuminated in accordance with Department of Defense regulations, which specify 0.2 footcandles of illumination measured 6 inches above the ground in a horizontal plane 30 feet outside the outer fence. A series of retroreflective arrays was installed on the ground along a 100-foot section of the clear zone starting at a point 600 feet from the tower.

A very real cost associated with exterior lighting systems is that required to maintain an adequate level of illumination for the guards to perform their visual tasks. Another consideration is that if the illumination level is adequate to maintain security, it is sufficient enough to pinpoint the site's location, especially from the air. Sometimes it is not desirable to advertise the location of security sites to external observers. The problem is how to preserve an adequate visual environment for maintaining a high probability of detection and correct assessment while reducing the site's "signature" and utility costs. Using retroreflectors in those critical or poorly lighted areas might be the solution.

The retroreflective arrays used at Fort Belvoir were constructed from a commercially available retroreflective material. The material is made by embedding microscopic spherical glass beads in a durable, transparent plastic layer backed with a reflective coating that is secured to a protective liner. In operaton, incident light on the spherical beads reflects the light back toward the source, as shown in Figure 23–3. The retroflective material is readily available in sheets that can be cut to the desired width. The sheets are backed with either a pressure-sensitive adhesive layer or a coating that must be heat-treated for proper adhesion. The substrate to which the retroreflective material is secured must be clean, dry, smooth, rigid, nonporous, and weather resistant. Another advantage of the retroreflective material is that it is easily cleanable and very conformable.

The Belvoir Research and Development Center tests used 3-inch-wide pressure-sensitive adhesive strips of series 580 retroreflective material manufactured by the 3M Company. The 3-inch-wide strips were secured to aluminum strips, which were then secured to 10-foot-long 2-by-4s. The 10-foot long arrays were installed starting 700 feet from the guard tower. (Seven hundred feet was selected as the starting point because previous tests indicated that the probability of detection decreased at distances over 600 feet.) The 10-foot arrays were installed end to end, perpendicular to the fences and line of sight from the guard tower. The two 10-foot arrays together formed a 20-foot array as seen from the tower. Each array was staked into the ground, with the retroflective side facing the guard tower and so that the top of the array did not extend more than 6 inches from the ground. (If the array is higher than 6 inches, an intruder might be able to hide behind it and crawl through the clear zone undetected.) A second pair of 10-foot arrays was positioned 10 feet from the first pair, in the direction away from the tower and parallel to the first array. A third pair of arrays was posi-

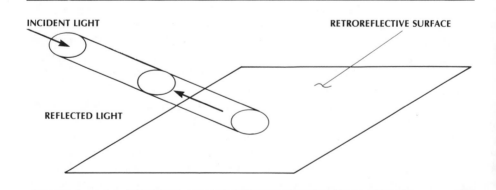

Figure 23–3 Retroreflective surface.

tioned 10 feet farther away from and parallel to the second array. This arrangement continued for a total of twenty-one 20-foot arrays, which covered 200 feet of the clear zone. As viewed from the tower, because of the acute angle of sight, the array appeared as a solid retroreflective surface 20 feet wide extending from 700 to 900 feet from the tower.

The test site luminaires were placed within the compound along the inside fence, as they are at most military installations. From this position, the light was directed downward into the clear zone from the luminaires, which were located about 30 feet above the ground. Overhead lighting illuminated the top of the head of a standing intruder and the back of a crawling intruder. It produced minimal shadows, which can improve detection. Consequently, a camouflaged crawling intruder would be very difficult to detect in this lighting scheme.

The retroreflective array concept tested at Fort Belvoir used three 12 VDC, 37½ watt instant-on tungsten iodide lamps mounted on the observation tower just above the security guard, as shown in Figure 23–4. The effectiveness of the light source in this location is strongly dependent on the bistatic angle formed by the light source beam, retroreflector array, and observer's line of sight. In general, this angle must be less than 1 degree for maximum efficiency, although enhancement capabilities are obtainable at bistatic angles approaching 30 degrees.

Tests were conducted at night during the month of December by having intruders run and crawl across the clear zone at ranges of about 700, 800, and 900 feet from the tower. Guards were cued to start a search by artificially generated alarms to simulate an intrusion detection system. False alarms also were generated to simulate real operational intrusion detection systems, but principally to preclude guessing by the guards.

The response of each guard was noted and recorded, along with the time required to make the detection or false alarm decision. The guards were required to state whether there was an intrusion attempt and, if in progress, whether the intruder was running or crawling and at what range. The ranges were indicated by markers placed along the test zone. Tests were conducted using different roadway lighting and retroreflective array lighting combinations. Results showed that regardless of whether the overhead lights were on or off, the retroreflective array presented a target in dramatic negative contrast. That is, the target appeared as a dark silhouette against a bright background. the target presentation was amplified even more when the array was illuminted by the colocated light source and the overhead roadway lights were off. This distinguishable target improved the probability of detection to almost 100 percent in all tests and lighting combinations. It also reduced the assessment time needed to identify the intrusion (or false alarm) from 5 or 10 seconds to only 2 or 3 seconds.

The effectiveness of retroreflective arrays is affected by the weather and environment, especially when they are installed on the ground. Rain will not affect the reflector's optical gain greatly unless it is submerged in water,

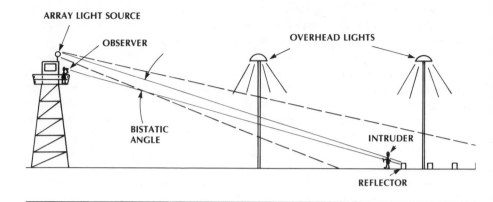

Figure 23–4   Retroreflector array concept.

but more than about 6 inches of snow will obscure the arrays. The clear zone area in which arrays are installed should be cleared of all vegetation that would otherwise obscure the arrays.

Retroreflective arrays can be used in almost any application where an improvement in the visual probability of detection is needed. This includes applications for general surveillance performed by either patrolling or fixed guards or by television for alarm assessment. When television cameras are used to conduct the surveillance or assessment function, the array light source must be colocated with each camera. Also, each camera must be located in a position where its view of the arrays is no greater than 30 degrees away from looking perpendicularly toward the array. Patrolling guards can carry lanterns or flashlights to illuminate the arrays. Only a small amount of light is required for effective illumination.

Another test using retroreflective arrays at Fort Belvoir was to determine how effective the arrays would be in improving the surveillance effectiveness of perimeter patrolling guards. In this test, 3-inch-wide, 10-foot-long arrays were installed on the inside of the perimeter fence at levels of 6 inches, 18 inches, and 36 inches above the ground. The arrays were aligned end to end to form a 100-foot array at each level. In a real application, the arrays could be installed end to end to form continuous arrays at each level around the site, or they could be installed only in perimeter sections where visibility was poor. The purpose of the arrays was to improve the patrolling guards' ability to detect anyone between the perimeter fence and the patrol road. As the guards patrolled the perimeter, they illuminated the arrays with a 6 volt hand-held lantern. Anyone standing between the fence and the observer was silhouetted and very detectable, even though the silhouette was broken into three narrow strips in the case of a standing man. His legs would be silhouetted on the bottom array, his hips or thighs on the middle array, and his chest or midsection on the top array. Even though the silhouette is broken, it is very distinguishable. A crawling intruder would be silhouetted against the bottom array as an elliptical or long silhouette, depending on his relative position. The test proved that it was very easy to detect anyone inside the fence, whether standing or crawling, from distances up to 200 feet from the fence and at angles as much as 45 degrees from perpendicular to the fence. For fixed observation points, however, a maximum angle of 30 degrees from perpendicular to the array is still recommended.

Retroreflectors are an inexpensive way to improve surveillance and alarm assessment effectiveness. The imagination is the only limiting factor in their use. When guards are observing dark areas with only a flashlight, from distances of 100 to 200 feet, it is very unlikely they will detect an intruder unless he is moving. But with retroreflectors, the intruder instantly becomes very distinguishable if the area is clear of obstacles. Possible uses are in dark corners around buildings, around industrial equipment, and in storage areas. Retroreflective tape can be installed on metal strips, as it was for the Belvoir Research and Development Center tests, and the strips installed on the buildings. Alternatively, the tape can be secured directly to an item in the area being viewed—for example, on metal equipment or storage tanks.

Chapter 24

Closed Circuit Television

Closed circuit television systems are the primary means of providing security force personnel with remote surveillance and intrusion alarm assessment in security applications. When properly designed, these systems permit rapid real-time display of remote locations for viewing and security personnel response when required. Binoculars and telescopes, including comparable night vision devices, can be used in special security applications for remote surveillance, but these devices are usually not part of the security force's operating equipment.

A basic CCTV system consists of one or more television cameras at the remote area, one or more camera display monitors at the monitoring area, and the signal transmission system to transmit the video information from the remote camera to the monitors. The basic function of the television camera and lens is to convert the visual scene focused on the camera image tube through the lens into an electrical signal. This signal is then transmitted from the camera to the central monitoring area, where it is converted into a visual image of the viewed scene on the display monitor.

For the scene to be viewed by the camera, it must be illuminated by natural or artificial light. A portion of that light must be reflected from the scene onto the camera lens. Light reaching the lens from the scene is focused onto the photosensitive surface of the faceplate or image tube target, where it is converted into an electrical or video signal. The amplitude of the video signal is proportional to the intensity of the impinging light on the image tube target. The rate of change of the video signal is proportional to the variation in the impinging light. Video motion detectors monitor this signal, looking for changes indicative of someone moving in the camera's field of view.

The viewed scene is captured from the photosensitive surface of the image tube target by the camera's scanning electronics. In a vacuum image tube, electrons are released from a heated cathode. These free electrons are accelerated from the cathode toward the photosensitive target by a positively charged focusing structure that focuses the electrons into a narrow beam. The narrow electron beam is guided by the camera's scanning electronics to scan the image target from left to right, starting at the top of the target and scanning down. The electron energy is released to the tube signal electrode from the point where the electron beam strikes the photosensitive surface. The amount of energy released is a function of the quantity of light from the viewed scene focused onto the photosensitive surface where the electron beam strikes. The resulting video signal varies in amplitude as the scene light changes on the photosensitive surface along the narrow path or line being scanned by the electron beam. In a black-and-white camera, which is normally used for security surveillance applications, the signal varies from 1 volt for a pure white picture to a low-level (near zero) voltage for a black picture.

The image tube target is scanned in equally spaced lines from top to bottom to form one field of video data. A second field is generated by scanning midway between the lines scanned in the first field. Combining the second field with the first field forms a full frame of data. Standard American specifications are 262½ lines per field and 525 lines per frame. The scanning rate in the United States for most television components is 15.750 kHz. This rate corresponds to sixty fields, or thirty full frames, of data per second. This means that between each field of data, the electron beam must be turned off or blanked during the retrace interval from the lower right side to the upper left starting point after each field trade. Phosphorescence of the monitor's CRT, along with the persistence of human vision, creates what appears to be a continuous picture of the original viewed scene when the electron beam is blanked during the retrace.

The newest type of CCTV cameras available are solid-state cameras. These use a solid-state, light-sensing element instead of the conventional vacuum vidicon tube. Solid-state cameras are small and rugged, making them appropriate for covert surveillance applications.

SLOW SCAN

Television video signals cannot be transmitted over normal telephone lines because video requires a wider bandwidth than that normally available on voice-grade telephone lines. Slow-scan transmitters send the video signal line by line to the monitor, similar to a facsimile machine. With slow scan a full frame of information is constructed every few seconds. If the camera is sensor activated, when there is an alarm, the camera basically captures the scene, hopefully showing what caused the alarm, and then transmits it through the telephone exchange to the monitor operator. Once that scene is viewed and acknowledged by the operator, the camera is reset, ready to capture and transmit another picture. The advantage of slow-scan transmission is that the video signal can be transmitted almost any distance over commercially available voice-grade telephone lines.

SCENE AND CAMERA FACEPLATE ILLUMINATION

Faceplate illumination is the amount of light energy necessary to achieve full camera performance. The actual amount of light required is a function of spectral distribution and brightness of the light illuminating the scene being viewed by the camera, the quantity of light reflected from the scene that is focused on the image tube target by the camera lens, and the relative sensitivity of the image tube.

Relative levels of scene illumination resulting from natural sources are an important consideration when evaluating the camera faceplate illumination. Table 24–1 provides approximate scene illumination levels for natural light sources.

The percentage of light reflected from a scene is dependent on the incident light angle and texture and the composition of the surface in the scene. Table 24–2 provides approximate ambient illumination reflectance for various scene surfaces. The reflectance is relatively independent of angle of incidence.

CAMERA TYPES

Cameras are generally classified according to the sensitivity and spectral response of the photosensitive surface of the image tube target. The more common classes of cameras are illustrated in Table 24–3 and discussed in the following paragraphs.

Conventional Cameras

Conventional cameras are used primarily for daylight or well-illuminated interior applications. The most popular daylight cameras use an antimony trisulfide material for the photosensitive target image surface. This material has a spectral response similar to that of the human eye. Image tubes using an antimony trisulfide target are classified as standard vidicon tubes. Vidicon tubes require a minimum of 0.1 footcandle of faceplate illumination to produce a clear picture. These tubes are, however, susceptible to target damage if they are exposed to very high target illumination. Therefore, care must be taken in positioning the cameras so that they never face bright lights.

Also, cameras using antimony trisulfide vidicon tubes can have the viewed scene permanently burned onto the photosensitive target in a relatively short time when the camera is fixed on a scene with high contrast and when the camera lens is sharply focused on a target. The actual time before damaging the tube depends on the target contrast and image sharpness. Burn-in will render the camera useless for assessment or surveillance

Table 24–1   Scene Illumination Levels

Illumination Source	Scene Illumination (Broad Spectrum)
Full sunlight	10^4 to 10^5 lumens/m^2
Overcast day	10^2 to 10^4 lumens/m^2
Twilight	1 to 10^2 lumens/m^2
Full moon (clear)	10^{-1} to 1 lumens/m^2
Full moon (overcast)*	10^{-2} to 10^{-1} lumens/m^2
Starlight (clear)	10^{-3} to 10^{-2} lumens/m^2
Starlight (overcast)*	10^{-4} to 10^{-3} lumens/m^2

*Man-made illumination in inhabited or industrial areas will typically produce greater scene illumination levels than those listed due to partial reflection of light energy from an overcast sky.

Table 24–2   Scene Reflectance

Scene Televised	Reflectance (percent)
Empty asphalt surface	7
Grass-covered area with trees	20
Red brick building or surface	30
Unpainted concrete building or surface	40
Smooth-surface aluminum building	65
Snow-covered field	75

because the viewed scene will appear the same on the monitor even if the camera lens is covered. The image burn-in problem can be minimized if the camera is operated in a continuous surveillance panning or oscillating mode rather than fixed on a specific scene, or if it is physically interchanged with another camera at least once every 3 or 4 months, or more often if dictated by the application. Vidicon cameras also exhibit lag characteristics or picture smear when viewing a moving scene or target. The degree of smear depends on the scene or target speed.

Vidicon tubes are less expensive than some more sensitive tubes, and they perform well in most well-illuminated areas. They also are rugged and easy to install, and they have a relatively long life, a good environmental operating temperature range, and good resolution characteristics.

Some vidicon tubes are slightly more sensitive than standard tubes. These require a minimum faceplate illumination of only 0.05 footcandle to produce a clear picture. Physically these tubes are identical to standard tubes, and they also are susceptible to target damage if exposed to very bright lights for a long time. They also exhibit picture smear when viewing a moving scene. Cameras using the more sensitive vidicon tubes can be used for outside or inside applications, but they are recommended primarily for inside use.

Table 24-3   Video Camera Light Range Comparisons

Faceplate Illumination (1m/m²)	10^5 10^4 10^3 10^2 10 1 10^{-1} 10^{-2} 10^{-3} 10^{-4}
Standard Vidicon	Antimony Trisulfide Target
Vidicon & Newvicon	Silicon Target
Single Stage Intensifier Vidicon	Antimony Trisulfide Target Silicon Target (SIT)
Two-stage Intensifier Vidicon	Antimony Trisulfide Target Silicon Target (ISIT)
Bright Sunlight Overcast Sky Twilight Moonlight Starlight	

Other vidicon tubes have special target elements consisting of several hundred thousand discrete LEDs. The silicon diode vidicon, for instance, is about ten times more sensitive than the conventional antimony trisulfide vidicon. It can operate satisfactorily with only about 0.01 footcandle of faceplate illumination. Silicon diode vidicons are generally more expensive than antimony trisulfide tubes, but they are immune to damage from very bright light sources and image burn-in. They may, however, suffer from blooming (sometimes called wash-out; the defocusing of regions of the video picture where scene brightness is at an excessive level) caused by impinging light sensitizing adjacent diodes on the image target surface.

There are advantages to using cameras with silicon diode vidicon tubes, especially in outside applications, in place of cameras using either a standard or a sensitive vidicon tube. Silicon diode tubes can operate under reduced lighting, especially lights with spectral energy that extends into the near infrared region. Cameras using silicon diode tubes operate satisfactorily in the areas illuminated with at least 1.0 footcandle of uniform horizontal illumination from either high- or low-pressure sodium vapor luminaires or incandescent luminaires.

Silicon diode array tubes are, as mentioned earlier, virtually impervious to target damage from exposure to bright light, but they might exhibit some blooming. Therefore, cameras used in surveillance applications should use silicon diode tubes so that if they are inadvertently directed into the sun or other bright lights while moving from scene to scene, the tube will not be damaged. The silicon diode tube exhibits lower lag characteristics, or less picture smear, at the monitor, which also makes it desirable for cameras operating in a movable surveillance mode. The silicon diode tube has a longer life expectancy than daylight vidicons and has good picture resolution.

Low Light Level Cameras

Low light level (LLL) cameras usually use image tubes with greater light sensitivity, wider spectral response, lower lag or picture smear, and greater resistance to image burn. Characteristically, they require as little as 0.005 lumens/meter square of faceplate illumination with spectral response extending into the near infrared region. These cameras do, however, require automatic light level controls to function effectively over a wide range of faceplate illumination levels. Video signal amplitude can be regulated by using automatic gain control (AGC) of the video amplifier stages and by using either neutral density spot filters, or optical filter wheels in the camera lens aperture.

Very Low Light Level Cameras

Very low light level (VLLL) cameras use image intensifiers just before the vidicon to amplify the existing light. There are two classes of VLLL cameras: silicon intensifier target (SIT) and intensified silicon intensifier target (ISIT). Silicon intensifier target cameras use a one-stage intensifier that allows them to operate with 0.0004 lumens/meter square of faceplate illumination, while ISIT cameras use an SIT tube light sensing device that is fiber optically connected to an image intensifier. This tube can be used with as little as 0.00002 lumens/meter square, but because image intensifiers are used, the tube has no spectral response into the near infrared region.

Bright lights in the viewed scene can reduce visibility because the automatic brightness control used to control blooming at the monitor reduces the faceplate illumination, causing a loss of background contrast. Also, as each stage of image intensifier is added, the camera's horizontal resolution decreases. Horizontal resolution is defined as the maximum number of vertical back-and-white bars that can be resolved in three-quarters of the raster width. The higher the number of lines of resolution, the sharper the image. (Raster is the pattern of scanning lines covering the area where the camera image is projected on the CRT in the television monitor.)

Solid-State Cameras

Solid-state cameras derive their name from the fact that they use a solid-state light-sensing element consisting of a series of either charge-coupled devices

(CCDs), charge-priming devices (CPDs), metal oxide silicon (MOS) devices, or charge-induced devices (CIDs) in place of a vacuum tube. Some solid-state have the same sensitivity as silicon diode cameras and, like silicon diode cameras, can operate under very high illumination levels. The light-sensing element is responsive to near infrared energy, so the camera operates most effectively under incandescent or sodium vapor lighting. These cameras are unaffected by tube-related problems, they provide less-distorted pictures, and they are more reliable than tube cameras.

Color Cameras

Color cameras can produce acceptable color with as little as 0.2 lumens/ meter square of illumination focused on the image tube faceplate. Color enhances feature recognition for objects of identical brightness and contrast that might be difficult to recognize on a monochromatic monitor. The additional information provided by chrominance and hue might make these features more distinguishable, even though the resolution of color systems is more limited than that of monochrome systems. Although color systems are available for a wide variety of usages, they have not been adequately evaluated in terms of their effectiveness in alarm assessment or surveillance.

LENSES

The basic function of a camera lens is to focus the light from the viewed scene onto the photosensitive area of the camera image tube. This is where the scene light is converted into the electric video signal that is proportional in amplitude to the light level. Although a lens is referred to as a single lens, it is actually a precision assembly of several lenses carefully mounted in relationship to each other to focus the scene light onto the photosensitive image surface. This assembly is sometimes referred to as a compound lens.

The distance between the optical center of the lens assembly and the photosensitive image surface of the camera tube is the focal length, usually expressed in millimeters. The focal length determines the distance the camera can see and the angle of coverage. The greater the focal length, the farther the camera can see, but the narrower the field of view or viewing angle. Consequently, the target under assessment or surveillance is difficult to track, especially if it is moving rapidly through the narrow field of view.

Lenses vary from telephoto to wide angle. Telephoto lenses have a long focal length and consequently a narrow field of view for a fixed distance. Wide-angle lenses have a short focal length and a closer and wider field of view. The lens for any application should be determined based on the distance to the scene of interest and the size of the target to be viewed. Therefore, the lens should be selected based on where the camera will be positioned with respect to the area to be viewed, the size of the area to be viewed, and the desired target size. Once the camera's position is determined, a trade-off must be made between the desired area of coverage and target size because the lens viewing angle and target size are directly related. Cameras used in outside applications in fixed positions to assess a given area usually use standard 25mm, 50mm, or 75mm lenses. Both 16mm and 25mm lenses are popular for inside applications.

Camera tubes are standardized for two sizes of photosensitive areas on the image faceplate. The smaller area is a ⅔-inch format, and the larger area is a 1-inch format. Only a portion of the total image tube is used for scanning purposes; this area is referred to as the image tube target. These dimensions are meaningless with respect to actual image format size, but both image format areas do maintain the traditional 4 to 3 aspect ratio.

The size of the format is independent of the lens type and focal length. An in-focus image will be the same distance from the optical center of the lens regardless of the format size. The smaller ⅔-inch format simply means that the scene covered will be smaller than it would be for a tube with a 1-inch format.

There are both fixed and zoom camera lenses. A fixed lens has a fixed focal length and, consequently, a fixed viewing angle. A zoom lens allows the viewer to vary the focal length, which varies the viewing angle. The angle can be extended from wide angle to telephoto, while the viewed image remains in focus. Zoom lenses are rated by the operating range of the focal lengths. For instance, most zoom lenses change in focal length from 20mm to 80mm for a 4.1 zoom or from 15mm to 150mm for a 10.1 zoom. Therefore, a particular viewed target can be amplified 4 to 10 times from the wide-angle position, depending on the zoom lens ratio. The greater the focal length range, the lower the aperture rating and, usually, the more expensive the lens assembly. A focusing adjustment is provided on zoom lenses to compensate for overall assembly tolerance. Once focused, however, the lens should remain in reasonable focus throughout the zoom range without additional adjustment. When cameras are located away from the operator, the zoom lens assembly is operated by a miniature electric motor remotely controlled by the operator.

Most television cameras are rated in faceplate illumination. This is the amount of light required on the tube faceplate to achieve full camera performance. Faceplate illumination is a function of lens speed, or f-stop, which determines the amount of light the lens can pass, or the ability of the lens to collect light from the viewed scene. Bright scenes require a smaller aperture, or higher f-stop, to achieve full performance. The f-stop is derived from the ratio of the focal length of the lens to the diameter of the maximum lens opening. The f-stop of a lens determines the depth of field—that is, the distance at which an object will appear in focus. The narrower the aperture, the greater depth of field the lens will have, but more scene illumination will be required to maintain the camera's performance.

TRANSMISSION SYSTEMS

The basic function of a video signal transmission system is to transmit the video information from remote cameras to the CCTV monitors and to communicate articulated camera control information from the camera control unit to the remote cameras. Video information can be transmitted by video cable, microwave link, or optical transmission.

Video Cable

Triaxial and coaxial 75 ohm cable and twin-axial 124 ohm video cable are available for video transmission. The most popular transmission medium for security CCTV applications is 75 ohm coaxial cable. This cable provided optimum picture quality because it can transmit the full video signal frequency content describing a particular scene with minimum transmission losses. Coaxial cable must be terminated in its characteristic impedance to eliminate reflections and optimize the quality of the received video signal at the monitor. If the cable termination is not properly matched to the cable, reflected energy from the termination will cause double images or ghosts to appear on the monitor screen. Therefore, when 75 ohm coaxial cable is used, it must be terminated in its characteristic impedance, or a 75 ohm load.

Coaxial cable is usually constructed with a solid copper or plated copper center conductor, surrounded by a braided copper outer conductor, which is separated from the center conductor by a low-loss dielectric material. Some cables have a stranded center conductor for applications requiring improved flexibility. The characteristic impedance of a coaxial cable is a function of the inner and outer conductor diameters. Since no cable can be perfectly manufactured, small variations in the inner and outer conductor diameters will result in differences in impedance. Smaller-diameter cable will be affected more by these variations than larger cable. Because larger cable, such as RG-11/u, exhibits more uniform characteristics and less signal transmission loss, it should be used for long transmission lines.

The composition and structure of the cable's outer cover depends on the application. Cable for exterior applications has an exterior jacket of polyethylene suitable for direct burial or continuous exposure to weather. In areas where rodents may be a problem, armor-shielded cable should be used. This cable is wrapped with a polyethylene-covered steel sheath.

Regardless of the coaxial cable diameter, there is a finite degradation in the video signal as it travels from the camera to the monitor. This degradation, which is in the form of high-frequency attenuation, electromagnetic interference, and phase addition, can alter the transmitted scene information displayed on the monitor. Care should be exercised when installing coaxial cable to avoid kinks or sharp bends in the cable, which also can cause degradation in the video signal. High-frequency attenuation reduces image detail or picture resolution, while phase addition might cause image smear similar to the ghosting caused when incident and reflected signals combine from cable or equipment with impedance discontinuities. High-frequency electromagnetic interference appears as snow on the monitor screen. Low-frequency electromagnetic interference, such as the interference caused by power lines, appears on the screen as black or white horizontal bands called *hum bars.* Both forms of interference should be minimized because they partially obscure the image on the monitor screen.

These signal degradations can be compensated for by inserting signal conditioning equipment in the coaxial signal transmission cable between the camera and monitor. Video equalizers can be installed in the transmission path at the cable input from the camera, at intervals along the cable, or at the cable output. The equalizer, as the name implies, equalizes the low or high video signal as necessary to restore the output signals so that the amplitude versus frequency relationship is the same as the camera's output signal.

Power line frequency hum is a common problem encountered with video transmission over long cable runs. This occurs because the signal paths to ground at separate locations are often not identical in electrical potential. These ground potential differences at the opposite ends of a video cable shield cause 60 Hz currents to flow in the shield. Since the shield is part of the signal path with 75 ohm unbalanced coaxial cable, the video signal will be amplitude modulated at the 60 Hz rate, producing hum bars. The imposed 60 Hz signals can be removed from the coaxial cable by hum clampers or clamping amplifiers. These devices remove the 60 Hz signal from the composite video and hum signal, leaving a relatively hum-free video signal on the monitor. Low levels of hum can be removed by using isolation transformers to ground the video cable at one point, thereby eliminating ground loops that are the source of the hum interference. A good ground should have a resistance value less than 25 ohms and preferably less than 10 ohms.

The maximum distance a video signal can be transmitted over coaxial cable is about 2 miles under ideal conditions. Broadband video amplifiers can be used to increase this distance. When a single camera's video output is to be sent to several remote monitors, a video distribution amplifier can be used to provide isolation between the input and output video signal and between the individual video outputs to eliminate coupling interference. Video distribution amplifiers also can be used at a remote location to distribute single camera video signals to multiple monitors. This can be accomplished without signal reduction and impedance mismatching. For long cable runs, equalizing amplifiers having frequency and phase characteristics complimentary to those of the coaxial cable can be installed in the coaxial transmission line to maintain signal quality.

When transmitting video signals over long cables and in extreme electromagnetic environments, an unbalanced 75 ohm video signal may be converted through a passive balanced line transformer to a push-pull signal for transmission over a 124 ohm balanced line. A corresponding transformer is, however, required to reconvert the signal to a standard video output for display or recording. In this transmission arrangement, any noise induced on the line affects both cable leads equally so that 60 Hz hum and other induced noise is effectively eliminated.

RF Transmission

Transmitting the video output from a large number of cameras over relatively great distances using video cable with the appropriate signal enhancement equipment would be extremely expensive. For such applications, it might be most cost-effective to modulate the video signal and transmit it by frequency division multiplexing (FDM) over a single cable or a microwave link. The single cable transmission is similar to commercial cable television systems.

The modulators and demodulators used at either end of the transmission lines are expensive, but their costs are somewhat offset by the savings when using a single cable instead of multiple coaxial cables. The video output from up to twelve separate cameras can be transmitted over a single cable, which is another cost savings. In the final analysis, the costs associated with using a single cable RF transmission system must be compared with the costs of using a coaxial transmission system with multiple cables. The installation cost for each technique must be included in the analysis to determine the total cost-effectiveness of an RF system.

Cable transmission is effective for distance up to 5 miles. Longer video transmission distances can be achieved by transmitting the signals over a microwave link. A microwave link is formed by directing a highly directional microwave transmitter toward a corresponding receiver located in a line-of-sight path up to 50 miles away. Amplifier and repeater stations can be used along the transmission path to extend the transmission range, but they too must be located in each other's line of sight. Microwave transmission systems can be expensive, and they do require FCC licensing.

Optical Transmission

Optical transmission of television surveillance and assessment video information is a relatively new development. Transmission is accomplished by amplitude modulating a light beam with the camera's video signal. The light beam does not necessarily have to be visible. One optical transmission system uses an infrared LED to generate an invisible infrared light beam. In this system the infrared energy emanating from the LED is focused by a lens assembly into a flashlight-type beam and directed toward the receiver. The light beam is then focused onto a photodetector by a similar lens arrangement at the receiver. The video signal is reconstructed by the photodetector's output signal, which varies in rate and amplitude with incident infrared light intensity variations. The reconstructed video signal is then ready for recording or for display on a television monitor. Optical video transmission equipment is much less expensive than microwave transmission, and it does not require FCC licensing. But the range is limited to about 3,000 feet, even under ideal operating conditions.

A typical optical transmission system as described in Chapter 19 consists of a transmitter, receiver, and fiber-optic cable. The transmitter converts the electrical video signal to a light of varying intensity through a light emitter. The optical signal is received by a photodetector and amplified to reconstruct the video signal. The fiber-optic cable carries the optical signal from the transmitter to the receiver. Because of the rapid progress in fiber-optic technology, a manufacturer of video optical systems should be consulted for detailed design information.

Fiber-optic systems provide low-loss, high-resolution transmission of video signals without use of amplifiers and can transmit signals over significantly longer distances than coaxial cable. Cables are available for indoor and outdoor aerial and direct burial applications. Camera zoom and pedestal pan/tilt controls can be transmitted over the same cable as the video signal. Another advantage of fiber-optic systems is that there is no electrical connection between the camera and monitor, so hum bars are eliminated. There also are no power line phase problems or lighting or other electromagnetic interference problems.

The decision to use fiber optics is usually a combination of economics (material and labor costs), harsh environment (corrosive atmosphere or large sources of electromagnetic energy), and physical limitations (limited cable and conduit routing available).

AUXILIARY VIDEO EQUIPMENT

Video Switching Equipment

Video switching equipment can be used to switch the video information from multiple cameras to one or a combination of display monitors. With CCTV zone assessment applications, the video switcher can be interfaced with individual sensors to switch any camera to any monitor automatically. Multiple alarms can be processed in a similar manner, but for such a system to be effective, there must be additional monitors to accommodate the individual cameras, or the video information from each sensor zone in alarm must be recorded for viewing. By recording the video information, the operator can switch from one camera scene to another to try to determine the cause of the alarm. In applications having high-priority sensor zones or protected areas, priority switching control equipment should be used to switch in those cameras covering high-priority areas in a prioritized sequence.

Several types of video switchers are available. The simplest switcher can connect a single camera input to a single output bus. Multiple output switchers can switch one or more camera inputs to the switcher to any combination of output buses. In a fully loaded switcher, any camera input can be switched to any output, one camera input can be connected to all the switcher outputs, or different camera inputs can be connected to each output.

Both passive and active switchers are available. In a passive switcher, the switching is accomplished by manually actuated push-button contacts. The video signal is routed through the switcher without electronic conditioning or timing. In an active switcher, the switching route for the video signal is through relay contacts or semiconductors. Active switchers can have input and output amplifiers to provide signal isolation, impedance matching, and amplitude control. Electronic processing of the video signal also is available in some active switchers to control the timing of switching between different camera inputs. Active switchers can be controlled either locally or remotely. If they are remotely controlled, it is necessary to transmit the switcher control signals from the monitoring area to the remotely located switcher.

Video switchers are available using gap switching and lap switching. In gap switching no signal is present on the output bus during switching because the first video input is terminated prior to connecting the second input. This signal interruption, if too long, could result in losing synchronization at the monitor, which will cause picture instability.

In lap switching the synchronization is not interrupted because both input signals exist on the output bus during switching. Overlapping preserves the synchronization timing required by the monitor. Having both signals on-line at the same time does cause jitter and transients that might be noticeable on the display screen. But these transients can be reduced by slowly facing out one input while increasing the intensity of the other. Switching is normally timed to overlap one field of video data.

Pan/Tile Pedestals

A pan/tile pedestal is a movable camera-mounting platform that can be remotely controlled to position the camera toward the scene of interest. Panning moves the camera from side to side, while tilting moves it up and down.

Pedestals can be electrically articulated from a remote location using manual controls or automatically articulated to a programmed position. The automatically controlled pedestals in security applications are usually sensor activated. In this application, when an exterior sensor is activated, the alarm output activates the pedestal control, which then moves the pedestal control, which then moves the pedestal to the programmed coordinates covering the sensor zone in alarm. Once the camera has been correctly positioned according to the coordinates, it can be manually articulated by the operator to track a target or search the area.

Camera Enclosures

Enclosures provide camera mounting and protection for most security applications in interior and exterior environments. Indoor enclosures protect the camera against dust and tampering. The enclosures have both fixed and swivel bases to accommodate different camera-mounting positions. They are typically constructed from sheet metal, with vents to relieve camera heat and a window for camera optics. The enclosures have provisions for locking and tamper switches that, when connected into an alarm system, are meant to detect anyone opening the enclosure.

Outdoor enclosures must protect the camera in a more severe environment. To accommodate these conditions, enclosures can be equipped with heaters, blowers, and window cleaning, wiping, and defrosting accessories. Outdoor enclosures are usually painted white or left shiny to reflect the radiant energy from the sun. Sunshields can be installed on top of the enclosures, leaving space between the enclosure and shield for air circulation to eliminate radiant energy and further reduce the internal enclosure temperature. Thermostatically controlled blowers can be installed inside the enclosure to exhaust internal heat, and thermostatically controlled heaters can be installed to maintain the temperature above freezing. The window cleaning, wiping, and defrosting accessories keep the enclosure window clean in dusty and precipitating environments.

Camera enclosures also are available for special applications. Refrigerated enclosures are available for housing and cooling cameras that must be operated in hot environments. Explosionproof enclosures are available that meet the National Electrical Code for camera application in hazardous environments. Covert enclosures are available that either hide or disguise cameras to be used in covert applications.

Closed Circuit Television Monitors

The function of the monitor is to display the scene being viewed by the camera. The scene is generated in a manner opposite that of the video camera in that the scanning beam generates the visual scene on the CRT instead of extracting the scene information from the camera vidicon image tube target. The picture quality is determined by the contrast ratio and the resolution of the monitor, camera, and video transmission system. The scene to be viewed determines the required resolution for the camera and monitor.

Video Recording Systems

Video recording systems produce a permanent record of a scene for historical information or for subsequent viewing that can aid in real-time assessment by providing instant replay capabilities for the monitoring operator. Recordings can be used for preserving sensor zone scenes and security incidents and for training purposes. Two basic types of recorders are available: disc and helical scan. The helical scan system is the most common system and provides a high-quality recording for most security CCTV applications. The disc recorder is considerably more expensive than the helical scan recorder, but it does provide virtually instantaneous record capability, which might be vital in some assessment systems.

Information Display Equipment

Time/date source identifiers and environmental data generators are available for assisting the monitor operator in real time and for permanent video recording. This equipment converts electronic signal information to an alphanumeric video waveform for presentation or recording. Time/date generators can display alarm information in real time in hours, minutes, seconds, and tenths and hundredths of seconds, with dates in years, months (with automatic number of days per month correction), and days. Source identifiers generate an alphanumeric indication of individual cameras or alarm zones. Environmental data generators generate an alphanumeric display of environmental conditions such as wind speed and direction.

Video Motion Detectors

Intrusion in an area covered by a television camera can be detected by monitoring the camera's video signal for changes indicating movement into the protected area. Changes in a video scene are detected by comparing real-time scene information with a scene during a nonintrusion period. Since significant changes in brightness or contrast can cause an alarm, the reference scene is periodically updated to accommodate slow changes in lighting.

Surge Protection

Lightning and sudden changes in ground potential caused by activating or deactivating large electrical equipment can induce signals on video transmission and power lines that can damage the video transmission equipment and cameras. Surge protectors limit the input voltage to a safe level. The most common surge protection devices for video transmission lines use a network of zener diodes in conjunction with current-limiting resistors to limit the induced signals. Power line surge protection devices use gas discharge tubes, which ground the power lines when the line voltage exceeds the normal operating level. Surge protection is highly recommended for all CCTV video equipment, but especially for those systems operating in areas with frequent lightning activity.

TELEVISION APPLICATIONS

Television is used in security applications primarily for surveillance and alarm assessment. Surveillance applications include covert surveillance to detect adversary actions and perhaps identify responsible individuals for evidence purposes and overt surveillance to detect or deter intrusions, theft, or any adverse act. In some surveillance applications, cameras can be installed to monitor security activities during off-hours and to monitor operating activities such as safety, traffic flow, and plant operations during operating hours. The fact that the television cameras can be used to perform a dual function can be an attractive selling point for management.

Alarm assessment cameras are used to monitor areas protected by intrusion detection sensors. In these applications, when an alarm occurs, the cause can usually be determined without having to send a guard to assess the area. In case of an actual intrusion, depending on the camera type and placement and the intruder's location, the monitoring operator might be able to keep the intruder under surveillance and inform the responding guards about the intruder's activity.

Television cameras can be used for both interior and exterior surveillance and alarm assessment. In addition to covert operations, interior surveillance applications include monitoring functions such as department store shopper surveillance, personnel flow and access, merchandise and currency handling, and general plant operations. Exterior surveillance includes sensor zone alarm assessment, perimeter surveillance, traffic flow, vehicle and personnel access, and equipment and merchandise handling. Both fixed and articulated pedestal-mounted cameras are used for surveillance applications.

An operational problem that must be considered when using surveillance cameras is that it is very difficult for an operator to be attentive to the monitor display for long periods. His attention span depends on the complexity of the visual task and whether he is expected to perform the task continuously or only at various times during his shift. For instance, if the operator is expected to observe a group of monitors or even a single monitor continuously, looking for an incident that might never occur, his attention span will be less than a half hour. If for some reason the application requires continuous monitoring, the security task should be divided between at least three operators so that each one can be relieved for about an hour after spending no more than a half hour observing the displays. This schedule will improve the operator's concentration. If the monitoring task requires articulating the camera to observe larger areas, then the attention span might be a little longer because of the physical involvement. Any type of continuous monitoring is not recommended.

Both interior and exterior alarm assessment is accomplished by using television cameras to view areas protected by intrusion detection sensors for the purpose of assessing alarm causes. In alarm assessment applications, the cameras can be fixed to observe a specific area or mounted on a pan/tilt pedestal so that it can be articulated to cover a larger area. Also depending on the application, multiple cameras can be connected to a single monitor or several monitors in which the operator switches the camera covering the area in alarm to the appropriate monitor either automatically or manually.

Another operational concept is to have a dedicated monitor for each camera covering a sensor zone. Of course, this concept would be influenced by the number of cameras required to cover the total protected areas. An operator can effectively view sixteen monitors (sixteen sensor zones) when cued to the monitor covering the sensor zone in alarm and when the corresponding sensor zone false alarm rate is less than one alarm per hour. Higher false alarm rates become unmanageable with almost any alarm assessment system, especially as the number of sensor zones and corresponding cameras increases above sixteen. This assessment problem will be discussed in the following paragraphs. Basically, an above normal false alarm rate will require using a video recorder to record the camera scene covering the sensor zone where the alarm occurred for delayed assessment by the operator when that zone is called up. If the false alarm rate is high in inclement weather, contingency procedures should be established to increase the number of patrolling guards and, if required, to station guards at sensitive areas until the weather improves and the alarm rate returns to normal. Taking neither design nor operating contingency measures to complement the alarm assessment system during periods of high false alarms leaves the protected areas, especially exterior perimeters, very vulnerable to intrusions.

Another alarm assessment option is to decide whether the monitors will be left on continuously for casual viewing when there are no alarms or left off and automatically switched on when covering an area in alarm. As with most application decisions, there are two schools of thought. One would leave the monitors off, believing the operator would become complacent while viewing the monitors even casually. When there is an alarm, the operator would then lack the alertness to assess the scene adequately to determine the alarm cause. The second school would leave the monitors on because the operator might at any time detect someone in the protected area or detect something that might cause the sensors to false alarm.

I agree with the first school of thought for cameras covering interior protected areas, assuming the areas have adequate protection to detect the perceived threat and have a low false alarm rate. But for outside camera applications where the false alarm rate is high, I agree with the second school: Leave the monitors on. With the monitors operating, the operator might detect something that could cause a false alarm and correct it before the alarm occurs. Some operators like having the monitors on for outside cameras, especially for those cameras covering the perimeter, because they can occasionally observe the monitors to determine what, if anything, is happening at the perimeter. Another consideration is that the eyes are especially adept at detecting motion, even peripherally. Therefore, even with only casual observation of the monitors, the operator might detect someone or something entering the protected area prior to sensor detection. An underlying consideration is the number of cameras the operator must observe. If the number is greater than sixteen with sixteen monitors, then perhaps some monitors could be dedicated to specific cameras located in areas of high interest and the remaining cameras switched between other monitors. Each monitor also should have an indicator light that will be illuminated by the alarm monitoring system when an alarm occurs to direct the operator to the appropriate monitor.

The adequacy of a television system for performing the surveillance and alarm assessment functions certainly depends on the quality of the equipment and installation. But it also depends on the thoroughness of the system design. Therefore, the following paragraphs will discuss the basic CCTV system design considerations, equipment selection, acceptance specifications, and some performance and maintenance considerations. The discussions will address interior and exterior CCTV systems for surveillance and alarm assessment, while concentrating on exterior alarm assessment systems. Television systems are used often in exterior intrusion detection systems and are relatively difficult to design. Many of the design and operational considerations are applicable to all CCTV systems.

Design Considerations

The CCTV system design must be totally integrated with the intrusion detection sensors and display system, and with the site's physical layout and operating requirements. When designing an exterior alarm assessment system, it would be desirable to have the freedom to lay out the perimeter fences, select the intrusion detection sensors, define the sensor zones of detection, select and position the luminaires, and establish the alarm display at the same time that the television assessment cameras are being selected and located and the television monitor display is being chosen. Of course, these design freedoms are not always possible, and, consequently, the alarm assessment system is usually not as cost- or operationally effective as when the freedom to design the total system is available. In fact, when designing an alarm assessment system for a site with an in-place lighting and intrusion detection system, it might be cost-effective to redesign all or at least part of the existing systems to improve the overall effectiveness of the total system. The design considerations discussed here will address applications to achieve maximum assessment performance regardless of whether the system is for an existing intrusion detection system or a new installation.

Site Layout

The first assignment is to review the location, ground contour, and configuration of the fence line. For security purposes the fence should be located as far as possible, within reason, from the protected assets to maximize the time the security forces have to respond to intrusions. For optimum visual and television alarm assessment, the fence lines should be straight to allow full zone coverage with single or dual cameras. If a double fence is being considered, the separation between the inner and outer fence should be uniform with a minimum separation of 30 feet. This spacing will accommodate both invisible barrier and buried line intrusion detection sensors, and it allows adequate space for visual and television alarm assessment.

The ground contour around the perimeter should be as level as possible and without obstacles or ditches in the sensor zones, where possible intruders could hide from view. If the ground is not level and cannot be made level, then the intrusion detection sensor zones should be limited to a nominal 330-foot length so that the total sensor zone can be viewed from a point at one end of the zone. Vegetation in the sensor zones should be maintained at a length that will not interfere with the sensor operation or the operator's visual assessment. The area can be sterilized to remove the vegetation and then covered with gravel to maintain the surface. Having a uniformly colored surface, especially of light color, improves the reflectivity, which in turn increases the camera faceplate illumination and picture quality. Improved picture quality improves the operator's visual assessment task.

Lighting

The placement, quantity, and quality of light sources are very important considerations when designing a television assessment system. Lighting was discussed in greater detail in Chapter 23, but features affecting exterior television systems will be reviewed here in less detail. The type of luminaire lamp should complement the camera's image tube spectral response, and it also must be compatible with the lighting concepts. There are two lighting concepts: one is to leave the lights on continuously, and the second is to turn the lights on only in the event of an alarm and only in the zone or zones in which the alarm occurs.

Each concept has advantages and disadvantages. One advantage of leaving the lights on continuously is that high-intensity discharge energy-efficient lamps can be used in the luminaires. Having the lights on continuously complements the general surveillance capability and also acts as a deterrent to certain types of threats. A distinct disadvantage of using the energy-efficient lamps is that during temporary or even a momentary loss of power, it could be 3 to 20 minutes before the lamps restrike and reach full brightness. This characteristic eliminates their consideration for the instant-on lighting required for the second alarm assessment concept. During power outages, incandescent lamps operated from the power line or emergency generators can be used to illuminate the perimeter. When the high-intensity discharge lamps regain full brightness, the incandescent lamps can be turned off.

The alarm assessment concept using inefficient instant-on lamps reduces power consumption by having the lights on only when an intrusion detection sensor initiates an alarm. One major disadvantage is that when the lights come on, they provide information on the system's alarm rate and the alarm response practice to outside observers. Another disadvantage, depending on the camera's iris opening, is that rapid changes in the light level will delay assessment from 1 to 5 seconds until the iris adjusts to the increased light level. If camera power is left off and turned on only when an alarm occurs, there will be an additional delay while the image tube warms up. Another distinct disadvantage is that during periods of high false alarms, the site will probably resemble Las Vegas with its flashing lights.

Once the decision whether to use continuous or instant-on lamps to support the television surveillance and assessment system has been made, the lighting requirements must be established. There are four specific requirements: horizontal illumination, vertical illumination, light-to-dark ratio, and spectral response.

Horizontal illumination is that light impinging perpendicular to the horizontal surface. It is the light that illuminates the back of an intruder crawling under the lighting system, and it accounts for most of the camera faceplate illumination when reflected from the surface or ground cover under the lights. Therefore, the intensity of the horizontal illumination must be sufficient to illuminate the camera faceplate adequately. A minimum horizontal illumination level of 1 footcandle measured 6 inches above the ground in the horizontal plane is usually adequate to accommodate a camera with good day and night resolution. The illumination level depends on the spectral output of the illuminating sources, the spectral response of the camera image tube, the lens speed, and the ground surface reflection characteristics.

Vertical illumination is that light impinging normally on a vertical surface. It illuminates the front of an intruder walking or running toward a lighting system. The quantity of vertical illumination required to support the television observation task is difficult to define because it is so dependent on the observation task. But the vertical illumination requirements are usually satisfied by any system satisfying the horizontal illumination requirements.

The *light-to-dark ratio* requirement for television systems is as important as, and perhaps even more important than, the illumination level. The light-to-dark ratio is the difference between the brightest area and the darkest area in the camera's field of view. If the light-to-dark ratio is excessive, the bright areas will provide too much camera faceplate illumination, causing blooming or washout of scene detail. Likewise, dark areas will not provide sufficient illumination for adequate resolution. These deficiencies exist because the camera's automatic light control iris adjusts to accommodate the average scene illumination, and it does not have the dynamic range to accommodate the light extremes. The light-to-dark ratio should not exceed 6 to 1.

The *spectral response* of the camera image tube is similar to the human eye in that both are sensitive only to a limited portion of the light spectrum. Therefore, the lighting system luminaire lamp selected should have the maximum amount of illumination in the region of the light spectrum where the image tube is most sensitive. Otherwise, there will be a loss of illumination efficiency because more light will be required to achieve the same picture quality that would be provided by a properly matched luminaire lamp and camera image tube.

The following lamp types are popular for exterior lighting systems supporting television surveillance and assessment systems because of their particular characteristics, such as instant-on capability, energy conservation, and light spectrum output.

Incandescent Lamps.   Light is emitted from a heated filament inside an evacuated globe. A moderate amount of the spectral output exists as visible light. The relative power of the light increases almost linearly across the visible light spectrum, starting in the 400 nanometer wavelength region and increasing to nearly maximum intensity in the 800 nanometer wavelength region, where the magnitude starts leveling. From the spectral output curve description, it is apparent that most of the energy exists in the infrared frequency range starting in the 700 nanometer wavelength region and continuing to longer wavelengths. Because of this abundance of infrared energy, incandescent lamps are used as the light source for infrared illuminators.

Fluorescent Lamps.   The fluorescent lamp is an electrical discharge source in which light is produced predominantly by fluorescent powders activated by ultraviolet energy. The energy is generated by an electric arc inside a long, mercury vapor–filled glass tubular bulb. The low-pressure mercury vapor emits some visible light, but mostly invisible ultraviolet radiation that is converted into visible light by fluorescent powders on the inner surface of the tube. Most of the spectral output exists as visible light covering the entire visible light spectrum, with distinct spectral lines at wavelengths of approximately 440, 545, and 580 nanometers. The distinct spectral lines are fixed, but the remaining light distribution varies depending on the lamp type. For most fluorescent lamp types, the majority of the spectral output exists as yellow light.

High-Intensity Discharge Lamps. High-intensity discharge lamps (HID) include the family of lamps known as mercury, metal halide, and high- and low-pressure sodium lamps. Light is generated in the HID lamps by direct interaction of an arc with the gas in the bulb. Argon gas is normally added to the basic gas to improve starting. Powders or other gases may be added to the basic gas to improve color rendition. High-intensity discharge lamps do not generate a continuous spectrum of light, as do incandescent lamps. Instead, they have unique spectral lines in which the energy exists at one or several specific wavelengths in the electromagnetic energy spectrum.

In mercury lamps, light is produced by passage of an electric current through mercury vapor. The spectral output of the lamp in the visible region of the light spectrum exists as distinct spectral lines at wavelengths of approximately 405, 435, 545, 560, and 570 nanometers. The shorter wavelength spectral lines exist in the blue-green region of the light spectrum, and the 570 nanometer wavelength approaches the yellow region of the spectrum. The positions of the spectral lines account for the greenish blue light emitted from mercury vapor lamps.

Metal halide lamps are very similar to mercury lamps. The major difference is that the metal halide arc tube contains various metal halides in addition to mercury. The spectral output of the lamp in the visible region exists as spectral lines at wavelengths of about 435, 535, and 590 nanometers for lamps using sodium, thallium, and indium iodide halides. Again, the shorter wavelength spectral lines exist in the blue-green region of the visible light, and the 590 nanometer wavelength line approaches the yellow region. This combination of spectral lines accounts for the greenish blue light. Halides such as tin might produce a continuous spectrum across the visible region instead of distinct spectral lines.

In high- and low-pressure sodium lamps, light is produced by passage of an electric current through sodium vapor. High-pressure sodium lamps radiate some energy across the visible spectrum, but they have distinct spectral lines at wavelengths of about 490 and 530 nanometers, with broader spectral energy bands with peaks at wavelengths of about 560 and 590 nanometers. The majority of the spectral output is at wavelengths between 550 and 650 nanometers. This accounts for the golden white color of the high-pressure sodium vapor lamp.

Low-pressure sodium discharge lamps produce light by passing the arc through the vaporized sodium. The light produced by the low-pressure sodium arc is almost monochromatic, meaning that the light output is at one wavelength. Low-pressure sodium lamps radiate at two distinct wavelengths— 589 and 589.6 nanometers. The position of the spectral lines accounts for the yellowish red light generated by the low-pressure sodium vapor lamp. Because the two spectral lines are so close together, low-pressure sodium vapor lamps are basically monochromatic, and it is impossible to distinguish colors in areas illuminated by them.

Camera Placement

Before camera placement can be considered, you must decide whether to use fixed or articulated cameras to perform the desired viewing task. The task can be surveillance, alarm assessment, or both. Articulated cameras are normally used for surveillance because the camera pedestal can be panned and tilted to direct the camera toward the scene of interest, and if detailed viewing is required, the camera lens can be zoomed in on the scene for closer surveillance. Fixed cameras also can be used for surveillance if the area to be protected can be viewed adequately without scanning. Of course, multiple cameras can be used to cover larger areas. Articulated cameras can perform alarm assessment functions, but in most assessment applications, fixed cameras dedicated to a specific sensor zone are used.

Camera placement for indoor applications, whether in surveillance or alarm assessment applications, is usually relatively easy. It is easy because the area to viewed is usually small compared with outdoor 330-foot perimeter sensor zones. Indoor environmental and lighting condition also are relatively fixed. For indoor applications, cameras should be mounted at a height and in a position where they give a full view of the area of interest and are not facing bright lights. Camera placement for outdoor surveillance task is for small areas away from bright lights or for large areas that can be viewed by articulated cameras with appropriate lighting.

The most difficult camera placement design is for systems that must assess alarms from perimeter intrusion detection sensors. It is difficult because the camera, like the human eye, has an angular or cone-shaped field of view. Consequently, when the camera is mounted on a mast, there will be a blind area under the camera, as shown in Figure 24–1. The size of the blind

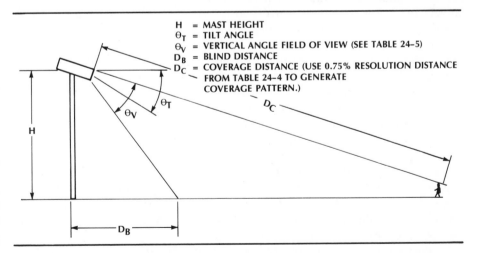

Figure 24–1 Vertical field of view.

area and the vertical and horizontal fields of view are a function of the camera lens focal length, the camera mast height, and the camera tilt angle.

Because of the camera's angular field of view, the camera must be off-set from the sensor zone it is viewing. Providing this offset distance in an installation can be a problem, especially in applications where the detection sensor is for volumetric detection as with bistatic microwave barrier detectors. For instance, the optimum camera position to accommodate the necessary offset to have full view of one sensor detection zone will be in the adjecent sensor detection zone. This location will not only interfere with sensor performance, but it will partially block the field of view of the camera covering that zone. One consideration to alleviate the problem is to offset the camera mast laterally inward from the sensor zone at a distance where it will not interfere with either the sensor performance or the adjacent camera's field of view. The actual distance will depend on the sensor detection zone. From this position the camera will have to be tilted down and directed out toward the zone. Also, the camera lens focal length will have to be selected to accommodate the offset viewing angle.

Another consideration in alleviating the offset problem is to mount the camera on an arm extending from the mast at a distance that will accommodate all, or at least part of the necessary lateral offset distance (maybe 8 to 10 feet). The reason for limiting the offset distance is that the mast and arm will have to be constructed rigidly to minimize camera oscillations in the wind. Increasing the mast rigidity, however, increases design and construction costs.

Another design problem is that of providing adequate camera offset at the corners where adjacent sensor zones interface. Sometimes it is desirable to install cameras outside the perimeter fence, looking back and along the sensor zone. But perimeter sensors are normally located around the site's outer bounderies, and consequently, they cannot be installed outside the fence. In these cases, if adequate lateral offset cannot be achieved because the ideal camera position will interfere with the camera in the adjacent zone, two cameras might be required to cover the sensor zone. One camera would be located in the corner, looking down the sensor zone; the second camera would be located away from the corner in a position to view the dead zone in the area of the corner camera. The corner camera mast also could be used to mount the camera for the adjacent corner sensor zone.

Still another camera positioning problem is that of determining where to locate the cameras to assess fence-mounted sensor alarms. Positioning the cameras to assess alarms from capacitance sensors mounted on top of the fence or electric-field and taut-wire sensors installed on the inside of the fence is basically the same as positioning for volumetric-type sensors because they are in full view of the camera.

Positioning the cameras to assess fence disturbance sensor alarms presents a different set of problems. Fence disturbance sensors detect the mechanical vibrations generated by anyone climbing, cutting, or lifting the fence fabric. If the cameras are positioned inside looking down the fence fabric, they will be in a position to view the top and inside of the fence but not the outside. The fence fabric becomes a solid barrier beyond about 50 feet when looking down the fence line. Therefore, if the cameras are located inside the fence looking toward and down the fence line, they will not be able to see through the fence fabric. The monitoring operator might have to wait when there is an alarm to see whether someone is actually cutting through the fabric or assume that it was just a false alarm. In the absence of more convincing evidence, the latter assumption would probably be made most of the time.

The best camera position for assessment of fence disturbance sensor alarms, assuming the fence line is straight and there are no obstacles, such as barbed tape, on top of the fence to blind the camera's view, is to mount it directly above the fence, looking down the fence line. From this position, the fence appears as a straight line on the monitor, making it easy to view both sides of the fence.

A disadvantage of mounting the cameras above the fence, as voiced by some security people, is that the camera mounting arm can be used by an intruder as a climbing aid to get over the fence without disturbing the fence sensor. In this scenario the adversary lassos the camera-mounting arm with a rope and swings over the fence. The chances of an intruder attempting such an intrusion are probably low because it would be as easy, if not easier, to bring a stepladder to the fence, climb the ladder, and jump over without touching the sensors. Even this scenario has a very low probability if the fence is 10 feet high as recommended, instead of the standard 7 feet. Also, fence disturbance sensors, when used alone, are recommended to detect only low-skill intruders who will climb the fence to gain access, not skilled intruders, who most likely will attempt to bypass the sensors. An inner sensor line should be established in conjunction with fence disturbance sensors to detect skilled intruders.

Because the perimeter sensor zones form a closed loop around the perimeter, camera coverage also must form a closed loop. With this configuration, there might be times of the year when some of the cameras will be looking directly into a rising or setting sun. During this time the camera facing the sun will be blinded. This coverage problem can be eliminated by installing a camera at each end of zones lying east and west of the affected camera. In this configuration, the sensor zone can be viewed by the camera facing away from the rising or setting sun. A less expensive way to accommodate the blinding sun problem is to have a guard or guards patrol the affected zone during the time the camera is blinded.

Normally, sensor alarm assessment is accomplished by using cameras dedicated to monitor-specific sensor zones, as described in the previous paragraphs. This concept is necessitated because the perimeter sensor zones are either too close to the areas requiring protection or there are obstacles, such as trees or bright lights, between the building and sensor zones that preclude using articulated cameras. But this is not always the case, and there are advantages to using articulated cameras, besides the fact that the assessment task can be accomplished with fewer cameras. For instance, if there is a distance of at least 330 feet between the building being protected and the perimeter sensor zones, and if the area is reasonably level and clear of trees and large shrubs, articulated cameras can be used to assess alarm causes, zoom in on the target if necessary, and track any intruder approaching the areas of interest. These additional capabilities certainly enhance the assessment function.

Some camera pedestals can be programmed to position the camera on command according to a set of coordinates to view a specific sensor zone or area. By properly programming the coordinates for each sensor zone being assessed, the pedestal will automatically position the camera for the sensor zone in alarm when activated by an alarm signal. The camera lens might be set initially for wide-angle viewing so that the monitoring operator will first have a full view of the sensor zone in alarm and much of the area between the camera and sensor zone. Once the operator has assessed the full sensor zone, he may manually articulate the camera pedestal and lens to view specific areas or targets of interest. If there is an intruder in the area, the operator can keep him in view by manually articulating the pedestal and camera controls. He can then inform the responding security force of the intruder's position and direction.

Camera Masts

Camera mounting masts or poles should be capable of positioning the camera between 15 and 20 feet, nominally 18 feet, above the ground but below the area lighting. The mast should be as rigid as is reasonably possible and well anchored to minimize camera motion. Excessive camera motion will degrade performance. A low-frequency motion, although annoying to the operator, can be tracked by the eye. But a high-frequency motion, which is too fast for the eye to track well, results in a blurred image on the monitor. The high-frequency resonant motion might exist in windy weather when a camera is installed on an offset mounting arm extending from a mast or building. If a camera installation has a high resonant frequency, then it might be better to replace the bracket or mount with a less rigid one having a low resonant frequency that the eye can track.

Poles should be at least class 1 wooden poles buried well into the ground or steel poles or braced steel masts anchored to concrete foundations that extend well below the local area frost line. In installations where the camera mast must be offset from the sensor zone, a braced steel mast that can adequately support the camera mounting arm is recommended. The mast and arm assembly must be capable of supporting the camera's weight and the torsional loads induced on the mast and mounting foundation when the wind blows the offset camera.

A very important consideration when designing the camera mast is camera maintenance. How will the maintainer reach the camera when it is mounted 15 to 20 feet above the ground? If the camera is mounted on the mast, it can be reached by a built-in ladder or an auxiliary ladder. In either case it is very difficult to handle a camera standing on a ladder. When the camera is mounted on an offset arm, it is even more difficult to service the camera from a ladder.

Two possibilities other than ladders exist for servicing cameras mounted on masts. One possibility is to use a cherry picker to lift the maintainer to the camera. Of course, this means having a cherry picker available, and there must be adequate space so that it can be driven to and maneuvered around the mast to a position where the bucket can reach the camera. The second possibility is to design the mast so that it can be tipped over in a controlled manner so the maintainer can service the camera from ground level. One design has the mast pivot point located about 4 feet above the ground, with the mast extending to ground level and a counterweight at the bottom of the mast to minimize the force required to lower it to the ground. With this design, the cable to the camera is flexible and has a service loop to accommodate lowering the mast, or the cable has an interconnecting connector to disconnect the camera cable.

Another maintenance consideration related to mast design is a service box at the base of the mast where the maintainer will have access to the video signal and have a 110 volt convenience outlet for plugging in any electronic maintenance equipment. Lightning protection devices also can be installed in the service box. Because the video and power signals are conveniently available here, the box should be locked and tamper protected to minimize unauthorized access.

Alarm Assessment

Designing a video assessment system to assess interior sensor alarms where the alarm and false alarm rates are low is reasonably straightforward. With low alarm rates, there is a low probability of simultaneous alarms where the operator would have trouble or be unable to assess each alarm cause. Also, when the alarm rate is low, there will probably be a reasonable amount of time for the monitoring operator to assess each alarm. In this case the alarms can be assessed according to some established priority, which could be simply on a first-in/first-out basis. If there are critical areas that must be assessed, however, then the established sequence will have to be interrupted so that the critical area alarms can be assessed immediately.

Designing an assessment system becomes much more difficult when considering simultaneous alarms, which is the case with most exterior perimeter intrusion detection systems, especially large ones. When exterior systems are exposed to inclement weather, the false alarm rate usually increases, and the probability of having simultaneous alarms is extremely high. The possibility of having multiple simultaneous alarms also is high.

Some number of simultaneous alarms will overload the assessment system to the point where the monitoring operator will not be able to assess each alarm cause. This number is a function of the number of sensor zones, the number of cameras covering each zone, the number of video monitors and monitoring operators, and the perceived threat. The overload number is so site specific in terms of equipment and operator numbers that it would be difficult to quantify the number even for a general case. Basically, if there are more than two alarm zones waiting to be assessed by any one operator, the system is probably overloaded.

The reason for such a small number is that it requires time to acquire the alarm signal and switch in the corresponding camera, and it requires additional time, usually 5 to 7 seconds, for the monitoring operator to assess the camera scene to determine the alarm cause. The 5 to 7 seconds is based on actual intrusion tests when the alarm cause was not immediately obvious, which is usually the case in reality. Ignoring the time rquired to acquire the alarm signal and identify the appropriate camera, and considering only the assessment time, it will take the operator about 10 to 14 seconds to assess the first two alarms. This means that by the time he switches to a third camera, at least 10 seconds have elapsed, and in all probability whatever caused the alarm has disappeared, especially if it was an intruder. An intruder moving at a fast walk of only 3 feet per second will travel 30 feet in 10 seconds, which will clear most camera viewing scenes.

There are two possible approaches to accommodating the overload problem. One is to dispatch guards to patrol the perimeter during times when the alarm rate overloads the system. The second is to control the camera switching and video recording with a computer to preserve the alarm scene needed for assessment. Even this system has inherent delays due to delays in computer processing, video switching, and disc recorder start-up. Therefore, it is important to have adequate perimeter barriers to delay the adversary. Perimeter barriers are needed for any assessment system, whether they are on-site guards or video monitors.

Resolution

Selecting hardware for a video assessment system must start with determining the degree of resolution required for the specific application. Resolution requirements for most security applications can be divided into three levels: detection, recognition, and identification. Detection must be at least adequate to allow the monitoring operator to detect an object in the camera's field of view. Recognition requires increased resolution over detection so that the operator can determine whether the object is a person, animal, or just debris. Identification requires even greater resolution so that the operator can identify the object based on details of appearance.

All three levels of resolution depend on object size and proximity to the camera. Obtaining the desired level of resolution for most interior security applications is relatively easy because the object size of interest is usually a person, not some small animal. Moreover, target proximity relative to the camera is contined to the limits of the room. Object size and proximity to the camera are much more critical for exterior video assessment systems, even when the monitoring operator is alerted to the presence of the object by an intrusion detection sensor. Detecting an object moving through the camera's field of view, if it is within reasonable proximity to the camera, is usually not difficult because the eye is well adapted to detecting motion. Recognizing whether the object is a person, small animal, or blowing debris can be much more difficult. If the object is a person walking or running through the scene, he will be easy to detect and recognize as a person. But if the object is a skilled intruder who moves very slowly, keeping a low profile by crawling, and if he is camouflaged to match the ground cover, he will be much more difficult to detect. Therefore, when designing a video assessment system for exterior applications, the methods an intruder might use to penetrate the perimeter must be considered when establishing the level of resolution needed for detection and recognition. Resolution can be improved by selecting a longer focal length lens, which will make the intruder appear larger at any distance. Remember, however, that lenses having a long focal length reduce the width and height of the field of view.

Resolution of television cameras is generally expressed in terms of the number of resolvable lines in the picture. This is the maximum number of alternating light/dark bands that can be imagined on the camera tube target surface and subsequently recovered from the camera video's output. The amount of monitor scene detail in the horizontal direction depends on the number of alternating light/dark vertical bands recoverable in scan line form. Scene detail in the vertical direction depends on the corresponding number of recoverable light/dark horizontal bands. The light/dark bands contain all the scene information imaged on the target surface that is available for scanning, while scan lines transmit the fraction of this information that is contained in the video signal for reproduction of the scene on the monitor screen.

All scene information imaged on the tube target surface is not represented in the scan lines displayed on the video monitor. Some horizontal band information is lost due to gaps between adjacent scan lines and other deficiencies in the scanning process. Vertical band information is lost due to less than ideal horizontal bandwidth. The maximum number of horizontal or vertical light/dark bands that can be resolved in the camera output or displayed on the monitor screen describes the video resolution. Resolution is expressed as a number (N) of TV lines. For instance, 340 vertical lines describes the resolution for a 525 scan line system.

The broadcast television industry has adopted a standard camera transmission of 525 scan lines per frame with about a 4.5 MHz bandwidth. The

4.5 MHz bandwidth resolves into about 360 vertical lines of resolution, assuming 1 MHz of bandwidth is required to achieve 80 vertical TV lines of horizontal resolution for a 525 scan line system. Closed circuit cameras are available that transmit anywhere from 450 scan lines per frame up to 1,225 scan lines per frame and vary in bandwidth from 4.5 MHz to 30 MHz. Cameras with 650 TV lines of resolution should be adequate for most security applications. For special applications, such as personnel identification, higher resolution might be required.

It is generally agreed that a given object in the camera's field of view must occupy more than one picture element to be recognized. Five scan lines (four picture elements) are normally adequate for recognition if other assessment conditions, such as the illumination level and contrast ratio, are met. With this as a basis, the minimum object size for recognition at the required camera viewing distance can be calculated for lenses with a given focal length. If the calculated object size is larger than the actual object size, then either the viewing distance will have to be shortened or the camera lens changed to ensure that the object occupies at least five scan lines. In general, the minimum detectable object size for a 650 TV line system should occupy at least 0.75 percent of the horizontal field of view. Table 24–4 gives the distance at which a 0.190-meter-square contrasting target would satisfy this condition for various lenses.

There are situations, however, where 0.75 percent might not be adequate because the specific degree of resolution depends on a large number of variables. For instance, cameras are generally mounted above ground level on poles or walls and tilted backward to view the scene of interest. This mounting arrangement results in nonsymmetrical images because the scan line distribution over the field of view is more dense in the near field than in the far field. Because of this density difference, resolution becomes a function of the camera's height and the distance to the specific object of interest. This means that the minimum object size to achieve five raster lines in the far field will have to be larger than if it was in the near field.

Table 24–4 Distance Limits for Five-Line (0.75%) Object Resolution

Lens Focal Length (mm)	0.75% Object Distance (m)
12.5	25
25.0	50
50	100
75	150
100	150
150	300
300	300

Video Equipment Selection

Proper camera and ancillary equipment selection are prime considerations when designing a television surveillance or alarm assessment system.

Cameras

When selecting cameras for exterior surveillance and alarm assessment applications, a big consideration is whether to use low light level cameras supported with artificial lighting or very low light level SIT or ISIT cameras operated with very low scene illumination. For most surveillance applications, the cameras are pedestal mounted so that they can be articulated to view large areas. In these applications it is usually difficult to have adequate scene illumination to cover all areas where surveillance is desired.

If low light level cameras are planned and the area lighting is inadequate, one option is to mount an active infrared light source on the pedestal with the low light level camera to illuminate those area where the existing light is poor. Both narrow beam and wide beam luminaires are available for this application. Narrow beam luminaires generate a spotlight-type beam to illuminate small areas or targets up to about 400 feet from the camera. This type of luminaire is useful when the camera zooms in to view specific targets. Wide beam luminaires generate a floodlight-type beam that is good for viewing areas within 200 feet of the camera where the existing illumination is not adequate to provide proper scene illumination. An advantage of the infrared luminaire is that the light is invisible to the human eye in the area being illuminated. Any intruder in the camera's field of view would probably not realize that he is visible unless he looked at the luminaire and noticed the reddish glow.

The infrared light is generated by a high-intensity lamp that produces light in the visible and near infrared frequency range. The visible light is virtually eliminated by placing infrared filters over the luminaire lens. The filters do not block all the visible light, and consequently there is a red glow in front of the luminaire. Since most of the visible light is restricted by the filter, the resulting heat produced by the visible light must be absorbed by the luminaire housing. This requires that the housing be relatively large and heavy to absorb and dissipate the heat.

When using low light level cameras supported by an infrared luminaire, consideration must be given to the additional luminaire weight and surface area when selecting the camera pedestal. Heavy-duty pedestals should be used to carry the camera and luminaire. Pedestal counterweights and wind sails might be needed to compensate for the imbalance weight and wind loads produced by the offset luminaire.

If very low light level SIT or ISIT cameras are planned for the surveillance operation, care must be taken to ensure that the cameras are not exposed to bright light sources that can damage the tube when the cameras are articulated from one scene to another. Exposure can be minimized by mounting the cameras below the area lighting and perhaps limiting the tilt angle so that the monitoring operator cannot accidentally point the cameras into the lights. The operator also should be warned about pointing the cameras at bright lights or the sun.

Because excessive scene brightness can cause permanent tube damage with subsequent loss of resolution to certain image tubes, burn-free or burn-resistant image tubes should be used in low light level cameras. The image tubes recommended for outside alarm assessment applications, because of their good resolution in both daylight and at night with the proper lighting, are silicon diode target and Newvicon tubes. Both tubes are relatively insensitive to image burn-in, with the Newvicon somewhat superior because it produces less blooming from bright scenes, but it exhibits more lag. The tube has a greater spectral response to near infrared illumination than the Newvicon tube, thereby making it more desirable for low light level surveillance applications when supported by a comounted infrared luminaire.

Although both low light level and very low light level cameras can be used for perimeter alarm assessment, low light level cameras are recommended when supported by a perimeter lighting system that meets the illumination and light-to-dark uniformity requirements. Camera procurement and maintenance costs also are significantly less than for very low light level cameras. Low light level cameras also are less prone to tube damage when exposed to bright light sources. Perimeter illumination provided for low light level cameras is a psychological deterrent to some threats, and it projects shadows that could increase the monitoring operator's probability of detecting someone in the area.

Lenses

Two types of lens assemblies—zoom lenses and fixed lenses—are available for television surveillance and alarm assessment applications. Zoom lenses are usually used for general surveillance because the field of view can be remotely adjusted by the monitoring operator to accommodate his viewing task. They are usually not considered for primary alarm assessment systems because, in the event of an intrusion, they will usually not be set at the proper focal length for immediate target assessment. Time would then be wasted adjusting the lens. An important overall objective is to keep the number of lens types at a minimum to accommodate camera maintenance with interchange of units and reduce parts inventory.

Fixed lenses that have been selected to accommodate the configuration of a clear zone and intrusion detection sensor zone are usually recommended for alarm assessment applications. Proper lens selection is crucial in obtaining optimum alarm assessment. In general, lens selection should be based on imaging as much of the clear zone as possible to minimize the number of cameras, while retaining an acceptable degree of overall resolution. It is also recommended that the sensor zones be configured so that one camera will cover a single zone. This interdependence is why the system designer should consider video assessment and intrusion detection system designs simultaneously.

Although lenses can be designed to accommodate different focal lengths and lens spreads, standard lenses such as the 25mm, 50mm, and 75mm should be used for the assessment cameras, if possible, to reduce costs. This means that the designer might have to adjust the clear zone view and sensor zone length to use a standard lens.

Generally, the lens format should match or exceed that of the image tube target format. One-inch and ⅔-inch lens formats are available, but there are two distinct advantages to selecting 1-inch formats even when ⅔-inch formats are being used. One advantage is that there is generally a greater variety of 1-inch format lenses available, allowing a greater degree of design freedom in lens selection. The second advantage is an increase in resolution because of the reduction in lens edge caused by using only the central area of the tube target. If wide-angle lenses are used, this improvement will be even more apparent because geometric distortions also are reduced. Cameras using tubes and lenses with a ⅔-inch format are usually selected for size and lower initial cost, but they result in a reduction in resolution.

Lens focal length is the most important factor in proper lens selection. It determines the relative magnification of objects in the field of view and defines the angular field of view for any object distance. If the object distance is known, the height and width of the perpendicular camera's field of view at that distance can be determined. As mentioned under resolution, the longer the lens focal length, the larger an object appears at any given distance, thereby increasing the resolvability of the object.

The horizontal (l_H) and vertical (l_V) angular fields of view for various standard lenses using a 1-inch format are shown in Table 24–5.

A convenient way to determine the proper lens focal length and to establish the sensor zone configuration is to make a scale drawing of the site showing the perimeter fences and clear zones. Then generate patterns of the horizontal angular fields of view for several different lenses with standard

Table 24–5 Angular Fields of View*

f (mm)	Θ_V (degrees)	Θ_H (degrees)
12.5	41.71	53.86
25	21.57	28.50
50	10.88	14.48
75	7.27	9.68
100	5.45	7.27
150	3.64	4.85
300	1.82	2.43

*Assumes 1-inch-format lens.

focal lengths that might be used to view the perimeter sensor zones. Since the angular field of view is a function of the lens format and focal length, it is independent of the site drawing scale. Therefore, the pattern can be drawn on transparent paper using a conventional protractor to lay out the proper viewing angle for each lens type. A list of the horizontal angular field of view of various standard lenses is given in Table 24–5. Remember that these calculations are for cameras pointed parallel to the ground. In actual applications the cameras are usually pole mounted and pointed down-ward. This means that any horizontal angular field of view will be slightly less, depending on pole height, than the corresponding value shown in the table.

Each lens type has a maximum distance at which a small target will occupy five raster lines on the monitor screen. These distances are identified in Table 24–4 for several standard focal length lenses typically used in alarm assessment applications. The appropriate target distance for each lens type, not exceeding the 0.75 percent resolution threshold, should be indicated on the respective field of view pattern using the same scale for the viewing distance as was used for the site drawing (see Figure 24–1). This distance should be compared with the maximum viewing distance from which a standing person can be seen in the vertical field of view. This distance can be calculated, but it is also a function of the camera's height and tilt angle, as well as the lens's vertical angular field of view. The shorter of these two distances should be used as the maximum viewing distance. The blind zone distance that exists in front of the camera, which is a function of the camera's height, tilt angle, and lens type, also should be marked on the lens pattern. Remember that these distances are for a flat terrain. Ground undulations must be taken into account when fixing camera positions.

Now the fun begins: trying to fit the field of view pattern to the desired sensor zone. There should be a layout to ensure that cameras have an adequate viewing distance without blind zones. This is no easy task, especially for large sites with uneven terrain, when trying to minimize the number of cameras by using only one camera per sensor zone.

Ancillary Camera Equipment

Various pieces of equipment are needed for long-term support of television cameras. A partial list includes automatic light controls, remote camera controls, camera enclosures, and pan/tilt systems. Three types of automatic light controls are generally available, including auto-iris, neutral density spot filter, and filter wheel. Automatic iris is a standard feature of most low light level cameras. Neutral density spot filters are recommended to provide the necessary dynamic range to accommodate varied lighting. They are recommended because of their overall excellence and the poor reliability of filter wheels.

Specifications for remote camera controls are a function of the particular camera. Self-adjusting cameras are preferred, however, since every additional remote control typically provides another source of reliability degradation. Functions adjusted by drive motors should be avoided wherever possible.

Camera enclosures are required for outdoor use of nonenvironmentally rated cameras. When selecting an enclosure, remember that the size must be adequate to accommodate not only the camera's body dimensions, but also the lens, especially the full range of a zoom lens. Size considerations also must include cable connections, cable service loops, and all other camera options. Cameras with an integral housing need an external enclosure only in applications where weather extremes exist, such as very high or low temperatures and hig winds combined with blowing sand, rain, or snow. Enclosures to accommodate these conditions include waterproofing with or without pressurization, wipers, washers, blowers, dehumidifiers, and heaters.

Selection and application of camera-mounting pedestal pan/tilt controls are relatively straight forward. Articulated pedestals should be used to extend the surveillance capabilities of cameras but should not be used to replace fixed cameras for alarm assessment. They can be used in alarm assessment to supplement the fixed camera system to obtain more detailed target information. But as with zoom lenses, too much time can be wasted manipulating the pedestal, except perhaps when there is an adequate distance between the camera and sensor zones and the area is clear.

Pan/tilt pedestals are normally rated for both electrical and mechanical performance. Several important parameters to consider when selecting a pedestal follow.

Pan Range.   This is the pedestal angular displacement in the horizontal plane, and it is usually limited to less than 360 degrees rotation, which is usually adequate for most surveillance applications.

Pan Speed and Torque.   This is the speed of the pan/tile pedestal at its maximum rate of angular displacement. The rate is normally an unloaded figure expressed in degrees per second and is somewhat lower with the camera and enclosure mounted. For this reason, a torque figure is provided for calculating the angular speed for a fully loaded pedestal.

Tilt Range.   This is the maximum angular displacement in the vertical plane and is usually limited to ± 90 degrees as needed to point the camera straight up or straight down when the pedestal is mounted in the horizontal plane.

Tilt Speed and Torque.   This is the rate of angular displacement in the vertical plane and is generally lower than the pan speed. Tilt torque is normally higher than pan torque because of the difference in weight distribution. Pan torque moves the camera and enclosure weight about a vertical axis, while tilt torque must oppose the torque generated by the camera and enclosure weight offset from the horizontal tilt axis.

Limit Switches.   Camera image tubes can be damaged if pointed at excessively bright objects or the sun. Limit switches are normally installed on the pedestal so that the user can adjust or limit the pan and tilt angles to minimize the possibility of tube damage from bright lights and to limit the camera coverage to areas of interest. In cases where zoom lenses are used on a pan/tilt equipped camera, limit switches may be installed to return the lenses automatically to a preselected focal length when the zoom control is released.

Sync Generation Equipment

The choice of a synchronization technique for an assessment system depends primarily on the system's size and complexity and the available budget. The choices are to use random or local camera-interlaced sync or to provide a master sync source. Local sync is the easiest, least expensive, and most reliable means of dealing with the sync question. It does, however, produce the least aesthetically pleasing monitor display and limits the system's capabilities. It is displeasing because when more than one camera must be either alternately selected for monitor viewing or simultaneously viewed or processed through the system, the respective sync pulses, although very close in frequency, occur at different times. Because of this time difference, vertical rolling may appear on the monitor screen for a short time after switching, and complete loss of monitor sync will probably occur if two such camera signals are simultaneously displayed. Videotape recorders and, more importantly, disc recorders may lose vital assessment information due to sync lock-up lag immediately following system activation. In addition, local sync is not compatible with many video motion detectors.

Master sync instruments provide horizontal and vertical synchronized scanning information to drive the cameras, video recorders, and ancillary equipment. There is nothing particularly unique about these generators as compared with the generators in cameras, except that they are almost always fully interlaced and possess excellent stability. Individual units might be capable of driving more than one device, but they are usually operated with distribution amplifiers. Options include separate horizontal and vertical sync signals, generator lock, which allows the generator to be phase locked to an external source, and various test signals. Master sync allows high-quality switching, display, and recording. It does, however, require a cable to each camera, which increases system cost.

Sync distribution instruments provide the means to distribute the master sync signal to all cameras in a system. These are commonly available in module form to accommodate system expansion. Options include pulse regeneration and pulse delay for timing signals over varying transmission line lengths.

Transmission Systems

Selection of video signal transmission equipment includes consideration of the variety of transmission methods available, the physical layout and environment of the transmission system, and the bandwidth requirements for the video signal. Video cable, signal conditioning equipment, and RF and optical transmission equipment are all part of the transmission system.

The design consideration for bandwidth should relate to the overall quality of the input and output components, specifically cameras and monitors. For example, assuming 80 lines of horizontal resolution is approximately equivalent to 1 MHz of bandwidth, a camera with a specification of 600 lines of horizontal resolution will require 7.5 MHz of bandwidth. It would be difficult to justify this quality in a camera if the transmission system bandwidth was only 4 MHz. Similarly, there is no advantage to providing a 12 MHz bandwidth transmission system for a 7.5 MHz camera. The bandwidth capabilities of all system components should match. Monitor resolution and bandwidth capabilities are generally stated in lines of horizontal resolution, but of the two component types, the camera is usually the limiting factor for system bandwidth. Once the bandwidth is determined, the total system must be reviewed to be certain that no portion will compromise overall system quality, including high-frequency losses in long transmission lines.

Most video signals for security applications will be transmitted over balanced 124 ohm or unbalanced 75 ohm video cable. Sometimes coaxial, twin-axial, or core configurations are used, depending on the particular application. For installations where electromagnetic interference is a problem, the interference phase cancellation properties of balanced twin-axial cable or the additional shielding capabilities of triaxial cable may be desirable. Triaxial cable for television systems is normally 124 ohms and will generally require use of matching transformers or amplifiers. If properly used, matching or signal isolation transformers also will eliminate AC ground currents in the video signal paths of coaxial, twin-axial, or triaxial cable runs. All cable, even armored semirigid coaxial cable, should be handled with care to prevent kinks or dents, which will result in an impedance mismatch and signal degradation, and the cable should be well grounded.

Selection of signal conditioning equipment is based primarily on the amount of attenuation experienced by the video signal during cable transmission and the amount of noise picked up during this transmission. These include video equalizers, hum clampers, video transformers, and video distribution amplifiers.

Video equalizers provide both preequalization and postequalization. Preequalization is generally used in conjunction with postequalization rather than in lieu of it, while postequalization is frequently used alone when cable loss permits. Combined equalization is usually used in extremely long cable runs where postequalization alone cannot correct high-frequency attenuation.

Postequalization is commonly used alone in installations since many cable losses are usually correctable with one equalizer at the receiving end. At this location, the equalizer alignment is much simpler because the equalizer output can be adjusted while the video test signal is being monitored.

Intermediate equalization is normally used on extremely long cable runs where the compensation obtained by combined pre- and postequalization is not sufficient for the desired overall amplitude versus frequency relationship.

The importance in selecting a hum clamper is its relative ability to remove hum from the video input signal. Ideally, the resultant hum level should not significantly degrade the overall signal-to-noise ratio. This ratio places a limit on the maximum permissible input hum-to-signal ratio that a single clamper can tolerate without adversely affecting system performance.

Clampers are commonly employed at the video cable head. This requires that the input impedance or connector configuration be compatible for both the clamper and the associated transmission cable. Matching transformers or amplifiers may be required if the selected manufacturers cannot provide the necessary modifications.

Signal isolation and impedance matching are two of the more common applications for video transformers in television systems. In general both functions may be obtained in a single transformer. They are frequently employed at the local and remote cable heads as an interface between unbalanced 75 ohm video lines and the balanced or unbalanced transmission cable. Video transformers then act not only to match and isolate the two lines, but also as a bandwidth-restricting element for the entire system. For this reason, careful attention must be given to the total bandwidth to ensure a performance level compatible with that of the overall system.

Most transmission equipment available for video applications is either 75 ohm unbalanced or 124 ohm balanced. Transformers designed primarily for isolation will typically have somewhat improved hum rejection over transformers designed specifically for impedance matching. Similarly, bandwidth, connector type, and cost restrictions are often difficult to satisfy simultaneously with a single commercial unit. The usual choice, therefore, will be a compromise between one or more of the various selection parameters.

Another important factor to consider in transformer selection is whether or not phase inversion between the primary and secondary windings may be tolerated. Transformers are available in both forms and should be selected to meet the requirements.

Most distribution amplifiers are provided with a high-impedance looping input and four or more 75 ohm outputs. Adjustable gain is normally included to vary the output level on all outputs simultaneously.

Radio-frequency transmission equipment is normally specified only in systems requiring widespread distribution of a few video signals. A separate modulator/demodulator pair is required for each channel, but the system range is essentially unlimited, with the availability of commercial line extenders. A major disadvantage is that the bandwidth is limited to 9.8 MHz, or about 400 lines. Some wideband modulator/demodulator pairs are available on special orders.

Microwave transmission is technically fesible, but it is not usually considered an economical alternative for video transmission. System cost is extremely high due to the complexity of both the electrical and mechanical components. Overall economic considerations generally prohibit the use of microwave over distances of less than 4 to 6 miles, and the local terrain might not provide the required line-of-sight path between the transmitter and receiver over distances greater than several miles. For installations where a large number of video signals must be transmitted over long line-of-sight distances or where cable transmission is impractical, microwave may be an acceptable alternative. Single-channel microwave links are available because of the increase in commercial usage of remote reporting of television news. This hardware suffers the same bandwidth limitations as other commercial broadcast hardware, however.

Optical transmission is accomplished by modulating an infrared beam. Its limitations are cost per channel, usable range, and susceptibility to heavy fog. Its use may be advantageous, however, at installations where a small number of video signals must be transmitted through extremely adverse electromagnetic environments that prohibit the use of cable transmission. Some commercial units can transmit one of the two video signals at distances of up to ½ mile, but as with microwave, an unobstructed line-of-sight path is required.

Video Switching Equipment

Both passive and active switchers are available. Passive switching is, however, useful only in systems having a limited number of cameras or no requirement for immediate assessment. Active switchers are available in a variety of configurations suitable for a wide range of applications. These are discussed below in order of increasing complexity.

Manual Switching.   Manual control of an active switcher has the same qualifications as passive switching, although the video quality may be higher. It is, however, both beneficial and satisfying to be able to switch any system manually when necessary.

Sequential Switching.   These units allow a number of cameras to be automatically scanned, either for monitor display or historical video recording. The scanning can be programmed for selected cameras, not necessarily all the cameras included in the switching sequence, and for the appropriate dwell time for each camera. These switchers are useful if the video system is being used for detection or random surveillance as well as assessment. A form of video line supervision also is effected.

Alarm Activated Switching. These features may be incorporated in a sequential or conventional routing switcher to present the alarm zone camera information to the output regardless of the selected input before alarm activation. This switching technique provides rapid alarm switching. Interfacing of alarm outputs should be accomplished according to the manufacturer's specifications, but it typically requires only a simple contact closure. This type of switching is ideally suited to assessment systems. It can be controlled by simple sensor logic outputs to an alarm processing computer.

Remote Switching. Remote switching fulfills two requirements. First, it can free equipment space in the display and control console. The bulk of the switcher can be installed in an equipment enclosure, leaving only the controls at the operator console. Second, remote switching allows spatial separation of parts of the switch matrix. This is useful in eliminating duplication of long transmission runs between cameras and consoles. For example, if twenty cameras are installed but only five will be observed at one time, part of the switcher can be located near the cameras. Only five cables then need to be run to the console. Remote switching also is required for the addition of computer control.

Computer-Controlled Switching. This feature, although complex and expensive represents the ultimate in state-of-the-art sophistication for video assessment system control. The improved switching capability is an excellent example. Prioritization of multiple alarm sector displays, automatic recording control, sequential switching pattern control, and other features also are possible.

Switchers of all types are characterized by common performance specifications. These include speed of activation, output drive capability, and differential gain across the switcher points. Relay and mechanical contact switching has good noise immunity and high bandwidth but is limited in switching speed. Electronic switching has a more limited bandwidth but is faster and far more common in assessment equipment because of improved reliability over relay switching. Three switcher timing techniques are used with video assessment systems: random, lap, and vertical interval. *Random switching* should be used only in systems with a small number of cameras, minimal recording capabilities, and no requirement for instantaneous assessment. *Lap switching* is suggested for most systems since it provides a quality of video signal that can be displayed and recorded with essentially no problems with loss of sync. *Vertical interval switching* provides the maximum quality video signal, but its cost should be justified by the need for video free of discontinuities.

Video Monitors

The monitor is where the camera's output signal is converted to a visual scene for the monitoring operator. A level of performance compatible with other system components is an important concern. The level of performance or quality of the picture viewed is determined by the resolution, bandwidth, gray scale response, and automatic frequency control.

Resolution.   Monitors, like video cameras, use television lines as the dimensions for resolution. The vertical resolution of both monitors and cameras is limited by the number of lines containing picture information, or active scan lines. This number is normally 340 TV lines for a 525 scan line system. Therefore, only the horizontal resolution needs to be specified. Monitor resolution is frequently expressed in conjunction with a certain level of screen brightness, with separate degrees of resolution specified for the center and corners of the screen. Monitors having 700 to 800 TV lines of horizontal resolution are often employed in 525 scan line systems operating at up to 10 MHz of horizontal system bandwidth.

Bandwidth.   Bandwidth ratings on video monitors normally consider only the video amplifier and may or may not agree exactly with the 80 lines of resolution per 1 MHz of bandwidth used in the earlier example for resolution. The accuracy in using this rule of thumb is usually acceptable.

Gray Scale Response.   The number of unique discernible shades of gray that a monitor can display is a criterion of selection occasionally overlooked. An ideal monitor would be capable of displaying white, black, and an infinite number of shades in between, and a worst case monitor could display only white or black regardless of video input. Monitors capable of ten discernible shades of gray or better are usually acceptable for security surveillance and alarm assessment systems.

Automatic Frequency Control (AFC).   The internal horizontal oscillator may free-run in most monitors, with the instability of loss of composite video or sync input signals. An AFC is frequently incorporated into the horizontal oscillator to make the monitor less sensitive to slight variations in horizontal sync pulse frequencies commonly found in videotape recorder (VTR) output signals. The time constant of this AFC should be compatible with the format used by the particular VTR.

Once the video monitor's level of performance has been determined, the monitor's screen size must be selected. This is based on the console arrangement and operator's viewing position. The size is primarily a function of the operator's viewing distance, viewing angle, and viewing task. For general surveillance and assessment purposes, industry has found that the maximum vertical angle between the operator and the screen for optimum viewing is 30 degrees. In addition, the farther the operator is seated from the center of the monitor screen, the greater is the image distortion. Therefore, a maximum horizontal angle of 45 degrees from the center is recommended to maintain a reasonable distortion-free picture. When it is necessary to have a distortion-free picture, the maximum horizontal angle should not exceed 30 degrees. If the viewing task requires a larger screen, then a 14- to 19-inch screen should be located directly in front of the operator, where he can switch in any individual monitor scene for closer scrutiny. Table 24–6 shows the recommended maximum and minimum operator viewing distances for the standard size monitor screen.

Video Recording Systems.

Most video assessment systems will require some type of video recorder, if only to provide historical data for review. The recorder can provide other useful functions, including stop frame, slow motion, precise event/time correlation, and an almost instantenous record capability. Both videodisc and videotape recorders are intended for storing video data, but their characteristics and capabilities are entirely different.

Videotape recorders provide long-term storage of large quantities of video data. They can store up to several hours of real-time video data, and the tape can be removed for later review on other machines if required. The mechanical components and tape interface of videotape recorders will not support continuous real-time recordings. Daily maintenance is required to preserve good quality recording capabilities if the machine is set in a ready-to-record mode.

Videodisc machines can provide nearly instantaneous recording since the low-mass (lightweight) head can be retracted from the disc surface when not used. The only moving part is a high-mass disc driven by a motor rated for continuous operation. Since the disc is continuously turning, when a command to record is given, the head can be positioned on the disc in a few milliseconds and start recording as soon as the next video field appears. Videodiscs can store only about two hundred frames of video data, and discs are often not interchangeable between machines. Disc recorders are re-

Table 24–6   Maximum and Minimum Operator Viewing Distances

Screen Size (inches)	Maximum Viewing Distance	Minimum Viewing Distance
9	7'0"	3'0"
12	10'0"	3'4"
14	12'0"	3'7"
17	14'9"	3'9"
19	16'9"	3'10"
21	19'0"	4'10"
23	19'4"	4'11"

quired when nearly instantaneous recording is required to satisfy security assessment requirements.

Information Display Equipment

Insertion of auxiliary information on the video scene can help verify the time and place of origin of each alarm and identify weather contributions to high sensor alarm rates. Selection of a time-date generator, zone and sensor identifiers, and weather status indicators are as important as selecting any video equipment. Since the video signal loops through the hardware, it is important to choose equipment that does not degrade the video signal or cause its loss if the information display unit fails. The information should be displayed in a nonessential area of the picture and in contrast to the background if possible.

Video Motion Detectors

Motion detectors monitor the video signal from a camera or the resulting scene brightness on the monitor screen. When there is a change in the signal or picture brightness resulting from motion within the camera's field of view, an alarm sounds and the scene is visible on the respective monitor. Various types of video motion detectors are available. Some have small photodetectors that can be positioned anywhere on the screen to monitor scene brightness. When there is a small change in brightness, an alarm is sounded. Other more sophisticated detectors monitor the video signal from the camera at positions equivalent to several hundred light-sensitive spots throughout the camera's field of view. If desired, some or all of the positions can be desensitized to allow for moving objects in the field of view. Fine-grain comparison-type video motion detectors are generally more sensitive than integrated comparison hardware. The false alarm rate also might be higher.

Digital motion detectors provide direct capability for sophisticated computer processing of the video scene. This technique will increase sensitivity while holding the false alarm rate to a minimum. This type of motion detector provides excellent detection and is recommended for interior applications. The scene is basically fixed for valid motion, or perhaps a change in scene brightness resulting from a lamp burning out, that would initiate an alarm.

Some of the less sophisticated video motion detectors might function satisfactorily for many interior applications, but they are not currently recommended for exterior applications. They may be used in selected applications where the camera's field of view can be controlled to eliminate light or scene brightness changes from cloud motion, windblown objects passing through the scene, or camera vibrations. All these conditions cause false alarms. Digital motion detectors that might be able to function adequately in these environments are being developed.

Miscellaneous Equipment

Other items are needed to complete the video system. These include connectors, surge protectors, and line supervision. Connector selection is determined by cable and equipment mating connectors. Crimp and solder connections are available for most connector types. Both types are adequate, but crimp connectors usually result in fewer installation problems than solder joints.

The need for surge protection is determined by the local electromagnetic conditions, particularly power line surges and lightning. In any area with lightning, video equipment should have lightning protection to minimize system failures from nearby lightning strikes. Surge suppressor selection depends on carefully tailoring the suppressor to the video equipment requirements. Video and sync lines can tolerate only a small amount of parasitic capacitance without significant signal degradation. In addition, the clamping voltage for surge suppression is much closer to the operating voltage than is necessary on power lines. Some experimentation might be necessary to determine allowable capacitance levels, since this specification is not usually given by manufacturers.

Line supervision devices added in the signal line should not degrade the quality of the video signal or cause loss of signal if the detector fails.

System Specifications

Establishing appropriate acceptance and performance specifications is essential to obtaining and maintaining a high-quality, reliable television system. The security business is a relatively small part of the extremely large and dynamic video equipment industry. Consequently, only a few manufacturers are interested in totally customizing equipment. Detail component specifications must, to a large degree, be based on the manufacturer's equipment capabilities. It is recommended that both general and component acceptance specifications that detail acceptance testing and predelivery documentation be generated to ensure that the equipment, when installed, has a high probability of meeting system requirements.

To ensure quality performance of the television system after acceptance and installation, the system should be tested to verify the adequacy of the initial design criteria. For example, if an alarm assessment system's design requirement is to provide adequate resolution for an operator to detect objects in the field of view and recognize whether they are animals, blowing debris, or humans, representative objects should be passed through the camera's view to determine whether the operator can perform the detection and recognition tasks. These tests should be documented in a performance specification.

It is also recommended that some form of performance testing be conducted at regular intervals of at least every 6 months, if not otherwise specified, to ensure continued system quality. One way to judge the quality on a continuing basis is to make a video recording of all typical day and night camera fields of view. The recording should represent the maximum overall performance level attainable with the system, considering, for example, video bandwidth, tape format, and relative scene illumination. The recording can then be periodically compared with real-time camera video output on a standard video monitor. Observed differences would identify possible system degradations, such as changes in camera positioning, image tube target deterioration, poor focus, and dynamic range losses. These interval tests should be documented in a performance specification, and the resulting test data should be documented on data sheets and saved for reference.

An even simpler way to judge monitor picture quality periodically is to take a photograph of the normal camera scene on the monitor when it is first installed. The photograph can be used to compare current picture quality.

Maintenance

A preventive maintenance procedure and schedule should be established for every installation and updated as required to ensure continuous trouble-free operation of the television system. The following guidelines are presented to aid in establishing an effective maintenance program.

Software Operational Tests

To ensure acceptance and continuing quality performance of the assessment system, it is necessary to perform periodic functional evaluations to assess performance deviation, as indicated in the paragraph on performance specifications. This practice will establish dynamic overall component compatibility, ensure continued quality performance by identifying potential component deficiencies, and expedite isolation and subsequent repair or replacement of components contributing to degradation.

Preventive Maintenance

To maintain the quality of performance required of the video system, components most subject to electrical and mechanical degradation must be periodically serviced or replaced. The nature and degree of preventive maintenance required will depend on individual unit design, system complexity versus desired level of performance, environmental and weather conditions, and the maintenance program versus the availability of required test facilities. The preventive maintenance procedures also should incorporate the manufacturer's recommended maintenance practices. The manufacturer should be consulted for specific recommendations for maintenance and spare parts for complex items such as cameras and lenses.

Corrective Maintenance

Corrective maintenance responsibilities and procedures should be established prior to system installation to ensure adequate parts inventory and appropriate manufacturer's literature and documents to support the maintenance concept. There are two basic maintenance concepts: Develop an in-house capability, or establish a maintenance contract with a local repair and calibration center or equipment manufacturer. Developing an in-house capability requires a considerable investment for test equipment, parts inventory, and manpower. Therefore, this concept might best be reserved for large television systems or for sites with critical security systems requiring an absolute minimum downtime. Choosing a maintenance contract might require a smaller investment, but downtime is typically increased. This could increase security guard time to provide the assessment capability, and it could increase the required number of operational spare equipment.

Each maintenance concept requires a different level of personnel. To isolate equipment failures to the component level, both concepts will require personnel familiar with basic video theory, components, and test equipment. Even when maintenance is contracted, an in-house person might be required to isolate the failed item and replace it with a spare unit. The failure should be documented to establish the failure rate or failure pattern for future system evaluation. The failed unit is then returned to the manufacturer or contractor for repair.

The in-house maintenance person must be highly trained to perform relatively complex repair and alignment of individual components. A theoretical understanding and working knowledge of television would be an asset.

Chapter 25

Application Guidelines

The intent of this summary is to present a list of basic guidelines to assist in the selection, design, installation, and operation of exterior lighting and television systems for surveillance and intrusion detection applications. It concludes with a checklist for evaluating television assessment and surveillance systems.

EXTERIOR LIGHTING

1. Luminaires must be positioned and directed so that they will not create glare problems for the guards or television cameras performing their security function or for the population outside the protected site.
2. Lighting should be considered for its deterrent effect on some intruders.
3. Incandescent lamps are instant-on but are economically inefficient to operate because of their power consumption.
4. Incandescent lamps have good spectral match to support both human and television camera surveillance and alarm assessment.
5. Lighting uniformity should be on an average ratio of 3 to 1, not to exceed 6 to 1 in the area being viewed by the television camera.
6. Emergency generators must be considered for those times when primary power is not available.
7. Directing light toward the building or area requiring illumination improves off-site guard patrolling effectiveness.
8. Ground level lighting for building illumination improves the guard's ability to detect intruders approaching the building.
9. Direct lighting toward the perimeter when guards patrol inside the site.
10. Direct perimeter lights so that there is little or no backlighting that could cause glare or illuminate the patrolling guard.
11. Light for fixed alarm assessment guards or television cameras should be located above the guard or camera or far enough away to prevent glare interference.

12. High-masted luminaires are very effective in area lighting because they produce such uniform illumination.
13. Security guards or television cameras should be located close to high-value assets because target size is very important in visual assessment tasks.
14. The clear zone around the protected site should be at least 30 feet wide to encourage the intruder to keep moving and improve the observer's chance of detecting him.
15. A highly reflective background enhances camera faceplate illumination and intruder detection.
16. Lighting uniformity is best achieved with equal intensity lights equally spaced around the perimeter.
17. There are three major lamp categories for exterior applications:
    a. Incandescent lamps have good color reduction for both human and television camera viewing tasks. A security application advantage is that they illuminate instantly, but they are expensive to operate.
    b. Fluorescent lamps have good color rendition for visual surveillance, and they are much less expensive to operate than incandescent lamps. Special temperature compensation is preferred for outside applications.
    c. High-intensity discharge lamps produce light by direct interaction of an arc with a gas. The color spectrum varies for the different types of HID lamps. Mercury vapor lamps produce a blue-gray light. Metal halide lamps produce a white and more intense light; they have excellent color rendition and should be used where color identification is important. These lamps are more efficient than mercury lamps but their longevity is lower than other HID lamps. High-pressure sodium vapor lamps produce a warm golden white color. The color spectrum is well matched to television cameras, using silicon diode array tubes. Low-pressure sodium vapor lamps produce a warm golden white color. This color spectrum also is well matched to television cameras using silicon diode array tubes. Low-pressure sodium vapor lamps are very efficient to operate, but they are monochromatic and should never be used where color information is needed.
18. There are four basic types of lighting units that should be considered for exterior lighting systems:
    a. Floodlights direct light in one basic direction and are used to illuminate small and irregular-shaped areas and when the light must be confined to specific areas.
    b. Streetlights or roadway luminaires are located above the area requiring illumination and are directed downward to project a rather uniform pattern. Several different roadway luminaire types are available. They produce different shaped beam patterns to accommodate different lighting requirements.

    c. Fresnel lens luminaires direct light outward in a 180-degree horizontal and 15- to 30-degree vertical pattern.

    d. Searchlights are narrow beam lights usually used in security applications to illuminate areas of interest.

19. Light loss factors such as burnout, reflector surface depreciation, and dust must be considered when designing a lighting system.

20. A maintenance plan is necessary to keep the lighting system output near its initial level.

21. Both intensity and contrast can be enhanced for both visual and television surveillance and assessment by reducing vegetation and applying a light-colored artificial ground cover such as crushed stone in the clear area.

22. High illumination levels can quickly reveal high-security sites, especially from the air.

23. Retroreflector arrays can be used to help patrolling security guards or television cameras see in poorly illuminated areas.

CLOSED CIRCUIT TELEVISION

1. Cameras using a vidicon tube with an antimony trisulfide target surface are usually used in well-illuminated areas, but they are susceptible to tube damage if exposed to bright lights.

2. Cameras using a silicon diode tube are more sensitive to low light levels, immune to damage from bright lights, and recommended for outdoor fixed and surveillance applications.

3. Low light level silicon intensifier target (SIT) and very low light level intensified silicon intensifier target (ISIT) cameras are used for special applications in which illumination enhancement is impractical or undesirable.

4. Solid-state cameras are small, rugged, and very applicable in covert surveillance situations.

5. Color cameras are available for a wide variety of uses, but their effectiveness in alarm assessment and surveillance applications has not been adequately evaluated.

6. The camera lens focuses light from the viewed scene onto the camera image tube. Lenses range from telephoto to wide angle.

    a. Telephoto lenses have a long focal length and, consequently, a narrow field of view for a fixed distance.

    b. Wide-angle lenses have a short focal length and a closer and wider field of view.

7. Lenses should be determined based on camera placement, distance to the scene of interest, and size of the target to be viewed.

8. Standard 25mm, 50mm, or 75mm lenses are popular for outside applications.

9. Camera image tubes are available in ⅔-inch and 1-inch formats. One-inch tubes are recommended because of their increased coverage.

10. Zoom lenses can be varied from wide angle to telephoto while the viewed image remains in focus for surveillance applications.

11. The most popular transmission cable for security applications is 75 ohm coaxial cable.

12. Coaxial cable must be terminated in its characteristic impedance to eliminate reflections and to optimize the quality of the received video signal at the monitor.

13. Cables for exterior applications should be suitable for direct burial or continuous exposure to weather. Armor-shielded cable should be used in burial applications where rodents are a problem.

14. Care must be exercised when installing coaxial cable to avoid kinks or sharp bends, which can cause degradation in the video signal.

15. An equalizer restores the video output signals so that the amplitude versus frequency relationship is the same as the camera's output signal.

16. Hum clampers can remove 60 Hz signals on the coaxial cable's outer conductor.

17. Balanced 124 ohm transmission cable should be used for long cable runs in extreme electromagnetic environments.

18. Radio-frequency transmission should be considered when transmitting a large number of camera scenes over a great distance.

19. Optical transmission of video signals should be considered for applications where it is difficult to run coaxial cable over distances less than ½ mile.

20. Future optics transmission systems provide low-loss, high-resolution transmission of video signals over significantly longer distances than coaxial cable.

21. Video switchers are used to switch video scenes from multiple cameras to one of a combination of displays.

22. A pan/tilt pedestal is a remotely controlled camera-mounting platform.

23. Camera enclosures are available to provide camera mounting and positioning for applications under most interior or exterior environmental and climatic conditions.

24. Television monitors display the scene being viewed by the camera. The monitor's tube size should be commensurate with the number of cameras being deployed and the visual assessment test of the operator.

25. Video recording systems provide permanent records of video information.

26. A time/date and source generator should be considered to assist the monitoring operator in real time and for permanent video recording.

27. Video motion detectors can detect changes in a camera scene. These devices are recommended for indoor applications, where the weather and the environment will not affect their performance.

28. Current surge protection is recommended for all outdoor cameras, especially at sites where lightning or another large source of electromagnetic interference is a potential problem.

29. Continuous monitoring of several monitors or even one monitor by an operator in an attempt to detect intrusions, especially exterior perimeter intrusions, is not recommended.

30. A dedicated monitor for each camera is recommended for installations with sixteen or fewer cameras.

31. Contingency plans should be prepared for those times when above normal false alarms will reduce the effectiveness of the television system and when the system is malfunctioning.

32. This is a controversial issue, but I recommend that television monitors be left on to monitor exterior alarm assessment cameras.

33. Straight fence lines are vital for optimum fence line camera coverage.

34. The minimum double fence separation for optimum sensor performance and camera coverage is 30 feet.

35. Obstacles should not obscure the camera's field of view.

36. Perimeter lighting can be sensor activated to turn on lights covering the sensor zone in alarm to accommodate television assessment, but leaving the lights on continuously also has advantages.

37. Emergency generators should be considered to support both lighting and television.

38. Articulated cameras are normally used for surveillance applications, while fixed cameras are used for alarm assessment.

39. Perimeter assessment cameras must be strategically positioned and directed, with adequate overlap and offset to accommodate their cone-shaped field of view.

40. General-purpose barbed tape or concertina wire should not be installed on top of fences where television cameras are used to assess fence-mounted sensors.

41. Either additional cameras or on-location security guards should be considered for those sensor zones covered by east and west looking cameras that will be blinded by a rising or setting sun.

42. Cameras must never be pointed toward bright lights.

43. Articulated cameras are normally used for surveillance applications, but they can be used for alarm assessment if there is about 330 feet of clear zone between the camera and perimeter sensor zones.

44. Cameras are normally mounted between 15 and 20 feet above the ground.

45. A camera's mounting mast or structure must be rigid to prevent excessive camera motion in the wind.

46. Maintenance accessibility must be considered when selecting or designing a camera mast.

47. In alarm assessment, critical areas that require immediate assessment

should have an interrupt capability to call up the camera covering the sensor zone in alarm.

48. Either additional patrolling guards or video recording should be considered for those times when the sensors are experiencing a high false alarm rate.

49. Camera resolution must be commensurate with the application, whether the camera is used for detection, recognition, or identification.

50. Five monitor scan lines of information are normally adequate for recognition with adequate lighting.

51. Lens focal length is the most important factor in proper lens selection because it determines the relative magnification of the objects in the field of view and defines the angular field of view for any object distance.

52. Camera enclosures should be considered in areas that experience weather extremes such as high or low temperatures, blowing sand, rain, or snow.

53. Pan/tilt camera pedestals must be reviewed with respect to pan and tilt range, speed, and torque; limit switches; electrical power; and mechanical load.

54. Infrared light sources may be affixed to surveillance cameras where lighting conditions are limited.

55. Bright lights can severely damage sensitive very low light level SIT and ISIT cameras.

56. Low light level cameras supported by a properly designed lighting system are recommended over SIT and ISIT cameras for perimeter alarm assessment.

57. Silicon target and Newvicon tubes are recommended for low light level cameras used in outdoor applications.

58. Zoom lenses are normally used with surveillance cameras.

59. Fixed lenses, in particular 25mm, 50mm, and 75mm, are normally used for perimeter alarm assessment cameras.

60. Camera image tube target formats of 1 inch and ⅔ inch are available, but the 1-inch format is recommended.

61. Local camera synchronization is the easiest, least expensive, and most reliable synchronizing method, but picture rolling might occur on the monitor screen for a short time after switching.

62. Master camera synchronization possesses excellent stability and should be considered in applications where loss of vital assessment information would be detrimental to the site.

63. Video signals are usually transmitted over unbalanced 75 ohm video cable except in high-electromagnetic environments, where balanced 124 ohm cable is normally used.

64. Signal isolation and impedance matching are two of the more common applications of video transformers in television systems.

65. Microwave transmission is feasible, but it is not usually considered as an economical alternative for distances of less than 4 to 6 miles.
66. Optical transmission is limited by its cost per channel, usable range, and susceptibility to heavy fog.
67. Manual, sequential, alarm-activated remote, and computer-controlled switching are available for displaying the scenes from multiple cameras on single or multiple monitor recorders.
68. Video monitor performance is determined by resolution, bandwidth, gray scale response, and automatic frequency control.
69. Video monitor screen size is based on the console arrangement, the monitoring operator's viewing position, and the operator's visual surveillance or assessment task.
70. Video recording systems can provide historical data and nearly instantaneous record capability for multiple alarm assessment.
71. Video motion detectors monitor the video signal for changes indicating that someone is moving in the camera's field of view.
72. Video motion detectors are presently not recommended for exterior applications.
73. Performance testing should be conducted periodically on the television system to evaluate system degradation.
74. A maintenance concept, either in-house or contracted, should be established during system design to ensure minimum downtime for repair.

TELEVISION EVALUATION CHECKLIST

1. Are enough cameras being used to view the perimeter continuously and completely?
2. Assuming an intrusion detection occurs at the boundary or within a protected zone, are the cameras arranged, mounted, and focused so they can cover the appropriate sensor zone?
3. Is the CCTV system designed so that an effective assessment capability exists without resorting to pan, tilt, and zoom controls, which are normally reserved for surveillance functions?
4. Is the viewing angle between television monitors and the operator satisfactory and without glare?
5. Is picture quality satisfactory, or is it fuzzy, dull, too bright, or too dark, with horizontal lines across the screen? An iris control for the camera lens might improve the picture by automatically controlling the amount of light entering the camera.
6. Does the television picture at each monitor have satisfactory resolution? At least 500 scanning lines per frame are desirable.
7. Is artificial lighting in all parts of the protected zone sufficient to allow assessment under adverse weather conditions?

8. Are all lamps directed away from the cameras and the cameras directed away from bright sunlight?

9. In the clear zone, could changes in backdrop color be affected to improve color contrast and thus provide a better target silhouette?

10. With respect to camera locations and enclosures, how well are the cameras tamperproofed?

11. Are outdoor cameras adequately protected and equipped for the environment in which they must function?

12. Is each camera covered by at least one CCTV monitor?

13. How many cameras are connected—that is, sequenced into each television monitor? Is this number more than the operator can effectively monitor?

14. Assuming that multiple cameras are being sequenced into a television monitor, is the console operator equipped to select the desired camera manually in the event of a suspected or apparent intrusion at any point?

15. Is a videotape recorder available that can be activated and switched to any camera? A recorder can provide a valuable record of activity for later in-depth analysis.

16. Are the video transmission cables secure and placed in grounded dedicated conduits, if necessary, to avoid high electromagnetic interference?

17. Is the transmission system compatible with the cameras and monitors as far as frequency bandwidth and signal-to-noise ratio are concerned?

PART VI

Access Control

Access control systems do not detect intrusions, but they are a very important part of a total security system needed to reduce the risk to valuable assets operating or stored in an area. They are usually thought of as controlling people's access or egress from an area. But in many applications, control of the access and egress of vehicles, access of weapons and explosives, and egress of valuable property or materials such as special nuclear materials (SNM) at a nuclear plant is of prime importance.

CONTROL TECHNIQUES

The simplest way to control personnel access is to display signs such as KEEP OUT, RESTRICTED AREA, or AUTHORIZED PERSONNEL ONLY. Signs alone are usually not totally effective. More meaningful access control is accomplished by guards or automated control systems. The guards and more sophisticated systems can control not only who enters and where, but also when they can enter. Guards normally control access by comparing the photograph and personal characteristics described on an identification badge with the characteristics of the individual requesting access. Entrance is granted or denied based on the guard's visual assessment. Guards also can control when individuals enter areas if the badges are appropriately marked or color coded to identify to what area and when the individuals have access.

A guard's ability to control an entrance can be upgraded to satisfy specific needs by adding equipment to detect weapons or explosives entering a controlled area and to detect unauthorized removal of valuable property. Such equipment includes metal detectors, X-ray baggage search systems, explosives detectors, and SNM monitors. An upgraded system would be comparable to an airport access control system.

Having a guard at each entrance who monitors only personnel access can be costly, especially in low-traffic areas or even during periods of low traffic at normally busy entrance points. In these areas it might be cost-effective to have the guard monitor a video comparator system or automate the access control. This system basically contains one or more television cameras at the entrance and two television monitors or a single split screen monitor. With this system, the guard can compare the real-time image of the individual requesting access to either a stored video image or a photo identification. The operator, who can be located away from the entrance in a central monitoring station, can compare the two images and either grant or deny access. Access is usually accomplished by activating an electric strike securing the entrance door.

Automated recognition systems control access without the aid of a monitoring operator. These systems grant or deny access based on their recognition of a memorized code, a coded access card, personal characteristics of the individual requesting access, or a combination of these techniques. Memorized codes are used with cipher locks and with keyboards that usually provide the first level of access to a multiple level system. Automated systems include coded card readers and positive verification of identity. Automated recognition systems are the primary subject of this section.

As with intrusion detection sensors, there are several application factors that should be considered when selecting access control systems. The vulnerability of the system to counterfeiting is important. Precautions should be taken against more than the authorized individual entering the controlled area when the door is opened. A very important, and probably the most important, consideration is the throughput rate into the controlled area. If the number of people entering the controlled area each day is small, problems are reduced. But as the number increases, the problems of correctly identifying and granting access to each requester increases. If the entry process is too long and people are waiting to enter, they will probably be unhappy and deliberately abuse the equipment. But if the entry process is eased to allow large numbers of people to enter, then the error rate for allowing unauthorized individuals to enter might be high. Also, if the control system is too simple, an authorized individual might enter and then hand his coded card to someone outside the controlled area so he too can enter. Thus, designing an access control system that will satisfy all your security needs requires much consideration.

CONTRABAND DETECTORS

Metal detectors are used primarily to detect weapons, but they also can be used to detect other metal objects such as tools. Active and passive metal detectors are available. Passive detectors have limited detection capabilities and are unsuitable for most access control applications. They respond to changes in the ambient earth's magnetic field resulting from the presence of ferromagnetic metal objects. Unlike passive detectors, active detectors can detect all metals. They generate an electromagnetic field and detect changes resulting from introducing metallic objects into the field. Because the active detector responds to changes in its electromagnetic field, it is susceptible to changes produced by external sources such as large electrical equipment, power line transients, and even flickering fluorescent lights. Moving machinery in close proximity to the active metal detectors can generate false alarms.

Explosives detectors use trace vapor techniques to detect the presence of vapors given off by explosives in an ambient atmosphere. They are vulnerable to failure because the technical capabilities needed to detect all explosives in all quantities do not exist. There are just too many explosive compounds. Explosives detectors are considered necessary at nuclear plants, where they are useful in detecting explosives that can be used to gain access to protected or vital areas.

X-ray baggage search systems are often used to detect contraband contained in packages or luggage being transported into or out of controlled areas. An example is the baggage inspection system used at airports. These systems use pulsed X-ray techniques that produce images of the baggage contents based on the density and absorption characteristics of the articles inside. The images are produced on a fluorescent screen or stored in an image-retention device.

Chapter 26 will discuss the basic principles of operation and application of access control systems.

Chapter 26

Access Control Systems

The primary function of access control systems is to control access to and sometimes egress from critical areas. They accomplish this function by identifying and permitting only authorized individuals to enter the areas. Besides the normal access control functions, automated systems can monitor time and attendance, execution of industrial functions and guard tours, and the safety and security of personnel through points of entry and exit. But for access control systems to be totally successful, they must be sold to the employees or users and be supported by management.

Both guards and automated access control systems can perform this function. Guards can be stationed at entry points to control access directly, or they can control access indirectly by comparing those requesting access with their identification credentials, using a video comparator access control system. Guards sometimes support entry control by searching individuals requesting access and their packages and vehicles.

Two other functions usually performed by guards are providing access to visitors and emergency vehicles. Visitor control is vital because a visitor could become a threat. Each visitor's credentials should be validated to the greatest extent possible, the person whom he is visiting should be contacted to verify the visit, he should be given a visitor's badge, and, depending on the level of security control, someone should escort him to his destination in the controlled area. Handicapped individuals might need special assistance in gaining access if they cannot be accommodated by the access control system.

Fire and rescue equipment must be allowed to enter and exit a controlled area in the event of an emergency. The level of control for these events are site dependent. Administrative procedures should be established, probably requiring a guard to escort the vehicles within the controlled areas. These procedures and all other site-specific safety and security procedures should be coordinated with the local fire, police, and rescue departments.

Besides these access control functions, the guards also must respond to alarms. When there is an alarm from an automated control point, a guard must respond to the point to determine whether it is an unauthorized individual attempting to gain access or an authorized individual who has been denied access; or he might have to respond to an area where a door was left open too long.

Guards are an essential part of controlling access and should be well trained in the essential functions of access control and in the operations and vulnerabilities of access control systems and search equipment. All access control systems, and search equipment in particular, have vulnerabilities, especially if they are not properly installed or applied. In some cases this vulnerability can be minimized with proper use. Therefore, the manufacturer of each piece of equipment should provide operation and application training and identify possible vulnerabilities.

Automated access control systems can sometimes reduce the number of guards by eliminating the need for them at some entrance points. Their success depends on the system selected, however. Therefore, this chapter primarily addresses automated access control systems and the supporting search equipment. The actual type of control system chosen depends on the level of security, number of personnel requiring admittance, and their entrance and, where required, exit schedule. No single system can satisfy all these factors for all applications. A system suitable for one facility might not be suitable for another.

The designer must evaluate the access application factors and select either guards, a video comparator systems, an automated central or automated control system using positive personnel identity verification, or some combination of these. For complete access control, these systems might sometimes require search support by metal detectors, explosives detectors, X-ray baggage search units, and special nuclear material monitors. Before discussing individual access control systems, general control techniques will be discussed.

CONTROL TECHNIQUES

Automated recognition systems are the primary subject for this discussion. They control access without the aid of a monitoring operator. They grant or deny access based on their recognition of a memorized code entered at a keyboard, a coded access card, the personal characteristics of the individual requesting access, or a combination of these techniques. Automatic recognition systems include keyboard and memorized codes, encoded cards and card readers, video comparators, and positive personnel identity verification.

A number of factors should be considered when selecting an access control system. The most important is the resistance of the system to compromise or counterfeiting. The degree of resistance required is a function of the criticality of the area being controlled and the value of the assets being protected in the controlled area. Resistance to counterfeiting is a measure of the difficulty required to synthesize necessary identification characteristics to gain access. Speech, retina, and signature recognition systems are considered the most resistant to counterfeiting because of the dynamic interaction required for individual recognition. Fingerprint and hand-geometry recognition systems are considered high to medium. When used alone, access cards, video comparators, and memorized codes offer relatively low resistance to counterfeiting.

Besides counterfeiting, precautions should be taken against compromise due to the portal remaining open longer than the time required for one person to enter the controlled area. With the door open, other people can enter the area unchallenged. Some systems initiate an alarm if the door remains open longer than a predetermined time established as an adequate entry time. Another possibility for reducing this compromise is to install a turnstile gate at the entrance. Attractive, see-through turnstyles that will not detract aesthetically from normal interior entrances are available.

An additional consideration is the throughput rate. The throughput rate is the inverse of the average verification time for an individual to be granted access to a controlled area. For instance, if it requires on an average of 3 seconds for a system to verify and grant access to an individual, then the throughput rate would be one individual per 3 seconds. It would require at least 30 seconds for ten people, one minute for twenty people, etc. In this example, the 3-second access time does not include the time for the requesting individual to punch in a memorized code on a keyboard.

Throughput rate is an important consideration when large numbers of people have to be granted access or if an emergency should arise in the controlled area requiring the rapid access of a number of individuals to handle the emergency. In the case of a large population, the rate could be increased by installing dual systems, or perhaps guards could be located at the high-traffic access areas during peak traffic flow. In the case of an emergency, a guard might be able to respond to the critical area in time to control access.

Still another factor is the door lock. Electromagnetic locks are replacing electric door strikes because they are fully fail-safe. Locking and unlocking is positive and instantaneous, without residual magnetism or moving parts that might stick, jamb, or bend. Their operational reliability allows the user to leave critical exit doors locked at all times when the doors are controlled by a fail-safe fire control system that will automatically unlock the doors in the event of a fire. The locks also are easily integrated with security access control systems for door control.

The lock assembly consists of a powerful electromagnetic and a rigid armature. The electromagnetic is usually installed in a position horizontal to the top of the door frame in the inside corner, opposite the hinge side of the frame, so the door opens away from the magnet. The armature is mounted on the door directly opposite the electromagnet. When the door is closed and power is applied to the lock, the armature is attracted to the electromagnet creating the holding force. The actual holding force depends on the efficiency and size of the magnet. Available models grip with 500 to 3,000 pounds of force.

There are no moving parts with electromagnetic locks, so wear is not a problem. But like any magnetic device, misalignment between the electromagnet and armature can create a problem. For proper operation the lock must be properly aligned and the interfacing surfaces must be near parallel. A warped door or one out of alignment can cause such problems. Newer models are designed to compensate for minor misalignments between the door and its frame.

The following paragraphs describe prominent features of the various types of access control systems. These features might vary from model to model.

Keyboard and Memorized Codes

Systems using only memorized codes that must be entered in a proper sequence at a push-button keyboard provide only a relatively low level of security. Operationally, when the code is properly entered to satisfy associated logic circuits, access is granted to the controlled area by activation of the electric door strike that releases the door gate or turnstile. A vulnerability of these simple systems is that once the door is open, more than one person can enter, usually unchallenged. Some systems offer additional security by initiating an alarm if the door remains open longer than the few seconds necessary to gain access.

Depending on the application, a single memorized access code might be used by all individuals authorized to enter the controlled area, or each authorized person may be assigned his own individual code. The group code is most useful when the number in the group is small and the controls are primarily to keep out the general public. Group codes are too vulnerable for applications providing access to the most critical areas. Individual codes are often used with other types of access control systems, especially those that require and recognize personal characteristics. In these cases the code identifies the individual requesting access so that the characteristics necessary for comparison can be retrieved from the reference data base.

Encoded Cards and Card Readers

Most access control systems use encoded cards and card readers, which identify the cardholder by means of the card being inserted into or presented to the reader. The encoded cards, the "keys" of the access control system, generally resemble a credit card in size, thickness, and appearance. Although the card memory technique varies depending on the manufacturer, they all have the capability of storing millions of scrambled cryptically encoded combinations. The card memory is encoded either magnetically or electronically with the data necessary to admit the cardholder. Often the cards carry a photograph and personal characteristics of the holder for supplementary badge-type identification.

Card readers are used to open both mechanical door locks and electro-mechanical locking mechanisms. Mechanical door releases are used in many systems where stand-alone or off-line card reading terminals operate doors, gates, or turnstiles. Card readers also are finding widespread application in on-line systems where centralized data processors are linked with remote card readers. A typical on-line card reading system consists of multiple card readers, a processor with data storage, an access controller, and a system logger. The controller, containing a microcomputer with memory for data storage, can control the access and egress of thousands of employees using card readers at many scattered locations. When a card is presented to a reader, the reader electronically senses the information on the encoded card and transmits it to the controller. The controller receives the information and compares it with the stored data, and in a few milliseconds it decides whether to grant access. When access is granted, the controller commands the reader to release the door lock, thereby allowing access through the controlled portal.

A computer-controlled access system can accommodate a wide range of software design goals. For example, a week can be divided into an arbitrary set of time intervals to control the "when" of access at all reader terminals within the system. Each weekly cycle can be divided into as many as 125 such time zones. In addition to such time constraints, individual employees or groups of employees can be assigned status levels designating accessibility to restricted areas based on their security clearances, work assignments, etc. With these computer-controlled capabilities, the system can control who enters where, and when they enter. It also can be programmed to accommodate a two-person control procedure required at some vital facilities, such as nuclear plants.

Activity loggers or printers provide a hard-copy record of all activity, with date, time, and location. Unsuccessful access attempts are printed in red, and entries are printed in black. Reasons for denial of access also are recorded.

The controller console enables the operator to perform many functions, one of which is to cancel lost or stolen cards. From a security standpoint, it is important that cancellation of cards be done easily, as with simple push-button controls. There should be minimal delay in ridding the system of lost cards. For operational expediency, some models offer features that will simultaneously void batches of one hundred or more cards.

An additional feature, sometimes referred to as *antipassback*, will not allow a card to be used to gain access until it has been used to exit the controlled area. With this feature, the card cannot be passed from an employee inside a protected area to a person on the outside for him to gain access.

Good security dictates that each reader continually report its status to the controller. Thus, if a door remains open too long, if the communication link between a reader and the controller is broken, or if a reader is tampered with, the condition is annunciated for the monitoring operator.

Card readers identify the card, not the authorized cardholder. The most common vulnerability of the encoded card access system is the lost card and the possibility that the owner might not realize he lost it. The combination system that requires the encoded card as well as a memorized code is a more effective means of reducing this vulnerability. But it is still possible to defeat the system by collusion. Even this vulnerability is reduced by the use of the system logger, which provides a permanent record of identification numbers correlated with all entries and exists.

Cards can be coded to provide information about the individual's identity, job function, and where and when he is permitted acces. The most popular access cards are discussed below.

Photo Identification Card

The most common credential is a color-coded or symbol-coded card with a photograph of the cardholder that can be visually inspected by a guard. It is difficult to quantify the effectiveness of such a card because it depends on the diligence of the guard when he examines it. A guard's diligence usually varies depending on his alertness and the number of personnel wishing to gain access at the same time.

A disadvantage of photo ID cards is that they are rather easy to counterfeit. For this reason, it might be beneficial to use a badge exchange system, which not only minimizes the possibility of the card being counterfeited, but also minimizes the possibility of the card being lost or stolen. With this system, duplicate cards are held at each access location. When an employee requests access, the guard matches the individual to the photo on the exchange card held at the access control point. If the cards match, the guard exchanges badges and grants access. The employee's badge is held at the access control point until he leaves the area. Then the badges are exchanged again. With this procedure the exchange badge worn within the controlled area never leaves the area. But if a badge is stolen, this exchange system does not preclude someone with similar characteristics from altering his or her facial features to match the image on the stolen badge to gain unauthorized access.

Magnetic Coded Cards

These cards contain a sheet of flexible magnetic material sandwiched between plastic sheets on which an array of spots has been permanently magnetized. The card code is determined by the polarity of the magnetized spots. When the card is inserted into a reader, it is read by either magnetic sensors, which are interrogated electronically, or magnetic reed switches, which are mechanically read when the magnetized spots on a property coded card are located adjacent to the read. The magnetic spots can be accidentally erased if the card is exposed to a strong magnetic field. Experience has shown that this is not a significant problem in normal applications, but it is possible to duplicate the code pattern of magnetic spots and fabricate a false badge.

Magnetic Strip Cards

Systems using magnetic strip cards similar to bank credit cards are in wide use. The cards have a strip of magnetic material along one edge that is encoded with the badgeholder's data. Some systems use alphanumeric coding, allowing the holder's name to be included in the card data along with the badge member. The card is read into a tape recorder–like head reader as the magnetic strip moves past the read head. A vulnerability of this type of card is that the magnetic data can be decoded and duplicated rather easily. The magnetic strip also is sensitive to accidental erasure.

Wiegan Effect Cards

These cards use a coded pattern of short-length magnetic wires embedded in the card to generate the code. Each wire, which contains a bit of data, is twisted under tension and heat tempered and has a magnetic snap action. The cards are difficult to duplicate and are immune to magnetic fields. When the card is passed through the reader head, the sensing device reads the magnetic code and sends the data to the reader for decoding. The card contains 26 bits, which makes millions of code combinations possible.

Optical Coded Cards

These cards are coded by a geometric array of printed stripes that are spaced to represent coded data. This type of code is now found on most grocery items, which are automatically read by an optical reader at the supermarket. The advantage of optical bar codes is that they do not require a sophisticated optical character reader, but they can be read by passing a hand-held photodetector over the code.

A disadvantage of early bar code cards was that the code was visible to any observer and consequently easy to duplicate. Recent versions have been introduced for security applications that encode the card so that they are readable only by ultraviolet or infrared light patterns of frequencies produced by the resonant circuit. The card code is then relayed to the remote card reader, which translates the pattern into the access information.

Proximity Cards

Proximity systems use coded cards that do not have to be inserted into a reader to gain access. These systems relay access codes through electromagnetic, optical, or ultrasonic transmission. Electromagnetic transmission is probably the most popular proximity system. It uses electrically coded cards and a stationary interrogation unit, which generates a weak electromagnetic field. When the card is placed near the interrogation unit, this field activates the passive electric circuit embedded in the card. The interrogator unit senses the code and sends it to the control unit. If the code is valid, the unit grants access to the cardholder.

A distinct advantage of proximity systems is that the card does not have to be inserted into a slot to be read. It only has to be held in close proximity (2 to 4 inches) to the interrogation unit. Because the interrogation unit does not have exposed openings, it is less vulnerable to tampering and physical abuse. It can be mounted behind shock-resistant plastic sheets or even concealed within a wall, which improves security and architectural flexibility. The principal disadvantage of this type of system is that the cards can be decoded and counterfeited, and they are more expensive than magnetic-type cards.

Video Comparator

One of the four common types of access control systems uses CCTV in combination with personnel identification badges. These systems provide manned rather than automated access control at multiple entrances that can be remotely located. In operation, no one can gain access to a controlled area without a positive decision from the operator on an individual basis. The monitoring station operator is equipped with one or more television monitors. Each monitor is dedicated to an entrance that is under access control. Labor costs are reduced because one guard or operator is able to monitor several access terminals. The time required to monitor and manually respond to several discrete television monitors and associated door controls is an operational limitation.

The time to process each person requiring access is a disadvantage of manual positive access controls. They require more access time than control systems using encoded cards and readers. According to one manufacturer, experienced operators can handle up to 150 personnel in 15 minutes, equivalent to an average of 6 seconds per person. It is recommended that control terminals be manned during peak traffic periods, however, such as intervals when there is a substantial change in the work force.

From an operational standpoint, a working system usually uses three cameras installed at the entrance booth. One camera is mounted overhead in the ceiling, and two cameras are located behind a glass mirror, one for a face view and the second to view the ID card. For each entrance booth, the monitoring operator is equipped with a television monitor and, for identification purposes, is provided a split-screen simultaneous view of the identification badge and the subject's face. The overhead camera monitors the number of people in the enclosure and also exposes to view the articles they might be carrying. Since three cameras are dedicated to each monitor, the operator must select his television picture with a push-button control. He must choose between the split-screen view using two cameras or the view from the single overhead camera.

The sequence for gaining access via the TV system is straightforward:

1. The person desiring entrance at the booth pushes the entry request button, which alerts the guard via a signal light and audible tone.
2. The guard pushes the entry door unlock button and, using the overhead camera, watches the person enter the booth.
3. After entering the booth, the person looks into the mirror and places the ID card on the badge viewer.
4. The guard switches to split-screen television and, after identifying the person, pushes the exit door unlock button.
5. The person hears a tone and leaves the booth. The door automatically closes and locks as the guard, using the overhead camera, watches the exit and makes sure the booth is clear and closed.

Only one door at a time can be unlocked and opened, making it almost impossible to bypass the system. Additional security is provided by visual and audible alarms that inform the guard of the system status, such as doors being open or closed and locked with the bolt in place.

The functional reliability and vulnerability of the overall CCTV system depends on the dedication, concentration, and overall proficiency of the monitoring operator. It is the operator's responsibility to study and compare the separate televised pictures of the subject's face and ID card and to judge the authenticity of the matchup. The security risk is greatest when personnel traffic is heavy. Familiarity with the faces in the daily flow of traffic is a valuable asset. Some vulnerability exists in the prospect of a stolen or forged badge on which the imposter's photograph is superimposed.

Positive Personnel Identity Verification

Automated access control systems that rely on intrinsic personal characteristics are regarded as the ultimate control for high-security locations where relatively few people require access. Systems of this type are identity verification systems, which use various unique personal characteristics such as fingerprints, hand geometry, voice pattern, or signature dynamics to verify identity. Manufacturers of these systems stress that high security ideally demands verification of the *person*, not a card or a code. With controls of this type, identity is not based on badges, codes, or cards, which can become available to unauthorized individuals by theft or other means.

All control methods of this type require storage of numerous digitized data related to certain unique characteristics of each identified user. In practice, the user desiring entrance at the access terminal signals the computer with a card or code claiming his identity. He is then tested or measured for conformance with the stored data. The input information is digitized and processed at high speeds for comparison with the reference data. Based on this comparison, within a few seconds the access control system makes a decision as to whether the person desiring entrance is the individual with the alleged identity. If identity is verified, the door, gate, or turnstile is released for access.

Unfortunately, operating statistics show that short-term variations in the physical characteristics of people occur. For example, fingerprints might be affected by injuries, weather extremes, and surface abrasions attributable to the person's occupation and other activities. Voice and signature patterns are affected by stress and fatigue. As a result, the user must tolerate errors in system performance. It is customary to refer to functional errors as being either Type I or Type II. Type I errors keep out the authorized individual, while Type II errors allow the imposter to gain access. In general, verification systems that operate on unique personal characteristics have error rates ranging from 1 to 5 percent, including errors of both types.

Although a 1 or even 2 percent false acceptance rate with a Type II error might appear low, the possible consequences of admitting even one unauthorized person should be carefully considered. For instance, if a system is controlling access to a sensitive area, the entry of one unauthorized person might put him or her in proximity to the sensitive items or materials with the potential for loss of life, assets, and public confidence.

A Type I error might occur due to correlation statistics that are marginal and outside the tolerance limits due to a slight mismatch in fingerprints, signatures, or other personal characteristics on which verification is based. To cope with this, systems usually have an adjustment to control the limits of correlation required to verify identity. As correlation requirements are relaxed with this control, the incidence of Type II errors increases. Therefore, in practice, there ordinarily is a trade-off of Type I error for Type II error, or vice versa, and the owner settles for what he considers an acceptable compromise.

Type I errors might occur in voice and signature verification systems as a result of requester stress and fatigue. They also can occur with fingerprint recognition systems if its requester injures his finger or as a result of weather extremes.

A brief discussion of fingerprint, signature, hand geometry, voice pattern, and eye retina recognition systems follows.

Fingerprint Recognition Systems

These systems take fingerprints in an inkless manner by optically scanning an area of a fingerprint, digitizing it, and then transmitting this information to a central controller. Automatic identification for access control is based on computer analysis and comparison of fingerprint minutiae. Minutiae are the tiny interruptions, ridge endings, and branches, which number approximately one hundred, on the print of a typical finger. After a matching decision is made, the central control transmits an acknowledge signal to the terminal.

Before a system of this type can be useful, one or more fingerprints of each individual must be enrolled in the computer memory as reference standards for comparison purposes. Enrollment usually requires prints of a minimum of two separate fingers if a high level of security is an objective. The enrollment procedure is accomplished by compilation of the finger minutiae and computer analysis after the selected fingers are scanned several times at the access terminals and the images are transmitted to the central controller. The enrollment procedure also involves assignment of identification numbers, authorization levels, and possible time constraints, which restrict entry to selected hours. All such information and the standard minutiae are entered and on file at the central controller. The storage capacity of coded data often exceeds that required for one thousand people and is generally expandable.

For a typical system the access terminal contains a lighted display panel, a keyboard or card reading mechanism, a palm and finger positioning plate, and an electro-optical scanner for obtaining a definitive well-informed image of the fingerprint. By using the keyboard or card reader, the individual desiring entrance will initially announce his alleged identity with the preassigned identification number. The display panel then provides sequential instructions and also informs the individual of the status of the request to enter. The designated primary finger is always used for admittance unless delay develops and use of an alternate finger is requested at the access display panel.

The central controller requires considerable electronic equipment, including a preprocessor and control processor for control of the remote terminals, for processing fingerprint data, and for data storage. When an individual seeks entrance at one of the access terminals, the preprocessor at the central controller is used to detect minutiae in the scanned fingerprint. A matching algorithm in a small computer than correlates the minutiae with the reference minutiae. If the matching score is high enough to satisfy tolerance limits built into the system—that is, if the fingers match—identity is verified. Then, assuming that the user is seeking entrance at an authorized time and meets other authorization requirements, the control processor signals the appropriate terminal, and the electric door strike or other locking mechanism is released for admittance.

Various controls at the central station are used to delete user data, enter new data, and activate or disable access terminals. A terminal controller polls the access terminals to determine which are active and to detect tampering or malfunction. Also, the various alarm messages are displayed at the control panel.

With the aid of the computer, the response time of a typical fingerprint verification system is fast. Identity is verified or denied in a few seconds after the ID number is entered and the user's finger is in place.

Signature Recognition Systems

Systems of this type measure, with respect to time, the pressure and speed of the person signing his or her name. Two techniques are used to identify signatures. One uses a special pressure-sensitive writing table that senses the forces aplied to the table during signing. No special pen is required with this system. The second technique uses a special pen that senses the pen tip motion as well as the pressure applied by the signer. The pressure pattern and pen motion are sufficiently individualized and repeatable to ensure with a high degree of certainty that a signature is authentic. Forgery of a genuine signature is difficult because writing speed and pressure are not directly related to the appearance of an individual's signature.

Personnel designated for access are initially enrolled by having each person execute several signatures to develop the enrollment data base. Often a person's signature will vary with time on a long-term basis. For this reason, the system has provisions for automatic and continual updating of the reference standard to adjust for this change. The updating occurs in the normal daily or weekly usage of the system without causing inconvenience to the user. Besides the signature enrollment, an identifying code and selected authorization levels also can be assigned to each individual.

Operationally, the individual desiring access initially enters his identifying code at the terminal via a keyboard, or possibly enters an access card. When directed by a signal from the controller, the individual signs his name. The data are digitized and transmitted to the computer, where they are processed in accordance with one or more specifically designed computer algorithms. Following numerous computer calculations, signature data are compared with those of the enrollment data base, and if the correlation statistics are found to be within predetermined limits, and if other authorization requirements are satisfied, the door or gate is released for access.

Hand-Geometry Recognition Systems

This system uses hand geometry as a means of recognizing those individuals authorized access to the controlled area. The system can be programmed to operate in a number of configurations, but basically it measures the finger lengths on either hand for recognition. The finger measurements are made photoelectrically when the hand is properly positioned and the fingers aligned with the four slots in a top-lighted panel. Light, illuminating the photodetector device located beneath the top-lighted panel, is partially obscured by the fingers. Before the measurement is made, a capacitive switch located on the top-lighted panel in the palm area must sense the presence of the hand. When the switch is activated, the photodetector device scans the slots to detect the presence of light. This location is then compared with the reference data collected during enrollment.

In operation, when an individual wishes to gain access to the controlled area, the individual enters his identification through either a card reader or keyboard. The central controller then requires the addressee to place either the right or left hand on the top-lighted panel. The processor indicates which hand by illuminating the appropriate indicator light on the lighted panel. The addressee places the appropriate hand on the panel and aligns his fingers in the slots. After the capacitive switch is closed, the finger measurements are made. These measurements are compared to the reference file data and, if the actual measurements and the reference measurements match within a predetermined tolerance, access is granted.

Speaker Verification Systems

This is a stand-alone system that consists of a terminal and a minicomputer. The terminal consists of a keyboard microphone, speaker, and voice-signal preprocessor. Operationally, when an individual wishes to gain access to the controlled area, he enters a soundproof booth and enters his identification through the keyboard. A prerecorded voice message requests the individual to repeat a four-word phrase selected at random from a file of thirty-two phrases constructed from sixteen monosyllabic words. Each phrase is approximately 2 seconds in duration. The individual then repeats the phrase into the microphone. It is processed and compared with the stored enrollment data. The system compares the amplitude of the speech waveform as a function of frequency and time. If the input phrase is verified, the individual is permitted access, and the individual's enrolled data base is updated to reflect minor changes in his voice. If the individual is rejected on the first phrase, he is prompted with another phrase. The number of attempts to repeat the phrase before access is denied and an alarm is sounded is programmable.

Eye Retina Recognition System

This system analyzes the blood vessel pattern in the retina of the eye of the individual requesting access to the controlled area. The manufacturer of this system states that each individual, even an identical twin, has a widely divergent, unalterable retinal eye pattern. Because of this unique characteristic, the chance of false acceptance in the verification mode (a Type II error) is as low as 0.0001 percent, or one in a million, and the chance of false rejection of an authorized person (a Type I error) is as low as 0.1 percent, depending on system threshold settings and proper use.

The system offers three operational modes: enrollment, personal identification, and recognition. During initial enrollment, the person being authorized access simply looks into an eye camera, focuses on an alignment point, and presses a button that initiates the retinal scan. The camera scans a circular area of the retina with a beam of ultralow-intensity infrared light. Light reflected back from the eye is focused on a photosensor, which measures the magnitude of the light at 320 distinct points along a 450-degree scan. The resulting waveform described by these 320 data points is analyzed by a microprocessor and stored for future verification.

According to the manufacturer, there is no health problem associated with either the enrollment or identification process. Each procedure typically requires only a few seconds while the system electronically records the retinal and choroidal vasculature at the back of the eye. The scan emits no laser light or potentially harmful rays. In fact, it emits only about as much light to the eye as one would receive when opening a refrigerator door.

The system is equipped with a twelve-digit keypad to permit optional entry of personal identification numbers. An eight-character display indicates acceptance or nonacceptance.

During personal identification, the individual requesting access enters his personal identification code using the twelve-digit keypad. Then he looks into the eye camera and focuses on the alignment point, as is done when enrolling in the system. Once aligned, he presses the scan button. The waveform representing the live eye signature is then matched with the stored eye signature of the individual requesting access. If a match is made, the system activates release of the security mechanism involved.

During recognition, the waveform representing the live eye signature is compared with all the stored eye signatures, and the person is recognized or rejected depending on whether or not a match exists. Upon signature recognition, the system automatically allows access.

The time required for individual processing in the recognition mode varies, depending on the number of individuals on file. With fifty individuals, identification would typically take less than 2 seconds. The personal identification mode is faster because just the verification of the individual's identification code and eye waveform is involved. In this mode, with twelve hundred signatures on file, verification would take about 1½ seconds. These times do not include the time for each individual to position himself at the unit, enter his identification code, if applicable, and look into the eyepiece and focus on the alignment point.

The eye retina recognition system is designed to operate as a stand-alone unit or in conjunction with existing card access systems. The system is not designed to provide access to low-security areas but to control access to critical security areas.

Automated Access Control Portal Systems

These systems handle routine personnel processing automatically and require security force action only to assess alarms and provide user aid. Portal systems can be configured using remotely controlled access and

CCTV for identity verification. In operation, the requester enters the portal, places his badge against a viewing window, and positions himself so that he is properly aligned with a split-image camera, which projects his image and badge onto a screen for comparison. Once these are verified, the viewing guard grants him access. This is not, however, an automated system. An automated system usually consists of a central control, a video and audio communication network, a portal system, and a bypass system. The actual level of security provided depends primarily on the sophistication of the portal verification system and somewhat on the video and audio communication network and central control.

Central control is normally located inside the protected area at the security control center. This is where the portal control that manages personnel access is located and where the portal alarm status and video and audio information is annunciated and displayed for the security control operator. Central control is capable of monitoring the status of a number of portal systems. The exact number depends on how much personnel verification information is processed at the portal control versus the portal verification reader. At one extreme, minimal information capability exists at the portal. For this case, data are transmitted from the portal to the portal control, where all verification and command decisions are made. At the other extreme, significant verification capability is designed into the portal system, and command decisions are made totally at the portal. In all cases, portal system status and alarm signals should be sent to the portal control for processing and displaying. Portal control also should perform functional tests of the portal systems to verify that each is functioning properly.

In the course of normal personnel processing at the portal, situations that require guard assistance arise. For this reason CCTV cameras are installed at some portals to provide visual coverage of the portal interior for the central control operator's assessment. An audio communication network is usually installed in all portal systems to allow communication between the person in the portal and the central monitoring area guard. Both the television and audio link are recommended to enable the guard to assess the portal and to assist personnel having difficulty getting through the system.

Portal systems in general consist of a number of entry control portals and a bypass portal. A portal is an enclosure area that contains verification readers, television assessment cameras, and an audio communications network. The interior of the portal is isolated by two interlocking doors. One door functions as a barrier between the portal interior and the controlled area, and the other door serves as a barrier between the entrance area and portal interior. These doors are secured by electric strikes controlled by the personnel verification system, with overriding control at the central monitoring area. Some special purpose portals are equipped with contraband detectors. For instance, portals at nuclear facilities might be equipped with metal detectors, explosives detectors, and SNM monitors to reduce the risk of such materials entering the facility.

Automated portal systems need status assessment equipment to control normal portal traffic and to detect attempted entry by deceit. This equipment includes weight scales, presence detectors, tamper alarms, door position indicators, and occupancy timing systems. The primary purpose of the weight scale is to guard against multiple portal occupancy. This system requires that the weight of authorized individuals be stored as part of their personal characteristics file. This way the portal's weight scale reading can be compared with the individual's weight information to determine the occupancy number. The information also can be used as a crude form of additional personnel identity verification. The weight scale should not be the only means of determining portal occupancy. Door position sensors and a door locking mechanism, along with the weight scales, should be adequate to control personnel processing. Tamper alarms are intended to detect attempts to defeat the portal system, but some defeat possibilities might go undetected. For this reason, door position sensors should be used to provide additional evidence of tampering or unauthorized entry. Timing systems limit the amount of time an individual can remain in the portal before an alarm is sounded at the central monitoring area.

Portal identity verification is probably the most important function of the portal system. The verification system usually consists of a magnetic strip badge and a memorized four- or five-digit code to identify the person requesting access at the portal. The badge is encoded with the badgeholder's name, badge number, and any other information desired by security or management, such as a photograph of the holder. The memorized code and badgeholder's access authority should not be encoded on the badge.

On entry into the portal, the requester presents his access card to the reader and enters his memorized code at the keyboard. This information initiates access to the individual's personal characteristics stored at the portal control. These data can then be compared with the corresponding data from the portal's personnel identity verification system. If the requester's access card and memorized code information match the personal characteristics of the person requesting access, the portal exit door is released. Automated systems use any of the eye retina, fingerprint, voiceprint, hand-geometry, or signature verification systems described earlier in this chapter.

Automated access control systems normally grant access with few problems unless the portal is equipped with contraband detectors. In this case access occasionally will be denied because a contraband detector alarms or identity is not verified. The most probable cause of rejection is a false alarm. False rejection rates for personnel identifiers vary from 1 to 5 percent, depending on the verification reader. As a result, one to five authorized individuals out of one-hundred processed will be denied access. The rejection might not be totally random because some individuals have more trouble adapting to the identity verification system than others. A need therefore exists for a means of processing rejected personnel. Also, handicapped personnel who cannot use the portal system must be processed. A manual bypass or portal bypass system is required to accommodate these persons.

The location of a portal bypass depends primarily on the number of employees requiring access and the number of different entry points and their location around the facility. If all employees enter at the same entry area, then the bypass should be located there. But if there are several entry locations around the facility, depending on the number of employees using each entry, a bypass portal at each location is probably not justified. In this case a centrally located portal bypass is probably more cost-effective.

The portal bypass can constitute the weak link in an access control system if it is not designed correctly. Care must be taken to ensure that the portal bypass security is as good as or better than the portals it bypasses. Access through the bypass should be discouraged, and consequently it should be more difficult and time-consuming. Otherwise, everyone will by using the bypass instead of the portals to gain access to the facility.

The equipment associated with the portal bypass should include an alternate identity verification system and appropriate contraband search equipment where required. Additional procedures should be implemented at a bypass portal where personal characteristic verification systems are not used. One procedure would be to call the requester's supervisor for verification of identity and perhaps have the supervisor come to the portal to admit the individual. Personnel requesting access through the bypass portal should be suspected of being unauthorized outsiders.

Power outages will affect the automated access control system. The first consideration is to determine what happens to a person in the portal. Even if emergency generators are used for emergency power, there will be a power interruption. The length of the interruption depends on the time required to start the generator or bring it on-line. Therefore, when there is a power failure, the electric door strike controlling the exit door to the controlled area should be fail-secure. The entrance door strike should be fail-safe or automatically open so the occupant can exit.

The second consideration is to determine how to handle individual access while the power is off. If an emergency generator is used, it is only a matter of waiting a few minutes until power is restored. Otherwise, contingency plans must be made to accommodate access. These plans might require that everyone enter at a central bypass point or that temporary bypass portals are put into operation at the desired entrance points. The exact measures depend on the number of individuals requiring access to the facility. In most cases where the security level dictates using automated access control portals, the most cost-effective measure to handle power outages is to use an emergency generator.

When automated access control systems are used to control access at a critical facility, guard assistance in the portal can be requested at any time. Using the audio communications link to control the monitoring area can be burdensome and time-consuming. Training of employees using the system will minimize the need for assistance and alarms resulting from improper use.

PERFORMANCE TESTING

Access control systems should be checked daily by operating them both in a valid and an invalid mode. That is, you could test a card reader by using a valid card to gain access, then use an invalid card to ensure it is denied. Keyboards can be checked in a similar manner by entering valid and invalid codes. Personnel verification systems can be checked by introducing a valid card and valid code to gain access to the system and then verifying the valid requester. You could then repeat the access procedure but attempt to verify an invalid requester. These are basic tests to ensure that the system is performing satisfactorily. Tamper alarms associated with the access system should be tested at least monthly.

MAINTENANCE

When an automated access control system fails, access control must be performed by guards, who can be costly. To minimize downtime, spare units or modules should be maintained on-site to ensure quick repair. Whether spare units or spare modules are maintained depends on the complexity of the access control system and the capability of the maintenance personnel.

Access control systems, depending on the level of control, can be complex electronic systems that require competent on-site technicians to perform maintenance. If the maintenance force is unable to repair the system, a maintenance contract with either the manufacturer or an authorized contractor is in order. The maintenance contract should include operational spares to minimize downtime.

CONTRABAND DETECTORS

The following paragraphs discuss the most popular types of equipment used to support contraband control. This equipment includes metal detectors, explosives detectors, package search systems, and SNM monitors. The operation of this equipment is usually unique for each manufacturer; therefore, the discussion addresses only typical features and functions of such equipment. The manufacturer must provide detailed operational and application information.

Metal Detectors

Metal detectors are normally used to detect the presence of metal objects, usually concealed weapons. But they can detect any metal objects and can be used in loss prevention applications to detect theft of metallic objects or even contraband. Metal detectors are essential in access control systems at prisons and nuclear facilities, but they are best known for airport security applications.

Both walk-through and hand-held detectors are available to perform these functions. The difference between walk-through and hand-held detectors is obvious. With a walk-through detector, the person to be searched must walk through a stationary tunnellike structure or an open door frame structure. The hand-held detector is passed over in close proximity to the person being searched.

Metal detectors are classified as passive or active. The difference between them is their basic operating principles. Passive detectors respond to perturbations of the ambient earth's magnetic field caused by passing ferromagnetic objects in close proximity to the detector. Because passive detectors will detect only ferromagnetic metals, their usefulness in access control applications is limited.

Active metal detectors do not rely on the earth's magnetic field. They generate their own electromagnetic field and detect changes in that field caused when metal objects are introduced into it. Unlike passive detectors, which detect only ferromagnetic metals, active detectors will detect any metal object.

Active detectors use either continuous wave (CW) or pulse generators to generate the low-strength electromagnetic field between the transmit or search coils and the receive or sense coils. Continuous wave systems produce fixed frequence sinusoidal signals in the search coil within the frequency band of 100 Hz to 25 kHz. Pulse systems excite the search coil with a fixed frequency pulse train in the 400 to 500 Hz frequency band.

A typical walk-through active detector consists of a search coil and one or a combination of sense coils located a few feet apart in the archway. In a CW system, the transmit coil is driven by an oscillator that produces a low-frequency sinusoidal signal that generates the low-strength electromagnetic field. This field induces a signal into the sense coil or coils that is monitored by the detection circuit. A metal object introduced into the magnetic field produces phase and amplitude changes in the signal monitored by the detection circuit. The magnitude of these changes depends on the size of the metal object, the conductive and magnetic properties of the object, how rapidly the object is moving through the field, and the object's position and orientation in the field. Depending on the detector type, when any or a combination of these parameters satisfies the detection criteria, an alarm is sounded.

The detectors have a self-balancing network that compensate for external metallic objects placed near the detector. To compensate for this self-balancing feature, the detector processes only signals produced by metallic objects moving rapidly through the detector. The primary differences between active walk-through metal detectors are the transmitter or search coil and receiver or sense coil size and arrangement, the uniformity of the field created within the walk-through space, and the operating frequency.

Performance and operational check tests should be conducted periodically to ensure the quality of detection and to verify that the detector is functioning. Performance tests are more detailed than operational checks and should probably be conducted at least semiannually by a maintenance person. Since the operational check simply verifies that the detector is operating, it should be conducted daily by the guard.

These procedures are already established for those facilities regulated by the Federal Aviation Administration (FAA), NRC, and the Department of Energy. Facilities that use metal detectors but are not regulated should generate their own performance and operational check procedures.

All detection performance tests should be conducted by a metallic clean tester or by some mechanical means of passing metallic test samples through the detector. The clean tester should not carry any metallic objects, such as keys, coins, watches, or even metal-frame eyeglasses. The tester should start from a position about 10 feet from the detector and walk at a speed of 3 feet per second through the detector, without hesitating, to a position 10 feet beyond the detector. The operational check can be performed by having the guard carry a realistic test sample (one that represents a real threat) through the detector once or twice to verify that it is operating. Performance testing should be conducted by having the tester carry each test sample through the detector an adequate number of times or in accordance with the manufacturer's recommendation. Test samples could represent different size handguns, knives, or whatever the detector is supposed to detect.

The detector also should be installed in accordance with the manufacturer's installation procedures. It should not be installed near large sources of electromagnetic energy or moving metal.

Explosives Detectors

Explosives detectors are considered an essential element of any access control system at nuclear facilities or any facility where explosives can be used to gain entry into vital areas. They detect the vapors given off by the explosives. The probability of detecting an explosive is directly proportional to the rate of escaping vapors or volatility of the compound. Volatility depends on the explosive's composition, partial pressure of the various component vapors, and temperature of the bulk explosive.

Explosives are very difficult to detect because there are so many different types and their escaping vapor rate is so low. Vapor escape rates are low because of the explosive's low vapor pressure. The vapor escape rates are reduced even further by the explosive's casting materials packaging materials and transport container. Detection is made even more difficult because the minute quantities of escaping vapors quickly diffuse in the air.

The problem of explosives detection is complicated even more by the variety of objects or containers requiring search. For instance, detectors suitable for examining briefcases might be ineffective for examining people. In brief, the technical capability to detect all explosives in all quantities does not exist.

The vapor collection and detection method varies between manufacturers. Therefore, the capabilities, advantages, and disadvantages of each detector type should be discussed with the manufacturer. The manufacturer should supply the performance and operational test procedures and train guards in the use of the detector.

Package Search Systems

The most familiar package search system is used by airport security to inspect baggage, but this type of system can be used in any application where it is vital to search packages entering or leaving areas for weapons, explosives, SNM, or valuable assets.

In systems typical of those used by airlines, trained personnel view images produced by sensors positioned opposite a penetrating, pulsed X-radiation source. The contents of a package are identified by an inspector, who considers the density and shape of the images projected on a video screen. In an automatic package search system, a visual image is not produced, since the detection system will generate an alarm based on computer processing of the search data.

Package search systems are specialized, and their operation, application, and testing should be discussed with the manufacturer.

Special Nuclear Materials Monitors

Special nuclear materials monitors, when used at access or entry control areas in nuclear facilities, detect concealed SNM on persons, in packages, or in vehicles leaving controlled areas. Commercially available monitors detect SNM by measuring gamma radiation resulting from the natural radioactive decay in the SNM. A monitor usually consists of a detector scintillator and photomultiplier tube, along with its electronic signal processing and alarm circuit. The scintillator material absorbs gamma rays and emits light pulses that are converted to electric charge pulses by the photomultiplier tube. The associated electronic circuit counts the gamma rays to determine whether an alarm condition exists.

Special nuclear materials monitors are very specialized units, and their operation, application, and testing should be discussed in detail with the manufacturer.

ACCESS CONTROL APPLICATIONS

Access control systems can restrict employee and visitor access to vital areas where valuable assets are being stored. They will not totally eliminate risk, but if properly designed, they can reduce the risk and losses to an acceptable level. Access control systems are finding many new applications beyond their use at government facilities. They are being used to monitor and control access to areas such as parking lots, buildings, elevators, computer rooms, hazardous areas, utility rooms, pharmacy storage rooms, and offices.

When designing an access control system, the designer must first identify each area requiring control. Then he must establish the level of security required for each area and identify who (not individuals but the functional element) requires access. Probably the most important consideration, and one that is sometimes neglected, is to determine the number of individuals who require access to each area and their access schedule. These are the primary considerations affecting the selection of an access control system, but other related factors must be considered.

The security level of each area requiring access control can be classified as Level A, B, C, or D in accordance with the criteria defined in Chapter 4. Levels A and B require the highest level of control because they must protect against a highly skilled internal threat and a highly skilled external threat, respectively. Level C requires medium level control to protect against a skilled internal and an unskilled external threat. Level D requires only the minimum level of control to protect against unskilled internal and external threats.

When considering an access control system for Level D areas, one fact to consider is whether a highly visible or a low-profile system is desirable. A highly visible system will be a psychological deterrent to some unskilled threats. For this reason, it might be desirable to have a visible system, especially at main entrance points to buildings and parking lots, to discourage theft and vandalism. Quantifying the deterrent effectiveness of access control systems, as with any other security measure, is difficult. But the FAA's airport systems demonstrate that this deterrent exists. There has not been a successful hijacking using metal weapons since the FAA imposed the antihijacking measures. Psychological deterrents will not stop determined adversaries, but they might be quite effective against less determined persons. Access control visibility would not be desirable in other areas where it would identify a secure facility for a would-be adversary.

The throughput rate is the number of individuals that must pass through an access point in a unit of time. It is usually expressed as individuals per minute. For instance, for Level D areas where fewer than one-hundred people will require access at any one time, a single card reader will probably satisfy the need. Card readers can read a card in about 3 seconds. This is called the verification time. Several seconds should be added to the verification time for the requester to move to the reader and insert or pass his card through it and for him to exit the door or turnstile. The total time for him to gain access is the enrollment time. Assuming the requester has his card ready and does not have any trouble, the enrollment time will be about 5 seconds. This means twelve individuals can enter in 1 minute, which is the throughput rate. At this rate, it will take about 9 minutes for the one-hundred people to gain access. This time estimate might be a little to conservative or liberal, but it illustrates the importance of considering the throughput rate. The throughput rate can be doubled or tripled by adding additional access control points. If people have to wait too long to gain access (get to work), they might become disgruntled and abuse the system.

The throughput rate becomes even more important as the level of access control increases. For instance, Level C access control using a card reader in conjunction with a keyboard and memorized code will require about 3 seconds to read and verify the card and another 3 seconds for the requester to enter his memorized code. Several additional seconds will be required for him to move to and through the access point. The enrollment time could easily double from 5 to 10 seconds, meaning the throughput rate will drop to six requesters per minute, and the time for the one-hundred individuals to gain access will double to 18 minutes.

When systems that recognize personal characteristics are required, the access time increases appreciably. Depending on the exact combination of readers, the access time can range from about 5 to 10 seconds for a combination of readers using a card reader and a hand-geometry or fingerprint reader, to 10 to 20 seconds for systems using a card reader and signature or eye retina verification reader. The eye retina or signature reader is usually used for Level A and B areas in conjunction with a card reader and keyboard with a memorized five-digit code. At this level the requester has to insert his card in the reader, enter his memorized code, then register at the eye retina verifier or sign in at the signature verifier. This procedure could easily take 15 seconds. With this system, the throughput rate will be only four per minute. These access times assume that the system functions reliably and that the requester finds his card, puts it in the reader correctly, enters the correct five-digit code at the keyboard, and executes the personal verification function correctly.

For low-security Level D areas, the system designer must decide whether to use off-line or on-line readers. Off-line readers simply open the door either mechanically or by activating an electric strike for authorized cards. On-line readers are connected to a central computer that can identify who is entering, determine whether he is allowed to enter at that location and time, turn intrusion detection systems off, register the fact that the

Table 26–1   Threat/Access Control Matrix

Level	Guard	Automated
A and B	Photo identification with badge exchange	Access control portals with Wiegan effect cards and card reader; keyboard and five-digit memorized code; either an eye retina recognition, speech verification, or signature verification system
C	Photo identification with badge exchange	Proximity or Wiegan effect cards and card reader with either a fingerprint or hand-geometry recognition system or a keyboard and a four- or five-digit memorized code
D	Photo identification	Any access card and card reader

requester has entered, and not allow the card to be used again until the requester exists the area he has entered. The computer manages these functions by maintaining a record of the access authorization for each badge-holder and checks the record each time an access request is made. Because this authorization checking is automated, a detailed set of access levels can be easily implemented. Also, most code credential systems provide the capability to restrict access based on time of day, day of week, or entry point.

There are still other advantages. Computer-managed access control system programs can be quickly changed to meet new security needs. If a card is lost or stolen, it can be easily voided and replaced without having to rekey the entire system. Because the system has such a complete access authorization record, it prevents a cardholder from entering an area and passing his card back for someone else to use. Most access control computers can be programmed to monitor the night watchman's patrol tour. With such a system, all the areas that must be checked are registered in the computer in the patrol sequence, with a time window assigned to each area. When the guard makes his rounds, he uses his own card to clock in at the area's card reader. He must register at each area in the proper sequence and within the allocated time, or an alarm sounds at the console. Then another guard can respond to determine what happened. To minimize possible collusion, the watchman need not know the programmed tour until he goes on duty.

Computer-managed access control systems can be used not only to control access to areas, but also to control access to equipment. With such a system, only authorized individuals would be able to physically operate the controlled equipment. For instance, a computer room or manufacturing area might contain specific computers or manufacturing equipment that only a few individuals are authorized to operate. By having an on-line card reader connected to the equipment, the computer can turn the computer or equipment on for the authorized card and hopefully the authorized cardholder. Misusing or losing the access card is a vulnerability of any card system.

Another design consideration is to integrate the access control system with the intrusion detection system. Many false alarms are caused by innocent employees entering a secured area and initiating an intrusion alarm. By having the intrusion detection system access controlled by an access control system, the authorized cardholder can enter the secured area without initiating a false alarm. This also will eliminate the need to call the console operator prior to entering a secure area. It is probably still desirable to call in, however, especially if entry is at an abnormal time. It should be noted that not all access control systems can be fully integrated with other security equipment.

Table 26–1 recommends the minimum level of access control for security levels A, B, C, and D. Both levels A and B are considered to require the highest level of access control because they must protect against a highly skilled internal threat. The internal threat is the predominant one for access control systems.

Chapter 27

Application Guidelines

Following is an unprioritized list of reminders and considerations for designing an access control system.

1. The primary consideration when designing an access control system is to identify areas requiring protection, the level of security, and the number of individuals requiring access.
2. No single system can be recommended for all applications.
3. Ease of counterfeiting credentials is a vital consideration.
4. Guards can certainly control access based on some identification criteria, but their inattention after a period of routine work might jeopardize the site's security.
5. Guard verification criteria can vary from a simple credential check to a badge exchange procedure.
6. Guards must respond to alarms occurring at access locations.
7. Emergency vehicles must be allowed to enter and exit controlled areas in the event of an emergency.
8. Visitor access and control is vital because these visitors could become a threat.
9. Many vulnerabilities associated with access control can be minimized with appropriate procedures and personnel training.
10. Maintenance is an important consideration. The question is whether to use in-house maintenance or contract it to a qualified company.
11. Access control systems are psychological deterrents to some threats.
12. Access control systems, like intrusion detection systems, must be designed to minimize the number of false alarms.
13. Most commercial coded credentials systems provide the capability of restricting access based on time of day or access point.
14. An occupant list can be maintained to serve as a master list in case of an emergency.
15. Antipassback can be eliminated by maintaining an occupant list and not allowing a badge to be used for two successive entrances and exits.
16. Any type of coded badge can be counterfeited if sufficient money and talent are devoted to the attempt.

17. Resistance to counterfeiting is not as important if the badge is used in conjunction with a separate personnel identification system.
18. Access card readers are vulnerable to attack if a personnel identification verification system is not used.
19. Card readers without personnel identifiers should be provided with tamper sensors.
20. Communication lines between the card reader and central monitoring area should be supervised.
21. A system that can accommodate the required number of access cards, card readers, and access levels should be selected.
22. The manufacturer's distance limitations between the location of the card reader and the monitoring console should be observed.
23. A periodic test procedure to ensure proper operation of the access control system should be implemented.
24. Type I errors are the rejection of a valid requester, while Type II errors are the acceptance of an invalid requester.
25. Throughput rate is the inverse of the average verification time, excluding the time to request access.
26. Enrollment time is the time an individual is required to remain in the enrollment center of a personnel identity verification system and is longer than the verification time.
27. Video comparator systems use a guard to verify an individual's identity based on visual characteristics securely stored for later comparison with the real-time image of the individual requesting entry.
28. Access readers should not be installed outdoors unless they are designed for it.
29. With any access control system, provisions must be made to handle visitors and handicapped personnel.
30. Access control portals should be temperature and humidity controlled.
31. Turnstiles are effective in reducing dual entry.
32. The most common vulnerability of access card systems is when the cardholder loses his card and does not realize he has lost it.
33. Automated access control systems can be manned during peak traffic periods to increase the throughput rate.

METAL DETECTORS

1. Metal detector performance is degraded when the detector is operated near another detector if the two are not mutually shielded.
2. The false alarm rate of metal detectors will increase if they are operated near moving metal parts.
3. Metal detectors should come with a list of test items that should be detected and those that should not be detected.
4. Testers should be clean of all metallic objects.

5. Detectors should be installed at least 33 feet from equipment operating with electric motors, timing devices, or relays.
6. Detectors should be installed at least 10 feet from television cameras or monitors.
7. Flickering fluorescent lights within 10 feet of a detector might cause it to false alarm.
8. The detector should not be operated from power lines prone to frequent power surges.

EXPLOSIVE DETECTORS

1. Dynamite is easily detected by explosives detectors.
2. To maximize its sensitivity, the detector should be installed in accordance with the manufacturer's installation instructions.
3. The detector should be installed and operated in a relatively dust- and smoke-free environment.
4. The detector should be installed and positioned for ease of maintenance.
5. Hand-held detector searches involve scanning the entire person with a particular emphasis on the waist and pocket areas.
6. Package searches should include all seams or cracks in the package.

PACKAGE SEARCH SYSTEMS

1. Search systems used in conjunction with personnel access should be selected to accommodate the package size and not impede the throughput rate.
2. Search systems for packages or letters alone also should be selected to accommodate package size and required search rate.

SPECIAL NUCLEAR MATERIALS MONITORS

1. Detectors should be located and positioned so that detection sensitivity is as uniform as possible over the detection area.
2. Detectors should be located in as low and as steady a background environment as possible to improve sensitivity and reduce false alarms.
3. Power line transients and pulsed electromagnetic radiation can cause a monitor to false alarm.

PART VII

INTRUSION DETECTION SYSTEM APPLICATIONS

This section will describe how to design a security system for several hypothetical facilities, with an emphasis on designing the intrusion detection system. An intrusion detection system is, however, only one part of a total security system. A total security system requires the proper integration of locks, safes, physical barriers, lights, television, and access controls, as well as the intrusion detection system. In fact, intrusion detection systems can provide adequate protection only when they are properly integrated in a security system that has an effective response force, proper maintenance, and, particularly, total management support.

When designing a security system, the first task is to establish the security system requirements based in part on allowable costs. Included as part of the requirements is a definition of the type of threat—vandalism, burglary, terrorism, etc.—and the anticipated mode of operation or skill level of the adversary. Once the security requirements have been established, a site survey should be conducted to determine the system's operational requirements. These requirements will be determined by the facility's physical and environmental parameters, such as plant layout and construction, the terrain and climate, and the facility's operational parameters, such as the nature of the operations, operating schedule, and security guard response time and functions.

After the design requirements have been established, the security equipment can be selected, procured, and installed. For an intrusion detection system this means selecting the sensors and alarm transmission system and procuring and installing the equipment by using in-house resources or contracting this effort in total or in part. If the effort is contracted, the contract terms and conditions and the system specifications should be well defined by someone technically qualified to ensure that the system will satisfy the security and operational requirements. In fact, it is recommended that the equipment and system contract specifications be performance-oriented toward satisfying the facility's requirements. It is also recommended that there be constant interaction between the user and designer during the design, implementation, and acceptance phases. Technical support also should be considered to provide assistance during the initial operational phase.

The design concept will be illustrated by discussing the rationale for establishing the security and operational requirements and for selecting the security equipment necessary to satisfy these requirements for three types of installations. The first security system will be designed for a public school complex consisting of high schools, intermediate schools, elementary schools, an administrative building, a maintenance garage, and bus parking areas. The second illustration will discuss the security system design for a nuclear reactor plant, where the security requirements are imposed by the NRC. The last security system design will be for an office building.

These three types of installations were selected because they represent facilities where the threat ranges from vandalism at the schools to a terrorist attack on a nuclear plant. They also represent both single and multiple building complexes that require different alarm transmission system considerations, and they have requirements for both interior and exterior sensors. As with most real installations, more than one type of sensor or alarm transmission system can be used to protect the hypothetical installations. Therefore, several types of sensors or signal transmission systems will be discussed as ways to protect certain areas. The systems described should be considered only as examples and not as prescribed and approved security systems. Predesign of security systems is not recommended because there are too many specific site requirements that need consideration in order to provide effective security.

Chapter 28

Public School Complex

The hypothetical school complex covers both city and suburban areas. There are twelve high schools, twelve intermediate schools, fiftyeight elementary schools, an administrative office building, a maintenance garage, and two bus parking areas divided between the city and suburbs. For this illustration, the city and suburban areas are divided into four districts identified as North, East, South, and West. Each city district has one high school, one intermediate school, and four elementary schools. Each of the four suburban districts has two high schools, two intermediate schools, and eight elementary schools. The administration building is located in the western part of the city just inside the city limits. The maintenance garage is located several miles west of the administration building in the suburbs. One bus parking area is in the suburbs northeast of the city, and the second area is in the southwest area, about five miles outside the city limits.

The school complex has a security administrator who is responsible for the security of the total school complex. He has an assistant, a secretary, eight security patrol officers, three radio communications officers, and an electronics technician to assist in this function. The security administrator and his staff are located in the administration building. The administrator and his assistant are located in two adjoining offices on the first floor, and the secretary is in an open area outside the offices. The patrol officers' lounge, the radio control room, and the equipment maintenance area are located in the basement.

The patrol officers are on duty during the evening hours and at night when the schools are either closed or being used for other activities such as sporting events and adult education classes. The eight patrol officers are divided between two work shifts starting at 4 P.M. and ending at 8 A.M. Two officers are assigned to patrol and inspect the city schools, and the other two officers are assigned to cover the suburban facilities on each shift. Each patrol officer has a radio-equipped patrol car so that he can communicate with the radio operator in the administration building.

The officers on the evening shift are responsible for inspecting each school after the evening schedule to ensure that the facilities are properly secured. The remainder of their shift is spent patrolling each school, the maintenance garage, and the parking areas on a random schedule. The officers on the second shift assume these duties at midnight. If a patrol officer needs law enforcement assistance, he notifies the radio operator, who in turn notifies the local police.

The local police in each school district also patrol the school facilities. But because of the limited time resulting from their other law enforcement duties, their surveillance is usually limited to observing the facility as they drive by. Even with the support of the local police, school vandalism and burglary at the hypothetical school complex are becoming excessive and costly.

The cumulative costs to repair the damage from vandalism and to replace the stolen equipment have been reviewed by the security administrator, and based on these costs it is apparent that the security measures at each of the schools should be improved to reduce vandalism and theft. One way to improve security is to install an intrusion detection system in each school to alert the police when there is an intrusion. This will improve the effectiveness of the security guards in maintaining security at the schools. Some of the administrator's concerns are: How should the system be designed? What equipment should be selected? How should the system be implemented?

The following paragraphs will address these concerns by describing a systematic approach to designing an intrusion detection system for the hypothetical school complex.

THEFT ANALYSIS

The first step in designing any security system, including the intrusion detection system, is to conduct a threat analysis. The purpose of this analysis is to identify the threat to the schools and supporting facilities. The threat can be either internal or external, or a combination of both. The second purpose of the analysis is to establish the level of sophistication of the threat. Based on recent security investigations, it is evident that the external threat to the school facilities ranges from unsophisticated, where the intruders break windows to gain entrance, to a more sophisticated approach, where the intruders cleverly defeat the door locks to gain entrance. Vandalism is usually the intent of the unskilled intruder, while the more sophisticated intruder is usually after typewriters, video equipment, cameras, projectors, etc. These pieces of equipment are also targets for internal theft in most of the schools, especially the high schools.

The type and sophistication of the threat varies between schools; therefore, the threat problems should be identified for each school and supporting facility. The most effective way to conduct the analysis is to visit each facility and interview the principal or another responsible individual who knows about the crime problems. If the security administrator is not conducting the survey, he should certainly visit the schools to participate in the interview. The local police officer who knows about neighborhood crime also should be included in the interview because he can provide information on the area crime trends. The interview can be conducted separately or along with the site security survey.

SITE SURVEY

A site survey should be conducted at each school or facility requiring an intrusion detection system to establish the particular security and operational requirements. Since many of the schools are physically similar, with exterior windows, windows in the exterior doors, and door locks, many of the physical security requirements pertaining to locks and window protection can be generalized. But the operational requirements should not be generalized because each school probably has unique operational schedules that could jeopardize the effectiveness of the intrusion detection system.

For instance, many school facilities are used in the evening for adult education, sports events, and meetings. In such cases, if all the intrusion detection sensors are connected to a single transmitter, the entire school will by unprotected when any part of the school is open. This type of vulnerability can be eliminated if the system designer knows which areas are being used in the evenings. Then he can divide the school into zones where only that part of the school being used will be exposed. Anyone entering a protected room would be detected, and an alarm would be annunciated at the central monitoring station.

A site survey will be conducted at East City High School to illustrate the concept of establishing security and operational requirements. The requirements for the remaining schools will be discussed collectively to reveal the nature of the threat and operational problems.

EAST CITY HIGH SCHOOL

East City High, as the name implies, is located in the east city school district. It is a large two-story building that provides classroom space for approximately two thousand students. Besides the full-time day activities, the school is used in the evening for adult education classes. With the addition of the normal after-school activities, the school is fully utilized.

East City High was selected for this example because it has the highest rate of vandalism and theft of any school in the hypothetical school complex. Therefore, establishing the security and operational requirements for such a school will best illustrate the methodology for protecting all the schools.

During the discussion among the principal, security director, and police chief, the principal described a number of specific thefts, the disastrous results of some of the vandalism, and the methods of breaking and entering, which were often about the same. Typewriters, video equipment, and motion picture cameras were the most expensive items taken. In fact, the theft of this equipment has been so extensive that the school is inadequately equipped to meet the present classroom demands. Besides this equipment, musical instruments have been taken from the band rooms, tools taken from the shops, and school supplies and typewriters taken from the principal's office.

The principal indicated that some of the equipment, and especially the musical instruments and tools, has been taken during normal school hours. Although all rooms containing valuable items are supposed to be locked, the principal has on many occasions found the rooms open and unoccupied. The school has on several occasions been broken into at night, with a resulting loss of typewriters, video equipment, and movie cameras. Usually an entrance door was broken or forced open to gain access to the school. Inside the school, the door to the rooms where the targeted items were located was forced open. On several occasions, however, when equipment was taken, including items in the principal's office, the locks were apparently compromised because there was no evidence of physical damage to the door or locks.

Vandalism is a constant problem at the school, even during normal school hours. But the most destructive vandalism has been at night after the school is closed. Vandals enter the school either by breaking a window to climb through or by breaking a door window and releasing the door lock from inside. Once inside the school, they can run rampant through the halls, entering any classroom. If the doors are locked, they can force their way into any room. The library has been a target for vandals on several occasions.

The police chief indicated that vandalism and theft would probably be a continuing problem at the school. He is trying to discourage anyone from intruding by increasing the police patrol. But because of their demanding schedule, some nights they may patrol the school only once or twice. Even then they only drive by the front of the school. On occasion the officers drive through the school parking lot so they can at least see one side and part of the back of the school. The police chief also stated that some of his men have complained that the lighting along the side and back is inadequate for them to check those areas from their patrol cars.

During the security discussion the principal described the hectic school operating schedule. In addition to adult education classes, which might be held in the classrooms and shops, the school is open at least one evening of the week during the school year for sporting events. Even during the outside sporting events, the school is open to provide bathroom facilities for attendees. Anyone can enter the building under these circumstances, and the principal admitted that he often found students roaming the halls.

An analysis of the facts gathered during the interviews showed that the exterior threat ranged from unskilled, where the intruders used force to gain access to the school or targeted equipment room, to semiskilled, where they were able to compromise the door locks. The skill level of the interior threat with respect to access to the targeted items is unknown because they were probably taken from open, unoccupied rooms. The thieves were certainly daring, however, as they carried out the thefts during school hours.

The security requirements necessary to combat both the external and internal theft and vandalism should be, at a minimum, to improve the penetration resistance of the doors; to restrict access internally to all sections of the school; to reduce the accessibility of potential items for theft; to improve visibility around the school at night; and to detect and alert the police of all unauthorized school entries.

Establishing the security requirements is a rather simple task once the security problems are identified. But determining a cost-effective way to correct the security vulnerabilities and to implement an intrusion detection system to detect all unauthorized entries is not simple. Correcting the vulnerabilities in the hypothetical schools means installing outside doors as well as doors that cannot be easily compromised at the equipment rooms and the principal's office.

The requirement for restricting personnel access to all parts of the school can be satisfied by installing roll-up screen barriers at strategic locations along the school corridors. For instance, during the survey of the school, the principal identified the classrooms being used at night for the adult education classes. They are scattered all over the school on both the first and second floors. The principal was asked whether it was really necessary to use the classrooms on the second floor. He said that the English, foreign language, and math rooms were on the second floor, but it was not necessary that they be used for the adult education classes. He followed by saying that all evening classes could meet on the first floor. This being the case, roll-up screens can be installed at the heads of the stairs to deter anyone from entering the second floor.

Another place that roll-up screens can be installed is at the end of the corridor adjacent to the gym. Proper use of screens in this location will restrict anyone attending a sporting event from entering the main portion of the school. Security measures of this type will certainly reduce the vandalism that occurs during sporting events.

The requirement for reducing the accessibility of potential theft items such as typewriters, video equipment, and motion picture cameras can be accomplished by locking the items to a secure structure. For instance, locks are available for securing typewriters to a desk. Individual television sets and motion picture cameras can be physically secured and locked to a mobile cart in such a way that the equipment can be moved and operated where necessary with little or no inconvenience to the user. At night the equipment carts can be locked together in the storage room.

The requirement to improve visibility at night for the patrolling police officers and for the school security patrol can be satisfied by installing additional lighting outside the school. For this application it is recommended that a roadway-type lighting system be installed around the school. The light should be directed away from the school to illuminate the parking lot and surrounding area.

Floodlights should be installed atop the telephone poles and directed toward the school to illuminate the sides of the building, especially in entrance door areas. This type of lighting system will silhouette anyone near the building to improve the police officers' assessment.

These types of physical improvements will not prevent all theft and vandalism, but they will delay the thief or vandal and, most likely, deter other intruders. The purpose of this application example is not to elaborate on physical security but to discuss the design considerations and equipment selection rationale for an intrusion detection system that will detect unauthorized entry and alert the police.

Before the intrusion detection system can be designed for East City High, the yearly school schedule should be reviewed. The normal school year is from the first of September to the end of May, with breaks for vacations and school holidays. During this time the students attend classes from 8:30 A.M. to 3 P.M.; however, there are many after-school activities that require classroom space. The teacher opens the classroom in the morning and is responsible for locking it before leaving the school. Those teachers sponsoring or in charge of after-school activities are responsible for locking their rooms. Summer school is part of the normal school schedule, but the same opening and securing procedures apply.

The adult education classes meet year-round, generally between the hours of 7 and 10 P.M. The same classes do not meet every night, but the school is open almost every evening for some classes. A custodian has a schedule of which classrooms are used each evening. He unlocks these rooms before 7 P.M. and secures them at 10 P.M., or after the classes are finished. When the normal custodial duties are completed around 11 P.M., the custodian secures all the exterior doors. The district school security patrol officer checks all the exterior doors shortly after the custodian leaves.

Based on East City High's full operating schedule, one of the primary intrusion detection system requirements is that the alarm transmission system be capable of monitoring and separately identifying multiple protected zones. A separate zone will be required for the video and motion picture equipment room, typing room, auto repair shop, machine shop, band room, library, principal's office, and each of the corridors on the first floor. Each corridor should be separately zoned to assist the police in responding to an alarm initiated in a corridor. For instance, if someone was in one of the side corridors and the police responded to the front or opposite side of the school, then whoever was in the school would probably have time to escape. By dividing the corridors into separate zones of detection, the police would know which doors to cover. Each protected room should be on a separate zone to accommodate the operating schedule and also to assist the police in responding to an alarm.

Several additional subjects that could influence the intrusion detection system's operational requirements were discussed during the site survey. They included temperature extremes inside the school, especially in the winter; length of time the electrical power has been off in the school; possible sources of electromagnetic energy near the school; and the availability of telephone circuits.

The temperature extremes should be known in order to establish the equipment's operating temperature. When considering what the temperature extremes might be inside the school, consider what the temperature might be if the heat were off for some extended period. It is not unreasonable to expect the electrical power to be off for 6, 8, or 10 hours because of thunderstorms or severe winter weather. The outside temperature in the area of the hypothetical school complex rarely goes below 0°F, which is well within the intrusion detection equipment's normal operating temperature range. Therefore, the specified operating temperature of – 30°F to ± 120°F is quite adequate for equipment to be used in the hypothetical school complex.

The lengthof time the electricity might be off is an important consideration when establishing the standby battery operating requirements. The longest power outage that the security director could remember was about 48 hours. This occurred several years ago in the winter, when there was a severe ice storm. Some of the schools had power sooner, but several of the schools in the suburbs were without power for several days. Usually the electrical power is off only 2 or 3 hours; the ice storm was a worse case.

Most security equipment has a standby battery capacity that will operate the equipment for about 4 hours. Batteries are rated based on use at a fixed temperature. As the battery operating environment temperature decreases, the battery capacity decreases. For some batteries the capacity is reduced to only 70 percent of its rated capacity at freezing. Therefore, the operational requirements for the standby battery should be specified based on the equipment's operating at a realistic low temperature that could be anticipated with the heat off for an extended period. The standby battery operating time for the equipment used in the hypothetical school complex will be 4 hours at 32°F. Four hours of standby battery is quite adequate for the majority of power outages. The additional cost for each battery capacity to operate the equipment for an extended period, such as during the extreme ice storm, could not be justified. It was decided by the security director that on such occasions the school security officers would work longer hours and increase school security patrols.

The interviewees also were asked if they knew of any large sources of electromagnetic energy near the schools. Typical energy sources are electrical substations, radio transmitters, and radar systems that operate at airports or military installations. The security director indicated that there was a radio transmitting tower near West City High. Although the transmitted energy would not affect East City High, it could cause false alarm problems for the intrusion detection system at West City High. One consolation is that the radio transmits at a single specified frequency and at a fixed broadcast wattage. Because the transmitted electromagnetic energy is at a single frequency, any related equipment problems should be easy to identify and correct.

Knowing the availability of telephone circuits in the school is important when selecting the type of alarm transmission system. All of the telephone circuits entering East City High are being used, but spare circuits are available in the telephone junction box located on the pole in front of the school. Because of the proximity of the junction box and the fact that the telephone line enters the school above ground, there will be little problem supplying telephone circuits for security implementation.

The rationale for establishing security and operating requirements for East City High have been discussed in some detail to illustrate the concept of conducting a site survey. Some additional tasks that should be completed during the site survey will be discussed in the paragraphs on system design. But first, the security and operational requirements should be established for the remaining school facilities. These requirements will be discussed collectively for the facilities to identify their unique security problems and to establish the intrusion detection system requirements.

Most of the high schools have a full operating schedule, like that at East City High, and suffer from similar security problems. The primary difference is that theft and vandalism are less severe at the other high schools. Security problems at the intermediate and elementary schools are even less severe simply because they do not have the equipment required by the high schools. Their operating schedules are not as demanding because the facilities are not used for adult education. On the average, they are used one evening a week for Scout meetings, and maybe once a month for a school function or community meeting. These meetings usually involve only the school cafeteria and, in some schools, the gym.

Since the nature of the security problems is about the same at all the schools, with only a variation in the severity, the security measures recommended for East City High should be implemented to the degree necessary at all the schools. The operating schedules for the high schools are much more demanding than for the intermediate or elementary schools, but the intrusion detection system requirements should be about the same. The primary difference will be that the intermediate and elementary schools will not require as many protected zones.

OTHER FACILITIES

The remaining facilities in the hypothetical school complex are the vehicle maintenance garage, two parking areas, and the administration building. The maintenance garage is located inside a 300-foot by 500-foot fenced compound adjacent to the 300-foot-long back fence. The entrance into the site is at the front side of the compound facing Roberts Road. The garage is a large metal building that has six vehicle repair bays, an open shop area, an equipment storage room, and two offices on the end of the building. The area in front of the garage is used for parking. The fence around the compound is 7 feet high and is topped with three strands of barbed wire supported on 45-degree outriggers.

According to the maintenance supervisor, the security problems are theft of tools and test equipment from the garage, theft of gasoline from the school buses, and vandalism to the buses. All intruders that entered the compound have either climbed over the fence or lifted the fence fabric and crawled under, because there was never any physical damage to the fence or gate resulting from the intrusion. The fence and gate were examined during the site survey and were found to be in good condition. The bottom of the fence fabic was within about 2 inches of the ground, and there were no washouts or gaps under the fence. It was recommended, however, that a bottom rail be installed between the fence posts around the compound with the fence fabric secured to the rail. This rail reduces the possibility of someone lifting the fence to crawl under. It also was recommended that the fence height be increased to 10 to 12 feet when the fence is eventually replaced. Securing the bottom of the fence and increasing the height will improve the penetration resistance effectiveness and deter some would-be intruders.

The theft of tools and equipment from the garage was the security problem or most concern to the supervisor, even though it probably was not the most costly. Someone had broken into the garage three times in the past year. Twice the intruder gained access by breaking an office window and releasing the window lock. On the third occasion the door lock was apparently compromised, as evidenced by the lack of physical damage to the door or windows. Each time the intruder broke into the mechanics' toolboxes and into the test equipment storage room, took the items, and left through the front door. It was obvious after surveying the garage that the windows were an easy way to gain access; therefore, it was recommended that heavy wire screens, expanded steel grilles, or bars be installed over the windows.

In the discussion of possible security improvements, the police chief said that several of his officers had complained about the poor lighting inside the compound. The one roadway luminaire at the gate and the other at the garage door did not adequately illuminate the garage and parking area. Under this lighting, intruders could lurk inside the compound without being observed by the police.

Based on the discussion and findings during the facility survey, several things can be done to improve the overall security. First, additonal lighting is required to illuminate the entire compound to an average illumination level of at least 0.5 footcandles measured in the horizontal plane at ground level. Also, the light unformity ratio should be a maximum of 6 to 1 between the light and dark areas. The uniformity ratio is important because an excessive difference between the light and dark areas will make it difficult to observe anyone in the darker areas, as the eyes tend to adjust to the brighter areas and cannot quickly adapt to the darker areas when scanning.

One way to improve the lighting inside the garage compound is to install high-pressure sodium floodlights on poles about 25 feet above the ground along the side fences. The first light pole should be installed inside the fence near the front of the compound. The floodlight atop this pole should be pointed down and toward the back of the compound. The second pole and floodlight should be installed farther down the fence line in a position to maintain the 0.5 footcandle illumination level with a maximum light-to-dark ratio of 6 to 1. By continuing this lighting arrangement for the remaining area, the last floodlights will illuminate the front of the maintenance garage. Locating the floodlights near the front of the compound and pointing them toward the back will eliminate the possibility of glare affecting the visibility of drivers passing on Roberts Road. It also will eliminate possible glare in the eyes of the police officers in their surveillance of the compound.

Another desirable security improvement for the maintenance facility would be intrusion detection systems to detect anyone climbing over the fence and entering the garage. In general, the same system operating requirements discussed for East City High would be applicable here except for the multiple zone monitoring requirements. Since the operating schedule for the garage is from 8 A.M. to 5 P.M., all the sensors can be monitored by the same alarm transmission system. To identify alarm sources, however, it would be advantageous to have a means of separately identifying each sensor zone. Then the alarm monitoring operator could differentiate between the exterior sensors and the sensors used to detect intrusions at the garage.

Another important operational requirement is that the perimeter intrusion detection system should be basically immune to false alarms caused by physical phenomena such as wind and heavy rain. This requirement is needed because the garage is in an out-of-the-way location for the security police. Therefore, responding to false alarms would reduce their morale and confidence in the equipment, as well as require time that should be spent patrolling the schools. The threat to the schools is much more severe and costly than it is to the maintenance facility.

Buses parked in the two parking areas also have been vandalized and have had gasoline taken from their tanks. The parking areas are enclosed by 7-foot-high chain-link fences topped with barbed wire, like that around the maintenance garage area. They are unlighted except for a couple of roadway-type luminaires in front of the lots. Therefore, it is recommended that floodlights be installed to illuminate the parking areas and that an intrusion detection sensor be installed on the perimeter fences. The sensors also must have low false alarm rates.

The last facility in the hypothetical school complex is the administration building. The security director said that there has not been a security problem here, probably because the security officers are in and out of the building all night and a radio operator is always on duty. Although there is no demanding need for an intrusion detection system at this time, the radio operator said that it would be desirable for him to know when someone enters the front door and who is entering.

It is recommended that a magnetically actuated contact switch be installed on the front door to activate a buzzer in the operations room when the door is opened. A television camera could be installed in the hall and positioned so that the camera's field of view would cover the total door area. The TV monitor could be installed in the operations room in such a location that it could be easily seen by the operator. With this installation, whenever anyone opened the door, the buzzer would sound, alerting the operator that someone was either entering or leaving the building. Then he could observe the monitor and respond if necessary.

Now that the security problems at the hypothetical school facility have been identified and the requirements that will alleviate or at least reduce the severity of the problems established, the recommended security measures should be designed and implemented. One of these measures was to install lights in outside areas to satisfy the requirement for improving visibility for the security guards on night patrols. But the security measure of primary interest for this discussion is the one to install an intrusion detection system at each of the facilities to detect unauthorized entries.

INTRUSION DETECTION SYSTEM DESIGN

An intrusion detection system should be designed to satisfy the facility's operational and environmental requirements established during the threat analysis and site survey. One of the first tasks in designing a system is to select the sensors necessary to detect intrusions into the sensitive areas. The second task is to determine the number of separate detection zones needed to locate the intrusion in the protected building or installation. Along with determining the number of zones, the placement of individual sensors must be established within the designated zones. Zone selection should accommodate the facility's operating schedule and take maximum advantage of the guard force's response effectiveness. The next task is to select the alarm monitoring system to transmit the protected area alarm and security status information to the monitoring station, where it will be received and displayed for the operator.

Several related functions that could affect the operational performance and ultimately the success of the intrusion detection system must be considered during the design phase. Probably the most important of these is to identify who will respond to the intrusion alarms and to define the limits of their responsibilities. For example, with regard to intrusion detection system operation, what legal action, if any, can the response force take when they respond to an intrusion? If private security guards are responding, their responsibilities should be coordinated with the local law enforcement agency to ensure legal compliance.

The next function is to develop the necessary operational and maintenance procedures required to support the intrusion detection system. Written instructions are recommended to establish operational procedures for opening and closing a protected area. Established procedures are needed to ensure that the system is operating satisfactorily at closing and to minimize the possibility of an authorized individual accidentally initiating an alarm when entering a protected area. Maintenance procedures must be established to ensure the operational readiness of the system.

A function that cannot be overemphasized when designing an intrusion detection system is to coordinate the proposed design and operational procedures with all individuals who will be involved in using the system. Without full operational and management support, the overall long-term success of the intrusion detection system will be doubtful.

There are no step-by-step rules for accomplishing these design tasks because each site has its own unique detection and operational requirements. There are, however, basic guidelines that should be followed when designing an intrusion detection system. Instead of listing guidelines here, general procedures will be discussed for designing the intrusion detection system for the hypothetical school complex. In particular, this section will discuss the system design for East City High, the maintenance garage, and the bus parking lots.

Intrusion Detection Sensor Selection

Sensors should always be selected based on their ability to satisfy detection requirements and to operate satisfactorily in the particular environment of the area requiring protection. This means that sensors should be selected for each protected area separately, even though many of the areas requiring protection might have the same or similar detection and operational requirements. For instance, all the high schools have the same basic system requirements, but the sensors will be selected after each school has been surveyed.

Separate sensor selection for individual areas is necessary to ensure that all sensors be compatible with the size, configuration, and arrangement of the equipment, supplies, or furniture in each area. Each area also has its own sources of energy or stimuli that could cause false alarms for some sensors. This is especially true for motion sensors and exterior perimeter sensors. Otherwise similar buildings and rooms could have heating and air-conditioning vents in different locations, an important consideration in eliminating false alarms. Therefore, each area should be surveyed prior to selecting and positioning any sensors. In each case of the high schools, many of the schools will use the same sensors, but they will probably be in different locations within the protected areas.

The first step in designing an intrusion detection system, even before selecting the sensors, is to obtain a drawing showing the layout of the site or areas requiring protection. The drawing should be available for the site survey. Appropriate notations can then be made as the areas requiring protection are identified and examined. Any likely false alarm stimuli sources can be shown, along with the furniture or equipment arrangements within the areas. The drawing also will be helpful for visualizing personnel traffic flow during the school's various activities. Once the areas requiring protection within a school have been identified and the traffic flow analyzed, the locations for the roll-up barriers to limit personnel access can be assigned.

The plan view of East City High is shown in Figure 28–1. The layout does not represent an architect's concept of a high school, but it shows the typical long corridors, entrance doors, and rooms requiring protection. During the site survey of East City High, it was determined that all school entrance doors, along with the first floor corridors, principal's office, typing room, band room, library, video and motion picture equipment storage room, and shops required protection. The level of protection established during the threat analyses required the system to deter, delay, and/or detect unskilled to semiskilled intruders. To achieve this level of protection, it was decided, at a minimum, to replace all school entrance doors and doors to the protected rooms with higher-security doors and door locks and to install intrusion detection sensors to detect anyone entering the school or protected areas.

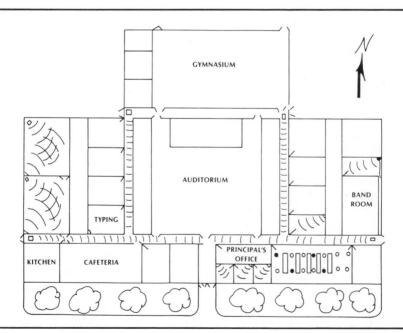

Figure 28–1 East City High School layout, first floor.

Selecting the intrusion detection sensors is the most difficult task for most people designing security systems because they are not technically knowledgeable about the principles of operation and application of the many available detectors. Therefore, the basic principles of operation will be reviewed, along with the rationale for selecting the sensors required to detect intrusions into East City High, the maintenance garage, and the bus parking lots.

All exterior entrance doors and interior doors to the areas requiring protection at East City High will have magnetic contact switches to detect anyone opening the doors. Motion inside the protected rooms will be detected by ultrasonic motion detectors. Motion along the first floor corridors and in the shop areas will be detected by microwave motion detectors. Loud intrusion-type noises will be received by audio detector receivers installed near all the entrance doors and close to the individually protected rooms. Once an alarm is initiated, regardless of whether it is initiated by an audio detector or motion sensor, the receivers can be used by the alarm monitoring operator to assess the alarm cause.

Ultrasonic motion detectors were selected to protect the individual rooms because ultrasonic energy is well contained within the room being protected. The rooms also are quiet with respect to stimuli that could cause the sensors to false alarm.

Although ultrasonic energy is well contained in the rooms, it might not be totally contained. Ultrasonic energy can leak through cracks around the door and windows. For this reason, the ultrasonic detectors located in adjacent rooms might have to be synchronized to prevent oscillator drift in one detector from causing a false alarm problem with the other detectors. Detectors using crystal-controlled oscillators usually do not have to be synchronized.

The most common stimulus that causes false alarms in ultrasonic detectors is air blowing from heating or air-conditioning ducts and from drafts around doors and windows close to the sensors. Fluttering mobiles, drapes, or anything that can oscillate within the sensor zone of detection also can cause false alarms. Hissing noises, such as the noise from a radiator relief valve, or whistling sounds caused by blowing wind passing through cracks around windows can cause false alarms. Ringing telephones or school bells are another possible source of false alarms. The ringing bell problem can be eliminated by replacing the telephone bell with a buzzer in the rooms having ultrasonic motion detectors.

You might be wondering why ultrasonic motion detectors were selected to detect intrusions in the protected rooms if they are so susceptible to false alarms. The reason is that they provide good protection at a reasonable cost and in reality have a low false alarm rate when the false alarm stimuli sources are recognized and eliminated or compensated for during the design, installation, and system operational tests. All sensors, especially motion or energy sensing sensors, are susceptible to false alarms generated by some stimuli other than those they are designed to detect. Therefore, it is important to understand sensor operation and the stimuli to which they are sensitive. Appropriate sensors can then be selected and strategically placed for optimum compatibility with the ambient conditions.

Two popular configurations of ultrasonic motion detectors are commercially available. One configuration uses single transceivers to transmit and receive ultrasonic energy. The second configuration uses separate transmitters to transmit the ultrasonic energy and separate receivers to receive the reflected energy for the signal processor. Each transceiver can detect motion in an area approximately 20 by 30 feet when it is wall or ceiling mounted. Detectors using a single ceiling-mounted receiver and transmitter can detect anyone moving in the same size space when the transmitter and receiver are separated by about 20 feet.

In the hypothetical complex, the outer offices and reception area in the principal's office will be protected by the transceiver-type ultrasonic motion detector. A single transceiver will be installed on the wall in the corner of each outer office, away from the windows and heating system air vents. In this position a single transceiver can detect anyone entering an office through a door or window. The transceivers in the reception area will be ceiling mounted to cover the areas on both sides of the reception counter and around the desks. Each transceiver will be connected to a single signal processor located in a closet in the reception area.

The individual equipment storage rooms also will be protected by the transceiver configuration motion detectors. In each room the transceiver will be located in a corner and pointed toward the center of the room to detect anyone entering or moving in the room. Two transceivers will be required to cover the band instrument storage area and the typing room. Two transceivers are needed in the band room to give total coverage between the instrument storage racks. The typing room requires two transceivers because the room size exceeds the 20- by 30-foot coverage for a single transceiver. The transceivers in each room will be connected to separate signal processors. Each processor will be locked inside a cabinet or closet in the same room where the transceiver or transceivers are located to reduce their vulnerability to tampering.

The library will be protected by the separate transmitter and receiver configuration ultrasonic motion detectors. The transmitters and receivers will be mounted on the ceiling between the rows of bookshelves and above the reading area. Remember, ultrasonic energy is contained or blocked by physical objects; therefore, the ultrasonic receivers and transmitters must be positioned so that the energy is not partially or totally blocked by the bookshelves. If the energy is blocked, the library or any area being protected by ultrasonic motion detectors will not be adequately covered.

Microwave motion detectors were selected to protect the school's main corridors and shop areas because of their large volumetric coverage. Some detectors can be equipped with an antenna that generates a long, narrow energy pattern or an antenna that generates a large teardrop-shaped radiated pattern. Detectors with the long, narrow pattern will be used to protect long corridors. The detectors will be positioned at the ends of the corridors, as shown in Figure 28–1.

Detectors with the large teardrop energy pattern will be used to detect motion inside the shop areas. A single detector has the coverage necessary to protect the shop area, but two detectors are used to reduce shadowing caused by the metal machines in the shops. The detectors will be mounted in adjacent corners in each shop near the ceiling and pointed down toward the center of the shop. In this position the detectors will give cross-coverage to detect anyone entering either shop.

An advantage, as well as a disadvantage, of microwave motion detectors is that microwave energy can penetrate many types of building materials. The degree of penetration depends on the material's density and the frequency of the radiated energy. For instance, glass, wood, and plasterboard provide very little attenuation for microwave energy in comparison to concrete or other high-density building materials. Also, microwave energy will not penetrate metal. For those materials that microwave energy can penetrate, lower-frequency microwave energy has a greater penetration ability than do higher frequencies. It follows that if it is desirable to detect motion behind partitions or walls invisible to microwave energy, detectors that operate at the lowest designated microwave frequency of 915 MHz should be selected.

An advantage of using microwave detectors to protect the shop areas in East City High is that the microwave energy will penetrate the Sheetrock partitions between the shop equipment and thereby detect motion anywhere in the shop. A disadvantage is that the low-frequency radiated energy can penetrate the exterior walls, doors, and windows and cause false alarms if the detectors are improperly positioned. For this reason, the microwave detectors in the shops are installed near the ceiling and pointed down toward the floor. In this position they provide adequate energy to detect motion near the exterior walls without causing penetration problems and possible false alarms from external activities.

If the detectors were pointed at the exterior walls, an adequate amount of energy might penetrate the doors and windows and cause false alarms from passing vehicles. When the police cruiser or security guard passes close to the rear of the shops, an adequate amount of energy could be reflected back to the detector from the car to initiate an alarm. It is very difficult for the microwave detector to discriminate between the Doppler signal produced by someone moving in the shop and the signal reflected from a passing car.

The microwave detectors in the corridors of East City High are directed away from the exterior doors to eliminate the possibility of energy penetration. Directing the detectors away from the doors in the main corridor, however, results in having two detectors pointing at each other. To eliminate possible radiated interference between these two detectors, the effective range of each microwave detector is limited to cover only one half of the corridor.

The threat to the maintenance garage area was determined to be primarily from unskilled intruders who would attack the exterior doors and windows to gain access to the garage. Therefore, magnetic contact switches will be installed to detect anyone opening either the entrance doors or overhead garage doors. Expanded steel grilles will be installed over all the exterior windows to deter anyone from entering the garage through a window.

In case someone does cut through a window grille or enters the garage undetected, pressure switch mats will be installed under the work mats in front of toolboxes and at the entrance to the test equipment storage room. Pressure mats can be easily defeated, if discovered, simply by not stepping on them. Therefore, it is essential that both the mats and signal wires be well concealed.

For anyone to reach the maintenance garage or any of the vehicles parked inside the compound, he must first penetrate the perimeter fence. It was assumed during the threat analysis that all the intruders who have entered the compound have climbed over or in some way jumped over the fence. Therefore, one of the security requirements was to install an intrusion detection system to detect anyone climbing over the fence. The system should be basically immune to false alarms.

A taut-wire fence detection system that will satisfy the false alarm requirement was selected to detect fence climbers. The taut-wire system consists of mechanical switches that support a single strand of barbed wire held in tension by the system terminators. When anyone pulls or cuts a strand of wire, the switch contact opens and initiates and alarm at the switch monitor. The system is not prone to false alarms because it requires about a 2-inch lateral displacement of the barbed wire to initiate an alarm. A multiple barbed wire fence detection system of this type can be constructed by assembling the switches on vertical columns.

Taut-wire switches will be installed on the outriggers supporting the three strands of barbed wire atop the chain-link fence around the maintenance garage compound. Each barbed wire strand will be supported by either a switch or an eyelet on every outrigger and terminated at the corner fence post. The completed system will be divided into four detection zones, one for each side of the compound.

The switch signal wires from each zone of sensors will be routed along the fence in metal conduit to the switch signal processor and alarm display located in the supervisor's office in the garage. The processor will separately monitor, annunciate, and display each alarm. In this way, if anyone climbs over the fence during the day, the shop supervisor will be alerted to the intrusion and the side where the intruder crossed. At night or when the system is in secure mode, the alarm zones will be collectively monitored and annunciated at the system monitoring station in the administration building. During this time the operator needs only to know that someone entered the compound. By the time the police arrive at the compound, the exact side the intruder crossed is insignificant. The important thing is that the intruder was detected climbing over the fence. Of course, if the intruder climbed something and jumped the fence without stepping on a barbed wire strand, or if he cut through the fence fabric, he would not be detected.

The fences around the two bus parking lots will also have taut-wire detection systems to detect anyone climbing over the fence. The only difference between these systems and the maintenance garage fence detection system is the location of the signal processor unit. Since there is no garage at either of these areas, the processor will be installed inside a weather-resistant enclosure. The electronic processor is designed to be used inside, protected from extreme weather conditions. For this reason, thermostatically controlled strip heaters will be installed inside the enclosure to maintain the temperature above $-20°F$ in the winter. A sunshield will be installed above the enclosure, and a blower will be installed inside to circulate the air over the critical electronic circuitry if the enclosure temperature should exceed $120°F$.

Alarm Monitoring System Selection

Selection of a monitoring system depends primarily on the number of protected areas reporting to the monitoring station, the availability of communication channels between the protected areas and the alarm monitoring station, and the required level of communications supervision. Other criteria are the type of display desired for the security status information and the need for an alarm assessment capability.

Communication channels to be considered include telephone, microwave, hard-wired or metallic lines, radio, and fiber optics. Telephone networks use all these communication channels except radio. Even radio is used to some extent for mobile telephones. Metallic lines constitute the major portion of the telephone networks, but complete networks of metallic lines are becoming extinct in many telephone exchanges. For this reason, DC and McCulloh transmission systems are becoming obsolete for control station applications. But DC systems are very popular for alarm transmission in proprietary-type applications where the transmission lines are not routed through the local telephone network.

Fiber-optic communication systems are becoming popular in the communications industry because fiber-optic cables are more economical to produce than copper cables and have other distinct advantages. For example, the diameter of the fibers is much less than that of copper wire, resulting in a smaller diameter multiple conductor transmission cable. An additional practical advantage of fiber-optic communication is that it is immune to electromagnetic interference on the signal lines. The fiber cables are fabricated from glass to pass the transmitted light or infrared signals. Glass is not an electrical conductor; therefore, electromagnetic energy from sources such as lightning, power cables, and radio stations will not distort or interfere with the light signals being transmitted over the fiber cables. This feature is especially important for a security alarm transmission system where any interference with communication could result in false alarms.

Besides the operational immunity to false alarms caused by electromagnetic interference, fiber-optic transmission systems are being developed for alarm transmission because they are difficult to compromise. The size of the fine fiber-optic lines makes them difficult to isolate and manipulate.

Both radio and telephone communication channels were considered for the hypothetical school complex alarm transmission system. Radio systems were eliminated because of the transmission difficulties between the alarm monitoring station in the administration building and some of the city schools. The tall buildings in the neighborhood prevented satisfactory radio communication.

All the schools and supporting facilities in the hypothetical school complex have telephone lines available for alarm transmission. A single dedicated line can be made available for the alarm transmission system in all the facilities, but all-metallic circuits are not available. This eliminates the use of DC and McCulloh transmission systems. Alternating current transmission systems also are eliminated because each school has several separate detection zones, and only one dedicated telephone line can be made available at each school. Alternating current systems require a dedicated voice-grade telephone line, not necessarily metallic lines, between the monitoring station and each detection zone.

The second consideration when selecting an alarm transmission system is signal line supervision. Since the level of threat to the hypothetical complex is judged to be unskilled or at most semiskilled, neither a high level of line supervision nor continuous line supervision is required. Although continuous line supervision is not required, the system should be capable of periodically reporting to the alarm monitoring station for a system operational check.

Digital dialers, or digital communicators as they are called by many manufacturers, satisfy all these operational requirements, as do multiplex transmission systems. But digital dialers were selected as the alarm transmission and monitoring system for the school complex because they can communicate over the existing telephone exchange. They construct the security status message in binary logic and transmit it over voice-grade telephone lines. This means that dedicated telephone lines will not be required in each of the school facilities.

With respect to the third selection consideration, the digital dialer will display the security access/secure and alarm status information on the front panel of the monitoring receiver and record the information on a paper tape printer. Each facility in the hypothetical school complex will be assigned a separate numeric identification number for each detection zone. This is the number that will be displayed and printed by the monitoring receiver to identify the location where the alarm or security status change occurred.

A map of the city will be installed on the wall in the radio communication and alarm monitoring room in the administration building. Each protected facility in the school complex will be identified on the map. The numeric identification numbers assigned to each facility will be listed along with its name. The map will assist the system operator in relating numeric identification numbers to the proper facilities.

The map will not, however, show individual facility detection zones. Therefore, individual drawings showing the basic outline of each facility and its detection zones with their numeric identification numbers will be bound in a loose-leaf notebook. Each drawing will be tabbed so that it can be located quickly. Then, in case of an alarm, the monitoring operator can identify the individual detection zone for the responding security officer.

The fourth selection consideration, alarm assessment, also is available with the digital dialer system. The dialer provides two-way communication between the transceiver in the alarm monitoring station and the digital dialers in the protected facilities. Two-way communication allows acknowledge and reset commands to be transmitted between the transceiver and the dialers. Once the communication channel has been established through the telephone exchange and the security message communicated, the same telephone line can be used to listen in through the receivers in the schools for noises that might verify that someone is in the school.

The digital dialer alarm transmission and monitoring system, in conjunction with the map display and individual facility detection zone drawings, provides an effective alarm monitoring system. When there is an intrusion alarm at any of the hypothetical school facilities, an alarm will be annunciated and displayed by the digital dialer transceiver and printed on the event recorder. The monitoring operator will focus on the displayed alarm zone identification number and then relate it to the corresponding protected facility using the large city map displayed on the monitoring room wall adjacent to the transceiver. Once the intruded facility has been identified, the operator will radio the school security officer on duty in that district and alert him to the alarm. He will then alert the local police.

If the alarm is initiated at a school, the operator will listen in for noises in the school to verify the validity of the alarm. Then using the notebook with the school outline drawings showing the individual zones of detection, he will index to the proper school and find the detection zone in alarm. This information will be radioed to the responding security officer to assist him in responding to the proper location at the school. With a trained monitoring operator, the complete series of events following the initial alarm annunciation should take only a few minutes to complete.

In operation, East City High will require four digital dialers to report individual detection zones needed to satisfy the normal school day and adult education schedule. During the site survey it was determined that the library and principal's office were closed every day about 5 P.M.; therefore, they will be connected to one four-zone digital dialer. With the four-zone identification capability, the ultrasonic motion detectors in the principal's office and the library and the magnetic switches on the doors of the rooms can be individually reported and identified at the monitoring transceiver.

Besides identifying the detection zones, having the capability to identify individual detectors will often assist the operator in judging the validity of an intrusion alarm. For instance, if there is an alarm from the door contact switch at the principal's office followed by an alarm from the ultrasonic motion detector inside the room after resetting the first alarm, the probability of someone being in the office is very high. In this case the security guard and police should be dispatched to the school, even if the alarm validity cannot be verified by listening for noises.

The auto shop, machine shop, and typing room will be connected to an eight-zone dialer. These three areas are connected to the same dialer because they are used every night when the adult education classes meet. The microwave motion detectors in each shop, the ultrasonic motion detector in the typing room, and the magnetic contact switches on the entrance doors to each room will be connected separately in the eight-zone dialer. This arrangement will provide the monitoring operator with separate zone identification, while accommodating the adult education class schedule.

The band instrument storage room and the video and motion picture equipment storage room will be in zones 1 and 2, respectively, of a single dual zone digital dialer. These two rooms are normally locked and opened only by authorized personnel. Depending on the demand, the rooms could be opened and closed many times during the day. To eliminate the need to transmit each opening and closing to the monitoring station, the dialer will be modified to have a remote display located in the principal's office. The display will annunciate and identify the alarm when the rooms are opened during normal school hours.

The remote display will be activated in the morning when the status of the digital dialer monitoring the band instrument and equipment storage rooms is switched from secure to access. With this modification the principal's office will be alerted when anyone opens the door and enters either room. A television camera will be installed in each room to view the entrance door. Corresponding television monitors for the two rooms will be installed in the principal's office. With this arrangement, when anyone enters the band room or audiovisual equipment storage room during the day, an alarm will be annunciated at the display to alert personnel in the principal's office that someone has entered one of the rooms. The office person can then use the television to identify the person who entered the room. During the evening hours when the digital dialer is in the secure mode, the standard opening and closing procedures will apply.

The fourth digital dialer will monitor and separately identify each of the four microwave motion detectors covering the corridors. The magnetic door switches on the exterior doors will be connected to the remaining four zones of the eight-zone dialer. The front door to East City High will be connected to the fifth zone, the east side door to the sixth zone, the two doors on the east side of the gymnasium to the seventh zone, and the two doors on the west side to the eighth zone. With the detection zones identified in this manner, the responding security officer and the police will know where to respond. The zones of detection will be established in a similar manner for the remaining schools.

The maintenance garage sensors will be connected to a dual-zone digital dialer. One zone will identify the door contact switches and pressure mats. The second zone will collectively identify the four zones of the taut-wire fence system. Single fence zone identification is desirable at the garage so that if anyone climbs over the fence during working hours, the supervisor will know which fence the intruder crossed. But when the garage is closed, single fence zone identification will not necessarily assist the responding police. By the time the police reach the garage facility, the intruder could be anywhere in the compound. With the garage and fence systems on separate digital dialer identification zones, the monitoring operator will know when someone climbs over the fence or enters the garage.

The four taut-wire sensor zones around the two parking areas will be monitored by a separate digital dialer at each site. Digital dialers are designed to operate indoors; therefore, they will be installed inside the heated weatherproof enclosure at each site, along with the taut-wire signal processor.

A primary consideration when designing an alarm monitoring system is the alarm transmission traffic to the monitoring station. This is especially true during peak transmission periods, when the number of messages could easily exceed the storage and display capacity of the receiver. For instance, in the hypothetical school complex, if the digital dialers communicated the opening of each and every school about 8 A.M. and the closing about 5 P.M., the transceiver in the monitoring station would be overwhelmed processing the messages. If there should be a bona fide alarm at one of the facilities during these times, it might not be received at the monitoring station. Therefore, to reduce the number of messages being transmitted, school openings after 7 A.M. and closings before 5 P.M. will not be reported to the monitoring station.

One advantage of having the digital dialers report daily openings and closings is to provide a daily system operational check for each dialer. Without this report the dialer might sit for weeks or even months without reporting to the monitoring station. To eliminate the long periods of idleness, a daily operational report will be programmed for the digital dialers used in the hypothetical school complex facilities. The dialers will be programmed to report a system test message to the transceiver daily. The reporting times for each dialer will be scheduled during the normally quiet hours each night when the school telephone lines are available. The reporting times will be assigned so that the transceiver will be capable of receiving all alarm messages. Operationally testing the digital dialers daily assures the monitoring operator that the dialers are functioning properly; this should increase confidence in the system.

The application of digital dialers can be expanded beyond just monitoring and reporting intrusion alarms and openings and closings. They can be used to monitor fire detectors, temperature and pressure gauges, or any sensing device that can activate an electrical relay or switch. It is planned to install fire detectors in all the hypothetical school facilities. They will be monitored by separate dialers in each facility. Multiple-zone dialers will be used because the fire detectors should be zoned in a manner similar to the intrusion detectors to identify any fire location for the responding fire department. It is also planned to monitor the refrigerator temperatures in each of the school cafeterias.

Response Force Functions

A primary consideration when designing an intrusion detection system is to determine who will monitor the system security status and respond to intrusion alarms. The manner of monitoring the system security status will likely influence the choice of the response force. For instance, if a commercial central station is selected to perform the monitoring function, its guards will probably respond to intrusions. The function of the security guards will depend on whether they are licensed and on the legal jurisdiction that accompanies any license. Since the jurisdiction varies between states, the functions and responsibilities of the security guards should be thoroughly reviewed with the contractor to ensure that they satisfy the security requirements. Also, if establishing a proprietary guard force is planned, it is prudent to obtain legal counsel or at least review the planned procedures for handling intruders with the local law enforcement agency.

In the hypothetical school complex, there are 86 facilities and about 135 detection zones that will require monitoring. Since normal openings and closings will not be reported, the system operator will only have to answer calls for early openings and late closings. With this operating procedure, monitoring the 85 facilities should be within the operating capability of the radio operator. For this reason, the radio operator will perform the monitoring function along with his other duties.

When there is an alarm at one of the schools or other facilities, the operator will contact the security guard in the district where the alarm originated. If the alarm is at a high school where there are multiple detection zones, the operator will pinpoint the alarm location inside the school for the benefit of the responding security guard. Knowing the intruder's location inside the school, the security officer can respond and guard the door where he thinks the intruder will exit. Then when the local police arrive, the security officer will open the school and assist the police in the search.

Contingency procedures have been established to manage security in the event of system failures. If there is a major power failure that exceeds the 4-hour operational capability of the equipment standby batteries, then the security guard duty schedule will be extended to increase the frequency of school patrols. Also, if the digital dialer's monitoring transceiver fails, the guard patrols will be increased. When there is a major equipment failure, the maintenance technician is immediately called in. Since the transceiver circuit is modular in design with convenient test points, the technician will only have to identify and replace the defective circuit. With a modular design, it should not take the technician long to diagnose and repair the transceiver trouble.

If there is a nighttime failure of a digital dialer at one of the schools or other facilities, the seriousness of the failure does not justify calling in the technician immediately. The repair can be made during normal working hours, but the security guard in the district where the failure occurred will be alerted so that he can increase his patrols of the affected facility.

The security response team, which might be composed of security guards, police, and military personnel in the case of military installations, is the most critical element in any successful security system. A building or area can be constructed with the most resistant materials, have the most effective locks to resist penetration and improve delay, and have the best intrusion detection and monitoring system to detect and report intrusions, but if response to the intrusion alarms is not swift and forceful, delay and detection are useless, except as a deterrent to low-level threats. Intrusion detection systems improve the effectiveness of the response team by alerting it to intrusions that might otherwise go unnoticed until after the purpose of the intrusion is accomplished. The real protection must be provided by the response team.

SUMMARY

A physical security system should be designed to deter, delay, and/or detect intruders who pose a threat to the items or facilities requiring protection. In some cases the nature and sophistication of the threat can be analyzed based on past or related experience. For instance, the threat to the hypothetical school complex was established by reviewing the history of security problems at each of the facilities.

In many cases, however, the areas requiring protection do not have a history of security problems to analyze. In these cases it is necessary to analyze the possible motivation of the threat to anticipate the sophistication of the intruders. For example, the threat to nuclear weapon sites and nuclear utilities cannot be identified. It is, however, assumed that these sites have a high value to groups trying to sway public opinion or attempting to force a desired concession on the part of a government, institution, or individual.

Therefore, the security system, and the intrusion detection system in particular, must be capable of protecting these sites from the most sophisticated team of intruders.

Once the threat has been analyzed and the skill level established, a site survey of the facility or area requiring protection should be conducted. The facility should be thoroughly examined from the perimeter to the sensitive area or item requiring protection. The survey should be conducted keeping in mind the nature and sophistication of the threat. In areas where the threat is unsophisticated, site vulnerabilities can usually be identified and corrected, such as with the hypothetical school complex. But in areas where the threat is assumed to be a highly skilled team, scenarios that could realistically be executed by the anticipated threat should be considered, while examining every aspect of the facility. If the site survey is conducted in this manner, many vulnerabilities that might otherwise be overlooked will be identified.

During the site survey but after the vulnerability has been identified, the appropriate security measures to correct the vulnerabilities must be designed and implemented. Assuming that one of the security measures is to install an intrusion detection system, the facility should then be surveyed for the appropriate types of sensors and an alarm monitoring system that will detect the anticipated intruder. A knowledge of the basic principles of operation and application of the available types of security equipment is required to accomplish this task. With this knowledge, sensors can be selected that will operate satisfactorily in the site environment while satisfying the security detection requirements.

The intrusion detection system design should be coordinated during the design phase with those people who must operationally support the system after it is installed. These people include not only those in maintenance who are responsible for ensuring the operational readiness of the system, but also those people who are operationally responsible for the areas where the sensors and equipment are being installed. These are the people who must properly access and secure the system and the ones who might be limited in their operation because of the system. They might be limited because of the particular motion sensor coverage or because of the placement of the equipment. Preliminary coordination could eliminate potential problems that might otherwise restrict the effectiveness of the system.

The intrusion detection system also must have management support—not only financial support but also judicial support for the security officers' enforcing of the security procedures. Financial support is certainly needed to implement the system, but it is also needed to operate and maintain it. Training is an essential part of this function, and it is often neglected by management for financial reasons. Training is especially important for the maintenance personnel who must maintain the intrusion detection system. It is also important for the security officers who are responsible for operating the system and enforcing the security procedures. Without total management support, not only will the effectiveness of the intrusion system be compromised, but the effectiveness of the security force in executing the security functions will be questionable.

Chapter 29

Nuclear Reactor Plant

A nuclear reactor plant was selected to illustrate the rationale for selecting a specific type of perimeter intrusion detector because every nuclear plant must have perimeter protection to be licensed by the NRC.

Every nuclear reactor plant is required to comply with the rules and regulations set forth in Title 10, Chapter 1, Code of Federal Regulations-Energy, Part 73, "Physical Protection of Plants and Materials." Part 73 covers a number of requirements, but this chapter on selecting perimeter intrusion detection systems will pertain only to section 73.55—"Requirements for physical protection of licensed activities in nuclear power reactors against radiological sabotage." This section sets forth the requirements for:

a. Physical security organization
b. Physical barriers
c. Access requirements
d. Detection aids
e. Communication requirements
f. Testing and maintenance
g. Response requirements

The perimeter security system design will address in particular the requirements set forth in paragraph (b), "Physical barriers," but the remaining requirements will be discussed as they pertain to perimeter security. The requirements in paragraph (b) are as follows:

> (1) The licensee shall locate vital equipment only within a vital area, which in turn, shall be located within a protected area such that access to vital equipment requires passage through at least two physical barriers. More than one vital area may be located within a single protected area.
>
> (2) The physical barrier at the perimeter of the protected area shall be separated from any other barrier designated as a physical barrier within the protected area, and the intervening space monitored or periodically checked to detect the presence of persons or vehicles so that the facility security organization can respond to suspicious activity or to the breaching of any physical barrier.

(3) An isolation zone shall be maintained around the physical barrier at the perimeter of the protected area and any part of a building used as part of that physical barrier. The isolation zone shall be monitored to detect the presence of individuals or vehicles within the zone so as to allow response by armed members of the licensee security organization to be initiated at the time of penetration of the protected area. Parking facilities, both for employees and visitors, shall be located outside the isolation zone.

(4) Isolation zones and clear areas between barriers shall be provided with illumination sufficient for the monitoring and observation requirements of paragraphs (b) (2), (b) (3) and (g) (3) of this section.

(5) Windows in walls and doors of the control room as well as the doors themselves, shall provide bullet penetration resistance. In addition, a means shall be provided for quickly locking all doors leading into the control room.

The referenced requirement in paragraph (g) (3), "Response requirements," is as follows:

(3) To facilitate initial response to detection of penetration of the protected area and assessment of the possible existence of a threat while affording protection of the security organization members who may be responding, a capability of observing the isolation zone and the clear area adjacent to the physical barrier at the perimeter of the protected area shall be provided, preferably by means of closed circuit television, or by other suitable means which limit exposure of responding personnel to possible attack.

The perimeter intrusion detection system will be designed for the hypothetical nuclear reactor plant shown in Figure 29–1. This plant is located in the northeastern part of the United States along the banks of the Noname River. The power plant and offices are located in the large central building. The reactor is on the right side of the central building adjacent to the power plant, and a warehouse is on the left side. The water inlet station is located behind the plant on the river bank. These structures are connected by a road that enters the compound next to the entrance building. An electrically operated gate that is controlled from the entrance building limits traffic into the plant.

PHYSICAL BARRIERS

The entire compound, including the work area around the outside of the water inlet station, is enclosed by a 10-foot chain-link fence. The fence has 45-degree outriggers supporting three strands of barbed wire. The barbed wire topping extends the effective height of the fence to 11 feet. The fence fabric is constructed from No. 9 AWG galvanized coated steel wire. The fence posts are spaced on about 10-foot centers and are set in concrete to a depth that exceeds the frost line. Extending the fence post foundation below the frost line reduces the fence movement, especially during spring thaws.

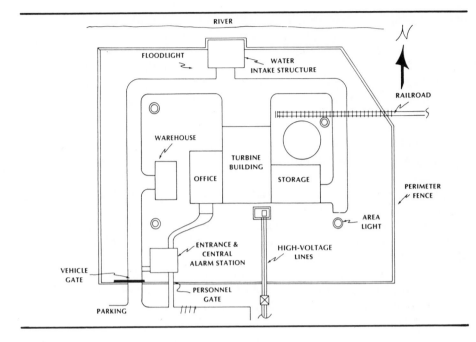

Figure 29–1 Hypothetical reactor plant.

The first requirement under (b), "Physical barriers," requires that vital areas be located inside of at least two physical barriers. Although a standard 7-foot chain-link fence, topped with barbed wire, around the perimeter would satisfy this requirement for the outer barrier, it has been demonstrated by the U.S. Army that such a fence can be crossed in about 3 seconds by an unassisted agile person. Raising the height of the fence to 10 feet will increase its effectiveness against climbing because the average person cannot simply grab the outrigger and quickly pull himself over the fence, as he can with a 7-foot fence. A climb-over penetration of a 10-foot fence would be more deliberate and easier to detect.

Fences also can be penetrated by lifting the fabric and crawling under or by cutting the fence fabric and crawling through. Unless the bottom of the fence is well anchored, anyone using a lever can lift the fence fabric and crawl under. Therefore, the bottom of the fence around the hypothetical reactor plant is anchored to a bottom rail as well as a top rail. While it is common practice to tie the fabric to the rails only about every 1½ to 2 feet, the fabric should be tied to the bottom rail about every 6 inches. This will prevent someone from simply cutting one tie and lifting the fabric over the rail far enough for a partner to crawl over the bottom rail and under the fabric.

To satisfy the second requirement under paragraph (b), the perimeter fence should be separated from all other barriers or structures. This way the facility security organization can respond to suspicious activity or to the breaching of any portion of the fence. The only barrier with which the fence perimeter comes in contact is the water inlet structure. Here the fence is secured to the inlet structure and is routed up the wall, which is about 5 feet above the fence, then around the front of the structure to the opposite side. Here the fence is routed down the wall and continues around the perimeter. In this location around the water inlet structure, the fence not only serves as a physical barrier for security, but it also serves as a safety barrier to prevent someone from falling off the structure into the river.

ISOLATION ZONE MONITORING

To comply with the third requirement of paragraph (b), an isolation zone will be maintained along the perimeter fence around the hypothetical reactor plant. A perimeter intrusion detection system will be installed within the isolation zone to detect the presence of individuals or vehicles. All sensor alarms will be annunciated and displayed by a monitor in both a central alarm station (CAS) located in the entrance building and a secondary alarm station (SAS) located in the main building. The monitor will alert the security operator of anyone penetrating the protected zone in time to allow response by armed members of the licensed security organization.

Perimeter Protection System Selection Analyses

The selection of a perimeter detection system for a particular application depends on the perimeter fence configuration and structural condition, terrain contour, vegetation around the perimeter, physical objects within the protected area, operations in and around the detectors, animals in the sensors' area of detection, and environmental conditions. For this hypothetical reactor plant, the fence is in excellent condition, and the fence lines are straight. The area inside the fence is clear of obstacles, except for the floodlight poles, which are installed about 20 feet inside the fence at the corners.

The terrain around the plant is generally level; however, it does drop off on the river side outside the perimeter road. The west side of the site is level along the fence from the front to within about 200 feet of the river. At this point the ground starts gradually sloping down until it is within about 15 feet of the river, where it drops another 15 feet to the river. The east side of the site is very similar to the west side, except the ground starts sloping closer to the front fence. The ground inside the fence and the area about 100 feet outside the perimeter fence is grass covered and well maintained.

In this application example, obstacles inside or outside the perimeter for at least 20 feet, other than lamp posts, which are too thin to hide behind, would be in violation of the isolation zone requirement of Part 73, paragraph 73.55 (b) 3. For other applications of perimeter intrusion detection systems, however, obstacles along the perimeter are very much a consideration when selecting perimeter sensors.

All plant operations are conducted inside the perimeter road, except for grounds maintenance, such as grass cutting and snow removal from the fence if drifting becomes a problem. With the snow accumulation and drifting occurring each winter at this site, microwave or infrared detectors would not be considered for the perimeter intrusion detection system. If one of these detectors were selected, accumulated wet snow or crusted snow deeper than 6 inches would have to be removed to maintain a high probability of detecting low-crawling or rolling intruders. This is not practical on a frequent basis for long or multiple zones of detection.

Operations, especially maintenance operations, should be considered when designing any perimeter intrusion detection system. If ground maintenance is considered in the sensor installation design, the inconvenience of having the detector along the perimeter can sometimes be minimized. For instance, if microwave detectors are selected to protect a perimeter, the concrete foundation for the detector's mounting column should be formed to extend out past the antenna at ground level far enough so that a mower can conveniently cut around the detector. If it is inconvenient to extend the concrete foundation, the area around the detector can be covered by asphalt. Also, the detector should be installed far enough away from the perimeter fence so that the mower can pass between the detector and fence.

Animals crossing the sensor zone of detection can cause severe false alarms or nuisance alarm problems, especially if the animals are large, such as cows, horses, or deer. It is very difficult for any perimeter sensor to distinguish between a man and a large animal. Smaller animals, such as dogs, rabbits, foxes, and birds, can cause nuisance alarm problems with microwave and infrared detectors. Microwave detectors that initiate an alarm only when there is a significant or total interruption of the beams are usually not bothered by small animals. But the more sensitive detectors can detect the smaller animals, depending on their position and motion in the zone of detection.

Infrared detectors also are sensitive to small animals because they are designed to initiate an alarm when the bottom beam is interrupted. The bottom beam detects low-crawling intruders, so it must initiate an alarm when it is interrupted. If animals are a problem, provision must be made either to get rid of them or to limit their access to the sensor area by installing another fence inside the infrared detector zones of detection.

In exterior sensor applications the environmental conditions include both man-made and climate-induced conditions that the sensors must survive. The most severe man-made condition at the hypothetical plant that might affect a sensor's performance is the large electromagnetic field generated under the high-voltage power lines exiting the plant on the south side. This electromagnetic field can induce electrical signals in the alarm transmission lines, detector power lines, or detector signal processors that could cause severe operational or false alarm problems. The electromagnetic interference (EMI) problem is most severe when the sensor line is positioned close to and in line with or parallel to the power lines.

At the hypothetical reactor plant, the power lines are perpendicular to the perimeter, which minimizes the EMI problem. The selection and placement of the sensors under the power lines still could be critical, however. If there is any doubt about a particular sensor's performance in this location, the candidate sensor or sensors should be temporarily installed and tested under the power lines before a final selection is made.

Climatic conditions are usually the most severe operating conditions that a perimeter intrusion detection system has to survive. In some applications severe climatic conditions might be seasonal. Unfortunately, the problem is year-round, for the hypothetical nuclear reactor plant is located in the northeastern United States. In this part of the country, the sensors have to survive winter cold, snow, and ice; spring rain, wind, and ground thaws; and summer heat and fog. If the sensors can perform reliably during these seasons, they can survive fall, except perhaps in some areas where falling and blowing leaves could initiate alarms if they interrupt the beams of an infrared detector.

Winter temperatures in the area of the hypothetical plant are about 15°F on the average, but it can get as cold as −40°F. Most exterior intrusion detection sensors will operate at temperatures only down to −30°F. Low temperatures most often limit the operation of the exterior detector electronics and not the detector transducers. Therefore, for the electronic assemblies to operate in the extreme winter cold at the hypothetical plant, thermostatically controlled heaters are required in any exposed electronics enclosures. Strip heaters or even lamps can be installed within such enclosures to maintain the temperature above −30°F.

Winter cold not only affects the electronics operation, but it also freezes the ground to depths of about 3 feet. Deeper frost lines have been measured in the area during extremely cold winters. Frozen ground usually does not affect microwave and infrared detector beam alignment once the ground is frozen. But during freezing, the ground expands, causing heaving that can move about anything that is not well anchored. As with the fence post installation, the beam-forming detector mounting column's foundation should extend well below the frost line to prevent or minimize misalignment. Proper installation of infrared detectors is especially important because the infrared beam is narrow and minor misalignment of either the transmitter or receiver column can redirect the beam until the detector is inoperative. Ground movement during the spring thaw causes the same alignment problems to occur. Therefore, the foundation design for infrared and microwave detector mounting columns is extremely important when these detectors are used in areas where the ground freezes.

A seasonal problem associated with accumulated snow is that during the day it might melt and then refreeze at night, causing severe icing. Icing also can accompany winter rains. Icing can be both operationally and physically hazardous to sensors. Ice forming on the radome of microwave detectors can distort or block the energy pattern until the detector will not function. Ice forming over the lens of an infrared detector will have similar results. Depending on the amount, ice can physically damage the sense and field wires of an electric-field sensor.

After surviving winter cold, ice, and snow, spring comes, bringing rain, wind, and ground thaws. Moderate rains are usually not a problem, but heavy rain can reduce the level of infrared energy transmitted to the infrared receiver to a degree that the detector will not function. Therefore, in areas of heavy rain, an infrared detector's operating range might have to be reduced below the manufacturer's specified maximum operating range to compensate for reduced infrared energy caused by the rain. About the only detectors affected by wind, other than high-velocity destructive winds, are fence disturbance sensors and sometimes seismic sensors. Winds above 25 mph often induce vibrations in the fence fabric that can cause alarms. Blowing trees and poles also induce seismic energy in the ground that can cause alarms. For this reason, seismic sensors should be installed at least 30 feet from tree lines and lamp poles.

The summer environment in the northeastern part of the United States is usually pleasant, causing few, if any, sensor operating problems. Because the hypothetical plant is located close to the Noname River, fog could be a problem, as it could affect the maximum operating range of infrared barrier detectors. Although the summer environment is mild in the Northeast, the summer heat in hotter parts of the country can cause severe sensor operational problems. As with the cold, heat primarily affects the signal processing circuitry. Exterior sensors will usually operate in temperatures up to 140°F. The temperature can easily exceed this limit inside an electronics enclosure if the equipment is exposed to the sun. Installing a sunshield over the enclosure is beneficial and might be adequate to reduce the enclosure temperature to acceptable levels.

Intrusion Detection System Selection Guidance

The NRC has developed Regulatory Guide 5.44, "Perimeter Intrusion Alarm Systems," to be used as a guide for selecting perimeter detectors. It describes six types of perimeter intrusion alarm systems and establishes acceptable performance criteria. The selection of a perimeter intrusion alarm system for the hypothetical plant shown in Figure 29–1 will be made using the guidelines in Guide 5.44. The description of each type of sensor will follow the guidelines with a rationale for either selecting or rejecting each type of system for this application.

An intrusion detection system generally consists of one or more line sensors or a number of transmitter and receiver combinations. Depending on the type of system, an intruder is detected when he comes in contact with a protected fence or crosses an invisible barrier or sensitive area along the ground. The proper detection probability for a detection system, as defined in Guide 5.44, is defined as the ability to detect an intruder with at least 90 percent probability for each segment of the isolation zone under the conditions stated in the performance criteria of each type of alarm system.

A brief description of each type of perimeter detector system will precede the rationale for selecting or rejecting that system.

Microwave Perimeter Alarm System

A microwave perimeter alarm system consists of a transmitter and receiver, along with a signal processor, alarm signal transmission system and power supply assembly, and a monitor. The microwave transmitter generates an electromagnetic energy pattern that is directed to a corresponding receiver. The receiver is located in the transmitter's line of sight but at the opposite end of the protected zone. A partial or total interruption of the microwave beam, or in some detectors, a distortion of the transmitted energy pattern, will initiate an alarm.

Rationale.   Microwave detectors were *not selected* to protect the hypothetical plant perimeter because the microwave energy will not penetrate wet or ice-crusted snow to detect crawling intruders. If the plant were located farther south, where there would be little or no snow accumulation, microwave detectors could be used to protect the perimeter along the level portions of the site on the east, south, and west sides. Using microwave detectors would be a good way to protect the perimeter under the high-voltage power lines. Assuming the zone length was limited to about 300 feet, the zone limits could be chosen so that the transmitter and corresponding receiver were equidistant from the power lines. This arrangement would minimize the effect the electromagnetic field associated with the power lines would have on the signal processor. Of course, the signal lines passing under the power lines should be shielded.

If microwave detectors were used to protect the perimeter, each transmitter/receiver zone would be overlapped far enough to prevent someone from crawling under the microwave pattern near the transmitter or receiver. Also, the detectors should be installed far enough away from the chain-link fence so that someone could not jump over the microwave beam from the fence top. This distance also should be far enough so that the reflected microwave energy from the fence or from passing vehicles on the nearby roads will not interfere with detector operation.

Microwave detectors are, however, used to protect the vehicle and personnel entrance into the hypothetical plant. In this application, and when microwave systems are installed in accordance with the manufacturer's instructions, they should be capable of detecting in accordance with the performance criteria. It requires that an intruder be detected passing between the transmitter and receiver at a rate between 0.5 and 16 feet per second, whether walking, running, jumping, crawling, or rolling.

Electric-Field Perimeter Alarm System

An electric-field perimeter alarm system consists basically of a field genera-tor, which excites a field wire or wires, and a combination of sense wires. In operation, the field wire generates a radical electric field along the length of the wire. Anyone approaching the wire array distorts the electric field, inducing an electrical signal in the sensing wires. If the induced signals are within the bandpass of human movement, an alarm is initiated.

Rationale. Electric-field systems were *not selected* to protect the hypothet-ical nuclear plant perimeter because of the heavy snow accumulation and drifting and the severe winter icing conditions. With the electric field installed on or near the perimeter fence, it would be very difficult to remove deep snow drifts along the inside of the fence without damaging the electric-field array. The field and sense wires would be vulnerable to breakage during snow removal. Heavy icing also might cause the sense and field wires to break, especially if high winds followed the icing.

The electric-field system will operate in snow, so if heavy snow accum-ulation and icing were not a problem, it could be used to protect the perim-eter. It would be especially effective along the fence line behind the plant where the ground is not level. The electric-field system is not a line-of-sight system and therefore can be installed along uneven terrain. The system can be mounted on fence-mounted insulated standoffs, or it can be mounted on separate posts to form a separate protective barrier away from the fence. The fence-mounted system has the advantage of following the fence line and occupying very little space inside the fence.

Electric-field systems used for personnel detection in the isolation zone around a nuclear reactor plant should consist of a minimum of one field wire and two sensing wires. When the system is installed in accordance with the manufacturer's installation instructions, it should be able to detect an indi-vidual weighing a minimum of 77 pounds, crawling and rolling under the lower sensing wire, stepping and jumping between the field and sensing wires, and jumping over the top sensing wire.

Ferrous Metal Detector Perimeter Alarm System

A ferrous metal detector system basically consists of a buried sensor cable, signal processor, power supply, and annunciator. The sensor cable is sensi-tive to changes in the earth's ambient magnetic field caused by ferrous metal being carried over the buried cables. Changes in the local ambient magnetic field induce a current in the buried cable, which is filtered and processed in the signal processor. When the induced signals exceed a predetermined threshold, an alarm is generated. The detector also is sensitive to changes in the ambient magnetic field caused by lightning, electrical power transmis-sion lines, or any high-energy source of electromagnetic energy. To minimize the effects of these extraneous sources of energy, the sensor cable is installed in the ground in a pattern forming loops, which are transposed at regular intervals. An optional inhibitor loop also can be used, along with transposing the sensor cable loops to reduce nuisance alarms from electromagnetic interference.

Rationale.   The ferrous metal detector was *not selected* to protect the hypothetical nuclear plant perimeter. In deep snow, someone walking on top of the snow might cross the sensor line without being detected. Ferrous metal detectors could be used in areas where there is less of a chance of the detector being bridged. They also can be used successfully in areas where there is minimum lightning and no strong source of electromagnetic energy close to the sensor line.

Ferrous metal detectors have several advantages. They are buried in the ground, where they will not interfere with site maintenance. Since they are buried, their exact location is not evident to an intruder. This makes the systems more difficult to bridge. Another, and probably the most significant, advantage is that ferrous metal detectors are not affected by animals unless there is metal on the animals, such as iron shoes on horses. For this reason, the detector can be used outside of a perimeter fence to detect anyone approaching the perimeter. In remote areas this would provide additional time for the response force to get to the perimeter.

Pressure/Strain-Sensitive Perimeter Alarm System

Buried pressure/strain sensors are designed to detect ground vibrations that occur when an individual passes above the sensors. Signals exceeding a pre-established threshold are processed by the signal processor, which then generates an alarm. Guide 5.44 states that the detector transducer may be a set of piezoelectric crystals, a fluid-filled flexible tube, a specially fabricated stress/strain electrical cable, or an insulated wire in a metal tube.

Rationale.   The guide does not mention geophone transducers, which also detect mechanical vibrations induced in the ground by anyone crossing the sensitive area in the proximity of the sensor line.

The strain-type detector system using geophone transducers is one of the sensor systems *selected* to protect the perimeter of the hypothetical plant. Geophones are very responsive to mechanically induced strain and seismic energy and are therefore sensitive to wind overpressure and wind-induced vibrations from the tree roots. But with the proper bandpass filters and signal processing, which the signal processor for the seismic sensor protecting the hypothetical plant will have, nuisance alarms caused by wind can be reduced.

Pressure/strain/seismic sensors do not require line-of-sight installation and can, therefore, be installed in uneven terrain. Installation of some types of traducers in rocky soil might, however, result in damage to the detector transducers. For this reason, the manufacturers and most buried line sensors recommend that the transducer line be installed between two layers of sand or rock-free soil. The sand protects the sensor line and also improves energy transmission between the ground and transducer.

A disadvantage of pressure sensors is that they will lose sensitivity when covered by snow, especially if a crust forms on the snow that will support a man's weight. In this case an individual could cross the sensor line with little chance of being detected by walking on the snow crust, which isolates the intruder from the buried sensor.

In accordance with Guide 5.44, pressure and strain sensors should be capable of detecting an individual weighing more than 77 pounds crossing the sensitive area of the system at a minimum speed of 0.15 miles per second, whether walking, crawling, or rolling.

Additional comments on the selection of a geophone detector system are included later in this chapter under system design.

Infrared Perimeter Alarm System

As in a microwave system, each zone of an infrared system is composed of two transmitter/receiver columns or a separate transmitter and receiver column, a signal processor, and an alarm annunciator. The transmitter in either detector configuration directs a narrow infrared beam of energy to a single dedicated receiver or to several receivers in a single column. If the infrared beam between the transmitter and receiver is interrupted, an alarm is generated. As with the microwave system, the infrared system is line of sight. Since the infrared beam does not diverge as significantly as does the microwave beam, multiple infrared beams between detector columns can be used to define the infrared barrier. When the barrier is penetrated by an individual, an alarm is initiated.

Rationale.   An infrared detector system was *not selected* to protect the perimeter of the hypothetical plant because of the severe snow environment. As mentioned earlier, fot attenuates the infrared beam and can cause nuisance alarms. Dust on the lenses or faceplates also will attenuate the infrared energy, as will an accumulation of condensation, frost, or ice on the faceplate. Heaters are usually installed inside the infrared optics in cold climates to alleviate the condensation and icing problem. Compensation for undesirable attenuation of the infrared energy can usually be achieved by moving the detector columns closer together.

Although the infrared detector was not selected for this application, it can be used in areas where the ground is level and there are no obstructions that will interfere with the energy beams. Because of their narrow, well-defined energy beams, infrared detectors are useful in protecting areas where nearby traffic or plant operations will affect other types of detectors.

Vibration or Strain Detector Perimeter Alarm System

A variety of devices that detect strain or vibrations are available as fence protection systems. These devices detect mechanically induced vibrations, such as those produced by anyone climbing or cutting the fence. In the simplest switch-type detection device, the vibration or strain makes or breaks electrical continuity by closing or opening a fence-mounted switch, and thereby generates an alarm. Detectors using piezoelectric and geophone transducers also are available as fence disturbance sensors.

Rationale.   A fence disturbance detector system *has been selected* along with the geophone detector system to detect penetration of the perimeter around the hypothetical nuclear plant. Fence disturbance sensors are susceptible to nuisance alarms caused by wind vibrating the fence or by hailstones or large pieces of trash or other objects blowing against the fence. Wind-induced nuisance alarms can be reduced by installing the fence rigidly to reduce vibrations. Having rigid fences is important, but the most effective method of reducing nuisance alarms is in the detector's signal processing. Using accumulator circuits in the switch-type fence disturbance detectors and bandpass filtering of the analog signals from the strain-type sensors is the most effective way to reduce nuisance alarms. The fence disturbance system used to detect perimeter penetrations at the hypothetical reactor site uses an accumulator circuit in the signal processor.

Guide 5.44 states that vibration or strain detector systems used for fence protection should detect an intruder weighing more than 77 pounds who is attempting to climb the fence. The system also should detect any attempt to cut the fence or lift the fence more than 6 inches above grade. The system should not generate alarms due to wind vibrations from a wind force of up to 30 miles/hour.

Additional comments on selection of the fence disturbance sensor will be discussed in the section on system design.

Ported Coax Cable Perimeter Alarm System

Guide 5.44 does not include information on ported coax cable sensors at this time, but the guide is being revised and will include this information in future issues.

The perimeter ported coax cable sensor is a buried field disturbance sensor that generates an electromagnetic field between a separate transmit and receive transducer cable. The energy radiates from the transmit cable and is received on the receive cable through small openings in the outer cable conductor. These cables are buried along the perimeter of the site. Anyone crossing the sensor zones produces perturbations in the electromagnetic field, and these are detected by the signal processor.

Rationale.   Although the pressure/strain-sensitive sensor, when used in conjunction with the fence disturbance sensors satisfies the requirements in regulation 73.55, the ported coax cable sensor has been selected to replace the pressure/strain-sensitive sensor in the site upgrade. A distinct advantage of the ported coax cable is that is operates as well in frozen ground as it does in thawed ground. Another advantage is that the low-frequency transmit RF energy, which generates the electromagnetic field, penetrates snow to detect anyone walking on top of it. Of course, if the snow accumulates to 3 or 4 feet, then someone might be able to cross the sensor line undetected. The ported coax cable sensor has the same advantages as any buried sensor: It follows the ground contour, is out of sight, and will not interfere with general maintenance, such as grass cutting or snow removal from around the perimeter.

PERIMETER LIGHTING AND SURVEILLANCE

The fourth requirement in 73.55 (b), "Physical barriers," states that the isolation zones and clear areas between barriers be sufficiently illuminated for monitoring and assessment of any activity in these areas. The fourth requirement of (b) refers to the third requirement of (g), "Response requirements." This requirement states that the security members must have the capability to observe the isolation zones and clear areas. It also states that the preferred means of observing the perimeter is by CCTV or another suitable means that limits exposure of responding personnel to possible attack.

Closed circuit television cameras will be installed around the perimeter fence of the hypothetical nuclear plant to provide the security force the capability to observe the perimeter isolation zones and quickly assess alarm indications. These cameras will be fixed-focus silicon vidicon cameras. They will be installed inside the fence and positioned to look down the fence line. There will be an adequate number of cameras to provide surveillance coverage along the total length of the fenced perimeter isolation zone.

Each camera will be connected to a dedicated video monitor in the CAS of the hypothetical plant. This will allow the CAS operator to observe the scene from any camera at any given time. Of course, having dedicated monitors might be unmanageable for some installations, since the required number of monitors might exceed the allowed space in the monitoring area or the number of monitors might exceed the operational capability of the CAS operator. If this is the case, more than one camera might have to be monitored on a single monitor. In this arrangement the cameras will have to be connected to the monitors through a coaxial switcher. Switchers can automatically sequence from one camera to the next, holding each camera scene on the monitor for only a few seconds, with the time being adjustable by the operator. These switchers also can be manually set to continually display the scene from any one camera. Commandable switchers can switch to a designated camera on command. For instance, a perimeter sensor alarm signal could command the switcher to call up the camera covering the zone protected by the sensor in alarm. The operator could then assess the scene on the monitor to determine the alarm cause.

Adequate illumination is a very important requirement, even for low light level cameras, which have good resolution in very low illumination for observing standing and walking targets. Their ability to provide adequate resolution to assess a low-crawling, camouflaged intruder is, however, limited. For this reason, the illumination level around the perimeter of the hypothetical plant will be a minimum of 1 footcandle within the isolation zones. Another very important lighting requirement, especially for CCTV surveillance, is illumination uniformity. Even illumination of an area is a vital requirement to achieve adequate target resolution where low light levels exist because of the limited intrascene dynamic range of the cameras. To achieve this, the contrast ratio between the light and dark areas at the hypothetical plant will be 3 to 1 on an average, with a maximum ratio of 6 to 1.

High-pressure sodium vapor lighting will be used for the isolation zones and the clear area between the barriers at the hypothetical nuclear reactor plant. The sensitivity and spectral response of the camera's photoconductive silicon target is well matched to the high-pressure sodium vapor lighting.

CONTROL ROOM WINDOWS AND DOORS

The fifth and final requirement of paragraph (b), "Physical barriers," requires the windows and doors of the control room to be made of bulletproof materials. To satisfy this requirement, the control room windows in the hypothetical plant are made of bullet-resistant glass or glass laminate, and the doors are steel laminated. The requirement also states that all doors leading into the control room should have a means of quick locking. Electrically actuated door strikes are installed in all the doors to satisfy this requirement.

PERIMETER SECURITY SYSTEM DESIGN

Selecting the security equipment was the first step in designing the perimeter security system to protect the hypothetical nuclear reactor plant. Normally the first design step is to identify the threat and establish the security requirements necessary to safeguard the assets. But in the case of nuclear reactors, the perimeter security requirements have already been specified by the NRC. The security equipment has been selected, and now it must be integrated into an effective perimeter security system that will satisfy the NRC requirements.

A 10-foot chain-link fence, topped with three strands of barbed wire extending the fence height to 11 feet, is the outer physical barrier around the hypothetical plant. The fence is protected by fence disturbance sensors to detect anyone climbing, cutting, or lifting the fence fabric to gain access to the plant. Since such sensors can detect those penetrations only when an intruder comes in contact with the fence, other detectors are required to detect attempts at fence circumvention by jumping over the fence from a ladder or some other object.

To alleviate the fence contact avoidance vulnerability, buried seismic sensors will be installed inside the perimeter fence. Now if an intruder jumps over the fence, he should be detected when he hits the ground, because he would have to jump from a height of about 12 feet to clear the 11-foot fence. From this height, his impact will induce a large seismic pulse that should be easy to detect. In the upgraded system, the intruder will be detected when he lands in the electromagnetic field generated by the ported coax cable sensor.

If it were not for the frozen ground and snow accumulation problems in the area around the hypothetical plant, seismic sensors alone would satisfy the detection requirements of NRC Guide 5.44. But frozen ground, which is a problem at the hypothetical reactor site, often reduces the sensitivity of such buried sensors, especially pressure sensors, by supporting an intruder's weight and therefore reducing the force on the sensor. The reduced sensitivity can usually be compensated for by increasing the detector's sensitivity. The frozen ground problem will be eliminated with the ported coax cable sensor, which also will minimize the snow accumulation problem unless the snow is allowed to accumulate to more than 3 feet.

Frozen ground is not of as much concern when using seismic sensors as is crusted snow that will support an intruder's weight. With crusted snow, the pressure or seismic energy generated by the crossing intruder is dissipated in the crust and completely isolated from the buried sensor. If the snow under the ice crust is firmly packed or the covering is solid ice, then some of the energy might reach the sensor. Regardless of whether the covering is crusted snow or solid ice, the seismic sensors used at the hypothetical site should detect the impact from anyone jumping from a height of about 12 feet.

If the snow is allowed to accumulate or drift to depths of 4 or 5 feet along the fence, the probability of detecting anyone jumping into the snow is probably low. Besides reducing the seismic sensor system's detection capability, deep snow can negate the effectiveness of the perimeter fence. Therefore, provisions have been made with the hypothetical plant maintenance supervisor to have snow more than 3 feet deep removed from along the perimeter fence.

These buried seismic sensors will be used in conjunction with the fence disturbance sensors to detect penetrations of the perimeter except at the water inlet structure and vehicle and personnel entrance. The water inlet structure shown in Figure 29–1 extends about 30 feet above the river. The fence is secured along the outside of the wall so that there is no ledge. It should be virtually impossible to scale the wall and cross the 11-foot fence around the edge of the structure without coming in contact with the fence. Therefore, the fence disturbance sensors should be adequate to detect anyone attempting to enter the structure from the river.

Microwave detectors will be installed across the vehicle and personnel entrances, as shown in Figure 29–2, to detect anyone entering the plant through these areas. The electrically operated vehicle gate is not protected by a fence disturbance sensor, but the fence on both sides is protected. Without the microwave detector across the vehicle entrance, someone could climb the gate and enter the plant without being detected. Seismic sensors are buried in the ground on either side of the entrance road, so if anyone climbs the gate and attempts to move along the fence to avoid the microwave detector, he would be walking across the seismic sensor line. The ported coax cable sensor also will detect anyone attempting to bypass the microwave detector.

The microwave detector protecting the vehicle entrance will be installed inside the fenced compound, with the transmitter positioned about 30 feet from the edge of the road on one side of the vehicle entrance and the receiver positioned in the same location on the opposite side of the entrance. At the personnel entrance gate, a transmitter will be positioned about 25 feet from the fence along the entrance walk, and the receiver will be positioned on the opposite side of the entrance about the same distance from the fence. Here the microwave energy will pass through the fence to detect anyone entering the entrance building. The fence should not affect the microwave detector's detection capability. Snow will have to be removed around the

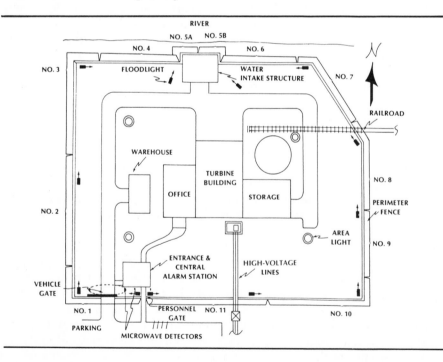

Figure 29–2   Hypothetical reactor plant with fence disturbance sensor and seismic sensor zones.

microwave detectors at both entrances so that it will not interfere with detector operation. But because of the limited detection zone length, snow removal will not be a major problem.

ZONES OF DETECTION

The fence disturbance sensor and seismic sensor zones of detection, or ported coax cable sensor zones in the site upgrade, coincide all the way around the plant perimeter. The zones are laid out as shown in Figure 29–2. Zone 1 starts at the personnel entrance gate and extends from there along the front fence to a point 75 feet from the corner on the west fence line. Zones 2 and 3 are each about 300 feet long and cover the remaining fence line on the west side of the plant and 75 feet of the fence along the river. Zone 4 covers the remaining 350 feet to the water inlet structure. Zone 5 covers only the 11-foot fence around the water inlet structure. Zones 6, 7, 8, 9, 10, and 11 range in length from about 250 feet for Zone 7 to about 350 for zone 10. Zone 12 covers only the sidewalk leading into the entrance building.

Zone 1 is protected by fence disturbance sensors on both sides of the entrance gate, seismic sensors or ported coax cable sensors in the ground on both sides of the entrance road, and a microwave detector across the road. Zone 1 seismic sensors could be extended across the road to detect anyone entering by the road. But the geophone transducers in that zone would then be installed both in soil and asphalt, which might compromise the detection capability. This change in the medium also will affect the ported coax cable sensors performance. Each of the sensor systems will be individually displayed, identified, and annunciated. In this way the central alarm station operator can identify each sensor alarm. The remaining zones, except for Zones 5 and 12, are protected by both fence disturbance sensors and seismic or ported coax cable sensors. Zone 5 has the fence disturbance sensors around the inlet structure, and Zone 12 is covered by the microwave detector.

Each zone of detection along the perimeter fence is covered by CCTV cameras, as shown in Figure 29–3. The cameras are located 15 feet above the ground and 2 feet inside the fence, aimed to cover the fence line and areas where the seismic or ported coax cable sensors are buried. From a height of 15 feet, or 4 feet above the fence, the cameras also have a good view of the area outside the fence.

Each camera is installed inside an environmental enclosure equipped with thermostatically controlled heaters to maintain the required camera operating temperature. The environmental enclosure and camera assembly is mounted on a 4-foot-long cantilevered arm extending toward the fence from a mounting pole 6 feet from the fence. The 6-foot space between the fence and camera pole allows the lawn mowing and snow removal equipment room to maneuver.

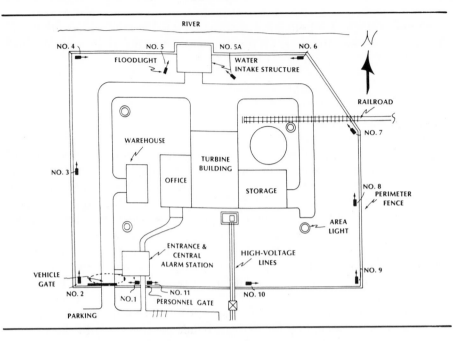

Figure 29–3 Hypothetical reactor plant with CCTV cameras.

The cameras are numbered to correspond to the zones of detection they cover. Camera 1 is mounted next to the fence at the personnel entrance and is aimed to cover the ground from the entrance road to the west fence and 100 feet of the corresponding fence line. Camera 2 is mounted 6 feet from each fence in the southwest corner and covers all of Zone 2. Camera 3 covers all of Zone 3, including 100 feet along the riverside fence. Camera 4 is mounted in the corner, like Camera 2, and covers the remainder of the riverside fence, or Zone 4. Camera 5 covers the fence along the top of the west side of the water inlet structure and at least half the fence along the river side. Camera 5A covers the fence on the opposite side of the structure. Each of the remaining zones of detection is covered by a single camera identified by the same number as the zone it is covering.

All cameras use 50mm lenses, except the cameras at Zone 5, which use 25mm lenses. From a height of 15 feet and tilted down at an angle of 2.6 degrees, the cameras with the 50mm lenses can adequately cover an area from about 75 feet out to 400 feet in front. The coverage actually extends out to about 700 feet, but a low-crawling target would be almost impossible to detect on the television monitor at this range. The 25mm cameras have a wider field of view but less range than the 50mm cameras. They will have full view of the fence around the water inlet structure when they are placed at a distance of about 100 feet from the structure.

Each surveillance camera is connected to a separate 9-inch television monitor in the CAS, where there is a total of twelve monitors. The monitors are mounted in six different chassis 19 inches wide, with two monitors in each chassis. The chassis are stacked two high in three 19-inch-wide racks arranged to form a desktop console, as shown in Figure 29–4.

The twelve television monitors are arranged to conform to the physical layout of the detection zones around the perimeter. Also, the monitors are identified by the camera numbers to which they are connected; Camera 1 is connected to Monitor 1, etc. Camera 1 is connected to the inner monitor in the lower left chassis. Camera 2 is connected to the outside monitor left of Monitor 1 and is designated Monitor 2. Camera 3's monitor is in the upper

Figure 29–4   Monitoring console arrangement.

left outside chassis above Monitor 2. Camera 4 is connected to the upper left inside monitor next to Monitor 3. Cameras 5 and 5A are connected to the upper two monitors in the center console rack. Cameras 6 and 7 are connected to the upper two right monitors. Cameras 8 and 9 are monitored on the lower two right monitors. Cameras 10 and 11 are monitored on the lower two center console monitors. With this monitor arrangement, the CAS operator can quickly associate a perimeter alarm with the proper television monitor to assess the cause of the alarm.

The alarm monitor for the fence disturbance sensors, seismic sensors, and microwave sensors are mounted in the 19-inch racks at desktop level just below the television monitors. The fence disturbance sensor alarm display chassis is mounted in the left chassis under Monitors 1 and 2. The seismic sensor and microwave detector alarm display panel is mounted in the center console rack, and an event recorder is in the right console. All controls—access/secure, acknowledge, and reset—are within easy reach of the CAS operator.

A 3-foot-square map display of the site is mounted on top of the center console and tilted down to be in easy view. The map depicts a plan view of the hypothetical plant and identifies each detection zone and televisicn camera. A separate red lamp is used to identify each sensor on the map. For instance, in Zone 1, a lamp is installed in the map along the fence in the center of the zone to identify the fence disturbance sensor. Another lamp is installed inside the fence in the center of the zone to identify the seismic sensor. A third lamp is installed in the center of the entrance road to identify the microwave detector. This type of lamp arrangement continues around the map to identify each sensor.

This console arrangement provides an effective operator/display interface. In a scenario with an intruder penetrating the perimeter, the intruder would first come in contact with the perimeter fence, initiating the fence disturbance sensor alarm. This alarm would be annunciated, displayed, and identified by a number on the fence alarm display. Simultaneously, the corresponding sensor lamp on the map display would be illuminated and the alarm annunciated. The operator would quickly acknowledge the alarm while identifying its exact location on the map display. Acknowledging the alarm silences the annunciator and changes the indicator lamp state from flashing to continuous. The operator then observes the corresponding television monitor to assess the alarm cause. By this time an intruder would probably be crossing the seismic or ported coax cable sensor line in full view of the television camera. The operator would then alert the response force. Concerning further alarm display events, when the intruder crosses the seismic or ported coax cable sensor line, the corresponding alarm would be displayed on both the alarm display panel and the map display. The operator would acknowledge the seismic or ported coax cable sensor alarm, and if the cause of the alarm had not been determined, he would observe the scene on the corresponding television monitor to assess the alarm cause. After the security response, the CAS operator would reset both the fence disturbance and seismic or ported coax cable sensor alarm indicator on the display.

SUMMARY

A nuclear reactor plant requires perimeter protection to comply with the security requirements as set forth by 10 CFR, Part 73. The requirements, along with the supporting guides, were developed to provide in-depth protection of nuclear plants from those who might attempt an act of radiological sabotage (causing a radioactive release harmful to the public).

Although these requirements were developed for nuclear plants, they provide excellent guidelines for designing any perimeter security system with a similar or lower threat to that specified in 10 CFR, Part 73. The hypothetical reactor plant perimeter security system was designed to comply with the objective of NRC perimeter security requirements and follows appropriate guidelines for selecting intrusion detection systems.

A northeastern United States location was selected for the hypothetical nuclear plant because of the severe winter environment. This is probably the most severe environment in which a perimeter security system must operate and still satisfy the objective of the NRC requirements. The NRC's objective is first to deter adversaries from attempting to enter a nuclear plant. If they are dedicated intruders, the objective is then to detect their presence in the isolation zone, where they will be confronted by the response force.

Detection becomes a primary problem in this northeast environment when the ground freezes and then is covered by deep snow. The performance criteria for perimeter intrusion detection systems state that a sensor system should detect ninety-five out of one hundred times under the performance conditions stated in NRC Guide 5.44 for each type of perimeter sensor. To satisfy the detection requirement objective and still be effective in deep snow, fence disturbance sensors and seismic sensors were selected to protect the perimeter of the hypothetical nuclear plant. Although neither of these systems individually would meet the detection performance criteria in the harsh winter environment, they should, as a composite system, satisfy the detection objective to detect ninety-five out of one hundred perimeter penetrations.

Under normal conditions, the ported coax cable sensor that replaces the seismic sensor in the site upgrade will detect ninety-five out of one hundred intrusions in accordance with the performance requirements of Guide 5.44. As stated earlier, the sensor would be vulnerable to compromise if snow was allowed to accumulate to 3 or more feet. Therefore, appropriate snow removal measures must be included in the site's contingency plan. Even though the ported coax sensor will satisfy the requirements of Guide 5.44 when properly maintained, the fence disturbance sensor will remain a part of the total perimeter intrusion detection system. Any attempted site penetrations will probably involve coming in contact with the fence, either by climbing, lifting the fabric (to crawl under), or cutting the fabric. The fence disturbance sensor should detect these penetration attempts and thus provide the security guards additional time to respond to the intrusion.

Television cameras are installed around the perimeter to provide complete surveillance coverage along the perimeter fence and isolation zone. Each camera is monitored on a separate monitor in the central alarm station. With cameras dedicated to individual monitors, the CAS operator can quickly assess the isolation zone around the entire perimeter. This type of surveillance is an excellent deterrent, especially if an adversary knows that if he attempts to penetrate the perimeter, he will be in full view on the television monitor. With this type of coverage, it would be unlikely that anyone would bring a ladder to the fence and attempt to jump over.

Although the hypothetical nuclear plant's perimeter security system satisfies the NRC requirements, it has not been approved by the NRC. The intent of this example is to review various perimeter intrusion detection systems and discuss the rationale for rejecting or accepting each type of sensor for the hypothetical plant.

Chapter 30

High-Rise Office Building

An architectural firm is designing a twenty-story office building where the owners want to emphasize security as one of their standard building features. The security system will include intrusion detection, access control, television surveillance, and security guards. Based on the size of the building and the desired security functions, the most effective way to monitor and control these functions is with a computerized monitoring system. Besides managing the security functions, the computer can monitor the fire detectors and control the building's environmental conditions.

The computerized monitoring system consists of a communication processor, CPU, memory, CRT display, and line printer. In operation, the communication processor sequentially polls each office or office complex transponder. When addressed, the transponder reports to the communicator the fire alarm status, the identification of anyone requesting access, and the temperature and humidity in the area. The communicator then transfers this information to the computer's CPU. The processing unit retrieves the programmed instructions from memory and executes the commands accordingly. Any changes in the area's access/secure status or alarms initiated by either the intrusion detection sensors or fire detection sensors or monitoring devices are displayed on the CRT display and printed on the line printer. The identity of any authorized individual requesting access to a controlled area also is printed on the line printer. The systematic integration of the computer components with the individual subsystems will result in an effective central control system.

The individual subsystems that will be managed by the computerized monitoring system will be discussed in the following paragraphs.

INTRUSION DETECTION SYSTEM

The intrusion detection system for each office or office complex will be designed to satisfy the tenant's specific security requirements. At a minimum, however, the entrance door to each office or office complex will have a magnetic door switch concealed in the door assembly to detect anyone opening the door. Concealing the switch obviously eliminates any cosmetic distractions in the door's appearance and also provides physical protection against abuse and tampering.

Since many of the tenants will require additional security for their offices, plans are made to accommodate their needs. The offices requiring motion detection will be protected by either ultrasonic motion or passive infrared detectors. Provisions are being made for installing the detector transducers by installing junction boxes above the ceilings in all the offices. Detector transducer selection depends on the office layout; therefore, the selection and transducer placement will be decided after the tenant submits a drawing of the layout.

Infrared beam detectors will be used in those offices that require only a minimum level of detection. In this application they will detect anyone moving freely through the office or anyone approaching a specific area or object without concern. To reduce the detectors' vulnerability to compromise by avoiding the infrared beam, the detectors will be concealed in the walls. The detectors will be installed to project an invisible beam across entrances and normal traffic paths. Some applications might require redirecting the infrared beam to increase the length of the barrier, but the beam will be limited to three directions. Redirecting the beam requires the use of mirrors, which can create operational problems if a mirror should become misaligned.

Passive infrared motion detectors will be installed in the foyer in front of the elevator entrances on each floor. They will detect anyone getting off or on the elevator, or anyone moving through the foyer after the floor has been secured. Ultrasonic motion detectors were considered for this application, but it was feared that escaping air around the elevator doors when the elevator approached and passed the floor might cause the detector to false alarm. Microwave motion detectors also were considered for this application but were not selected because it was believed their energy might penetrate the elevator shaft and consequently detect the elevators when they passed the floor. If additional detection is needed to cover the corridors, microwave detectors will be used, but they will be directed down the corridors away from the elevators. A television camera will be installed in each foyer to cover the elevator entrances and adjoining area so that when there is an alarm, the monitoring operator can observe the corresponding television monitor and assess the cause.

The intrusion detectors in each office or office complex will be connected to separate monitoring terminals in the transponder that monitor the sensors and control devices in that area. When the transponder is polled after an alarm has been initiated, the detector that initiated the alarm will be identified on the CRT and recorded on the line printer. The detector location will be graphically displayed and alphanumerically identified for the monitoring operator. The graphic display will depict the outline of the office or office complex where the alarm originated and also identify the location of the particular detector that is in the alarm state. Since many of the offices and office complex outlines on the various floors are identical, the floor and office must be identified in English text. Any special instructions for the monitoring operator will be displayed, along with the alarm location. With a system designed in this manner, the monitoring operator can quickly dispatch the response guard to the appropriate office.

ACCESS CONTROL SYSTEM

The access control system will provide the necessary level of security to accommodate each tenant's requirements. It will use encoded proximity cards and card readers to provide the basic level of access control. Although proximity cards are more expensive than magnetic-type cards, they are more difficult to counterfeit. They also can be read without having to insert them into or pass them through slot readers. This makes the proximity system more user friendly, reduces physical wear on the cards, and eliminates repairs to the readers caused by people jamming things into the slot. Over a period of time, the proximity card system is believed to be more cost-effective than magnetic card systems.

The proximity card alone will grant access to the parking lot and main entrance to the office building when the building is secure. But for the remainder of the building, the access control system will control who enters where, and where necessary, when they enter. Areas requiring medium level access security will be controlled by the access card, a keyboard with a five-digit memorized code, and perhaps a hand-geometry or fingerprint verification reader.

Areas requiring the highest level of access security will be controlled by a portal system, which will require card access and a five-digit memorized code to gain access to either an eye retina, voice, or signature verification reader.

TELEVISION SYSTEMS

Standard vidicon television cameras will be installed in strategic locations throughout the office building to assist the security guards in performing their surveillance function. Besides the cameras that view the elevator entrances in the foyer on each floor, additional cameras will be installed in the main lobby and parking areas. Two cameras will be installed near the ceiling, one on each side of the lobby, and positioned to view the main entrance and elevator entrances. Two articulated cameras with zoom lenses will be installed on each of the two building parking levels. One camera will be positioned near the ceiling to view the front elevator foyer entrance, and the second camera will be positioned on the opposite side of the parking lot to view the back foyer entrance. In these positions, the cameras can be articulated to view the entire parking area for general surveillance or for tracking anyone leaving the building until he reaches his automobile. Another camera will be positioned at the vehicle entrance on the first level to view the ramp and vehicle card access gate. Additional cameras will be installed as necessary to satisfy special tenant surveillance requirements.

The two lobby cameras will be connected to separate 9-inch broadcast-quality television monitors. These monitors will provide the monitoring operator with continuous surveillance of the lobby. The two articulated cameras and the fixed camera covering the entrance to the first parking level will be connected to a single 9-inch monitor through a sequential video switcher. A video switcher can automatically sequence the video signals from several cameras to one of several monitors for display. It also can be manually switched to one camera or from one camera to another, depending on the surveillance functions.

In operation, when the parking area cameras are not being used for selected surveillance, the video switcher will sequentially switch from one camera to the next. This arrangement will provide the monitoring operator with 10-second sequential views of the front and back entrances to the elevator foyer and the vehicle entrance to the first parking level. If the operator wishes to monitor just one entrance or use one of the articulated cameras for surveillance, he can switch the video switch from automatic sequencing to the desired camera. When finished with the specific surveillance function, he can switch back to the automatic switching mode. A sync generator will be used to synchronize the picture from each camera to eliminate flicker or roll on the monitor when switching from one camera to the next. The two surveillance cameras on the second parking level will be monitored in the same way.

The cameras, twenty in number, covering the elevator entrances in the foyer on each floor, will be monitored on six monitors. Video switching between the cameras and the six monitors will be computer controlled. In the normal operating mode the twenty cameras will be sequentially switched, and each camera will be periodically displayed on one of the six monitors. When there is an alarm, the computer will connect the camera covering the affected foyer and display it on the first of the six monitors. If another alarm occurs while the first scene is being displayed, then this foyer is displayed on the second monitor. It is very unlikely that six of the twenty foyers will be in alarm simultaneously. It is not planned to have video recording at this time, although it would alleviate the problem if more than six alarms should occur at any one time. Provisions are being made to add a video recorder if it is required by any of the tenants.

The twenty foyer cameras also will be synchronized to prevent picture flicker or roll when switching from camera to camera. When there is an alarm, the foyer where the alarm originated will be identified on the CRT display. But when the cameras are being sequentially displayed for general surveillance, the CRT will not be used in identifying the video. Instead, the monitoring operator can view a large number identifying the floor level. The number will be installed over the elevator door in full view of the camera in each foyer. Putting the numbers above the elevator doors will keep them from being blocked by normal personnel traffic entering and exiting the elevators.

Provisions are being made during the building design phase to accommodate almost any tenant video surveillance requirements. One such provision is the addition of video coaxial cables installed between the monitoring area and a central junction box located on each floor. Subsequently, if additional cameras are needed, new cables will only have to be routed through the ceiling from each camera to the central junction box. It is much easier to install spare cables when the building is being built than it is to add cables afterward. For this reason, spare transponder communication cables are being installed to accommodate other intrusion detection or building control systems.

The television monitors will be mounted above the computer console and CRT display. In this position the 9-inch monitors will be in easy viewing distance for the monitoring operator seated at the console. The video switcher control panel will be mounted just below the television monitors and to the side of the CRT display. The pan, tilt, and zoom controls for articulating the cameras in the parking areas will be located below the switcher control panel. Both the video switcher controls and the articulated camera controls will be within easy reach of the operator.

Another provision being made during the building design with respect to expanding the video surveillance capability is to allow adequate space in the monitoring room for additional monitors. The first ten additional monitors would be mounted above the existing monitors. If still more monitors are needed, the console will be extended on either side to accommodate them. Each time new television monitors or video controls are added, the console arrangement will be human-engineered to maintain a totally integrated system.

SECURITY GUARD PATROL SYSTEM

One function of the security guards is to conduct scheduled fire and security patrols through the office building. The security guard patrol function uses an integrated computer-managed reporting and communicating system. The guards will patrol each floor at least once every 4 hours. With this schedule, each floor will be checked three times each night during the week and six times during the weekend and on holidays. To ensure that the patrols are being conducted, the desired patrol schedule will be programmed into the computer instructions. Each floor will be assigned a time window during which a patrolling guard must patrol the floor or area and report to the computer.

The reporting is communicated by activating a card access reader. These readers are located in strategic areas on each floor where the guard should check the building's fire and security status. When the guard reports, the transmitted message identifies his location to the computer. The information is printed on the line printer, along with the reporting time. With this information, the monitoring operator can observe the guard's progress. If the guard does not report during the programmed time window, or if he reports in a sequence other than the programmed patrol route, an alarm will be initiated to alert the monitoring operator.

Communication between the patrolling security guard and monitoring operator in any security system is vital. For example, if a patrolling guard encounters any security or emergency hazard, he must be able to alert the monitoring operator or the proper authorities. Many installations provide their guards with portable radios, but radio communication will be limited in the high-rise office building because of all the steel and high-density building materials. Therefore, an intercom will be installed as part of the guard patrol system. The guard will be able to communicate with the monitoring operator by plugging a portable handset into the tour station telephone jack. Since it is often necessary for the monitoring operator to communicate with a patrolling guard, there will be a call-in lamp at each tour station, which can be activated on command from the control station.

FIRE CONTROL SYSTEM

The purpose of this discussion is not to describe a fire control system for the high-rise office building. That task requires someone who is knowledgeable about fire and building codes and standards, as well as the operation and application of fire control equipment. Instead, the purpose here is to describe the types of fire control devices that can be monitored by the computerized monitoring system. These devices include fire detectors and sprinkler systems. The computer can monitor the sprinkler water flow detectors, water temperature, air pressure in tanks and dry-pipe sprinkler systems, and water tank levels. There are two basic types of fire detectors—smoke and thermal detectors. The most important of these are the smoke detectors because they detect fires in the earliest stage of combustion, thus reducing the loss of life and property.

Smoke Detectors

Smoke detectors are required by Underwriters Laboratories (UL), Inc., to respond to gray smoke in concentrations of from 0.2 to 4.0 percent obscuration per foot. (Obscuration is the proportional reduction in transmitted light caused by smoke particles interposed between the light source and point of measurement at a stated distance from the light source).

The two most common types of smoke detectors that can comply with the UL requirement are ionization and photoelectric. Ionization smoke detectors contain a small amount of radioactive material safely sealed inside the detector's chamber. The radioactive material ionizes the air inside the chamber so that the air will be an electrical conductor. A precise electric current is passed through the ionized air and monitored by the detector. If smoke particles or particles of combustion enter the detector chamber, they mix with the ionized air and reduce the current flow. The reduction in the current flow is sensed, thereby initiating an alarm.

Photoelectric detectors sense the scattering of a light beam caused by smoke particles entering the beam. The detectors can either sense the attenuated light directly or detect the light scattered by the smoke particles. With both devices, a photosensitive cell detects either the attenuation of the direct light or the magnitude of scattered light impinging on the photosensitive cell. Detectors sensing the attenuated light illuminate the photocell directly and initiate an alarm when the smoke particles attenuate the light below a preset level. Detectors sensing the scattered light initiate an alarm when the light impinging on the photocell reaches a preset level.

Thermal Detectors

Thermal detectors sense the presence of fire when the ambient temperature rises above a preset temperature, usually about 135°F, or when the increase in ambient temperature exceeds a preset rate. The two detectors that sense these conditions are the fixed-temperature thermal detector and the rate-of-rise detector. Fixed-temperature detectors initiate an alarm when the ambient temperature reaches 135°F. They are available in both restorable and nonrestorable types. Restorable fixed-temperature detectors use replaceable fusible elements or are available with self-resetting bimetallic elements.

Rate-of-rise detectors initiate an alarm when the ambient temperature rises more than 15°F per minute. Most of these detectors also have a fixed temperature element in case the temperature rise is too slow to satisfy the rate-of-rise criteria.

ENVIRONMENTAL CONTROL SYSTEM

The computerized monitoring system also can be used to monitor building temperature and humidity and to control the heating and air-conditioning systems to maintain a comfortable working environment inside the office building.

EMERGENCY POWER

The building will have an emergency generator to provide power to essential equipment and lighting when commercial power fails. The intrusion detection system, access control system, CCTV, console control and monitoring system, and fire detection system are considered essential equipment. Emergency lighting, intrusion detection equipment, and fire detection sensors have standby batteries to provide power during power interrupt. But the television cameras and access control system's electric door strikes will be without power during this time.

This means that the access-controlled doors will have to fail-secure or fail-open during power interrupt. Electric-controlled parking lot gates will fail-open so that vehicles can exit and enter the lot unimpeded. Anyone can enter the lot during the time the gate is open, but at least authorized individuals will not be denied access and the emergency generator should be on-line within 2 or 3 minutes.

All controlled doors inside the building will fail-secure but will have inside manual releases so that occupants can exit the areas. Master control keys will be stored in a safe in the security office so they can be used to override the electric strike and gain access to any controlled area in an emergency.

SUMMARY

Computers have both a monitoring and a command and control capability that, when properly integrated, can provide a cost-effective way to manage security, access control, fire, and environmental control systems. There are, however, two important application considerations that could affect the computer system's operability and vulnerability. Operability can be affected if the maintenance plan is poorly conceived. There should be adequate spare modules available so that when there is a computer failure, making the computer operational is simply a matter of the technician replacing the failed module. The application might justify a spare computer that can assume control of the monitoring and control functions if the on-line system fails. Vulnerability is a prime consideration in high-security applications, so the number of functions performed by the computer should be limited to only those involved directly with security. Adding additional functions, especially functions that would involve other computer operators, will increase the vulnerability of the system to compromise.

Computerized monitoring systems, like all other intrusion detection sensors and monitoring systems, can improve security effectiveness only when they are properly designed and adequately supported by security personnel.

References

BOOKS

Broder, James F. *Risk Analysis and the Security Survey.* Stoneham, MA: Butterworth Publishers, 1984.

Fisher, A. James. *Security for Business and Industry.* Englewood Cliffs, New Jersey: Prentice-Hall, Inc., 1979.

Gigliotti, Richard J., and Ronald C. Jason. *Security Design for Maximum Protection.* Stoneham, MA: Butterworth Publishers, 1984.

Healy, Richard J. *Design for Security.* 2d ed. New York: John Wiley, 1983.

Illuminating Engineering Society. *IES Lighting Handbook.* 5th ed. New York: Illuminating Engineering Society, 1972.

Purpura, Phillip P. *Security and Loss Prevention.* Stoneham, MA: Butterworth Publishers, 1984.

San Luis, Ed. *Office and Office Building Security.* Stoneham, MA: Butterworth Publishers, 1973.

Walsh, Timothy J., and Richard J. Healy. *Protection of Assets Manual.* Santa Monica, CA: Merritt, 1974.

Weber, Thad L. *Alarm Systems and Theft Prevention.* 2d ed. Stoneham, MA: Butterworth Publishers, 1985.

REPORTS

Barry, Joseph A. *Personnel Fatigue in Closed Circuit Television Assessment.* Boston: The Loss Prevention Institute, Inc., June 1981.

Carpency, Frank M. *Fiber Optic Cable Applications in Security.* Gaithersburg, MD: NUS Corporation.

Fite, Robert A. *Commercial Perimeter Sensor Evaluation.* Report 2209. Fort Belvoir, VA: MERADCOM, May 1977.

Garrett, William C. *Infrared Motion Sensor Evaluation.* Report 2237. Fort Belvoir, VA: MERADCOM, March 1978.

Moore, R.T. *Penetration Resistance Test of Reinforced Concrete Barriers.* NBSIR 73–101. Washington, DC: National Bureau of Standards, December 1972.

Moore, R.T. *Penetration Tests on J—SIIDS Barriers.* NBSIR 73–223. Washington, DC: National Bureau of Standards, June 4, 1973.

Sandia Laboratories. *Intrusion Detection Systems Handbook.* Sandia 76–0554. Albuquerque, NM: Sandia Laboratories, November 1976.

Sandia Laboratories. *Entry-Control Systems Handbook.* Sandia 77–1033. Albuquerque, NM: Sandia Laboratories, September 1977.

PAPERS

Barker, Ben C., Jr. *Joint-Service Interior Intrusion Detection System.* Proceedings 1973 Carnahan Conference on Electronics Crime Countermeasures.

Barnard, Robert L. *Application for the Joint-Services Interior Intrusion Detection System.* Proceedings 1974 Carnahan Conference on Electronics Crime Countermeasures.

Blacksten, R., and R. Barnard. *Classification of Signal Transmission System Security for Modern Intrusion Detection Systems.* ADPA/IACSE Joint Government–Industry Symposium on Physical Security.

Duff, David J. *External Intrusion Detection Systems.* Proceedings 1973 Carnahan Conference on Electronics Crime Countermeasures.

Fite, Robert A., and Stuart Kilpatrick. *Final Report Joint-Service Perimeter Barrier Penetration Evaluation.* NBS Special Publication 480–24. The Role of Behavioral Science in Physical Security. The First Annual Symposium, April 29–30, 1976.

Galloway, Stephen L. *Response Force Selection and Training.* NBS Special Publication 480–32. The Role of Behavioral Science in Physical Security. Proceedings of the Second Annual Symposium, March 23–24, 1977.

Graff, A.J., and P. Nesbeda. *Illumination Criteria in Imaging System Design for Security Applications.* Proceedings 1978 Carnahan Conference on Electronics Crime Countermeasures.

Karber, Phillip A., and R.W. Mengle. *A Behavioral Analysis of the Adversary Threat to the Commercial Nuclear Industry—A Conceptual Framework for Realistically Assessing Threats.* NBS Special Publication 480–32. The Role of Behavioral Science in Physical Security. Proceedings of the Second Annual Symposium, March 23–24, 1977.

Miller, G. Kirby. *Development of Electret Transducer Line Sensors.* Proceedings 1974 Carnahan Conference on Electronics Crime Countermeasures.

Moore, R.T. *Computerized Site Security Monitor and Response System.* Proceedings 1980 Carnahan Conference on Electronics Crime Countermeasures.

Owen, James W. *The Use of CCTV for Perimeter Assessment.* Proceedings 1982 Carnahan Conference on Security Technology.

Pfleckl, Frances P. *Enforcement of Direct Visual and CCTV Surveillance/Assessment Functions at the Perimeter of Controlled Access Sites.* Proceedings 1983 Carnahan Conference on Electronics Crime Countermeasures.

Reiss, Martin H. *System Analysis and Design of Microwave Motion Detection Equipment for Premise Protection.* Proceedings 1971 Carnahan Conference on Electronics Crime Countermeasures.

Robertson, Marvin P., and Jay A. Rarick. *Application of Fiber Optics Technology to Physical Security.* Proceedings 1984 Carnahan Conference on Electronics Crime Countermeasures.

Rodems, J.D., and P.E. Harris. *Signal Processing and the False Alarm for Motion Detectors.* Proceedings 1971 Carnahan Conference on Electronics Crime Countermeasures.

Schwarz, Frank. *Design and Application of a Wide Field, Passive, Infrared Intrusion Detector.* Proceedings 1973 Carnahan Conference on Electronics Crime Countermeasures.

Shorrock, S., and N.I. Buckley. *Perimeter Intrusion Detection System of Microwave Energy.* Proceedings 1974 Carnahan Conference on Electronics Crime Countermeasures.

Zushin, Albert R. *Line Supervisory Techniques.* Proceedings 1974 Carnahan Conference on Electronics Crime Countermeasures.

PERIODICALS

"Bad Vibrations: The Key to Bacardi's Perimeter Protection." *Security World*, April 1979.

Baker, Hugh M. "The Economics of Multiplexing." *Security Distributing and Marketing*, May 1978.

Baker, Hugh M., Jr. "Multiplex: What's Happened to It?" *Security Distributing and Marketing*, February 1976.

Barget, R.J. "Multiplexing: Where Is It? Where Is It Going?" *Security Distributing and Marketing*, February 1976.

Barnard, Robert L. "Designing Your Intrusion Detection System, Part I." *Security World*, January 1978.

Barnard, Robert L. "Designing Your Intrusion Detection System, Part II." *Security World*, April 1978.

Barnard, Robert L. "Performance Standards for Ultrasonic and Microwave Motion Detectors." *Signal*, NBFAA (National Burglar and Fire Alarm Association) Third Quarter, 1975.

Barnard, Robert L. "When Security Covers the Expanded Picture." *Security World*, September 1977.

Bell, Everett. "Digital Is More Than Alarm Reporting." *Security Distributing and Marketing*, February 1978.

Bell, Everett. "Listening in Makes the Difference." *Security Distributing and Marketing*, April 1977.

Blattman, Daniel A. "The Invisible Protector." *Security Management*, October 1986.

Bordes, Roy N. "CCTV Lenses are Crucial to the CCTV System's Performance." *Security Management*, October 1982.

Bowers, Dan M. "Choosing the Right Card." *Security World*, June 1986.

"Buried Seismic System with Audio Listen-in Feature." *Security Distributing and Marketing*, April 1977.

Carroll, John M. "3 Missions for CCTV in Physical Security • Detection • Surveillance • Access Control." *Security World*, February 1979.

Cochran, Howard A. "Lighting for Closed Circuit TV Surveillance." *Lighting Design and Application*, March 1974.

"Computing Search Pays Off for Central Stations." *Security Distributing and Marketing*, October 1976.

"Cost-Effective Access Control." *Security World*, March 1979.

"Coverage at Low Light Levels." *Security Distributing and Marketing*, October 1979.

Crowther, Charles. "Better Cameras or More Lights." *Security World*, November 1976.

Day, Donald F. "Multiplexing and the Polling Computer." *Security Distributing and Marketing*, February 1976.

De Gennaro, Robert V. "CCTV 1986: Smarter, Simpler and Smaller." *Security World*, July 1986.

De Lia, Robert. "Fiber Optics, Advantages for CCTV–Long Distance, Interference Freedom." *AID*, June 1985.

"Digital Communications Come of Age." *Security Distributing and Marketing*, February 1978.

Dubois, Paul A. "The Design and Application of Security Lighting." *Security Management*, September 1985.

Egesdal, S.E. "The Basis of Fire Alarm Systems." *Security Management*, July 1980.

Evans, Sandy. "Masking the Message." *Security Management*, April 1986.

Fraden, Roger. "Ultrasonic Provides Cost-Effective Protection." *Security Distributing and Marketing*, June 1979.

Jaffe, Herbert M. "Selecting the Best Loudspeakers." *Security Distributing and Marketing*, July 1979.

"Keep Out Is Not Enough." *Security World*, June 1976.

Kellem, Carl. "Legislation vs. the False Alarm Problem." *Security Distributing and Marketing*, January 1978.

King, Claude. "Basic Considerations for Multiplexing Systems." *Security Distributing and Marketing*, February 1976.

Koegler, Charles. "High-Rise Fire Traps." *Security Management*, July 1980.

Le Nay, Tom W. "New Concepts in Multiplex Security." *Security Distributing and Marketing*, May 1978.

Lewis, Robert. "More Security, Less Cost." *Security World*, May 1978.

Luks, Henry J. "Audio Discrimination—Fact or Fiction?" *Security Distributing and Marketing*, April 1977.

Malec, Michael J., and Larry A. Thomas. "IR Catches EM Coming and Going." *Security World*, August 1979.

Matleson, Sally A. "Smoke Detectors Complete Industrial Fire Protection Circle." *Security World*, March 1979.

Meiners, Frank J. "One-Stop Shop for Electronics Physical Security, Energy Management Needs." *Security World*, February 1979.

Miller, Kenneth. "A Wide-Open Look at CCTV." *Security Management*, October 1986.

Moore, Michael H. "Audio—Can You Afford to be Without It?" *Security Distributing and Marketing*, April 1977.

Morgan, Jack B. "Remote Multiplexing Techniques." *Security Distributing and Marketing*, May 1978.

Nolte, John. "Security Corridors of Light." *Security World*, May 1978.

Osborne, W.E. "Passive Infrared Comes of Age." *Security World*, May 1977.

Petraglia, David. "Verified Technology: Sensors That Think Twice." *Security World*, February 1986.

"Proprietary System Provides Security and Energy Management at California College." *Security Distributing and Marketing*, October 1976.

"Reaping Protection Rewards from Audio Alarms and Invisible Beams." *Security World*, January 1979.

Sowder, Kathleen A. "CCTVs—A View of their Future." *Security Management*, March 1985.

Stewart, Layman L. "CCTV: Equipment and Applications." *Security World*, August 1983.

Stossell, George F. "Smart Security." *Security World*, June 1979.

Thorsen, J.E. "Considering the Sources." *Security World*, May 1978.

Vail, Kit. "Multiplex: Is It For You—Yet?" *Security Distributing and Marketing*, February 1976.

Warfel, George H. "Signature Dynamics for Access Control." *Security Management*, July 1980.

Williamson, William W. "Switch Line Systems for Central Station Signaling." *Security Distributing and Marketing*, February 1978.

Wilson, Stanley, Jr. "Distributed Processing with Microprocessors in Security Equipment." *Security Distributing and Marketing*, October 1976.

Index

Access control systems, 269, 357–89
 application guidelines, 387–89
 applications, 382–85
 automated, 362
 contraband detectors, 358–59, 378–82
 control techniques, 357–58, 362–78
 for high-rise office building, 443
 maintenance, 378
 performance testing, 378
 primary function of, 361–62
Accessibility, alarm signal display
  layout and, 259
Access roads, 9
Acoustical energy detectors, 22, 175–76
Active barrier detectors, 205–9
Active volumetric motion detectors,
  148, 151–76, 217–18, 406–9
Adaptation, transient, 285–86
Advanced level security, 47, 50, 64
Alarm activated switching, 342
Alarm assessment, 275–77, 318–20,
  329–30
Alarm response force, 10, 18, 53,
  415–16
Alarm station monitoring systems,
  25–31, 221–73
 alarm signal display, 25–29, 223–24,
  257–64, 273, 438
 application guidelines, 271–73
 commercial vs. proprietary, 25–26,
  30–31, 222, 223
 computer-managed systems, 29,
  223–24, 265–70, 273, 441–48
 functions, 221
 for public school complex, 410–15
 selecting, 24–34, 410–15

signal line vulnerability, 222–23
signal transmission systems, 26–29,
 222, 225–55, 271, 272
 See also False alarm
Alert function, 1, 2
Alternating current (AC) alarm
  transmission systems, 27, 239–40,
  272
Analog computers, 265
Analog signal of piezoelectric
  transducers, 88
AND gate logic, 185, 186, 187–89
Animals, 75, 138, 423
Annunciator panels, 261–62
Antennas, 96, 98–100, 103, 169–71,
  253, 254–55
Antipassback, 365
Applications. See High-rise office
  building; Nuclear reactor plant;
  Public school complex; specific
  detection systems
Articulated cameras, 325
Artificial lighting. See Lighting,
  surveillance and assessment
Assets, location of, 8–10
Asset value, 7–8
Audible alarm, local, 24–25
Audio detectors, 177, 181–84, 218
Audio listen-in feature, 124
Automated access control systems, 362
Automated recognition systems, 358,
  362–78
Automatic frequency control (AFC),
  343–44
Automatic gain control (AGC) circuit,
  100, 160

with sonic motion detectors, 176
with strain/magnetic line sensors, 130
with structural vibration detectors, 194
with ultrasonic motion detector, 160, 165–67, 406
Federal Communications Commission (FCC), 98, 168, 251
Fence disturbance sensors, 19, 20, 72, 83–94, 144, 326–27, 430, 432–33
Fences, 10–11, 20–21, 64–66, 72, 109–10, 420–22, 432–33
Ferrous metal detector perimeter alarm system, 427–28
Fiber-optic transmission, 228, 229–31, 314, 410–11
Fingerprint recognition systems, 370–72
Fire and safety officers, 42
Fire control system, 446–47
Fixed cameras, 325
Fixed lenses, 310, 334–35
Floodlights, 294, 398
Fluorescent lamps, 290–91, 323
Foil tape, 149, 197–99
Footcandle, 287
Frequency
control, automatic, 343–44
Doppler shift, 151–54, 156–61, 168
for microwave motion detectors, 168–69
radio-frequency systems, 251–55, 273, 313, 341
Frequency division multiplexing (FDM), 28, 240–41, 313
Frequency shift keyed (FSK) signal transmission, 241–42, 246, 248
Fresnel lens, 295

Gallium arsenide field effect transistor (GaAs FET), 186
Gallium arsenide LEDs, 206
Gap switching, 315
Gate openings, E-field sensor gate kits for, 116
Geophone transducers, 90–91, 121, 123–26, 145, 428
Glare, 280, 286, 287
Glass breakage detectors, 149, 195–96

Gray scale response, 343
Ground cover, 75
Guards, security, 70, 275–76
access control with, 357–58, 361–62
for high-rise office building, 445–46
lighting and, 279, 280–81
on-site, 31–34
in public school complex, 415–16
training, 31–34

Half-duplex digital multiplexing system, 242, 243
Hand-geometry recognition systems, 372–73
Heat sensors, 149, 196–97
Heavy wall conduit, 78
Helical scan system, 317
High-intensity discharge (HID) lamps, 277, 280, 291, 324
Highly skilled intruders, 54–55, 57–60
High-pressure sodium vapor lamps, 292–93, 324
High-rise office building, 441–48
High-risk facilities, design guide for, 59–60. *See also* Nuclear reactor plant
Horizontal illumination, 322
Hum clamper, 340

Identity verification systems, 368–74
Illuminance, 288
Illumination, 288. *See also* Lighting, surveillance and assessment
Incandescent lamps, 277, 289–90, 323
Industrial site, design guide for, 58–59
Information display equipment, video, 317, 345
Infrared detectors, 21, 95–97, 108–12, 144, 205, 429, 442
motion detectors, 177–81, 185–90, 218
Infrared energy, 96
Intensified silicon intensifier target (ISIT) cameras, 308
Interference, 79–80, 103–4, 116, 423–24
Interior barrier detectors, 23, 149–50
Interior intrusion detectors, 147–50. *See also* Barrier penetration